Java Methods

A & AB

Object-Oriented Programming
and
Data Structures

Maria Litvin

Phillips Academy, Andover, Massachusetts

Gary Litvin

Skylight Software, Inc.

Skylight Publishing
Andover, Massachusetts

Skylight Publishing
9 Bartlet Street, Suite 70
Andover, MA 01810

web: http://www.skylit.com
e-mail: sales@skylit.com
          support@skylit.com

Library of Congress Control Number: 2005910949

ISBN-10:   0-9727055-7-0
ISBN-13:   978-0-9727055-7-8

2 3 4 5 6 7 8 9 10   11 10 09 08 07

Printed in the United States of America

To Marg and Aaron

Brief Contents

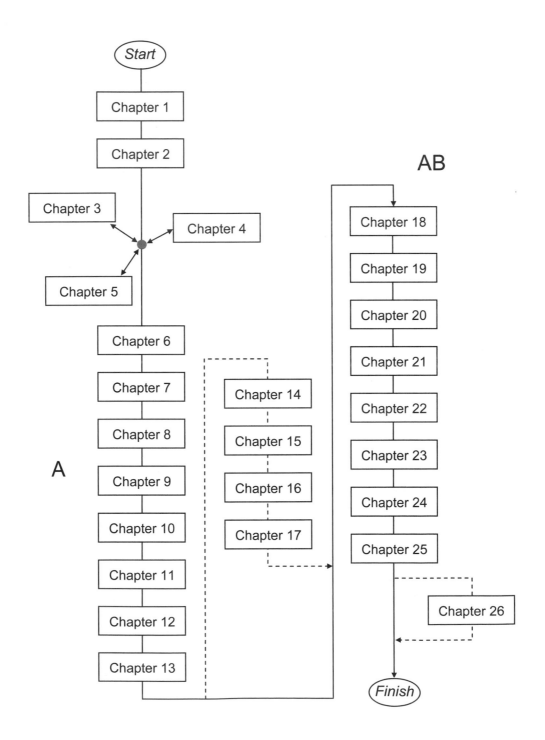

Contents

Chapter 6. Data Types, Variables, and Arithmetic | 121

Chapter 7. Boolean Expressions and `if-else` Statements | 153

Chapter 8. Iterative Statements: `while`, `for`, `do-while` | 193

Preface

This book offers a thorough introduction to the concepts and practices of object-oriented programming in Java. It also introduces the most common data structures and related algorithms and their implementations in the Java collections framework. As the title implies, the book covers the material in the A- and AB-level AP Computer Science course syllabus. This is equivalent to a two- or three-semester college course sequence in introductory programming and data structures for computer science majors. In addition to covering the AP curriculum in depth, we introduce several topics that are not required for the AP exams, including file input and output, graphics, graphical user interfaces, events handling in Java, and design patterns. This additional material gives students a better sense of real-world Java programming and makes case studies, labs, and exercises more fun.

This edition builds on our earlier books, *Java Methods: An Introduction to Object-Oriented Programming* (Skylight Publishing, 2001) and *Java Methods AB: Data Structures* (Skylight Publishing, 2003). In this edition we have organized all of the material into one volume. Besides incorporating new and useful features of Java 5.0, we have made many substantial changes that reflect the current thinking about object-oriented programming (OOP) among computer science educators and professionals. We have revised the sequence of topics for an earlier introduction of inheritance, class hierarchies, interfaces, and polymorphism; enhanced the discussion of object-oriented design; introduced new case studies and labs and updated and streamlined those we decided to keep from the previous edition; recast almost all examples from applets into applications; added a separate chapter on the Java collections framework; and made other improvements.

The book follows four main threads: OOP concepts and techniques, algorithms, Java syntax and style, and Java libraries. As in the software engineering profession itself, these threads are interwoven into an inseparable braid.

Our book strives to present the technical details while grounding them in clear explanations of the underlying concepts. OOP has an extensive conceptual layer and complex terminology. Fortunately, many OOP concepts are more straightforward than the terminology makes them appear. The notions of *objects* (entities that combine data elements and functions), *classes* (definitions of types of objects), *methods* (functions that handle certain tasks), *instantiation* (creating an object of a particular class), *inheritance* (one class extending the features of another class), *encapsulation* (hiding the implementation details of a class), *polymorphism* (calling the correct methods automatically for specific objects disguised as objects of more generic types), and *event-driven* applications (where the operating system, the user, or events in the program trigger certain actions) are actually quite intuitive.

We also emphasize good programming style, an element not mandated by formal Java language specifications but essential for writing readable and professional programs.

Our labs and case studies aim to demonstrate the most appropriate uses of the programming techniques and data structures we cover. OOP is widely believed to facilitate team work, software maintenance, and software reuse. While it is not possible for an introductory textbook to present a large-scale real-world project as a case study, the case studies and labs in this book offer a taste of how these OOP benefits can play out in larger projects.

We assume that at least two or three class periods each week will be held in a computer lab with students working independently or in small groups. A set of files, which we call *Student Disk*, downloadable from the book's web site, contains files for all the case studies, labs, and exercises in the book; downloadable *Teacher Disk*, available to teachers, provides complete solutions to all the labs and exercises.

Still, with all the examples and case studies, we leave a lot of work to you, the student. This is not a *Java-in-n-days* book or an *n-hours-to-complete* book. It is a book for learning essential concepts and technical skills at a comfortable pace, for acquiring a repertoire of techniques and examples to work from, and for consulting as needed when you start writing your own Java programs professionally or for fun.

Working through this book will not make you a Java expert right away — but it will bring you to the level of an entry-level Java programmer with a better than average understanding of the fundamental concepts. Object-oriented programming was originally meant to make software development more accessible to beginners, and *Java Methods A & AB* is written in that spirit.

Since our first book came out in 1998, many of our colleagues, too many to name, have become good friends. We are grateful to them for their loyal support, encouragement, and the many things they have taught us over the years.

Our sincere thanks to our reviewers, Don Slater from Carnegie Mellon University and Roger Frank from Ponderosa High School in Parker, Colorado, whose vision and attention to detail helped us improve this book and avoid many mistakes.

We thank the students in Maria's 2005-2006 introductory and AP Computer Science classes for their patience while studying from a draft of this book, catching some typos and mistakes, and making many useful suggestions.

Our special thanks to Margaret Litvin for her thorough and thoughtful editing.

Without further delay, let us begin learning object-oriented programming in Java!

About the Authors

Maria Litvin has taught computer science and mathematics at Phillips Academy in Andover, Massachusetts, since 1987. She is an Advanced Placement Computer Science exam reader and Question Leader and, as a consultant for The College Board, provides AP training for high school computer science teachers. Maria is a recipient of the 1999 Siemens Award for Advanced Placement for Mathematics, Science, and Technology for New England and of the 2003 RadioShack National Teacher Award. Prior to joining Phillips Academy, Maria taught computer science at Boston University. Maria is a co-author of *C++ for You++: An Introduction to Programming and Computer Science*, which became one of the leading high school textbooks for AP Computer Science courses, and of the earlier editions of *Java Methods* and *Java Methods AB*. Maria is also the author of *Be Prepared for the AP Computer Science Exam in Java*.

Gary Litvin is a co-author of *C++ for You++*, *Java Methods*, and *Java Methods AB* and a contributor to the 2006 edition of *Be Prepared for the AP Computer Science Exam in Java*. Gary has worked in many areas of software development including artificial intelligence, pattern recognition, computer graphics, and neural networks. As founder of Skylight Software, Inc., he developed SKYLIGHTS/GX, one of the first visual programming tools for C and C++ programmers. Gary led in the development of several state-of-the-art software products including interactive touch screen development tools, OCR and handwritten character recognition systems, and credit card fraud detection software.

How to Use This Book

The *Java Methods A & AB* companion web site —

```
http://www.skylit.com/javamethods
```

— is an integral part of this book. It contains four chapters and several appendices. It also has downloadable student files for case studies, labs, and exercises, assembled together in what we call *Student Disk*. Also on the book's web site are links, errata, supplemental papers, and syllabi and technical support information for teachers.

We have chosen to place Chapters 1, 16, 17, and 26 and the appendices on the web either because they rely on many web links or because the material they cover is less theoretical and handy to have online for reference.

⬟ The web symbol indicates a "webnote"; you will find it on the book's web site in the alphabetical list of webnote links.

J_M refers to the *Java Methods Student Disk*. For example, "you can find `HelloWorld.java` in `J`_M`\Ch02\Hello`" means the `HelloWorld.java` file is located in the `Ch02\Hello` subfolder in your student disk folder.

 This icon draws your attention to a lab exercise or a hands-on exploration of an example.

 "Parentheses" like these, in the margin, mark supplementary material intended for a more inquisitive reader. This material either gives a glimpse of things to come in subsequent chapters or adds technical details.

1.▪, 2.♦ In exercises, a square indicates an "intermediate" question that may require more thought or work than an ordinary question or exercise. A diamond indicates an "advanced" question that could be treacherous or lead to unexplored territory — proceed at your own risk.

(MC) We have included a few multiple-choice questions in exercises. These are marked (MC).

✓   A checkmark at the end of a question in an exercise means that a solution is included on your student disk. We have included solutions to about one-third of the exercises. They can be found in J_M\SolutionsToExercises (click on `index.html`).

Teacher Disk, which contains complete solutions to all the exercises and labs, is available for downloading free of charge to teachers who use this book as a textbook in their schools. Go to `skylit.com/javamethods` and click on the "Teachers' Room" link for details.

❖   ❖   ❖

(To a slightly different subject...)

How you use this book will depend on your background in computers. If you are familiar with computers and programming, you can glance quickly at Chapters 1 and 2 to see whether they fill any gaps.

Chapters 3, *Objects and Classes*, 4, *Algorithms*, and 5, *Java Syntax and Style*, can be covered in any order, depending on your taste.

If you know C++, Chapters 6, 7, and 8 will be easy for you. But do still read them for the sake of the case studies and labs, which cover broader concepts than the chapter headings imply. Chapters 14, *Streams and Files*, 15, *Graphics*, 16, *GUI Components and Events*, and 17, *Mouse, Keyboard, Sounds, and Images*, are optional as far as the AP exams are concerned. Chapter 18 begins the discussion of more advanced AB topics: big-O, the Java collections framework, and data structures. The concluding chapter, *Design Patterns*, aims to inspire you to study object-oriented design further, but it is optional, too — it can be read after the AP exam is behind you.

ch 001

An Introduction to Hardware, Software, and the Internet

1.1 Prologue

Have you ever opened that gray or black (or purple) box sitting on or beside your desk, with tangled wires snaking out of it in all directions? If you do, you will find a mostly empty box, with a power supply, a printed circuit board on the bottom connected by ribbon cables to a small disk drive and a few other devices neatly tucked away in their bays. And that's all. But it brings you an entire world.

The most important piece of a typical computer is the *Central Processing Unit* or *CPU*. In a personal computer, the CPU is a microprocessor made from a tiny chip of silicon, sometimes as small as half an inch square. Immensely precise manufacturing processes etch a huge number of semiconductor devices, called *transistors*, into the silicon wafer. Each transistor is a microscopic digital switch and together they control, with perfect precision, billions of signals — little spikes of electricity — that arise and disappear every second. The size of the spikes doesn't matter, only their presence or absence. The transistors in the CPU recognize only two states of a signal, "on" or "off," "high" or "low," "1" or "0," "true" or "false." This is called *digital electronics* (as opposed to *analog electronics* where the actual amplitudes of signals carry information).

The transistors on a chip combine to form logical devices called *gates*. Gates implement *Boolean* operations (named after the British mathematician George Boole, 1815-1864,[boole] who studied the properties of logical relations). For example, an *AND* gate takes two inputs and combines them into one output signal. The output is set to "true" if both the first <u>and</u> the second input are "true," and to "false" otherwise (Figure 1-1-a). In an *OR* gate, the output is set to "true" if either the first <u>or</u> the second (or both) inputs are true (Figure 1-1-b). A *NOT* gate takes one input and sets the output to its opposite (Figure 1-1-c). Note the special shapes used to denote each type of gate.

These three basic types of gates can be combined to make other Boolean operations and logical circuits. Figure 1-2, for example, shows how you can combine AND, OR, and NOT gates to make an *XOR* ("*eXclusive OR*") operation. This operation sets the output to "true" if exactly one of its two inputs is "true." In the late 1940s, John von Neumann,[vonneumann] a great mathematician and one of the founding fathers of computer technology, showed that all arithmetic operations can be reduced to AND, OR, and NOT logical operations.

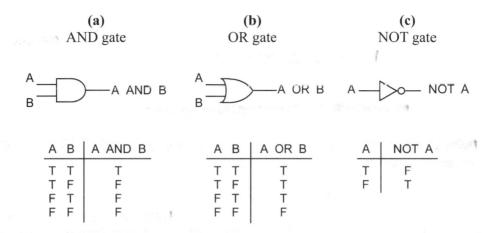

Figure 1-1. AND, OR, and NOT gates

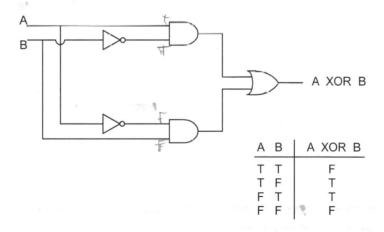

Figure 1-2. XOR circuit made of AND, OR, and NOT gates

The microprocessor is protected by a small ceramic case mounted on a *PC board* *(Printed Circuit board)* called the *motherboard*. Also on the motherboard are memory chips. The computer memory is a uniform pool of storage units called *bits*. A bit stores the smallest possible unit of information: "on" or "off," "1" or "0." For practical reasons, bits are grouped into groups of eight, called *bytes*.

One byte is eight bits.

There is no other structure to memory: the same memory is used to store numbers and letters and sounds and images and programs. All these things must be encoded, one way or another, in sequences of 0s and 1s. A typical personal computer made in the year 2005 had 256 "megs" (megabytes; 1 megabyte is 1,048,576 bytes) to 1 "gig" (gigabyte; 1 gigabyte is 1,024 megabytes) of *RAM* (Random-Access Memory) packed in a few *SIMMs* (Single In-Line Memory Modules).

The CPU interprets and carries out computer programs, or sequences of instructions stored in the memory. The CPU fetches the next instruction, interprets its operation code, and performs the appropriate operation. There are instructions for arithmetic and logical operations, for copying bytes from one location to another, and for changing the order of execution of instructions. The instructions are executed in sequence unless a particular instruction tells the CPU to "jump" to another place in the program. Conditional branching instructions tell the CPU to continue with the next instruction or jump to another place depending on the result of the previous operation.

Besides the CPU, a general-purpose computer system also includes *peripheral devices* that provide input and output and secondary mass storage. In a notebook (laptop) computer, the "peripheral" devices are no longer quite so peripheral: a keyboard, a display, a hard drive, a CD-ROM or DVD drive, a fax/modem, a touch pad, a microphone, and speakers are all built into one portable unit.

CPU, memory, peripherals — all of this is called *hardware*. It is a lot of power concentrated in a small device. But to make it useful, to bring life into it, you need programs, *software*. Computer programs are also miracles of engineering, but of a different kind: *software engineering*. They are not cast in iron, nor even silicon, but in intangible texts that can be analyzed, modified, translated from one computer language into another, copied into various media, transmitted over networks, or lost forever. Software is to a computer as tunes are to a band: the best musicians will be silent if they don't have music to play.

Take this amazing device with its software and connect it to the *Internet*, a network of millions of computers of all kinds connected to each other via communication lines of all kinds and running programs of all kinds, and you end up with a whole new world. Welcome to cyberspace!

↳ Gibson

In the rest of this chapter we will briefly discuss:

- The main hardware components: CPU, memory, peripheral devices

- What software is

- How numbers and characters are represented in computer memory

- What the Internet is

⬟ 1.2 - 1.7 ⬟

These sections are online at `http://www.skylit.com/javamethods`.

Exercises

Sections 1.1-1.4

1.   Mark T (true) or F (false) the output of each of the following circuits
      with the given inputs.

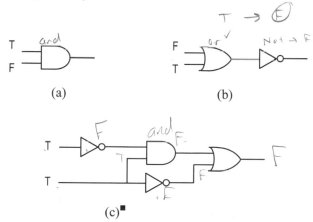

2.■   Let's say that two circuits are equivalent if they produce the same outputs for
      the same inputs. Draw a circuit equivalent to the one in Question 1-b using
      two NOT gates and one AND gate. ✓

3.◆   Simplify the circuit in Question 1-c to an equivalent one that has only two
      gates: one NOT gate and one AND gate.

4.   (a)■ Draw an alternative XOR circuit, different from the one in Figure 1-2, using two NOT gates, two OR gates, and one AND gate.   ⋛ Hint: at least one of the inputs, A or B, must be true, and at least one of the negated inputs, NOT A or NOT B, must be true, too. ⋛ ✓

      (b)◆ Draw a third XOR circuit using four gates: one OR gate, two AND gates, and one NOT gate.

5.   (MC) Computer memory is called RAM because:

      A. It provides rapid access to data.
      B. It is mounted on the motherboard.
      C. It is measured in megabytes.
      D. Its bytes can be addressed in random order.
      E. Its chips are mounted in a rectangular array.

6.   Mark true or false and explain:

      (a)   One meg of RAM can hold exactly as much information as one meg on a floppy disk. _____

      (b)   A factory-formatted floppy disk is split into a fixed number of files. _____ ✓

      (c)   In personal computers the operating system resides in ROM. _____ ✓

7.   Find an old discarded computer, **unplug the power cord**, and disconnect all other cables. Open the cover and identify the motherboard, CPU, RAM, USB, serial, and parallel ports (sockets for cable connectors), hard disk, CD-ROM, and other components and adapters, if present.

8.   Identify the following entities or devices as part of a computer system's hardware (H) or software (S).

      (a)   Operating system _____
      (b)   CPU _____
      (c)   GUI (Graphical User Interface) _____ ✓
      (d)   Modem _____ ✓
      (e)   Bus _____
      (f)   RAM _____
      (g)■ File _____

9.   Identify the operating system that is running on your current computer and some software applications installed on it: a word processor, an Internet browser, a spreadsheet program, e-mail, an image processing application, games, and so on.

Section 1.5

10.   Mark true or false:

(a)   Only data but not CPU instructions can be stored in RAM. _____

(b)   In ASCII code each character is represented in one byte. _____ ✓

(c)   16-bit binary numbers can be used to represent all non-negative integers from 0 to $2^{16}-1$. _____

(d)   Programs stored in ROM are referred to as "firmware." _____

11.   What is the maximum number of different codes or numbers that can be represented in

(a)   3 bits?   ✓
(b)   8 bits?   _____
(c)   2 bytes?   _____

12.   Assuming that binary numbers represent unsigned integers in the usual way, with the least significant bit on the right, write the decimal value and the hex representation of the following binary numbers. Example:

```
          Binary               Decimal        Hex

          00001000                8            08
          00011100               28            1C
```

(a)   00000010   _____   _____
(b)   00000111   _____   _____
(c)   10000000   _____   _____
(d)   00001011   _____   _____   ✓
(e)   11000011   _____   _____
(f)   11110101   _____   _____
(g)▪   00000101 10010010   _____   _____   ✓

13. An experiment consists of tossing a coin 10 times and its outcome is a sequence of heads and tails. How many possible outcomes are there?

14. How much memory does it take to hold a 512 by 512 gray-scale image with 256 levels of gray? ✓

15. When a printer runs out of paper, the eight-bit printer status register of the parallel interface adapter gets the following settings: bit 7 (leftmost bit), "BUSY," is set to 1; bit 5, "PE" ("paper end"), is set to 1; and bit 3, "ERROR," is set to 0. Bit 4 is always 1 when a printer is connected; bit 6 is 0; and bits 0-2 are not used. Write the hex value equal to the setting of the printer status register when the printer runs out of paper, assuming that bits 0-2 are 0.

16.▪ Design a method for representing the state of a tic-tac-toe board in computer memory. Can you fit your representation into three bytes? ✓

17.◆ In the game of *Nim*, stones are arranged in piles of arbitrary size. Each player in turn takes a few stones from any one pile. Every player must take at least one stone on every turn. The player who takes the last stone wins.

Games of this type always have a winning strategy. This strategy can be established by tagging all possible positions in the game with two tags, "plus" and "minus," in such a way that any move from a "plus" position always leads to a "minus" position, and from any "minus" position there is always a possible move into some "plus" position. The final winning position must be tagged "plus." Therefore, if the first player begins in a "minus" position, she can win by moving right away into a "plus" position and returning to a "plus" position on each subsequent move. If, however, the first player begins in a "plus" position, then the second player can win, provided he knows how to play correctly.

In Nim, we can convert the number of stones in each pile into a binary number and write these binary numbers in one column (so that the "units" digits are aligned on the right). We can tag the position "plus" if the number of 1's in each column is even and "minus" if the count of 1's in at least one column is odd. Prove that this method of tagging "plus" and "minus" positions defines a winning strategy. Who wins starting with four piles of 1, 3, 5, and 7 stones — the first or the second player? What's the correct response if the first player takes five stones from the pile of 7?

18.◆   The table below is called a *Greco-Roman square*: each of the three Latin letters occurs exactly once in each row and each column; the same is true for each of the three Greek letters; and each Latin-Greek combination occurs exactly once in the table:

Aγ	Bα	Cβ
Bβ	Cγ	Aα
Cα	Aβ	Bγ

Substitute the digits 0, 1, and 2 for A, B, C and for α, β, γ (in any order). Convert the resulting base-3 numbers into decimal (base-10) numbers. The base-3 system uses only three digits: 0, 1, and 2. The numbers are represented as follows:

Decimal	Base 3
0	0
1	1
2	2
3	10
4	11
5	12
6	20
7	21
8	22
9	100
. . .	. . .

Add 1 to each number. You will get a table in which the numbers 1 through 9 are arranged in such a way that the sum of the numbers in each row and column is the same. Explain why you get this result and find a way to substitute the digits 0, 1, and 2 for letters so that the sum of numbers in each of the two diagonals is also the same as in the rows and columns. What you get then is called a *magic square*. Using a similar method, build a 5 by 5 magic square.

19.   (MC) What does TCP stand for?

    A.   Telnet Control Program
    B.   Transmission Control Protocol
    C.   Transport Compression Protocol
    D.   Telephone Connectivity Program
    E.   None of the above

20.   Are the following entities or devices hardware (H) or software (S)?

    (a)   Host _____   ✓
    (b)   LAN _____
    (c)   Browser _____
    (d)   Search engine _____   ✓
    (e)   Router _____
    (f)■   TCP/IP Adapter _____   ✓

21.   Find and explore the home pages of some Internet and World Wide Web pioneers.

Chapter 2

An Introduction to Software Development

2.1 Prologue

One of the first computers, ENIAC,※eniac developed in 1942-1946 primarily for military applications, was programmed by people actually connecting hundreds of wires to sockets (Figure 2-1) — hardly a "software development" activity as we know it. (ENIAC occupied a huge room, had 18,000 vacuum tubes, and could perform 300 multiplications per second.) In 1946, John von Neumann developed the idea that a computer program can be stored in the computer memory itself in the form of encoded CPU instructions, together with the data on which the program operates. Then the modern computer was born: a "universal, digital, program-stored" computer that can perform calculations and process information.

Figure 2-1. Two technicians wiring the right side of ENIAC

(Courtesy of U. S. Army Research Laboratory)

Once program-stored computers were developed, it made sense to talk about programs as "written." In fact, at the beginning of the computer era, programmers wrote programs in pencil on special forms; then technicians punched the programs into punch cards※punchcard or perforated tape. A programmer entering a computer room with a deck of punch cards was a common sight. Fairly large programs were written entirely in machine code using octal or hexadecimal instruction codes and memory addresses. It is no coincidence that the same word, "coding," is used for writing programs and encrypting texts. Programmers were often simply mathematicians, electrical engineers, or scientists who learned the skill on their own when they needed to use a computer for their work.

In those days computers and "computer time" (that is, the time available for running programs) were very expensive, much more expensive than a programmer's time, and the high computer costs defined the rules of the game. For instance, only fairly important computer applications could be considered, such as military and scientific computations, large information systems, and so on. Programmers strove to make their programs run faster by developing efficient *algorithms* (the concept of an *algorithm* is described in Chapter 4). Often one or two programmers wrote the entire program and knew all about it, while no one else could understand it. Computer users were happy just to have access to a computer and were willing to learn cryptic instructions and formats for using programs.

Now, when computers are so inexpensive that they have become a household appliance, while programmers are relatively scarce and expensive, the rules of the game have changed completely. This change affects which programs are written, how they are created, and even the name by which programmers prefer to be called — "software engineers." There is still a need, of course, for understanding and optimizing algorithms. But the emphasis has shifted to programmers' productivity, professionalism, and teamwork — which requires using standard programming languages, tools, and software components.

Software applications that run on a desktop computer are loaded with features and must be very interactive and "*user-friendly*," (that is, have an intuitive and fairly conventional user interface). They must also be *portable* (that is, able to run on different computer systems) and internationalized (that is, easily adaptable for different languages and local conventions). Since a large team may work on the same software project, it is very important that teams follow standard development methodologies, and that the resulting programs be understandable to others and well documented. Thus software engineering has become as professionalized as other engineering disciplines: there is a lot of emphasis on knowing and using professional tools in a team environment, and virtually no room for solo wizardry.

A typical fairly large software project may include the following tasks:

- Interaction with customers, understanding customer needs, refining and formalizing specifications

- General design (defining a software product's parts, their functions and interactions)

- Detailed design (defining objects, functions, algorithms, file layouts, etc.)
- Design/prototyping of the user interface (designing screen layouts, menus, dialog boxes, online help, reports, messages, etc.)

- Coding and debugging

- Performance analysis and code optimization

- Documentation

- Testing

- Packaging and delivery

- User technical support

And, in the real world:

- Bug fixes, patches and workarounds, updated releases, documentation updates, and so on.

Of course there are different levels and different kinds of software engineers, and it is not necessary that the same person combine all the skills needed to design and develop good software. Usually it takes a whole team of software designers, programmers, artists, technical writers, QA (Quality Assurance) specialists, and technical support people.

In this chapter we will first discuss general topics related to software development, such as high-level programming languages and software development tools. We will discuss the difference between compilers and interpreters and Java's hybrid compiler + interpreter approach. Then we will learn how to compile and run simple Java applications and applets and take a first look at the concepts involved in object-oriented programming.

2.2   Compilers and Interpreters

Computer programmers very quickly realized that the computer itself was the perfect tool to help them write programs. The first step toward automation was made when programmers began to use *assembly languages* instead of numerically coded CPU instructions. In an assembly language, every CPU instruction has a short mnemonic name. A programmer can give symbolic names to memory locations and can refer to these locations by name. For example, a programmer using assembly language for Intel's 8086 microprocessor can write:

```
index   dw      0           ; "Define word" -- reserve 2 bytes
                            ;  for an integer and call it "index".
        ...
        mov     si,index    ; Move the value of index into
                            ;  the SI register.
        ...
```

A special program, called the *assembler*, converts the text of a program written in assembly language into the *machine code* expected by the CPU.

Obviously, assembly language is totally dependent on a particular CPU; *porting* a program to a different type of machine would require rewriting the code. As the power of computers increased, several *high-level* programming languages were developed for writing programs in a more abstract, machine-independent way. FORTRAN (F̲ormula T̲ranslation Language) was defined in 1956, COBOL (C̲ommon B̲usiness O̲riented L̲anguage) in 1960, and Pascal and C in the 1970s. C++ gradually evolved from C in the 1980s, adding OOP (O̲bject-O̲riented P̲rogramming) features to C.languagehistory Java was introduced in the mid-1990s and eventually gained popularity as a fully object-oriented programming language for platform-independent development, in particular for programs transmitted over the Internet. Java and OOP are of course the main subjects of this book, so we will start looking at them in detail in the following chapters.

A program written in a high-level language obeys the very formal *syntax* rules of the language. This syntax produces statements so unambiguous that even a computer can interpret them correctly. In addition to strict syntax rules, a program follows *style* conventions; these are not mandatory but make the program easier to read and understand for fellow programmers, demonstrating its author's professionalism.

❖   ❖   ❖

A programmer writes the text of the program using a software program called an *editor*. Unlike general-purpose word-processing programs, program editors may have special features useful for writing programs. For example, an editor may use colors to highlight different syntactic elements in the program or have built-in tools for entering standard words or expressions common in a particular programming language.

> **The text of a program in a particular programming language is referred to as *source code*, or simply the *source*. The source code is stored in a file, called the *source file*.**

Before it can run on a computer, a program written in a high-level programming language has to be somehow converted into CPU instructions. One approach is to use a special software tool called a *compiler*. The compiler is specific to a particular programming language and a particular CPU. It analyzes the source code and generates appropriate CPU instructions. The result is saved in another file, called the *object module*. A large program may include several source files that are compiled into object modules separately. Another program, a *linker*, combines all the object modules into one *executable* program and saves it in an executable file (Figure 2-2).

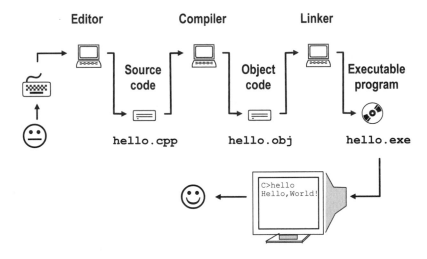

Figure 2-2. Software development cycle for a compiled program: edit-compile-link-run

For a compiled program, once it is built and tested, the executable file is distributed to program users. The users do not need access to the program's source code and do not need to have a compiler.

> **Java also uses a compiler, but, as we will explain shortly, the Java compiler does not generate object code.**

In an alternative approach, instead of compiling, a program in a high-level language can be *interpreted* by a software tool called an *interpreter*. The difference between a compiler and an interpreter is subtle but important. An interpreter looks at the high-level language program, figures out what instructions it needs to execute, and executes them. But it does not generate an object-code file and does not save any compiled or executable code. A user of an interpreted program needs access to the program's source code and an interpreter, and the program has to be interpreted again each time it is run. It is like a live concert as opposed to a studio recording, and a live performance needs all the instruments each time.

A particular programming language is usually established as either a compiled language or an interpreted language (that is, is either more often used with a compiler or an interpreter, respectively). FORTRAN, COBOL, Pascal, C++ are typically compiled; BASIC, Perl, Python are interpreted. But there is really no clear-cut distinction. BASIC, for example, was initially an interpreted language, but soon BASIC compilers were developed. C is usually compiled, but C interpreters also exist.

Java is different: it uses a mixed compiler-plus-interpreter approach. A Java compiler first compiles the program into *bytecodes*, instructions that are pretty close to a machine language. But a machine with this machine language does not exist! It is an abstract computer, a *Java Virtual Machine* (*JVM*). The bytecodes are then interpreted on a particular computer by the Java interpreter for that particular CPU. A program in bytecodes is not object code, because it is still platform-independent (it does not use instructions specific to a particular CPU). It is not source code, either, because it is not readable by humans. It is something in between.

Why does Java use a combination of a compiler and an interpreter? There is no reason why a regular Java compiler couldn't be created for a particular type of computer. But one of the main purposes of Java is to deliver programs to users via the Internet. A *Java-enabled* browser (that is, a browser that has a Java interpreter built into it) can run little Java programs, called *applets* (miniature applications). The many applets available free on the Internet, often with their source code, are one of the reasons why Java has become so popular so fast. When you connect to a web site and see some elaborate action or interactive features, it may mean that your computer has received a Java applet and is running it.

Java designers had to address the key question: Should users receive Java source code or executable code? The answer they came up with was: neither. If users got source, their browsers would need a built-in Java compiler or interpreter. That would make browsers quite big, and compiling or interpreting on the user's computer could take a long time. Also, software providers may want to keep their source confidential. But if users got executables, then web site operators would somehow need to know what kind of computer each user had (for example, a PC or a Mac) and deliver the right versions of programs. It would be cumbersome and expensive for web site operators to maintain different versions of a program for every different platform.   There would also be a security risk: What if someone delivered a malicious program to your computer?

Bytecodes provide an intermediate step, a compromise between sending source code or executables to users (Figure 2-3).   On one hand, the bytecodes' language is platform-independent, so the same version of bytecodes can serve users with different types of computers. It is not readily readable by people, so it can protect the confidentiality of the source code. On the other hand, bytecodes are much closer to the "average" machine language, and they are easier and faster to interpret than "raw" Java source. Also, bytecode interpreters built into browsers get a chance to screen programs for potential security violations (for example, they can block reading of and writing to the user's disks).

To speed up the loading of applets, a new software technology has emerged, called *JIT* (Just-In-Time) compilers. A JIT compiler combines the features of a compiler and an interpreter.   While interpreting bytecodes, it also compiles them into executable code. (To extend our music analogy, a JIT compiler works like a recording of a live concert.) This means an applet can be interpreted and start running as soon as it is downloaded from the Internet. On subsequent runs of the same applet, it can be loaded and run from its executable file without any delay for reinterpreting bytecodes.

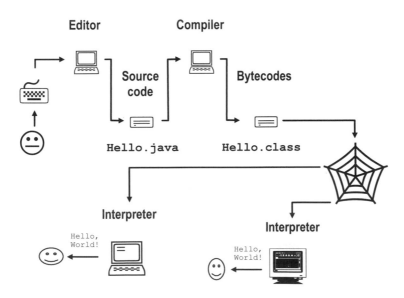

**Figure 2-3.   Java software development and distribution
through the Internet**

Naturally, bytecodes do not have to travel through the Internet to reach the user: a Java program can be compiled and interpreted on the same computer. That is what we will do for testing Java applications in our labs and exercises. We do not even have to use a browser to test an applet: the standard Java Development Kit (JDK) has a program, called *Applet Viewer*, that runs applets.

Modern software development systems combine an editor, a compiler, and other tools into one *Integrated Development Environment* (*IDE*). Some of the software development tools (a program editor, for example) are built into the IDE program itself; larger tools (a compiler, an interpreter) are usually stand-alone programs, for which the IDE only serves as a *front end*. An IDE has a convenient *GUI* (*Graphical User Interface*) — one mouse click on an icon will compile and run your program.

Modern programs may be rather complex, with dozens of different types of objects and functions involved. *Structure analyzers* and viewers built into an IDE create graphical views of source files, objects, their functions, and the dependencies between them. GUI *visual prototyping and design tools* help a programmer design and implement a graphical user interface.

Few programs are written on the first try without errors or, as programmers call them, *bugs* (Figure 2-4).

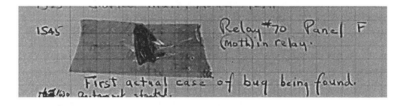

Figure 2-4. The term "bug" was popularized by Grace Hopper,[hopper] a legendary computer pioneer, who was the first to come up with the idea of a compiler and who created COBOL. One of Hopper's favorite stories was about a moth that was found trapped between the points of a relay, which caused a malfunction of the Mark II Aiken Relay Calculator (Harvard University, 1945). Technicians removed the moth and affixed it to the log shown in the photograph.

▌ **Programmers distinguish *syntax errors* and *logic errors*.**

Syntax errors violate the syntax rules of the language and are caught by the compiler. Logic errors are caused by flawed logic in the program; they are not caught by the compiler but show up at "run-time," that is when the program is running. Some run-time errors cause an *exception*: the program encounters a fatal condition and is aborted with an error message, which describes the type of the exception and the program statement that caused it. Other run-time errors may cause program's unexpected behavior or incorrect results. These are caught only in thorough testing of the program.

It is not always easy to correct bugs just by looking at the source code or by testing the program on different data. To help with this, there are special *debugger* programs that allow the programmer to trace the execution of a program "in slow motion." A debugger can suspend a program at a specified break point or step through the program statements one at a time. With the help of a debugger, the programmer can examine the sequence of operations and the contents of memory locations after each step.

2.3   Software Components and Packages

Writing programs from scratch may be fun, like growing your own tomatoes from seeds, but in the present environment few people can afford it. An amateur, faced with a programming task, asks: What is the most original (elegant, efficient, creative, interesting, etc.) way to write this code? A professional asks: What is the way to not write this code but use something already written by someone else? With billions of lines of code written, chances are someone has already implemented this or a similar task, and there is no point duplicating his or her efforts. (A modern principle, but don't try it with your homework!) Software is a unique product because all of its production cost goes into designing, coding and testing one copy; manufacturing multiple copies is virtually free. So the real task is to find out what has been done, purchase the rights to it if it is not free, and reuse it.

There are many sources of reusable code. Extensive software packages come with your compiler. Other packages may be purchased from third-party software vendors who specialize in developing and marketing reusable software packages to developers. Still other packages may be available for free in the spirit of an "open source" philosophy. In addition, every experienced programmer has accumulated his or her own collection of reusable code.

Reusability of software is a two-sided concept. As a programmer, you want to be more efficient by reusing existing code. But you also want to write reusable code so that you yourself, your teammates, your enterprise, and/or the whole world can take advantage of it later. Creating reusable code is not automatic: your code must meet certain requirements to be truly reusable. Here is a partial list of these requirements:

- Your code must be divided into reasonably small parts or components (modules). Each component must have a clear and fairly general purpose. Components that implement more general functions must be separated from more specialized components.

- Your software components must be well documented, especially the interface part, which tells the user (in this case, another programmer) what this component does and how exactly to use it. A user does not necessarily always want to know how a particular component does what it does.

- The components must be robust. They must be thoroughly tested under all possible conditions under which the component can be used, and these conditions must be clearly documented. If a software module encounters conditions under which it is not supposed to work, it should handle such situations gracefully, giving its user a clue when and why it failed instead of just crashing the system.

- It should be possible to customize or extend your components without completely rewriting them.

Individual software components are usually combined into *packages*. A package combines functions that deal with a particular set of structures or objects: a graphics package that deals with graphics capabilities and display; a text package that manipulates strings of text and text documents; a file package that helps to read and write data files; a math package that provides mathematical functions and algorithms; and so on. In Chapter 19, we will talk about Java collections classes, which are part of the `java.util` package from the standard Java library. Java programmers can take advantage of dozens of standard packages that are already available for free; new packages are being developed all the time. At the same time, the plenitude of available packages and components puts an additional burden on the software engineer, who must be familiar with the standard packages and keep track of the new ones.

2.4 *Lab:* Three Ways to Say Hello

A traditional way to start exploring a new software development environment is to write and get running a little program that just prints "Hello, World!" on the screen. After doing that, we will explore two other very simple programs. Later, in Section 2.6, we will look at simple GUI applications and a couple of applets.

In this section, we will use the most basic set of tools, JDK (Java Development Kit). JDK comes from Sun Microsystems, Inc., the makers and owners of Java.

> **JDK includes a compiler, an interpreter, the *Applet Viewer* program, other utility programs, the standard Java library, documentation, and examples.**

JDK itself does not have an IDE (Integrated Development Environment), but Sun and many third-party vendors and various universities and other organizations offer IDEs for running Java. *Eclipse, BlueJ, JCreator* are some examples, but there are dozens of others. This book's companion web site, `www.skylit.com/javamethods`, has a list of several development environments and *FAQs* (*Frequently Asked Questions*) about installing and using some of them.

> **In this lab the purpose is to get familiar with JDK itself, without any IDE. However, if you don't feel like getting your hands dirty (or if you are not authorized to run command-line tools on your system), you can start using "power" tools right away. Just glance through the text and then use an IDE to type in and test the programs in this lab.**

We assume that by now you have read Sun's instructions for installing and configuring JDK under your operating system and have it installed and ready to use. In this lab you can test that your installation is working properly. If you are not going to use command-line tools, then you need to have an IDE installed and configured as well.

This lab involves three examples of very simple programs that do not use GUI, just text input and output. Programs with this kind of old-fashioned user interface are often called *console applications* (named after a teletype device called a console, which they emulate). Once you get the first program running, the rest should be easy.

Our examples and commands in this section are for *Windows*.

1. Hello, World

JDK tools are *UNIX*-style *command-line tools*, which means the user has to type in commands at the system prompt to run the compiler, the interpreter, or *Applet Viewer*. The compiler is called `javac.exe`, the interpreter is called `java.exe`, and *Applet Viewer* is called `appletviewer.exe`. These programs reside in the `bin` subfolder of the folder where your JDK is installed. This might be, for example, `C:\Program Files\Java\jdk1.5.0_06\bin`. You'll need to make these programs accessible from any folder on your computer. To do that, you need to set the *path environment variable* to include JDK's `bin` folder. There is a way to make a permanent change to the path, but today we will just type it in once or twice, because we don't plan on using command-line tools for long.

Create a work folder (for example, C:\Mywork) where you will put your programs from this lab. You can use any editor (such as *Notepad*) or word processor (such as *Wordpad* or *MS Word*) or the editor from your IDE to enter Java source code. If you use a word processor, make sure you save Java source files as "Text Only." But the file extension should be .java. Word processors such as *Word* tend to attach the .txt extension to your file automatically. The trick is to first choose Save as type: Text-Only (*.txt), and only <u>after that</u> type in the name of your file with the correct extension (for example, HelloWorld.java).

In your editor, type in the following program and save it in a text file HelloWorld.java:

```
/**
 *  Displays a "Hello World!" message on the screen
 */
public class HelloWorld
{
  public static void main(String[] args)
  {
    System.out.println("Hello, World!");
  }
}
```

| **In Java, names of files are case sensitive.**

This is true even when you run programs in a *Command Prompt* window. Make sure you type in the upper and lower cases correctly.

In the little program above, HelloWorld is the name of a class as well as its source file. (Don't worry if you don't quite know what that means, for now.)

| **The name of the file that holds a Java class must be exactly the same as the name of that class (plus the extension .java).**

This rule prevents you from having two runnable versions of the same class in the same folder. Make sure you name your file correctly. There is a convention that the name of a Java class (and therefore the name of its Java source file) <u>always</u> starts with a capital letter.

> **The Java interpreter calls the `main` method in your class to start your program. Every application (but <u>not</u> an applet) must have a `main` method. The one in your program is:**
>
> ```
> public static void main(String[] args)
> ```

For now, treat this as an idiom. You will learn the meaning of the words `public`, `static`, `void`, `String`, and `args` later.

`System` is a class that is built into all Java programs. It provides a few system-level services. `System.out` is a data element in this class, an object that represents the computer screen output device. Its `println` method displays a text string on the screen.

> **Examine what you have typed carefully and correct any mistakes — this will save time.**

Save your file and close the editor. Open the *Command Prompt* window (you'll find it under *All Programs/Accessories* on your *Start* menu). Navigate to the folder that contains your program (for example, `Mywork`) using the `cd` (change directory) command, and set the path:

```
C:\Documents and Settings\Owner>cd \Mywork
C:\Mywork>path C:\program files\java\jdk1.5.0_06\bin;%PATH%
```

Now compile your program:

```
C:\Mywork>javac HelloWorld.java
```

If you have mistyped something in your source file, you will get a list of errors reported by the compiler. Don't worry if this list is quite long, as a single typo can cause several errors. Verify your code against the program text above, eliminate the typos, and recompile until there are no errors.

Type the `dir` (directory) command:

```
C:\Mywork>dir
```

You should see files called `HelloWorld.java` and `HelloWorld.class` in your folder. The latter is the bytecodes file created by the compiler.

Now run the Java interpreter to execute your program:

```
C:\Mywork>java HelloWorld
```

Every time you make a change to your source code, you'll need to recompile it. Otherwise the interpreter will work with the old version of the `.class` file.

2. Greetings

A Java application can accept "command-line" arguments from the operating system. These are words or numbers (character strings separated by spaces) that the user can enter on the command line when he runs the program. For example, if the name of the program is *Greetings* and you want to pass two arguments to it, "Annabel" and "Lee", you can enter:

```
C:\Mywork>java Greetings Annabel Lee
```

If you are using an IDE, it usually has an option, a dialog box, where you can enter command-line arguments before you run the program.

If you are already using your IDE and do not feel like figuring out how to enter command-line arguments in it, skip this exercise.

The following Java program expects two command-line arguments.

```java
/**
 *   This program expects two command-line arguments
 *   -- a person's first name and last name.
 *   For example:
 *   C:\Mywork>java Greetings Annabel Lee
 */
public class Greetings
{
  public static void main(String[] args)
  {
    String firstName = args[0];
    String lastName = args[1];
    System.out.println("Hello, " + firstName + " " + lastName);
    System.out.println("Congratulations on your second program!");
  }
}
```

Type this program in using your editor and save it in the text-only file `Greetings.java`. Compile this program:

```
C:\Mywork>javac Greetings.java
```

Now run it with two command-line arguments: your first and last name.

3. More Greetings

Now we can try a program that will *prompt* you for your name and then display a message. You can modify the previous program. Start by saving a copy of it in the text file Greetings2.java.

```
/*
    This program prompts the user to enter his or her
    first name and last name and displays a greeting message.
    Author: Maria Litvin
*/

import java.util.Scanner;

public class Greetings2
{
  public static void main(String[] args)
  {
    Scanner kboard = new Scanner(System.in);
    System.out.print("Enter your first name: ");
    String firstName = kboard.nextLine();
    System.out.print("Enter your last name: ");
    String lastName = kboard.nextLine();
    System.out.println("Hello, " + firstName + " " + lastName);
    System.out.println("Welcome to Java!");
  }
}
```

Our Greetings2 class uses a Java library class Scanner from the java.util package. This class helps to read numbers, words, and lines from keyboard input. The import statement at the top of the program tells the Java compiler where it can find Scanner.class.

Compile Greetings2.java —

```
C:\Mywork>javac Greetings2.java
```

— and run it:

```
C:\Mywork>java greetings2
```

What do you get?

```
Exception in thread "main" java.lang.NoClassDefFoundError: greetings2 (wrong
name: Greetings2)
        at java.lang.ClassLoader.defineClass1(Native Method)
        at java.lang.ClassLoader.defineClass(ClassLoader.java:620)
        at java.security.SecureClassLoader.defineClass(SecureClassLoader.java:124)
        at java.net.URLClassLoader.defineClass(URLClassLoader.java:260)
        at java.net.URLClassLoader.access$100(URLClassLoader.java:56)
        at java.net.URLClassLoader$1.run(URLClassLoader.java:195)
        at java.security.AccessController.doPrivileged(Native Method)
        at java.net.URLClassLoader.findClass(URLClassLoader.java:188)
        at java.lang.ClassLoader.loadClass(ClassLoader.java:306)
        at sun.misc.Launcher$AppClassLoader.loadClass(Launcher.java:268)
        at java.lang.ClassLoader.loadClass(ClassLoader.java:251)
        at java.lang.ClassLoader.loadClassInternal(ClassLoader.java:319)
```

Wow! The problem is, you entered greetings2 with a lowercase "G", and the Java interpreter cannot find a file called greetings2.class. Remember: Java is case-sensitive. You can see now why you might want some help from an IDE!

Try again:

```
C:\Mywork>java Greetings2
```

Now the program should run: it prompts you for your first and last name and displays a greeting message:

```
C:\Mywork>java Greetings2
Enter your first name: Virginia
Enter your last name: Woolf
Hello, Virginia  Woolf
Welcome to Java!
```

2.5 Object-Oriented Programming

In von Neumann computer architecture, a program is a sequence of instructions executed by a CPU. Blocks of instructions can be combined into *procedures* that perform a certain calculation or carry out a certain task; these can be called from other places in the program. Procedures manipulate some data stored elsewhere in computer memory. This *procedural* way of thinking is suggested by the hardware architecture, and naturally it prevailed in the early days of computing. In *procedural programming*, a programmer has an accurate picture of the order in which instructions might be executed and procedures might be called. High-level *procedural languages* don't change that fact. One statement translates into several CPU instructions and groups of statements are combined into functions, but the nature of programming remains the same: the statements are executed and the functions are called in a precise order imposed by the programmer. These procedures and functions work on separately defined data structures.

In the early days, user interface took the form of a dialog: a program would show prompts asking for data input and display the results at the end, similar to the *Greetings2* program in the previous section. This type of user interface is very orderly — it fits perfectly into the sequence of a procedural program. When the concept of *graphical user interface* (*GUI*) developed, it quickly became obvious that the procedural model of programming was not very convenient for implementing GUI applications. In a program with a GUI, a user sees several GUI components on the screen at once: menus, buttons, text entry fields, and so on. Any of the components can generate an event: things need to happen whenever a user chooses a menu option, clicks on a button, or enters text. A program must somehow handle these events in the order of their arrival. It is helpful to think of these GUI components as animated objects that can communicate with the user and other objects. Each object needs its own memory to represent its current state. A completely different programming model is needed to implement this metaphor. *Object-oriented programming* (*OOP*) provides such a model.

The OOP concept became popular with the introduction of Smalltalk,[smalltalk] the first general-purpose object-oriented programming language with built-in GUI development tools. Smalltalk was developed in the early 1970s by Alan Kay[kay] and his group at the Xerox Palo Alto Research Center. Kay dreamed that when inexpensive personal computers became available, every user, actually every child, would be able to program them; OOP, he thought, would make this possible. As we know, that hasn't quite happened. Instead, OOP first generated a lot of interest in academia as a research subject and a teaching tool, and then was gradually embraced by the software industry, along with C++, and later Java, as the preferred way of designing and writing software.

One can think of an OOP application as a virtual world of active objects. Each object has its own "memory," which may contain other objects. Each object has a set of *methods* that can process messages of certain types, change the object's state (memory), send messages to other objects, and create new objects. An object belongs to a particular class, and each object's functionality, methods, and memory structure are determined by its class. A programmer creates an OOP application by defining classes.

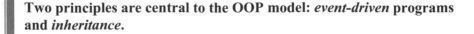

Two principles are central to the OOP model: *event-driven* programs and *inheritance.*

In an OOP program many things may be happening at once, and external events (for example, the user clicks the mouse or types a key, the application's window is resized, etc.) can determine the order of program execution. An OOP program, of course, still runs on sequential von Neumann computers; but the software simulates parallelism and asynchronous handling of events.

An OOP program usually defines many different types of objects. However, one type of objects may be very similar to another type. For instance, objects of one type may need to have all the functionality of another type plus some additional features. It would be a waste to duplicate all the features of one class in another. The mechanism of *inheritance* lets a programmer declare that one class of objects *extends* another class. The same class may be extended in several different ways, so one *superclass* may have several *subclasses* derived from it (Figure 2-5). A subclass may in turn be a superclass for other classes, such as `Music` is for `Audio` and `MP3`. An application ends up looking like a branching tree, a hierarchy of classes. Classes with more general features are closer to the top of the hierarchy, while classes with more specific functionality are closer to the bottom.

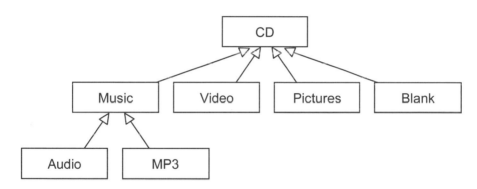

**Figure 2-5. A hierarchy of classes that represent
compact disks with different content**

Object-oriented programming aims to answer the current needs in software development: lower software development and documentation costs, better coordinated team development, accumulation and reuse of software components, more efficient implementation of multimedia and GUI applications, and so on. Java is a fully object-oriented language that supports inheritance and the event-driven model. It includes standard packages for graphics, GUI, multimedia, events handling, and other essential software development tools.

Our primary focus in this book is working with hierarchies of classes. Event-driven software and events handling in Java are considered to be more advanced topics. For example, they are not included in the Advanced Placement Computer Science course description. We will discuss events handling in Java and provide examples in Chapters 16 and 17.

2.6 *Lab:* More Ways to Say Hello

In Section 2.4 we learned how to run very simple console applications. These types of programs, however, are not what makes Java great: they can be easily written in other programming languages.

> **The features that distinguish Java from other languages are its built-in support for GUI and graphics and its support for object-oriented programming.**

In this section we will consider four more examples: two applications (one with a simple GUI object, another with graphics), and two applets (one with graphics and one with animation). Of course at this stage you won't be able to understand all the code in these examples — we have a whole book ahead of us! This is just a preview of things to come, a chance to get a general idea of what is involved and see how these simple programs work.

1. A GUI application

In this program, `HelloGui.java`, we create a standard window on the screen and place a "Hello, GUI!" message in it. Our `HelloGui` class *extends* the `JFrame` library class, which is part of Java's *Swing* package. We are lucky we can reuse `JFrame`'s code: it would be a major job to write a class like this from scratch. We would have to figure out how to show the title bar and the border of the window and how to support resizing of the window and other standard functions. `JFrame` takes care of all this. All we have left to do is add a label to the window's *content pane* — the area where you can place GUI components.

Our `HelloGui` class is shown in Figure 2-6. In this program, the `main` method creates one object, which we call `window`. The type of this object is described as `HelloGui`; that is, `window` is an object of the `HelloGui` class. This program uses only one object of this class. `main` then sets `window`'s size and position (in pixels) and displays it on the screen. Our class has a *constructor*, which is a special procedure for constructing objects of this class. Constructors always have the same name as the class. Here the constructor calls the superclass's constructor to set the text displayed in the window's title bar and adds a label object to the window's content pane.

```
/**
 *  This program displays a message in a window.
 */

import java.awt.*;
import javax.swing.*;

public class HelloGui extends JFrame      imitates
{
  public HelloGui()    // Constructor
  {
    super("GUI Demo");     // Set the title bar
    Container c = getContentPane();
    c.setBackground(Color.CYAN);
    c.setLayout(new FlowLayout());
    c.add(new JTextField(" Hello, GUI!", 10));
  }

  public static void main(String[] args)
  {
    HelloGui window = new HelloGui();

    // Set this window's location and size:
    // upper-left corner at 300, 300; width 200, height 100
    window.setBounds(300, 300, 200, 100);

    window.setDefaultCloseOperation(JFrame.EXIT_ON_CLOSE);
    window.setVisible(true);
  }
}
```

Figure 2-6. J_M\Ch02\HelloGui\HelloGui.java

The code in Figure 2-6 is a little cryptic, but still we can see roughly what's going on. Do not retype the program — just copy `HelloGui.java` form the J_M\Ch02\HelloGui folder into your current work folder. Set up a project in your favorite IDE, create a new class, `HelloGui`, and type in its code. Compile and run the program using menu commands, buttons, or shortcut keys in your IDE.

2. Hello, Graphics

We will now change our program a little to paint some graphics on the window instead of a text label. The new class, `HelloGraphics`, is shown in Figure 2-7.

```java
//  This program shows simple graphics in a window.

import java.awt.*;
import javax.swing.*;

public class HelloGraphics extends JPanel
{
  public void paintComponent(Graphics g)
  {
    super.paintComponent(g);  // Call JPanel's paintComponent method
                              //  to paint the background
    g.setColor(Color.RED);

    // Draw a 150 by 45 rectangle with the upper-left
    // corner at x = 25, y = 40:
    g.drawRect(20, 40, 150, 45);

    g.setColor(Color.BLUE);

    // Draw a string of text starting at x = 60, y = 25:
    g.drawString("Hello, Graphics!", 55, 65);
  }

  public static void main(String[] args)
  {
    JFrame window = new JFrame("Graphics Demo");
    // Set this window's location and size:
    // upper-left corner at 300, 300; width 200, height 100
    window.setBounds(300, 300, 200, 150);
    window.setDefaultCloseOperation(JFrame.EXIT_ON_CLOSE);

    HelloGraphics panel = new HelloGraphics();
    panel.setBackground(Color.WHITE);  // the default color is light gray
    Container c = window.getContentPane();
    c.add(panel);

    window.setVisible(true);
  }
}
```

Figure 2-7. `J`_M`\Ch02\HelloGui\HelloGraphics.java`

HelloGraphics extends a library class JPanel. Each JPanel object has a paintComponent method that generates all the graphics contents for the panel. paintComponent is called automatically whenever the window is opened, resized, or repainted. These events are reported to the program by the operating system.

By default, JPanel's paintComponent method only paints the background of the panel. Our class HelloGraphics redefines (overrides) paintComponent to add a blue message inside a red box. paintComponent receives an object of the type Graphics, often called g, that represents the panel's graphics context (its position, size, etc.).

> **The graphics coordinates are in pixels and have the origin (0, 0) at the upper-left corner of the panel (the *y*-axis points down).**

We have placed the main method into the same class to simplify things. If you wish, you can split our HelloGraphics class into two separate classes: one, call it HelloPanel, will extend JPanel and have the paintComponent method; the other, call it HelloGraphics will have main and nothing else (it doesn't have to extend any library class). Your project should include both classes.

3. Hello, Applet

Applets are small programs embedded in web pages and distributed over the Internet. From a programmer's point of view, the difference between an applet and a GUI application is minor. Instead of extending JFrame, your applet's class extends JApplet, a *Swing* library class that represents applet objects. An applet does not need a main method because the browser (or *Applet Viewer*) automatically constructs the applet object and displays it as part of a web document. Instead of a constructor, your applet class uses the init method to initialize your applet. Figure 2-8 shows the HelloApplet class adapted from the HelloGraphics class. This applet redefines JApplet's paint method to show graphics.

```
// This applet shows a string of text inside a box.

import java.awt.*;
import javax.swing.*;

public class HelloApplet extends JApplet
{
  public void init()
  {
    Container c = getContentPane();
    c.setBackground(Color.WHITE);
  }

  public void paint(Graphics g)
  {
    super.paint(g);      // call JApplet's paint method
                         //  to paint the background
    g.setColor(Color.RED);
    g.drawRect(25, 40, 150, 45);  // draw a rectangle 150 by 45
    g.setColor(Color.BLUE);
    g.drawString("Hello, Applet!", 60, 65);
  }
}
```

Figure 2-8. JM**\Ch02\HelloGui\HelloApplet.java**

The code for this applet is shorter than `HelloGraphics`. But now we need another
file that describes a web page that presents the applet. The contents and layout of
web pages are usually described in HTML (Hypertext Mark-Up Language). You can
find a brief HTML tutorial in Appendix C.✸ Here we can use a very simple HTML
file (Figure 2-9). Let's call it `TestApplet.html`. As you can see, some of the
information — the size of the applet's content pane — has shifted from Java code
into the HTML file. The title bar is no longer used because an applet does not run in
a separate window — it is embedded into a browser's (or *Applet Viewer*'s) window.
An applet does not have an exit button either (the browser's or *Applet Viewer*'s
window has one).

```
<html>

<head>
<title>My First Java Applet</title>
</head>

<body>
<applet code="HelloApplet.class" width="300" height="100"
   alt="Java class failed">
Java is disabled
</applet>
</body>

</html>
```

Figure 2-9. `J`ₘ`\Ch02\HelloGui\TestApplet.html`

You can either test your applet directly in your IDE or open it in your Internet browser. If you have a website, you can upload the `TestApplet.html` page to your site, along with the `HelloApplet.class` file, for the whole world to see.

> **You can adapt `TestApplet.html` to run another applet by replacing `HelloApplet.class` in it with the name of your new applet class and adjusting the applet's size, if necessary.**

4. Hello, Action

And now, just for fun, let's put some action into our applet (Figure 2-10). Compile the `Banner` class from `J`ₘ`\Ch02\HelloGui` and open the `TestBanner.html` file (from the same folder) in the *Applet Viewer* or in the browser to test this applet.

Look at the code in `Banner.java`. The `init` method in this applet creates a `Timer` object called `clock` and starts the timer. The timer is programmed to fire every 30 milliseconds. Whenever the timer fires, it generates an event that is captured in the `actionPerformed` method. This method adjusts the position of the banner and repaints the screen.

You might notice that unfortunately the animation effect in this applet is not very smooth: the screen flickers whenever the banner moves. One of the advantages of Java's *Swing* package is that it can help deal with this problem. We will learn how to do it in later chapters.

```java
// This applet displays a message moving horizontally
// across the screen.

import java.awt.*;
import java.awt.event.*;
import javax.swing.*;

public class Banner extends JApplet
  implements ActionListener
{
  private int xPos, yPos;  // hold the coordinates of the banner

  public void init()
  {
    Container c = getContentPane();
    c.setBackground(Color.WHITE);
    xPos = c.getWidth();
    yPos = c.getHeight() / 2;
    Timer clock = new Timer(30, this);  // fires every 30 milliseconds
    clock.start();
  }

  // Called automatically after a repaint request
  public void paint(Graphics g)
  {
    super.paint(g);
    g.drawString("Hello, World!", xPos, yPos);
  }

  // Called automatically when the timer fires
  public void actionPerformed(ActionEvent e)
  {
    Container c = getContentPane();

    // Adjust the horizontal position of the banner:
    xPos--;
    if (xPos < -100)
    {
      xPos = c.getWidth();
    }

    // Set the vertical position of the banner:
    yPos = c.getHeight() / 2;

    repaint();
  }
}
```

Figure 2-10. JM\Ch02\HelloGui\Banner.java

2.7 Summary

In the modern development environment, programmers usually write programs in one of the *high-level programming languages* such as C++ or Java. A program written in a high-level language obeys the very precise syntax rules of that language and must also follow stylistic conventions established among professionals. For compiled languages, such as C or C++, a software program called the *compiler* translates the source code for a program from the high-level language into machine code for a particular CPU. A compiler creates object modules that are eventually linked into an executable program. Alternatively, instead of compiling, a program in a high-level language, such as BASIC or Python, can be interpreted by a software tool called an *interpreter*. An interpreter does not generate an executable program but instead executes the appropriate CPU instructions immediately.

Java takes a mixed compiler + interpreter approach: the source code is compiled into code (called *bytecodes*) for the *Java Virtual Machine* (*JVM*). JVM is not a real computer; it is an abstract model of a computer with features typical for different computer models. Bytecodes are still independent of a particular CPU, but are much closer to a machine language and easier to interpret than the source code. A Java interpreter installed on a specific computer then interprets the bytecodes and executes the instructions appropriate for that specific CPU.

An *IDE* (*Integrated Development Environment*) combines many tools, including an editor, a compiler, and a debugger, under one convenient *GUI* (*Graphical User Interface*).

The software development profession has evolved from an individual artisan craft into a highly structured engineering discipline with its own methodology, professional tools, conventions, and code of ethics. Modern applications are built in part out of standard reusable components from available packages. Programmers strive to produce and document new reusable components that meet the reliability, performance, and style requirements of their organization.

One can think of an *OOP* (*Object-Oriented Programming*) application as a virtual world of active objects. Each object holds its own memory and has a set of *methods* that can process messages of certain types, send messages to other objects, and create new objects. A programmer creates an OOP application by defining classes of objects. OOP is widely believed to lower software development costs, help coordinate team projects, and facilitate software reuse.

Exercises

Sections 2.1-2.3

1.   Which of the following are the advantages of using a high-level programming language, as opposed to a machine language? Mark true or false:

   (a)   It is easier to write programs. _____
   (b)   It is easier to read and understand programs. _____
   (c)   Programs run more efficiently. _____   ✓
   (d)   Programs can be ported more easily from one hardware platform to another. _____

2.   Name four commonly used programming languages besides Java.

3.   Mark true or false and explain:

   (a)   The operating system compiles source files into bytecodes or executable programs. _____

   (b)   Each modern computer system is equipped with a compiler. _____   ✓

4.   (MC) Which program helps programmers enter and modify source code?

   A.   Editor   B. Compiler   C. Linker   D. Interpreter
   E.   None of the above

5.   (MC) What is a debugger used for?

   A.   Removing comments from the source code
   B.   Running and tracing programs in a controlled way
   C.   Running diagnostics of hardware components
   D.   Removing syntax errors from Java programs
   E.   Removing dust from the computer screen

6.   True or false: a modern IDE provides a GUI front end for an editor, compiler, debugger, and other software development tools. _____   ✓

7.   Describe the differences between a compiler, a JIT compiler, and an interpreter.

Section 2.4

8.   (a)   Replace the forward slash in the first line of the `HelloWorld` program with a backslash. Compile your program and observe the result.

      (b)   Remove the first three lines altogether. Compile and run your program. What is the purpose of the `/*` and `*/` markers in Java programs?

9.   Write a program that generates the following output: ✓

```
  xxxxx
 x     x
(( o o ))
 |  V  |
 | === |
  -----
```

10.   Make sure that JDK documentation is installed on your computer. Use "Help" in your IDE to access Java API (Application Programming Interface) documentation. Alternatively, outside of the IDE, navigate to the JDK's `doc` folder, double-click on `index.html`, and when the browser shows the index page, find a link to the API documentation. Find the description of the `Color` class. What color constants (`Color.RED`, `Color.BLUE`, etc.) are defined in that class? ✓

11.■   (a)   Write a program that prompts the user to enter an integer and displays the entered value times two as follows:

```
Enter an integer: 5
2 * 5 = 10
```

≶ Hint: You'll need to place

```
import java.util.Scanner;
```

at the top of your program. The Scanner class has a method nextInt that reads an integer from the keyboard. For example:

```
Scanner keyboard = new Scanner(System.in);
...
int n = keyboard.nextInt();
```

Use

```
System.out.println("2 * " + n + " = " + (n + n));
```

to display the result. ≷

(b)   Remove the parentheses around n + n and test the program again. How does the + operator work for text strings and for numbers? ✓

Sections 2.5-2.7

12.   Name the two concepts that are central to object-oriented programming.

13.   (a)   The program *Red Cross* (JM\Ch02\Exercises\RedCross.java) is supposed to display a red cross on a white background. However, it has a bug. Find and fix the bug.

(b)■   Using RedCross.java as a prototype, write a program that displays

in the middle of the window. ≶ Hint: the Graphics class has a method fillOval; its parameters are the same as in the fillRect method for an oval inscribed into the rectangle. ≷

14. ■ Modify *HelloApplet* (J_M\Ch02\HelloGui\HelloApplet.java) to show a white message on a blue background. ⸢ Hint: `Graphics` has a method `fillRect` that is similar to `drawRect`, but it draws a "solid" rectangle, filled with color, not just an outline. ⸣ ✓

15. ■ Modify the *Banner* applet (J_M\Ch02\HelloGui\Banner.java) to show a solid black box moving from right to left across the applet's window.

16. ◆ Using the *Banner* applet (J_M\Ch02\HelloGui\Banner.java) as a prototype, write an applet that emulates a banner ad: it should display a message alternating "East or West" and "Java is Best" every 2 seconds.

⸢ Hints: At the top of your class, define a variable that keeps track of which message is to be displayed. For example:

```
private int msgID = 1;
```

In the method that processes the timer events, toggle `msgID` between 1 and -1:

```
msgID = -msgID;
```

Don't forget to call `repaint`.

In the method that draws the text, obtain the coordinates for placing the message:

```
Container c = getContentPane();
int xPos = c.getWidth() / 2 - 30;
int yPos = c.getHeight() / 2;
```

Then use a conditional statement to display the appropriate message:

```
if (msgID == 1)
{
   ...
}
else  // if msgID == -1
{
   ...
}
```

⸣

Objects and Classes

3.1 Prologue

Non-technical people sometimes envision a computer programmer's job as sitting at the computer and writing lines of code in a cryptic programming language. Perhaps this is how it might appear to a casual observer. But there is structure to this job. Even in the earliest days of the computer era, when programs were written directly in machine code, a programmer first developed a more or less abstract view of the task at hand. The overall task was split into meaningful subtasks; then a set of procedures was designed that accomplished specific subtasks; each procedure, in turn was divided into meaningful smaller segments.

What a programmer works with is not just lines and pages of computer code, but an orderly structure that matches the task. He or she has to be able to see the big picture or to zoom in on more intricate details as necessary. Over the years, different software development methodologies have evolved to facilitate this process and to enable programmers to better communicate with each other. The currently prevailing methodology is *Object-Oriented Programming* (*OOP*). OOP is considered more suitable than previous methodologies for:

- Team work

- Reuse of software components

- GUI development

- Program maintenance

In OOP, a programmer envisions a software application as a virtual world of interacting objects.

This world is highly structured. To think of objects in a program simply as fish in the ocean would be naive. If we take the ocean as a metaphor, consider that its objects include islands, boats, the sails on the boats, the ropes that control the sails, the people on board, the fish in the water, and even the horizon, an object that does not physically exist! There are objects within objects within objects, and the whole ocean is an object, too.

The following questions immediately come to mind:

- Who describes all the different types of objects in a program? When and how?

- How does an object represent and store information?

- When and how are objects created?

- How can an object communicate with other objects?

- How can objects accomplish useful tasks?

We'll start answering these questions in this chapter and continue through the rest of the book. Our objective in this chapter is to learn the following terms and concepts: object, class, CRC card, instance variable or field, constructor, method, public vs. private, encapsulation and information hiding, inheritance, IS-A and HAS-A relationships.

3.2   Objects in a Program: An Example

The window in Figure 3-1 comes from a toy program called *Step By Step Dance Studio* that teaches a novice dancer basic ballroom dancing steps. Run the program by clicking on the $\text{JM}\backslash\text{Ch03}\backslash\text{FirstSteps}\backslash\text{DanceStudio.jar}$ file.

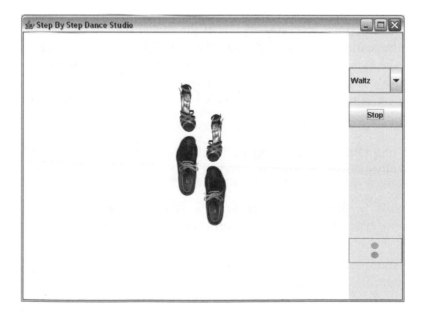

Figure 3-1. *Dance Studio* **program**

The user chooses a dance from the pull-down list, clicks on the "Go" button, and sees how dancers' feet move.

So how does one write a program like this in OO style? A good place to start is to decide what types of objects are needed.

> **An object in a running program is an entity that models an object or concept from the real world.**

Some of the objects in a program may model real-world objects, such as a dancer or a dancer's foot. There are also GUI objects that are visible or audible: buttons, menus, images, audio clips, timers, and so on. Other objects may represent more abstract concepts, such as a waltz or a coordinate system.

> **Each object in a running program has a set of attributes and behaviors. Each object's attributes hold specific values; some of these values can change while the program is running.**

For example, in the *Dance Studio* program, a dancer has two feet. A foot is an object with such attributes as location, direction, and screen image, and such behaviors as moving and turning. The image of a particular foot in the program remains the same, but the location and direction of a foot may change during a "dance."

A program often employs several objects of the same type. Such objects are said to belong to the same *class*. We also say that an object is an *instance* of its class. Objects of the same class have the same set of behaviors and attributes; they differ only in the values of their attributes. In Figure 3-1, for example, all four feet shown are objects (instances) of the same class `Foot`, but their locations, directions, and images are different.

In Java, a programmer must describe all the different types of objects used in a program in advance, in the program's source code.

> **A *class* is a piece of the program's source code that describes a particular type of objects. OO programmers write *class definitions*.**

Table 3-1 summarizes the concepts of a *class* and an *object* and the differences between them.

Class	Object
A piece of the program's source code	An entity in a running program
Written by a programmer	Created when the program is running (by the `main` method or a constructor or another method)
Specifies the structure (the number and types) of its objects' attributes — the same for all of its objects	Holds specific values of attributes; these values can change while the program is running
Specifies the possible behaviors of its objects	Behaves appropriately when called upon
A Java program's source code consists of several classes	A running program can create any number of objects of any class
Like a blueprint for building cars of a particular model	Like a car of a particular model that you can drive

Table 3-1. *Class* vs. *Object*

Now let us take a quick tour of the objects used in the *Dance Studio* program.

In *Dance Studio*, the most visible objects are of course the dancers. There is one male dancer and one female dancer. These two objects have similarities and differences: both make dance steps, but their pictures on the screen are different. Do they belong to the same class or different classes? Sometimes it is hard to decide whether two objects have serious "structural" differences and should be treated as different types or if they differ only in the values of some of their attributes. In OOP languages it is also possible to choose a compromise: two objects may belong to different subclasses of the same class. More on this later.

Each dancer has a left foot and a right foot. In this program, a foot is an object that can move and turn, and knows how to draw itself on the screen (from the picture given to it when the foot is created). Another object is the surface on which the dancers move, the "dance floor." This object is the GUI component on which the dancers are drawn.

The rest of the visible objects are GUI components. The area on the right side of the program window is a control panel object. It holds the control buttons and the pull-down list of dances. The buttons and the pull-down list are objects, too; they belong to classes defined in the Java library. In our implementation, it is the control panel's responsibility to capture "action events" generated by these GUI components.

Finally, we see an object that represents the whole window in which the program is running. This object holds both the dance floor and the control panel.

Dance Studio also uses more abstract types of objects. A "dance group" object represents the group on the dance floor as a whole. In this version of the program we have one male and one female dancer, but we have the flexibility to add more participants without changing other classes or GUI. A "band" object generates the beat. A "dance" object represents a sequence of steps. A "dance step" object represents one step in a dance. Finally, several types of objects represent different dances. Overall, the source code of the *Dance Studio* program refers to over 15 different types of objects defined by us and two dozen defined in the Java library.

❖   ❖   ❖

In OOP, a lot of the emphasis shifts from software development to software design. The design methodology, object-oriented design (OOD), matches the programming methodology (OOP). A good design makes implementation easier. But object-oriented design itself is not easy, and a bad design may derail a project.

The design phase starts with a preliminary discussion of the rough design. One of the informal techniques the designers might use is *CRC cards*. CRC stands for "Class, Responsibilities, Collaborators." A CRC card is simply an index card that describes a class of objects, including the class name, the main "responsibilities" of this type of object in the program, and its "collaborators," that is, other classes that it depends on (Figure 3-2).

At this initial stage, software designers do not have to nail down all the details. The responsibilities of objects are described in general terms. The need for additional types of objects may become apparent later in the process. In the *Dance Studio* program, there are objects that work behind the scenes. A coordinate system object, for example, will be brought in to represent a coordinate system associated with the image of a foot.

We will take a more detailed look at two classes from the *Dance Studio* project later in this chapter.

Dancer	
Controls the left and right foot.	Foot Dance
Learns dance steps.	
Knows how to start, make the next step, stop.	

Figure 3-2. A CRC card for the class Dancer

3.3 Classes

A formal description of a class is called a *class definition* or a *class declaration*.

Informally, we say that programmers write classes and that the source code of a Java program consists of one or several classes.

Each class is usually stored in a separate source file.

The name of the file must be the same as the name of the class, with the extension .java.

For example, a class Foot must be stored in a file named Foot.java.

In Java, all names, including the names of classes, are case-sensitive.

A class describes three aspects of an object: (1) the data elements (attributes) of an object of this class, (2) the ways in which such an object can be created, and (3) what this type of object can do.

> **An object's data elements are called *instance variables* or *data fields* (or simply *fields*). Procedures for creating an object are called *constructors*. An object's specific functions are called *methods*.**

The class describes all these features in a very formal and precise manner.

Figure 3-3 shows a schematic view of a class's source code. The source file may start with a few `import` statements, which tell the compiler where to look for the Java library classes used in this class. These are followed by a header that holds the name of the class, followed by the class definition body within braces.

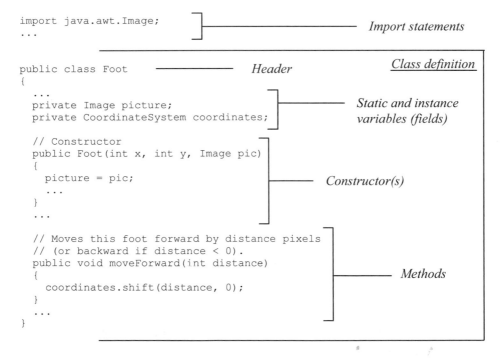

Figure 3-3. A schematic view of a class's source code

The header —

```
public class Foot
```

— states that the class `Foot` is `public`, which means it is visible to other classes.

The order of fields, constructors, and methods in a class definition does not matter for the compiler, but it is customary to group all the fields together, usually at the top, followed by all the constructors, and then all the methods.

> **Usually, the header of a class and each important feature of the class (constructor, method, public field) is preceded by a comment, which describes the purpose of that feature and how to use it.**

A class is sometimes compared to a cookie cutter: all objects of the class have the same configuration but might have different flavors. When the program is running, different objects of the same class may hold different values stored in their instance variables. A more apt comparison for a class, perhaps, would be a blueprint for making a specific model of a car. Like objects of the same class, cars of the same model have identically configured parts, but they may be of different colors, and when a car is running, the number of people in it or the amount of gas in the tank may be different from another car of the same model.

> **When a program is running, it is always executing some class's constructor or method.**

When a Java application starts, control is passed to the `main` method. A constructor or a method can create new objects — that's how new objects come into being. Once an object is created, a constructor or method can call this object's methods. The new object can in turn create other objects.

A new object is created by invoking (calling) a constructor of that object's class. The constructor sets the initial values of the object's instance variables. A programmer can pass parameters to the constructor, and the values of these parameters will be used to initialize some of the instance variables. The object's instance variables may remain constant over the lifetime of the object or they may change — that depends on how the object is used in the program.

A class definition does not have to start from scratch: it can *extend* the definition of another class, adding fields and methods or redefining (overriding) some of the methods. This feature of OOP programming languages is called *inheritance*. We will discuss inheritance in more detail in Section 3.6. Java programmers also make extensive use of Java library classes either by extending them or by creating and using their objects. For example, *Dance Studio*'s `ControlPanel` class extends a library class `JPanel`, and the "Go" and "Stop" buttons are objects that belong to a library class `JButton`.

Your class often refers to other classes in your project. For example, the `Dancer` class has two fields of the `Foot` type that represent the left and the right foot. So `Dancer` depends on `Foot`. The Java compiler automatically finds the definitions of the needed classes, as long as they are placed in the same folder. A programmer can also collect several compiled classes (`.class` files) in one *Java archive* (`.jar`) file and tell the compiler where to look for it.

Java library classes are collected in `.jar` files, too. If your class uses library classes, you need to put "import" statements at the top of your class definition file. For example, our `Foot` class uses the `Image` and `Graphics` classes from the `java.awt` package, so we put

```
import java.awt.Image;
import java.awt.Graphics;
```

at the top of `Foot.java` file. These statements tell the compiler that it can find the `Image` and `Graphics` classes in the `java.awt` package of the standard library. Or we could put

```
import java.awt.*;
```

Then the compiler would search the entire `java.awt` package for the class names that are undefined in the `Foot` class.

Without an `import` statement, you would have to use the *fully-qualified* name of the library class everywhere in your code, as in

```
public Foot(int x, int y, java.awt.Image pic)
```

instead of

```
public Foot(int x, int y, Image pic)
```

This would clutter your code.

❖   ❖   ❖

We are now ready to take a more detailed look at a complete class. But before you turn to the next page, we want you to know that you are <u>not expected</u> to understand all the details of the code. Trying to do that would be counterproductive at this stage. We want you to see the overall structure and the main elements of a class. After all, you can walk pretty well without knowing how every little bone in your foot works.

```
// Represents a foot, used for displaying walking creatures.

import java.awt.Image;
import java.awt.Graphics;
```
Uses Image *and* Graphics *classes from the* java.awt *library package*

```
public class Foot
{
```
Header with the class's name

```
  private Image picture;
  private CoordinateSystem coordinates;
```
Instance variables (fields)

```
  // Constructor
  public Foot(int x, int y, Image pic)
  {
    picture = pic;
    coordinates = new CoordinateSystem(x, y, pic);
  }
```
Constructor

```
  // Moves this foot forward by distance pixels
  // (or backward if distance < 0).
  public void moveForward(int distance)
  {
    coordinates.shift(distance, 0);
  }

  // Moves this foot sideways by distance pixels
  // (to the right if distance  > 0 or to the left
  // if distance < 0).
  public void moveSideways(int distance)
  {
    coordinates.shift(0, distance);
  }
```
Methods

```
  // Turns this foot (clockwise for degrees > 0).
  public void turn(int degrees)
  {
    coordinates.rotate(Math.PI * degrees / 180.0);
  }

  // Draws this foot in the appropriate coordinate system.
  public void draw(Graphics g)
  {
    coordinates.drawImage(g, picture);
  }
}
```

Figure 3-4. Anatomy of a Java class (JM\Ch03\FirstSteps\Foot.java)

The `Foot` class in Figure 3-4 represents a "foot" used for displaying a walking creature.

A `Foot` object can move forward or backward and sideways and it can turn. It has a picture that can be displayed on the screen. When we wrote this class, we tried to create a *reusable* class. We will see shortly how this class can be used in several different programs. In fact, `Foot` can be used for moving and turning any picture on the screen. In other words, our class is rather general: it represents a certain level of abstraction. More general means more reusable, but if a class becomes too general, then it may become unusable altogether. You need to keep a balance between reusability and ease of use.

The details of moving and turning images in Java are rather technical. We have created another class, called `CoordinateSystem`, and hidden the technical details behind its simplified façade, to make our `Foot` class more presentable. (Something tells us that you might not be particularly interested in learning about `AffineTransform` objects at this point.)

`picture`, an object of the `Image` type, is a field in `Foot`. An OO designer would say that a `Foot` HAS-A(n) (has an) `Image` and would show this relationship between classes in a UML (Unified Modeling Language) diagram:

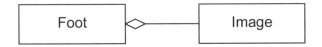

3.4 Fields, Constructors, and Methods

As we said earlier, the definition of a class describes all the *instance variables* of objects of the class. Instance variables are also called *data fields* or simply *fields*, from the analogy with fields in a form that can be filled in with different values.

Each field has a name, given by a programmer, and a type. A `Foot` object, for example, has two instance variables:

```
private Image picture;
private CoordinateSystem coordinates;
```

Think of an object's instance variables as its private "memory." (This is only a metaphor, of course: in reality, when a program is running, its objects are represented by chunks of RAM.) An object's "memory" may include other objects, and also numbers and text characters. (In Java, numbers and text characters are usually not represented by objects; for them Java provides special data types, `int`, `char`, etc., called *primitive data types*.)

An object is created with the `new` operator, which invokes (calls) one of the constructors defined in the object's class. For example:

```
Foot leftFoot = new Foot(5, 20, leftShoe);
```

This statement may belong in a constructor or a method of some class that uses `Foot` objects. It creates a new `Foot` object at location $x = 5$, $y = 20$, with an `Image` `leftShoe`.

A constructor is a procedure, usually quite short, that is used primarily to initialize the values of the instance variables for the object that is being created.

A constructor must always have the same name as its class.

A constructor can accept one or more parameters or no parameters at all. The latter is called a "no-args" constructor (parameters are often called "arguments," as in math, or "args" for short). `Foot`'s constructor accepts three parameters, `x`, `y`, and `pic`:

```
public Foot(int x, int y, Image pic)
{
  picture = pic;
  coordinates = new CoordinateSystem(x, y, pic);
}
```

This constructor assigns the value passed to it in the parameter `pic` directly to the field `picture`. For the second field, `coordinates`, it creates a new `CoordinateSystem` object, passing the same three parameters to it.

A class may have several constructors that differ in the number and/or the types of parameters that they accept.

For example, we could define another constructor for `Foot` that takes only one parameter:

```
// Creates a Foot object at the (0, 0) location
public Foot(Image pic)
{
  picture = pic;
  coordinates = new CoordinateSystem(0, 0, pic);
}
```

The number, types, and order of parameters passed to the new operator when an object is created must match the number, types, and order of parameters accepted by one of the class's constructors.

Each Java class has at least one constructor. If you don't define any, the compiler supplies a default no-args constructor that initializes all the instance variables to default values (zeroes for numbers, `null` for objects, `false` for `boolean` fields).

When an object is created, a chunk of RAM is allocated to hold it, and `new` returns a *reference* to that location, which is basically the object's address. The reference may be stored in a variable (Figure 3-5), and a constructor or a method can pass it along to other constructors or methods as a parameter. Eventually several variables may hold references to the same object. If you compare an object to a web page, a reference is like the page's URL (web address). Many users may have that URL saved somewhere in their "favorites" or their web pages.

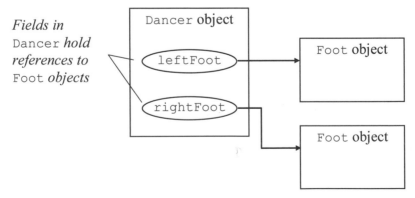

Fields in `Dancer` *hold references to* `Foot` *objects*

Figure 3-5. Fields in a `Dancer` object hold references to `Foot` objects

A Java interpreter is equipped with a mechanism that keeps track of all the references to a particular object that are currently in existence in a running program. Gradually the references to an object may all cease to exist. Then the object is unreachable, because no other object in the program can find it or knows it exists. The Java interpreter finds and destroys such useless objects and frees the memory they occupied. This mechanism is called *garbage collection*.

Metaphorically speaking, an object can "send messages" to other objects. In Java, to "send a message" means to call another object's *method*. A method is a function that performs a certain task or computation. All of an object's methods are described in its class definition, and all the objects of a given class have exactly the same set of methods. The methods define what an object can do, what kind of "messages" it understands.

Does a method belong to an object or to a class? The terminology here is not very precise. When we focus on a <u>running</u> program, we say that an <u>object</u> has a method, meaning that we can call that method for that particular object. When we focus on the program's source code, we say that a <u>class</u> has a method, meaning that a programmer included code for the method in the class definition.

Each method has a name, given by the programmer. Like a constructor, a method may accept one or more parameters. For example, once we have created an object `leftFoot` of the `Foot` class, we can call its `moveForward` method:

```
leftFoot.moveForward(10);
```

This statement moves `leftFoot` forward in its current direction by 10 units (pixels). The compiler understands this statement because we have defined the following method in the `Foot` class:

```
// Moves this foot forward by distance pixels
// (or backward if distance < 0).
public void moveForward(int distance)
{
  coordinates.shift(distance, 0);
}
```

Parameters passed to a method must match the number, types, and order of parameters that the method expects.

Empty parentheses in a method's header indicate that this method does not take any parameters. Such a method is called with empty parentheses. For example:

```
amy.firstStep();
```

A method may return a value to the caller. The method's header specifies whether the method returns a value or not, and if it does, of what type. For example, the Foot class could have a potentially useful method distanceFrom that would calculate and return the approximate distance of this foot from a point (*x, y*):

```
public int distanceFrom(int x, int y)
{
  int d;
  ...    // calculate the distance d
  return d;
}
```

This method returns an int value. When we call this method, we can assign the returned value to a variable:

```
int dist = leftFoot.distanceFrom(480, 600);
```

> **The keyword void in the method header indicates that the method does not return any value.**

For example, the moveForward method is declared void, because it does not return a value.

A method can call other methods of the same object or of a different object. For example, moveForward calls coordinates method shift (which here actually does all the work):

```
public void moveForward(int distance)
{
  coordinates.shift(distance, 0);
}
```

The shift method is defined in the CoordinateSystem class, and coordinates is an object of that class. Recall that the coordinates object was created in Foot's constructor.

The Foot class provides a well-defined functionality through its constructors and public methods. The user of the Foot class (possibly a different programmer) does not need to know all the details of how the class Foot works, only how to construct its objects and what they can do. In fact all the instance variables (non-static fields) in Foot are declared private so that programmers writing classes that use Foot cannot refer to them directly. This technique is called *encapsulation* and *information hiding*.

There are several advantages to such an arrangement:

- `Foot`'s programmer can change the structure of the fields in the `Foot` class, and the rest of the project won't be affected, as long as `Foot`'s constructors and public methods have the same specifications and still work as before;

- `Foot`'s programmer can document the `Foot` class for the other team members by describing all its constructors and public methods; there is no need to document the implementation details;

- `Foot`'s programmer can test the `Foot` class separately from the rest of the project.

In fact, let us do just that: test the `Foot` class. We have written a small class for that called `FootTest`. You need to set up a project in your IDE that would include the `Foot.java`, `CoordinateSystem.java`, and `FootTest.java` files from `JM\Ch03\FirstSteps`. Place the `leftshoe.gif` image file from `JM\Ch03\FirstSteps` into the same folder where your IDE places the compiled classes. Compile and run the program. The test should show several images of a shoe arranged in a circular pattern with a crosshair cursor drawn through the center of the first image.

3.5 *Case Study and Lab:* **First Steps**

We are now ready to proceed with our *Dance Studio* project. Before we learn how to dance, though, we need to learn how to walk! The window in Figure 3-6 shows *First Steps*, an "early prototype" of the *Dance Studio* program. Instead of dancing, two "walkers" just walk across the "dance floor."

We obviously need a `Walker` class for this program. A `Walker` object has two feet, left and right:

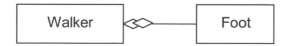

Figure 3-7 shows a CRC card for `Walker`. Note that handling the timer and animation are __not__ `Walker`'s responsibilities — they are handled by the `DanceGroup` and `Band` objects. But a `Walker` has methods for making steps and for drawing itself on the screen. These methods can be called to create animation effects.

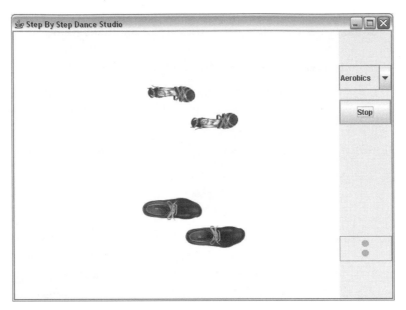

Figure 3-6.   *First Steps*, a prototype of the *Dance Studio* program

Walker	
Creates and controls its left and right foot.	*Foot*
Knows how to make the first step, the next step, and stop.	

Figure 3-7. A CRC card for the `Walker` class

Figure 3-8 shows the code for the `Walker` class (with some gaps). In general it is good when a class definition is not too long and fits on one or two pages. The full text of this one takes a little more than a page.

```java
// This class represents a walker with two feet.

import java.awt.Image;
import java.awt.Graphics;

public class Walker
{
  public static final int PIXELS_PER_INCH = 6;
  private Foot leftFoot, rightFoot;
  private int stepLength;
  private int stepsCount;

  // Constructor
  public Walker(int x, int y, Image leftPic, Image rightPic)
  {
    leftFoot =  new Foot(x, y - PIXELS_PER_INCH * 4, leftPic);
    rightFoot = new Foot(x, y + PIXELS_PER_INCH * 4, rightPic);
    stepLength = PIXELS_PER_INCH * 12;
  }
  ...

  // Makes first step, starting with the left foot
  public void firstStep()
  {
    leftFoot.moveForward(stepLength);
    stepsCount = 1;
  }

  // Makes next step
  public void nextStep()
  {
    if (stepsCount % 2 == 0)  // if stepsCount is even
      leftFoot.moveForward(2 * stepLength);
    else
      rightFoot.moveForward(2 * stepLength);

    stepsCount++;  // increment by 1
  }

  // Stops this walker (brings its feet together)
  public void stop()
  { < to be written by you > }

  ...

  // Draws this walker
  public void draw(Graphics g)
  { < to be written by you > }
}
```

Figure 3-8. ᴶM\Ch03\FirstSteps\Walker.java

The `Walker` class defines four fields: two objects of the `Foot` type, `leftFoot` and `rightFoot`, and two integers, `stepLength` and `stepsCount`.

`Walker`'s constructor creates `leftFoot` and `rightFoot`, placing them side by side around the specified point (*x*, *y*). It uses different images for the left and right foot, passed to the constructor as parameters. It also initializes `stepLength` — the distance that a walker advances forward in one step.

The `firstStep` method moves `leftFoot` forward by `stepLength` distance and sets `stepsCount` to 1. This method takes no parameters and does not return any value. The `nextStep` method moves a foot by `2*stepLength` (which advances the walker by `stepLength`); it moves `leftFoot` when `stepsCount` is even and `rightFoot` when `stepsCount` is odd. It then increments `stepsCount`.

Fill in the missing code in `Walker.java` from J~M~\Ch03\FirstSteps. `Walker`'s `stop` method is very similar to `nextStep`, but it makes a `stepLength` step. The `draw` method draws both feet in `Graphics g`. This is accomplished by calling each foot's `draw(g)`.

Set up a project with `DanceStudio.jar`, the completed `Walker.java`, and the rest of the source files in J~M~\Ch03\FirstSteps (except `FootTest.java`) and compile them. Copy all the `.gif` and `.wav` files from J~M~\Ch03\FirstSteps into the folder where your IDE places the compiled class files. Test the *First Steps* program — you should see two walkers walk across the floor.

3.6 Inheritance

A `Walker` from the previous section stops when it reaches the opposite "wall." It would be nice to be able to make it turn around and walk back. But a `Walker` does not have a method for changing direction. It would be easy to add a method `turnAround` to the `Walker` class. But there are several reasons why adding methods to a class may be not feasible or desirable.

First, you may not have access to the source code of the class. It may be a library class or a class that came to you from someone else without source. For example, if you didn't fill in the gaps in the `Walker` class from the previous lab, you don't have its complete source code, but your instructor can give you `Walker.class`. Second, your boss may not allow you to change a working and tested class. You may have access to its source, but it may be "read-only." A large organization cannot allow every programmer to change every class at will. Once a class is written and tested, it may be off-limits until the next release. Third, your class may already be in use in other projects. If you change it now, you will have different versions floating around and it may become confusing. Fourth, not all projects need additional methods. If you keep adding methods for every contingency, your class will eventually become too large and inconvenient to use.

The proper solution to this dilemma is to *derive* a new class from `Walker`.

> **In OOP, a programmer can create a new class by extending an existing class. The new class can add new methods or redefine some of the existing ones. New fields can be added, too. This concept is called *inheritance*.**

Inheritance is one of the fundamental OOP concepts, and all OOP languages support it.

> **Java uses the keyword `extends` to indicate that a class extends another class.**

For example,

```
public class Pacer extends Walker
{
   ...
}
```

If class *D* extends class *B*, then *B* is called a *superclass* (or a *base class*) and *D* is called a *subclass (or a derived class)*. The relationship of inheritance is usually indicated in UML diagrams by an arrow with a triangular head from a subclass to its superclass:

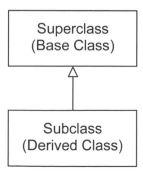

In Java you can extend a class without having its source code.

> **A subclass inherits all the methods and fields of its superclass. Constructors are not inherited; a subclass has to provide its own.**

In our example, we create a new class `Pacer` that extends `Walker`:

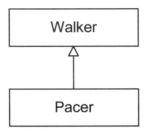

`Pacer` is a short class. It has its own constructor and adds one method, `turnAround` (Figure 3-9). We do not have to duplicate `Walker`'s methods and fields.

```
// A subclass of Walker that adds the turnAround method.

import java.awt.Image;

public class Pacer extends Walker
{
  // Constructor
  public Pacer(int x, int y, Image leftPic, Image rightPic)
  {
    super(x, y, leftPic, rightPic);
  }

  // Turns this Pacer 180 degrees
  // Precondition: the left and right feet are side by side
  public void turnAround()
  {
    Foot lf = getLeftFoot();
    Foot rf = getRightFoot();
    lf.turn(180);
    rf.turn(180);
    lf.moveSideways(-PIXELS_PER_INCH * 8);
    rf.moveSideways(PIXELS_PER_INCH * 8);
  }
}
```

Figure 3-9. JM\Ch03\FirstSteps\Pacer.java

You might notice two interesting things in this short class. First, its constructor simply passes all the parameters "up" by calling the superclass's constructor. This is accomplished by the statement

```
super(x, y, leftPic, rightPic);
```

> **super** is a Java reserved word. If **super**(...) is used, it must be the first statement in the subclass's constructor. If **super**(...) is not used, then the no-args constructor of the superclass is called automatically, and it must exist.

In our case, `Pacer`'s constructor takes the same number and types of parameters as `Walker`'s constructor. In general, this does not have to be the case.

Second, there is a paradox. `Pacer` has inherited all the fields from `Walker`. So a `Pacer` has a left foot and a right foot. However, these fields are declared `private` in `Walker`. This means that the programmer who writes `Pacer` does not have direct access to them (even if he is the same programmer who wrote `Walker`!). Recall that the `Walker` class is fully encapsulated and all its fields are private. It's like `Pacer` has feet but can't reach them. What do we do? `Walker`'s subclasses and, in fact, any other classes that use `Walker` might need access to the values stored in the private fields.

To resolve the issue, the `Walker` class provides two public methods that simply return the values of its `leftFoot` and `rightFoot` fields. We omitted these methods in Figure 3-8, but we can show them now:

```
public class Walker
{   ...
  // Returns the left foot
  public Foot getLeftFoot()
  {
    return leftFoot;
  }

  // Returns the right foot
  public Foot getRightFoot()
  {
    return rightFoot;
  }
  ...
}
```

> Such methods are called *accessor* methods (or simply *accessors*) because they give outsiders access to the values of private fields of an object.

It is a very common practice to provide accessor methods for those private fields of the class that may be of interest to other classes.

As you can see, the `turnAround` method in `Pacer` first requests and receives references to `leftFoot` and `rightFoot` by calling the respective accessor methods and stores the returned values in its "local" variables `lf` and `rf`.

```
Foot lf = getLeftFoot();
Foot rf = getRightFoot();
```

`Pacer` inherits the `getLeftFoot` and `getRightFoot` methods from `Walker`, so in the above statements this `Pacer` object in effect calls its own methods. That is why it can call them without any *objectName-dot* prefix.

After receiving references to the `leftFoot` and `rightFoot` fields, `turnAround` calls their appropriate methods to complete the turn. (Note that to turn around, it is not sufficient to turn each foot 180 degrees. Try it! The feet also need to swap places.)

Inheritance represents the *IS-A relationship* between objects. A `Pacer` IS-A (is a) `Walker`. In addition to the fields and methods, an object of a subclass inherits a less tangible but also very valuable asset from its superclass: its type. It is like inheriting the family name or title. The superclass's type becomes a secondary, more generic type of an object of the subclass. Whenever a statement or a method call expects a `Walker`-type object, you can plug in a `Pacer`-type object instead, because a `Pacer` IS-A `Walker`. For example, if you have a class `Promenade` with a method:

```
public void makeNSteps(Walker person, int n)
{
    . . .
}
```

then you can pass a `Pacer` to it as a parameter:

```
Pacer amy = new Pacer(20, 40, leftShoe, rightShoe);
makeNSteps(amy, 5);
```

Our project is growing. Figure 3-10 shows a diagram of the classes discussed so far and their relationships.

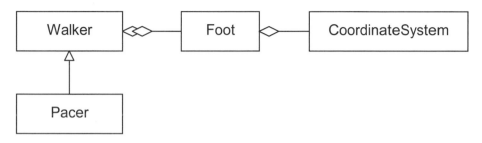

Figure 3-10. Some of the *First Steps* classes

In the new version of the *First Steps* program, we have created a class PacingGroup, adapted from WalkingGroup. In a PacingGroup, the two Walkers are replaced by two Pacers. We made them turn around when they reach a wall. Modify FirstSteps.java in JM\Ch03\FirstSteps, replacing WalkingGroup with PacingGroup. Compile and run this modified version of the program. You should see two pacers walk across the floor and turn around when they reach a wall.

We have made our first steps in OOP. But a lot remains to be learned. We will complete the *Dance Studio* project in Chapter 11.

3.7 Summary

An OOP program is best visualized as a virtual world of interacting objects. A program's source code describes all of the different types of objects used in the program. Objects of the same type are said to belong to the same *class*. An object is called an *instance* of its class. The source code of a Java program consists of *definitions of classes*.

The source code for each class is stored in a separate file with the same name as the class and the extension .java. It is customary to place all your classes for the same project in the same folder. Several compiled Java classes may be collected in one .jar file.

A *CRC card* gives a preliminary, informal description of a class, listing its name, the key "responsibilities" of its objects, and the other classes this class depends on ("collaborators").

The `import` statements at the top of a class's source code tell the compiler where it can find the library classes and packages used in that class.

A class definition begins with a header, followed by the class's body within braces. A class defines the data elements of an object of that class, called *instance variables*. Each instance variable has a name, given by a programmer, and a type. If an instance variable is an object, its type is the class of that object. An instance variable that holds a number or a text character has one of the primitive data types (`int`, `double`, `char`, etc.). The set of instance variables serves as the "personal memory" of an object. Their values may be different for different objects of the class, and these values can change while the program is running.

A class also defines *constructors*, which are short procedures for creating objects of that class, and *methods*, which describe what an object can do. When a program is running, it is always executing some class's constructor or method. When a Java application starts, control is passed to the `main` method.

A constructor always has the same name as its class. A constructor is used primarily to set the initial values of the object's fields (instance variables). It can accept one or several parameters that are used for initializing the fields. A constructor that does not take any parameters is called a *no-args constructor*. A class may have several constructors that differ in the number or types of parameters that they accept. If no constructors are defined, the compiler automatically supplies one default no-args constructor that sets all the instance variables to default values (zeroes for numbers, `null` for objects, `false` for `boolean` variables).

The program (the constructor or method that is currently running) creates a new object using the `new` operator. The parameters passed to `new` must match the number, types, and order of parameters in one of the constructors in the new object's class, and `new` invokes that constructor. `new` allocates memory to store the newly constructed object.

The functionality of a class — what it can do — is defined by its *methods*. A method accomplishes a certain task (much like a subroutine in BASIC or a function in C++). It can be called from constructors and other methods of the same class and, if it is declared `public`, from constructors and methods of other classes. A method can take parameters as its "inputs." Parameters passed to a method must match the number, types, and order of parameters that the method expects. A method can return a value of a specified type to the caller. A method declared `void` does not return any value.

In OOP, all the instance variables are usually declared `private`, so only objects of the same class have direct access to them. Some of the methods may be private, too. Users of a class do not need to know how the class is implemented and what its private fields and methods are. This practice is called *information hiding*. A class interacts with other classes only through a well-defined set of constructors and public methods. This concept is called *encapsulation*. Encapsulation facilitates program maintenance, code reuse, and documentation. A class often provides public methods that return the values of an object's private fields, so that an object of a different class can access those values. Such methods are called *accessor methods* or *accessors*.

A class definition does not have to start from scratch: it can *extend* the definition of another class, adding fields and/or methods or overriding (redefining) some of the methods. This concept is called *inheritance*. It is said that a *subclass* (or *derived class*) extends a *superclass* (or *base class*). Constructors are not inherited, but a subclass's constructor can call a superclass's constructor using the keyword `super`.

An object of a subclass also inherits the type of its superclass as a secondary, more generic type. This formalizes the *IS-A relationship* between objects: an object of a subclass IS-A(n) object of its superclass.

Exercises

Sections 3.1-3.4

1. Mark true or false and explain:

    (a) The name of a class in Java must be the same as the name of its source file (excluding the extension `.java`). _____

    (b) The names of classes are case-sensitive. _____

    (c) The `import` statement tells the compiler which other classes use this class. _____ ✓

2. Mark true or false and explain:

    (a) The *FootTest* program consists of three classes. _____ ✓

    (b) A Java program can have as many classes as necessary. _____

    (c) A Java program is allowed to create only one object of each class. _____

    (d) Every class has a method called `main`. _____ ✓

3.   Navigate your browser to Sun's Java API (Application Programming Interface) documentation web site (for example, `http://java.sun.com/j2se/1.5.0/docs/api/index.html`) or, if you have the JDK documentation installed on your computer, open the file `<JDK base folder>\docs\api\index.html` (for example, `C:\Program Files\Java\jdk1.5.0_06\docs\api\index.html`).

(a)   Approximately how many different packages are listed in the API spec?

(b)   Find `JFrame` in the list of classes in the left column and click on it. Scroll down the main window to the "Method Summary" section. Approximately how many methods does the `JFrame` class have, including methods inherited from other classes? 3? 12? 25? 300? ✓

4.   Explain the difference between public and private methods.

5.   Mark true or false and explain:

(a)   Fields of a class are usually declared `private`. _____
(b)   An object has to be created before it can be used. _____   ✓
(c)   A class may have more than one constructor. _____
(d)   The programmer names objects in his program. _____
(e)   When an object is created, the program always calls its `init` method. _____   ✓

6.   Modify the `FootTest` program (`JM\Ch03\FirstSteps\FootTest.java`) to show

(a)   four feet facing north, spaced horizontally 160 pixels from each other
(b)   four feet facing north, spaced vertically 160 pixels from each other
(c)   four feet aligned along the sides of a square, as follows:

Each side should be 160 pixels.

Sections 3.5-3.7

7. ■   (a)   Using the `FootTest` class as a prototype, create a class `WalkerTest`. Your program should display the same `Walker` in four positions, spaced horizontally by one full "step," facing east:

    ⋜ Hint: the distance of one full step is covered by calls to `firstStep`, `nextStep`, and `stop`. ⋝

   (b)   Change `WalkerTest` from Part (a) to show

8. ■   (a)   Change `WalkerTest` from Question 7 into `PacerTest`. This program should display four pairs of feet, as in Part (a), but facing west rather than east.

   (b)   Add the `turnLeft` and `turnRight` methods to the `Pacer` class (`JM\Ch03\FirstSteps\Pacer.java`) ⋜ Hint: for a right turn, turn each foot 90 degrees to the right, then move the left foot by `PIXELS_PER_INCH * 8` appropriately sideways and forward. ⋝

   (c)   Change the `PacerTest` class from Part (a) and use the modified `Pacer` class from Part (b) to show four pairs of feet, as follows:

9. ■   Add a third `Walker`, named `cat`, to the `WalkingGroup` class in `JM\Ch03\FirstSteps`. Position `cat` in the middle between `amy` and `ben`. `cat` should "walk" in sync with the other two. Change `cat`'s foot pictures to the ones from the `leftpaw.gif` and `rightpaw.gif` image files (in `JM\Ch03\Exercises`). Run *First Steps* to test `cat`.

10.■   (a)   Using the class `Walker` as a prototype, create a new class `Hopper`. A `Hopper` should move both feet forward together by `stepLength` in `firstStep` and `nextStep` and not move at all in `stop`.

(b)   Test your `Hopper` class by making `cat` in Question 9 a `Hopper` rather than a `Walker`.

11.■   Change the `PacingGroup` class (in `JM\Ch03\FirstSteps`) to make one `Pacer` walk counterclockwise along the perimeter of a square, turning 90 degrees after every few steps. Leave only `amy` in the `PacingGroup` — exclude the other pacers . Use a `Pacer` object with the `turnLeft` and `turnRight` methods, added to `Pacer` in Question 8 (b). ⋞ Hints: initially position `amy` at x = width/8, y = height*7/8; allow `amy` to travel in one direction for `danceFloor.getWidth()/2` pixels. ⋟ Repeat the exercise with a `Pacer` walking clockwise.

12.■   (a)   Write a subclass of `Walker` called `Bystander`. `Bystander` should redefine (override) `Walker`'s `firstStep`, `nextStep`, and `stop` methods in such a way that a `Bystander` alternates turning its left foot by 45 degrees left and right on subsequent steps but never moves the right foot. `Bystander` should also redefine the `distanceTraveled` method, to always return 0. ⋞ Hints: (1) To redefine (override) a superclass's method in a subclass, keep its header but change the code inside the braces. (2) Define a new field (for example, `tapsCount`), which will help determine the direction of the left foot's turn in each "step." (3) Do not duplicate the methods inherited from the superclass that remain the same. ⋟

(b)   Change a couple of words in the `WalkingGroup` class (in `JM\Ch03\FirstSteps`) to test your `Bystander` class. ⋞ Hint: turn one of the `Walkers` into a `Bystander`. ⋟

13.◆ Using the *Banner* applet from Chapter 2 as a prototype (`Banner.java` and `TestBanner.html` in J_M\Ch02\HelloGui), create and test an applet that shows a spinning foot.

≷ Hints:

1. Create a new class `SpinningFoot` adapted from `Banner`.

2. Use two fields: `Image pic` and `Foot foot`.

3. In the `init` method, load `pic` from an image file, for example, `leftshoe.gif`. Set up a timer that fires every 30 ms.

4. In the `paint` method, check whether `foot` has been created. If not yet —

```
        if (foot == null)
        {
          . . .
        }
```

— then set `foot` to a new `Foot` object in the middle of the content pane.

5. In the `actionPerformed` method, turn `foot` by 6 degrees.

6. Adapt `SpinningFoot.html` from `TestBanner.html`, changing `Banner.class` to `SpinningFoot.class` in its `<applet>` tag.

7. Add `Foot.java` and `CoordinateSystem.java` to the project. ≷

14.◆ The class `Circle` (`Circle.java` in J_M\Ch03\Exercises) describes a circle with a given radius. The radius has the type `double`, which is a primitive data type used for representing real numbers. The `CircleTest.java` class in J_M\Ch03\Exercises is a tiny console application that prompts the user to enter a number for the radius, creates a `Circle` object of that radius, and displays its area by calling the `Circle`'s `getArea` method.

Create a class `Cylinder` with two fields: `Circle base` and `double height`. Is it fair to say that a `Cylinder` HAS-A `Circle`? Provide a constructor that takes two `double` parameters, `r` and `h`, initializes `base` to a new `Circle` with radius `r`, and initializes `height` to `h`. Provide a method `getVolume` that returns the volume of the cylinder (which is equal to the base area times height). Create a simple test program `CylinderTest`, that would prompt the user to enter the radius and height of a cylinder, create a new cylinder with these dimensions, and display its volume.

15.◆ Create an application that shows a picture of a coin in the middle of a window and "flips" the coin every two seconds. Your application should consist of two classes: `Coin` and `CoinTest`.

The `Coin` class should have one constructor that takes two parameters of the type `Image`: the heads and tails pictures of the coin. The constructor saves these images in the coin's fields. The `Coin` class should have two methods:

```
// Flips this coin
public void flip()
{
    ...
}
```

and

```
// Draws the appropriate side of the coin
// centered at (x, y)
public void draw(Graphics g, int x, y)
{
    ...
}
```

The `CoinTest` class's constructor should create a `Timer` and a `Coin`. It also should have a `paint` method that paints the coin and an `actionPerformed` method that flips the coin and repaints the window.

᠄ Hints:

1. Use bits and pieces of code from the `Walker` class and from `Banner.java` and `HelloGraphics.java` in J_M\Ch02\HelloGui, and ideas from Question 16 in Chapter 2.

2. The class `Graphics` has a method that draws an image at a given location. Call it like this:

```
g.drawImage(pic, x, y, null);
```

This method places the upper-left corner of `pic` at (x, y). Explore the documentation for the library class `Image` or look at the `CoordinateSystem` class to find methods that return the width and height of an image.

3. Find copyright-free image files for the two sides of a coin on the Internet.

᠄

chapter ← 4

Algorithms

4.1 Prologue

Historically, software development was largely viewed as an activity focused on designing and implementing algorithms. A formal definition of an algorithm is elusive, which is a sure sign that the concept is fundamentally important.

> Informally, an *algorithm* is a more or less compact, general, and abstract step-by-step recipe that describes how to perform a certain task or solve a certain problem.

Algorithms are often associated with computer programs, but algorithms existed long before computers. One of the most famous, Euclid's Algorithm for finding the greatest common factor of two integers, dates back to about 300 BC. You may also recall the algorithm for long division of numbers, often used in the pre-calculator era. The question of whether computers have evolved the way they are to support the implementation of algorithms, or whether algorithms (as they are understood now) gained prominence due to the advent of computers, is of the chicken-and-egg variety.

A method of performing a task or solving a problem can be described at different levels of abstraction. Algorithms represent a rather abstract level of solving problems. A computer programmer can learn an algorithm from a book or from an expert. The "algorithmist" knows the capabilities of computers and the general principles of computer programming, but he or she does not have to know any specific programming language. In fact, an algorithm can be used without any computer by a person equipped with a pencil and paper. The programmer can then implement the algorithm in Java, C++, or any other programming language of choice.

The purpose of this chapter is to give you some feel for what algorithms are all about, to consider a few examples, to introduce methods for describing algorithms (flowcharts, pseudocode) and to review the main algorithmic devices: decisions, iterations, and recursion. At this stage, we are not going to deal with any complicated algorithms. We will discuss searching and sorting algorithms in Chapter 13.

4.2 Properties of Algorithms

Suppose we want to use a computer to calculate $1^2 + 2^2 + ... + 100^2$. Potentially, we could add up the squares of numbers from 1 to 100 by brute force, making our "algorithm" quite long (Figure 4-1).

```
sum ← 0
sq = 1 * 1; sum ← sum + sq
sq = 2 * 2; sum ← sum + sq
sq = 3 * 3; sum ← sum + sq
sq = 4 * 4; sum ← sum + sq
...
  (and so on, spelling out every
single line)
...
sq = 99 * 99; sum ← sum + sq
sq = 100 * 100; sum ← sum + sq
```

Figure 4-1. Brute-force "non-algorithm" for calculating
$$1^2 + 2^2 + ... + 100^2$$

But what good would it do to have a computer that could execute millions of instructions per second if we had to write out every single one of these instructions separately? You probably feel intuitively that there is a more concise way to describe this task: start with the sum 0 and the number 1; add the square of that number to the sum; take the next number, and so on: repeat for all the numbers from 1 to 100. It turns out your intuition is not far from a formal algorithm. Such an algorithm can be built around two *variables*: one that holds the accumulating sum of squares and another that holds the current number.

Think of a variable as a "slate" on which you can write some information. You can read the value currently written on the slate. When necessary you can erase that value and write a new one. In a computer implementation, a variable occupies a memory location, and there are CPU instructions to read a value stored in memory or to write a new value into it. In descriptions of algorithms, as in computer programs, we give names to variables for convenience. In this algorithm, let us call our two variables *sum* and *i*. At the beginning, we want to set *sum* to 0 and *i* to 1. Let's record these steps using a more formal notation, called *pseudocode*:

```
sum ← 0
i   ← 1
```

Now we want to compute i^2 and add it to *sum*. For extra clarity, let's introduce another variable that will hold i^2. Let's call it *sq*. So our next steps are

```
sq ← i * i
sum ← sum + sq
```

The last statement indicates that we are <u>updating</u> the value of *sum*. This is shorthand for the following instructions: read the value written in *sum*; add *sq* to it; write the result back into *sum*. That values of variables can be updated is the key for creating algorithms.

Now we want to "take the next number." How can we formalize that? Easily: to take the next number, we simply increment the value of the variable *i* by 1:

```
i  ← i + 1
```

The above three steps constitute the core of our algorithm. We need to repeat these steps as long as *i* remains less than or equal to 100. Once *i* becomes greater than 100, the process stops and *sum* contains the result. Thus, for each value of *i*, we need to make a decision whether to continue or quit. The ability to make such decisions is one of the devices available for implementing algorithms. A CPU has special instructions (called conditional branching instructions) that direct the CPU to take different paths depending on the result of the previous operation. It can, for example, compute $100 - i$ and then continue the computation if the result is non-negative or jump to a different set of instructions if the result is negative.

OK, suppose we have an algorithm for computing $1^2 + 2^2 + ... + 100^2$. But what if we need to compute $1^2 + 2^2 + ... + 500^2$? Do we need another algorithm? Of course not: it turns out that our algorithm, with a small change, is general enough to compute $1^2 + 2^2 + ... + n^2$ for any positive integer *n*. We only need to introduce a new input variable *n* and replace $i \leq 100$ with $i \leq n$ in the decision test.

Figure 4-2-a shows pseudocode for the final algorithm. Pseudocode can be somewhat informal as long as knowledgeable people understand what it means.

Figure 4-2-b represents the same algorithm graphically. This kind of representation is called a *flowchart*. Parallelograms represent input and output; rectangles represent processing steps; diamonds — conditions checked.

(a)   **(b)**

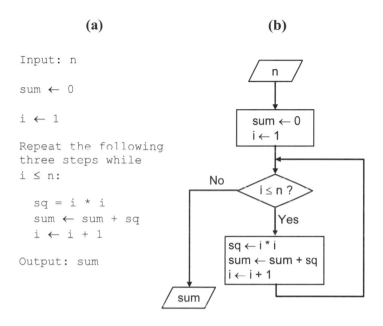

```
Input: n

sum ← 0

i ← 1

Repeat the following
three steps while
i ≤ n:

   sq = i * i
   sum ← sum + sq
   i ← i + 1

Output: sum
```

**Figure 4-2. Pseudocode and flowchart for an algorithm that
calculates $1^2 + 2^2 + ... + n^2$**

We can deduce several general properties from this simple example. First, an algorithm is rather compact. A reasonable algorithm folds the computation into one or several fragments that can be repeated multiple times. These repetitions, called *iterations*, execute exactly the same instructions but work with different values of variables. In the example in Figure 4-2 the algorithm iterates *n* times through three steps, updating *sum* and incrementing *i* by 1 in each iteration.

The second property of a good algorithm is that it is rather general. The brute-force "algorithm" in Figure 4-1 works for *n* = 100, but you have to change your program if you want it to work for, say, *n* = 500. The algorithm in Figure 4-2, a truly usable algorithm, works for any *n* without changing anything. The value of *n* is a parameter, an input value for the procedure. The running time of a program based on this algorithm will be different for different *n*, but the length of the program text itself remains the same regardless of the value of *n*.

The third property of an algorithm, as we have mentioned above, is that an algorithm is abstract: it does not depend on a particular programming language or computer system. Figure 4-3 shows how the same algorithm might be coded in Pascal and C++ functions and in a Java *class* with the `addSquares` *method*.

In Pascal

```pascal
function addSquares(n : integer)
        : integer;
  var
    i, sum : integer;
  begin
    sum := 0;
    for i := 1 to n do begin
      sum := sum + i * i
    end;
    addSquares := sum;
  end;
```

In Java

```java
public class MyMath
{
  public static int
          addSquares(int n)
  {
    int sum = 0;

    for (int i = 1; i <= n; i++)
      sum += i * i;
    return sum;
  }
}
```

In C or C++

```c
int addSquares(int n)
{
    int i, sum = 0;

    for (i = 1; i <= n; i++)
        sum += i * i;
    return sum;
}
```

**Figure 4-3. Pascal, C++, and Java, implementations of the
sum-of-squares algorithm**

At the same time, an algorithm does depend on the general computing model. For example, an algorithm for solving a problem with an abacus will be different from solving the same problem on a conventional computer, which in turn may be different from solving the same problem on a supercomputer with parallel processing capabilities.

❖   ❖   ❖

Different algorithms can solve the same problem. Because algorithms are abstract, we can study their properties and compare them for efficiency without ever implementing them on a computer. For example, we can see that in the sum-of-squares algorithm in Figure 4-2, a multiplication operation will be executed *n* times. Multiplication is in general a more time-consuming operation than addition. A slightly more efficient version of this algorithm can calculate the same result without any multiplications. This version is based on a simple observation that $(i+1)^2 = i^2 + k$, where $k = 2i+1$. To go from one value of *sq* to the next we need to add *k* to it. To go from one value of *k* to the next we need to increment *k* by 2. This way we can update the value of *sq* without multiplications (Figure 4-4).

```
Input: n

sum ← 0
sq ← 1
i ← 1
k ← 3

Repeat the following four
steps while i ≤ n:
   sum ← sum + sq
   sq ← sq + k
   k ← k + 2
   i ← i + 1

Output: sum
```

**Figure 4-4.   A version of the sum-of-squares algorithm
without multiplications**

We can verify that this algorithm indeed works by tracing its steps while keeping track of the values of the variables at the end of each iteration:

Iteration #	i	k	sq	sum
0	1	3	1	0
1	2	5	4	1
2	3	7	9	5
3	4	8	16	14
...	...	...	...	...

The gain in efficiency from this no-multiplications algorithm is insignificant, of course, when this task is performed on a modern computer, but it would save the day if we had to use an adding machine or the first ENIAC computer. Even now a slight improvement like this can make a difference in a computationally-intensive problem.

4.3 Iterations

As we have seen in the previous example, the ability to iterate over the same sequence of steps is crucial for creating compact algorithms. The same instructions are executed on each iteration, but something must change. Otherwise the iterations would never stop and the program would go into an "infinite loop." What actually changes are the values of at least some of the variables. Iterations stop when the specified condition is no longer satisfied.

High-level programming languages usually support iterations in one form or another. Java has a "while" loop —

```
while (<this condition holds>)
{
  ... // do something
}
```

— as in:

```
while (i <= n)
{
  sum += i * i;    // add i * i to sum
  i++;             // increment i by 1
}
```

There is also a "for" loop —

```
for (<initial setup>; <as long as this condition holds>;
            <adjust variable(s) at the end of each iteration>)
{
  ... // do something
}
```

— as in:

```
for (int i = 1; i <= n; i++)  // i++ means increment i by 1
{
  sum += i * i;   // add i * i to sum
}
```

We will discuss the complete syntax rules for Java's iterative statements in Chapter 8.

When you analyze loops, it is of course important to understand how the values of variables change. But it is also important to see what stays the same.

> A *loop invariant* is a relationship among the variables that is relevant to the purpose of the loop and that holds before the loop is entered and after each iteration through the loop.

Loop invariants help us ascertain that the loop is doing exactly what it is supposed to do. For example, you might notice that the algorithm in Figure 4-4 has two loop invariants: $k = 2i + 1$ and $sq = i^2$. In fact, this algorithm is specifically designed to have these invariants. Knowing these loop invariants helps us see that our algorithm works: we can be sure that the variables i, k, sq, and *sum* are initialized properly and updated properly on each iteration without tracing their values.

4.4 Recursion

According to "Common Notion" Number 5 in Book I of Euclid's *Elements*,^{*elements} "The whole is greater than the part." This may be true for the lengths of segments and the volumes of solids in geometry, but in the intangible world of computer software the whole is sometimes the same as the part, at least in terms of its structural description and use.

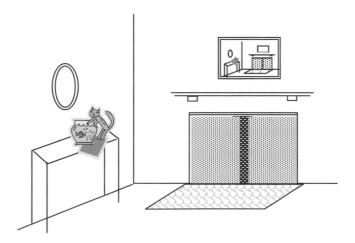

Figure 4-5. Some of the graphics elements are "primitives"; others are "pictures"

Consider the picture in Figure 4-5. As you can see, it consists of graphics elements. Some of these elements are "primitives": lines, circles, rectangles, and so on. But others are smaller pictures in their own right. In fact, you can have pictures within pictures within pictures... The overall complexity of the "whole" picture is greater than the complexity of each picture inside it, but the pictures inside have the same basic structure as the big one. This is an example of a *recursive* structure whose substructures have the same form as the whole. Such structures are best handled by *recursive* procedures, which operate the same way on a substructure as on the whole structure.

Recursion is a very powerful tool for describing and implementing algorithms.

> **A recursive solution describes a procedure for a particular task in terms of applying <u>the same</u> procedure to a similar but smaller task.**

A recursive solution also isolates simple situations (called the *base* or *stopping cases*) when a computation is obvious and recursion is not required.

For example, in the task of calculating $1^2 + 2^2 + ... + n^2$, recursive thinking would go like this: if $n = 1$, the result is simply 1 (base case); if $n > 1$, we can <u>calculate the sum</u> $1^2 + 2^2 + ... + (n-1)^2$, then add n^2 to it. The underlined phrase represents a recursive call to the same procedure for a smaller number, $n-1$.

To most people, though, this algorithm will seem totally unsatisfactory. They may ask, "Right, but how do I calculate $1^2 + 2^2 + ... + (n-1)^2$? The algorithm doesn't tell me anything about that!" In fact it does, because the same procedure applies to any input, and, in particular, to $n-1$. So in order to calculate $1^2 + 2^2 + ... + (n-1)^2$ you will calculate $1^2 + 2^2 + ... + (n-2)^2$, then add $(n-1)^2$. And so on, until you get down to 1, and you know the answer for $n = 1$.

> **For a recursive algorithm to work, it must have a base case (or cases) that do not need recursion, and the recursive calls must eventually reach the base case (or one of the base cases).**

Recursion may seem very tricky to an untrained eye, and some people never completely come to grips with it. But it is easy for computers.

> **A computer program handles recursion as a form of iterations, which however are hidden from the programmer.**

In high-level languages, such as Java or C++, recursion is implemented by means of functions calling themselves. In Java, for instance, the above recursive algorithm can be implemented as shown in Figure 4-6.

Computers have a hardware mechanism, called the *stack*, that facilitates recursive function calls. It is described in Chapter 21. Take a look at it now if you want to learn the technical details. At this point, suffice it to say that the compiler knows how to handle recursive functions without getting confused.

```java
public class MyMath
{
  public static int addSquares(int n)
  {
    if (n == 1)
      return 1;
    else
      return addSquares(n-1) + n * n;
  }
}
```

Figure 4-6. Recursive method in Java for computing
$1^2 + 2^2 + ... + n^2$ **(not recommended for this task)**

Some programming languages, such as LISP or Scheme, almost always suggest the use of recursion instead of explicit iterations. In Java, recursion is used in standard packages but programmers do not have to program recursive methods themselves very often. Still, knowing how recursion works is very useful for understanding certain common algorithms such as Mergesort (Section 13.7) or dealing with branching or nested structures (such as the structure of pictures within pictures in the above example).

You may notice that we said a recursive algorithm was "not recommended" for solving the sum-of-squares problem. Some people, once they understand it, find recursion so elegant that they are tempted to use it everywhere. Indeed, as Figure 4-6 shows, recursive solutions may be short and expressive. But they may be also more costly than iterative solutions in terms of running time and memory space, and in some cases this cost becomes prohibitive. In general, there is no need to use recursion when a simple iterative solution exists.

4.5 *Case Study:* **Euclid's GCF Algorithm**

Figure 4-7 shows a flowchart for Euclid's Algorithm, mentioned earlier, for finding the greatest common factor of two positive integers. This algorithm is based on the observation that if we subtract the smaller number from the larger number, and replace the larger number with the result, the GCF of the two numbers remains the same. In other words, $GCF(a, b) = GCF(a - b, b)$, assuming $a > b$.

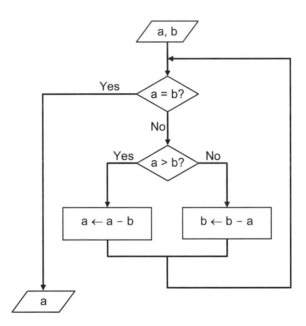

Figure 4-7. Euclid's Algorithm for finding the greatest common factor of two positive integers

Let us take an example, $a = 30$, $b = 42$, and see how this algorithm works:

Iteration #	0	1	2	3	4
a	30	30	18	6	6
b	42	12	12	12	6

An iterative implementation of this algorithm is shown in Figure 4-8. After each iteration through the `while` loop, both a and b remain positive but the larger of them gets reduced, so eventually they must become equal and the iterations stop.

In a recursive implementation (Figure 4-9), the `while` loop is replaced by recursive calls. But first we have to check for the base case, $a = b$. In that case the GCF is obviously a (or b). Again, the parameters passed to the recursive calls remain positive and the larger of them is reduced, so the recursive calls converge to the base case.

```java
// Returns GCF of a and b (iterative)
// Precondition: a > 0, b > 0
public static int gcf(int a, int b)
{
  while (a != b) // while a not equal to b
  {
    if (a > b)
      a -= b;      // subtract b from a
    else
      b -= a;      // subtract a from b
  }

  return a;
}
```

**Figure 4-8. Iterative implementation of
Euclid's Algorithm in Java**

```java
// Returns GCF of a and b (recursive)
// Precondition: a > 0, b > 0
public static int gcf(int a, int b)
{
  if (a == b) // base case: if a equals b
    return a;

  if (a > b)
    return gcf(a - b, b);
  else // if b > a
    return gcf(a, b - a);
}
```

**Figure 4-9. Recursive implementation of
Euclid's Algorithm in Java**

There is an operator % in Java, called the *modulo division operator*, that computes the remainder when a is divided by b. For example:

```
21 % 9 = 3 ( = 21 - 2 * 9 )
 9 % 21 = 9 ( = 9 - 0 * 21 )
```

The statement

```
a %= b;    // same as a = a % b;
```

replaces a with the result of a % b, which is equivalent to subtracting b from a as many times as possible while the result remains greater than or equal to zero. We could use the modulo division operator to make the code for both iterative and recursive gcf methods more efficient. This is left to you as an exercise.

4.6 Working with Lists

We deal with lists all the time — lists of things to do, shopping lists, guest lists, restaurant menus, and, sometimes, the proverbial "laundry lists." Computers deal with lists, too: lists of files, lists of words, lists of bank or credit card transactions, lists of people, students, courses, customers, subscribers, departing and arriving flights, and, yes, dry cleaning orders.

In abstract terms, a list is a data structure in which the items are numbered and we know how to get to the *i*-th item. One of the basic operations on a list is *traversal*, which means processing all the items in order (for example, printing out the list). A list traversal algorithm is straightforward:

```
Start at the beginning of the list
While more items remain in the list,
  process the next item
```

Such an algorithm presumably maintains a variable that refers to the "current" item in the list and shifts that variable to the next item once the current item has been processed. Java (starting with release 5.0) has a so-called "for-each" loop (also called the "enhanced for loop") that automates this process. For example:

```
for (String word : list) // for each word
                         // (character string) in list
{
   System.out.println(word);  // print word on a separate line
}
```

We humans can process short lists instantaneously. You can glance at a guest list for a small birthday party and immediately see whether you are invited or not. However, a computer needs to examine each item in the list to find a given target value or to ascertain that that value is not in the list. This type of process is called *Sequential Search*. If a list has 1,000,000 items arranged in random order, it will take, on average, 500,000 comparisons to find a particular item, and, if the target value is not in the list, then the computer will need to scan all 1,000,000 items to make sure it is not there. But if the list items are arranged in order (for example, words in alphabetical order or numbers in increasing order), there is a much more efficient search algorithm, called *Binary Search*.

The idea of Binary Search is familiar to anyone who has played the number-guessing game. Your friend thinks of a number between 1 and 100. You need to guess the number by asking questions like "Is your number greater than *x*?" How many questions, in the worst case, will you need to ask to guess the number? Seven, right? If I pick a number between 1 and 1,000,000, then you'll need to ask at most 20 questions!

The Binary Search algorithm in an ordered list is similar. Start looking for the target value at the midpoint of the list (Figure 4-10). If your target is greater than the middle item, continue searching in the right half; if it is less than the middle item, continue searching in the left half. Keep dividing the remaining search range into approximately equal halves until you find the target value or there is nothing left to search. This type of algorithm is called "divide and conquer." We will return to the Binary Search algorithm and its implementation in Java in Chapter 13.

In the Sequential Search algorithm, the number of comparisons in the worst case is roughly proportional to *n*, where *n* is the length of the list. In Binary Search, the number of comparisons is proportional to $\log_2(n)$. Suppose one comparison takes T_S time in Sequential Search and T_B time in Binary Search. Even if $T_B > T_S$, the Binary Search algorithm is still considered much better than Sequential Search because, for large *n*,

$$\frac{T_B \cdot \log_2(n)}{T_S \cdot n} \to 0$$

(approaches 0) regardless of the values of the constant factors T_S and T_B. It is said that Sequential Search is an $O(n)$ algorithm and Binary Search is an $O(\log n)$ algorithm. The "big-O" notation and its use for comparing algorithms is explained in Chapter 18.

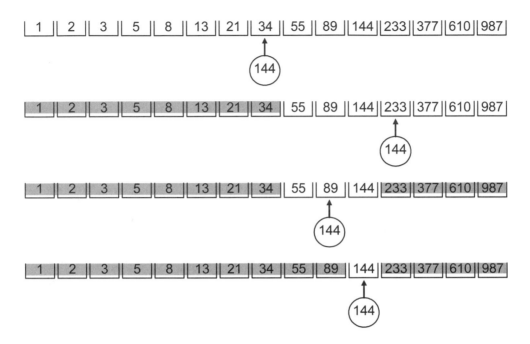

Figure 4-10. Binary Search

On each iteration, the target value (here 144) is compared to the value in the middle (or near the middle) of the remaining search range.   The gray areas indicate the values eliminated from the search range after a comparison.

❖   ❖   ❖

Another common task is arranging the list items in order (provided we have some method for comparing the items). This task is called *sorting*. Here is a simple algorithm for sorting a list of items:

```
Set n to the total number of items in the list
While n is greater than 1 repeat the following steps:
  Find the largest item among the first n items
  Swap that largest item with the n-th item
  Decrement n by 1
```

This algorithm is called *Selection Sort* (because we repeatedly <u>select</u> the largest item among the first *n* in the list). To better see how this works, you can enact this algorithm with a group of friends, arranging them, say, in order of their birthdays. Again, this is just a quick preview. A more detailed discussion of this and other sorting algorithms and their implementations in Java has to wait until we get to Chapter 13.

4.7 *Case Study:* **File Manager**

Recursion is especially suitable for handling nested structures. Consider for example the file system on your computer (Figure 4-11). A "file folder" is an inherently recursive definition: it is something that contains files and/or file folders! If you right-click on a folder and choose "Properties," you will see a screen that shows the total number of files in that folder and all its subfolders and the total number of bytes that the folder and all its files and all its subfolders take. How does your operating system do that?

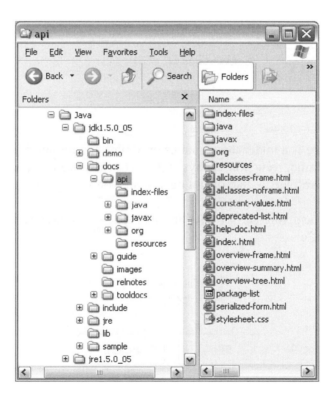

Figure 4-11.   A snapshot of the *Windows Explorer* screen

It is not easy to come up with an iterative algorithm to scan through all the files in all subfolders. When you jump into a deeper level, you need to remember where you are at the current level to be able to return there. You jump one level deeper again, and you need to save your current location again. To untangle this tree-like hierarchy of folders using iterations, you need a storage mechanism called a *stack* (see Chapter 21). But a recursive solution is straightforward and elegant. Here is a sketch of it in pseudocode:

```
fileCount(folder)
{
  count ← 0

  for each item in folder
  {
    if this item is a file
      count ← count + 1
    else (this item is a folder)
      count ← count + fileCount(item)
  }

  return count
}
```

The base case here is a folder that contains only files and no other folders. Since the file structure is finite, recursion always stops. (Luckily we can't have a folder that holds itself as a subfolder — the operating system won't allow that!)

Java/OOP is very appropriate for handling this type of structures. We can define a small hierarchy of classes:

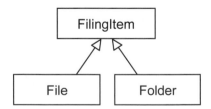

A `FilingItem` object can be a `File` or a `Folder`. As we say in OOP, a `File` IS-A (is a) `FilingItem` and a `Folder` IS-A `FilingItem`. A `Folder` also HAS-A list of `FilingItems`:

```
public class Folder extends FilingItem
{
  private List<FilingItem> items;
  ...
}
```

Let us define a `fileCount` method for both a `File` and a `Folder`. These methods have the same name but work differently. For a `File`, `fileCount` simply returns 1:

```
public class File extends FilingItem
{
  ...

  public int fileCount()
  {
    return 1;
  }
  ...
}
```

For a `Folder`, the `fileCount` method is recursive: it returns the sum of all counts for all items in its `items` list:

```
public class Folder extends FilingItem
{
  private List<FilingItem> items;
  ...
  public int fileCount()
  {
    int sum = 0;

    for (FilingItem item : items)  // for each item in items
      sum += item.fileCount();     //   add item's file count to sum

    return sum;
  }
  ...
}
```

Java will automatically call the correct `fileCount` method for each item in the `items` list, be it a `File` or a `Folder`. This feature is called *polymorphism*. Polymorphism is discussed later, in Chapter 11.

4.8 Summary

An *algorithm* is an abstract and formal step-by-step recipe that tells how to perform a certain task or solve a certain problem on a computer. The main properties of algorithms are compactness, generality, and abstraction. Compactness means that a fairly large computational task is folded into a fairly short sequence of instructions that are repeated multiple times through iterations or recursion. Generality means that the same algorithm can work with different sets of input data values. Abstraction means that the algorithm does not depend on a particular programming language.

Flowcharts and *pseudocode* are two popular ways to describe algorithms.

The three major devices used in algorithms are *decisions*, *iterations*, and *recursion*. A decision allows the algorithm to take different paths depending on some condition. Iterations and/or recursion help fold the task into one or several mini-tasks that are repeated multiple times. Any high-level programming language supports decisions, iterations, and recursion in some form. Java, for example, has the `if` statement for decisions, the `while` and `for` loops for iterations, and the liberty for a method to recursively call itself.

The computer may execute the same instructions on each iteration, but the values of at least some of the variables must change. The iterations continue while the values of the variables meet a specified condition.

Iterations are essential for handling *lists*. A list is a data structure in which the items are numbered and we know how to get to the *i*-th item. List traversal is a procedure in which we process all elements in the order in which they occur in the list. A sequential search for a particular value in a list of 1,000,000 elements, arranged in random order, takes, on average, 500,000 comparisons, if the target value is in the list, or 1,000,000 comparisons to establish that the target value is not in the list. For a list whose elements are arranged in some order (such as words in alphabetical order or numbers in increasing order) there is a much more efficient "divide and conquer" algorithm, called *Binary Search*. A binary search in a list of 1,000,000 elements needs only 20 comparisons!

Recursion is especially useful for handling nested structures, such as folders within folders or pictures within pictures. A recursive description of a data structure uses references to structures of the same type, and a recursive definition of a procedure that performs a certain task relies on applying the same procedure to a similar but smaller task. A recursive function calls itself, but the parameters passed to this recursive call must be somehow "reduced" with each call. A recursive function also has one or several simple cases that do not need recursion. These are called *base* (or *stopping*) *cases*. All recursive calls must eventually terminate with a base case.

Exercises

Sections 4.1-4.3

1.   Draw a flowchart and write pseudocode for an iterative algorithm that calculates $1+\dfrac{1}{2^2}+\dfrac{1}{3^2}+...+\dfrac{1}{n^2}$ for any given n. (This sum converges to $\dfrac{\pi^2}{6}$ as n increases.) ✓

2.   Draw a flowchart and write pseudocode for an iterative algorithm that calculates $1-\dfrac{1}{2}+\dfrac{1}{3}-...+(or-)\dfrac{1}{n}$ for any given n. $\dfrac{1}{k}$ is added to the sum if k is odd and subtracted from the sum if k is even. (This sum converges to $\ln 2$, the natural logarithm of 2.) ⸘ Hint: multiply $\dfrac{1}{k}$ by a factor that is equal to 1 or -1 before adding it to the sum. Flip the sign of the factor on each iteration. ⸘

3.   Design an iterative algorithm that, given two positive integers m and n, calculates the integer quotient and the remainder when m is divided by n. Your algorithm can use only $+$, $-$, and comparison operations for integers. Show your algorithm in pseudocode or draw a flowchart. ✓

4.   What is the output from the algorithm shown in the flowchart below when the input is $n = 37$, $b = 2$?

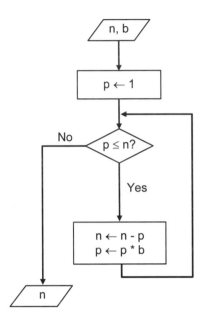

5.▪   Recall that $1 + 3 + ... + (2p - 1) = p^2$ for any integer $p \geq 1$. Using this property, come up with a simple iterative algorithm that finds out whether a given number is a perfect square. Your algorithm can compare numbers and use addition but don't use any other arithmetic operations. Show your algorithm in pseudocode or draw a flowchart.

6.▪   Add missing code to the following program:

```
/**
 *  This program prompts the user to enter
 *  a positive integer n and a line of text
 *  and displays that line n times
 */

import java.util.Scanner;

public class HelloNTimes
{
  public static void main(String[] args)
  {
    Scanner kb = new Scanner(System.in);

    System.out.print("Enter a positive integer: ");
    int n = kb.nextInt();
    kb.nextLine();  // consume the rest of the line

    System.out.print("Enter a line of text: ");
    String text = kb.nextLine();

    < missing code >
  }
}
```

Sections 4.4-4.8

7.   Consider the following recursive method:

```
public int mysterySum(int n)
{
  if (n == 0)  // if n equals to 0
    return 0;
  else
    return 3 + mysterySum(n - 1);
}
```

What value is returned when mysterySum(5) is called? ✓

8.▪   The questions below are paper-and-pencil exercises. You can use pseudocode or Java, but don't worry about the correct Java syntax.

Suppose you have a method `printStars`, such that `printStars(n)` prints *n* stars on one line. For example, a statement

```
printStars(5);
```

displays the line

```
* * * * *
```

(a)   Using the `printStars` method, write an iterative method `printTriangle` (or its pseudocode) so that `printTriangle(n)` prints a triangle with one star in the first row, two stars in the second row, and so on, up to n stars in the last row. For example, a statement

```
printTriangle(5);
```

should display

```
*
* *
* * *
* * * *
* * * * *
```

(b)   Write a recursive version of the `printTriangle` method, without iterations.

(c)   Modify the recursive version of `printTriangle`, so that `printTriangle(n)` displays

```
* * * * *
* * * *
* * *
* *
*
```

9.■   The following recursive method calculates 3^n:

```
// Precondition: n >= 0
public int power3(int n)
{
  if (n == 0)  // if n equals to 0
    return 1;
  else
  {
    int p = power3(n/2);
      // when n is odd, n/2 is truncated to an integer
      // for example, 7/2 gives 3 and 1/2 gives 0

    p *= p;  // multiply p by itself

    if (n % 2 == 1)  // if n is odd,
      p *= 3;        //    multiply p by 3

    return p;
  }
}
```

How many multiplications will be performed when the program calls
power3(15)?

10.   Let's pretend for a moment that Java does not support multiplication. Write
an iterative version and a recursive version of the following method (in
pseudocode, if you wish):

```
// Returns the product of a and b
// Precondition: a >= 0, b >= 0
public int product(int a, int b)
{
  ...
}
```

11. ■ Consider the following recursive method:

```
public int someFun(int n)
{
    if (n <= 0)
        return 2;
    else
        return someFun(n-1) * someFun(n-1);
}
```

(a) When the program calls someFun(5), how many times will someFun(3) be called?

(b)■ (MC) What does this method calculate when the input parameter n is a non-negative integer? ✓

A. n^2 B. 2^n C. 2^{n+1} D. 2^{2n+1} E. $2^{(2^n)}$

12. The numbers $\binom{n}{0}, \binom{n}{1}, \binom{n}{2}, ..., \binom{n}{n}$ in the expansion

$$(x+y)^n = \binom{n}{0}x^n + \binom{n}{1}x^{n-1}y + \binom{n}{2}x^{n-2}y^2 + ... + \binom{n}{n-1}xy^{n-1} + \binom{n}{n}y^n$$

are called *binomial coefficients*. For example,

$(x+y)^2 = x^2 + 2xy + y^2$, so $\binom{2}{0}=1, \binom{2}{1}=2, \binom{2}{2}=1$.

$(x+y)^3 = x^3 + 3x^2y + 3xy^2 + y^3$, so $\binom{3}{0}=1, \binom{3}{1}=3, \binom{3}{2}=3, \binom{3}{3}=1$.

$(x+y)^4 = x^4 + 4x^3y + 6x^2y^2 + 4xy^3 + y^4$, so

$\binom{4}{0}=1, \binom{4}{1}=4, \binom{4}{2}=6, \binom{4}{3}=4, \binom{4}{4}=1$.

$\binom{n}{k}$ is pronounced "n-choose-k" and sometimes written as $C(n, k)$. Binomial coefficients have the following properties: for any positive integer n,

$\binom{n}{0}=\binom{n}{n}=1$, and for any integers n and k, such that $0 < k < n$,

$\binom{n}{k}=\binom{n-1}{k-1}+\binom{n-1}{k}$.

Complete the recursive method binomialCoeff below, which computes a specified binomial coefficient (or write it in pseudocode).

```
// Returns the value of the binomial coefficient C(n, k)
// Precondition: 0 <= k <= n
public int binomialCoeff(int n, int k)
{
    ...
}
```

13.   The flowchart below describes the Sequential Search algorithm:

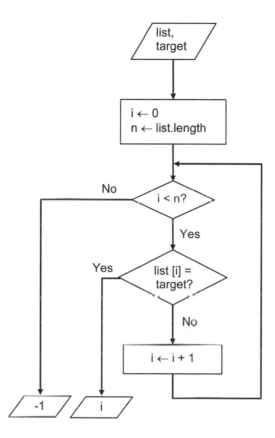

The algorithm finds the index *i* of the first element whose value is equal to *target*. If no such value is found, the algorithm returns –1. `list[i]` in the flowchart refers to the list's *i*-th element. <u>In Java, elements of a list are counted starting from 0.</u>

(a)   Modify the above flowchart for the algorithm that looks for two consecutive elements in the list, `list[i]` and `list[i+1]`, equal to each other. The algorithm should return the index of the first one, if such a pair is found, or –1, if no two consecutive values are equal.

(b)■   Draw a flowchart for the algorithm that finds in a list the index of the element with the maximum value. If several values are equal to the maximum value, the output should be the index of the first one of them.

Continued   ☞

(c)[♦] Draw a flowchart for the algorithm that determines whether a list has two duplicate (equal) values. The output should be *true* if found, *false* if not found. ⸘ Hint: for each *i* set `target` to `list[i]` and look for a duplicate `list[j]`, starting at $j = i + 1$. ⸘

14.■ In a bag of *n* coins, one is radioactive. In one trial we are allowed to measure the radioactivity of any pile of coins. (One radioactive coin makes the whole pile test positive for radioactivity.) Describe an efficient algorithm for finding the radioactive coin in the bag. Using your algorithm, how many trials are needed to find the radioactive coin in a bag of 1000 coins? ✓

15.♦ Suppose you have a precise balance scale and three coins. If two of the coins are of the same weight and the third one is lighter (a fake), it takes only one trial to identify the lighter one. How many trials are needed to find the lighter coin among 81 coins if the rest are all of the same weight? ✓

16.♦ The program *Ornament* (`JM\Ch04\Exercises\Ornament.java`) displays an ornament made of nested right isosceles triangles, as shown below:

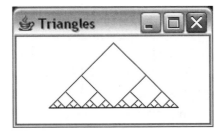

The half-length of the base of the largest triangle is 64, and the coordinates of the midpoint of the base are (100, 100). The half-length of the base of the smallest triangle is 4. Fill in the blanks in the `drawTriangles` method. ⸘ Hint: a statement

```
g.drawLine(x1, y1, x2, y2);
```

draws a line from point (`x1, y1`) to point (`x2, y2`) in the graphics context `g`. ⸘

```
/**
 *      Chapter 5
 */
```

Java Syntax and Style

5.1 Prologue

In Chapter 3 we discussed the main ideas of OOP methodology and worked through the general structure of a small program. There's much more than that, however, to writing working Java code. The text of a program is governed by very rigid rules of Java *syntax*, and every symbol in your program must be in just the right place. There are many opportunities to make a mistake. A compiler can catch most syntax errors and give error messages that provide somewhat comprehensible (or cryptic) clues to what is wrong with the code. However, some errors may look like acceptable code to the compiler even as they completely change how the code works. Programmers have to find and fix "bugs" of this kind themselves. Then there are honest logic errors in algorithms: you think your code works in a particular way, but actually it does something quite different. Java's run-time interpreter can catch some obvious errors (such as, when you divide something by zero); but most errors just show up in the way your program works (or rather fails to work).

Besides producing working code, a programmer must also pay attention to the program's *style*, a very important element of software engineering. The style is intended to make programs more readable. Technically, good style is optional — the compiler doesn't care. But the people who have to read or modify your program do care — a lot. As we say in Appendix A, ✤ *The 17 Bits of Style*,

> ... a programmer's product is not an executable program but its source code. In the current environment the life expectancy of a "working" program is just a few months, sometimes weeks. On the other hand, source code, updated periodically, can live for years.

In the following sections we will take a more detailed look at Java's syntax and style. We will discuss the following topics:

- How plain-language comments are marked and used in programs
- What reserved words are
- How to name classes, variables, objects, and methods
- Which rules come from syntax and which come from style
- How program statements are grouped into nested blocks using braces

In later chapters we will learn the specific syntax for declarations and control statements.

5.2 Using Comments

The first thing we notice in Java code is that it contains some phrases in plain English. These are *comments* inserted by the programmer to explain and document the program's features. It is a good idea to start any program with a comment explaining what the program does, who wrote it and when, and how to use it. This comment may also include the history of revisions: who made changes to the program, when, and why. The author must assume that his or her program will be read, understood, and perhaps modified by other people.

In Java, comments may be set apart from the rest of the code in two ways. The first format is to place a comment between /* and */ marks. For example:

```
/*  This is the main class for the Ramblecs game.
    Author: B. Speller  */
```

In this format, the comment may be placed anywhere in the code.

The second format is to place a comment after a double slash mark on one line. The compiler will treat all the text from the first double slash to the end of the line as a comment. For example, we can write:

```
if (a != 3)  // if a is not equal to 3
```

or

```
// Draw a rectangle with the upper-left corner at x, y:
g.drawRect(x, y, w, h);
...
```

> **Judiciously used comments are one of the most useful tools in the constant struggle to improve the readability of programs. Comments document the role and structure of major code sections, mark important procedural steps, and explain obscure or unusual twists in the code.**

On the other hand, excessive or redundant comments may clutter the code and become a nuisance. A novice may be tempted to comment each statement in the program even if the meaning is quite clear from the code itself. Experienced programmers use comments to explain the parts of their code that are less obvious. Self-explanatory code is better than well-commented obscure code (see Appendix A, ❈ *The 17 Bits of Style*, Bit 9).

Comment marks are also useful for *commenting out* (temporarily disabling) some statements in the source code. By putting a set of /* ... */ around a fragment of code or a double slash at the beginning of a line, we can make the compiler skip it on a particular compilation. This can be useful for making tentative changes to the code.

JDK supplies the *Javadoc* utility program (javadoc.exe), which generates documentation in HTML (HyperText Markup Language) format automatically from special "documentation" comments in the Java source. Documentation generated by *Javadoc* is ready to be viewed in an Internet browser.

A documentation comment must immediately precede an important element (a class, a constructor, a method, or a field) in order to be processed by *Javadoc*.

> **Documentation comments use the /* ... */ comment delimiters, but in addition they have to be marked by a second * after the opening /* so that *Javadoc* can recognize them.**

It is also common to put a star at the beginning of each line to make the comment stand out more. For example:

```
/**
 *   <code>MyMath</code> is a collection of math methods used in
 *   my algebra games applet.
 *   <p>
 *   All <code>MyMath</code> methods work with real numbers of
 *   the <code>double</code> type.
 *
 *   @author Al Jibris
 */
```

Or:

```
/**
 *   Returns the greatest common factor of positive integers
 *   <code>a</code> and <code>b</code>.
 *   <p>
 *   (This is a recursive implementation of Euclid's Algorithm.)
 *
 *   @param   a   the first number
 *   @param   b   the second number
 *   @return     the greatest common factor of a and b
 */
public int gcf(int a, int b)
{
    ...
}
```

Note how HTML formatting tags may be embedded in a documentation comment to make the final HTML document look better. *Javadoc* also understands its own special "tags": @param describes a method's parameter, @return describes the method's return value, and so on. There is a complete *Javadoc* tutorial☀javadoc at Sun's web site.

Any standard Java package is documented this way. Descriptions of Java library packages and classes in JDK's docs were generated automatically with *Javadoc* from the documentation comments in their code. Some programmers write documentation comments even before the code itself.

5.3   Reserved Words and Programmer-Defined Names

In Java a number of words are reserved for a special purpose, while other words are arbitrary names given by the programmer. Figure 5-1 shows a list of the Java *reserved words*, loosely organized by category.

Primitive data types:	Storage modifiers:	Classes, inheritance:	Exceptions handling:
char	public	import	try
byte	private	class	catch
int	protected	interface	finally
short	static	extends	throw
long	final	implements	throws
float		new	
double	Control statements:	this	Not used in this book:
boolean		super	
void	if	abstract	continue
enum	else	instanceof	package
	for		native
Built-in constants:	while		volatile
	do		transient
true	switch		synchronized
false	case		assert
null	default		
	break		
	return		

Figure 5-1.   Java reserved words

Each reserved word has a particular meaning and can be used only in its strictly prescribed way.

 All Java reserved words use only lowercase letters.

Figure 5-2 shows fragments of the HelloGui class with all the reserved words highlighted.

```java
/**
 *  This program displays a message in a window.
 */

import java.awt.*;
import javax.swing.*;

public class HelloGui extends JFrame
{
  public HelloGui()    // Constructor
  {
    super("GUI Demo");     // Set the title bar
    Container c = getContentPane();
    c.setBackground(Color.CYAN);
    c.setLayout(new FlowLayout());
    c.add(new JTextField(" Hello, GUI!", 10));
  }

  public static void main(String[] args)
  {
    HelloGui window = new HelloGui();

    // Set this window's location and size:
    // upper-left corner at 300, 300; width 200, height 100
    window.setBounds(300, 300, 200, 100);

    window.setDefaultCloseOperation(JFrame.EXIT_ON_CLOSE);
    window.setVisible(true);
  }
}
```

Figure 5-2. Reserved words in the HelloGui class

In addition to reserved words, there are other standard names and words whose meaning normally does not vary. These include all standard package names and names of classes from library packages. Examples include `java.awt`, `javax.swing`, `Object`, `String`, `Graphics`, `JFrame`, and so on. The names of methods from Java packages can be reused in your own classes, but you have to be very careful not to override a library method inadvertently when you derive your class from a library class.

> **A programmer gives names to his or her own Java classes, their fields and methods, and local variables inside methods. These names can use upper- and lowercase letters, digits, and the underscore character. No name may start with a digit. It is important to choose names that are somewhat self-explanatory and improve the readability of the program.**

It is also imperative to follow the Java naming convention.

> **All names of classes start with a capital letter; all names of methods and variables start with a lowercase letter. If a name consists of two or more words, all words starting with the second are capitalized. Names of "universal" or important constants may use all caps and an underscore character between words.**

For example:

```
public class VendingMachine               // class name
{
  private int depositedAmount;            // field
  ...
  public static final double TAX_RATE;    // constant
  ...
  public int getChange()                  // method name
  {
    int amt = ...                         // local variable
    ...
  }
}
```

> **Names of classes and objects usually sound like nouns, and names of methods usually sound like verbs.**

Names that are too short may not be expressive enough, but names that are too long clutter the code and make it harder to read. Java style experts do not mind a small set of standard "throwaway" names for temporary variables that are used in a small code segment, such as

```
int i, j, k;
double x, y;
Container c;
String str, s;
```

and so on. But variables used throughout the program should get more meaningful names.

> **It is a common practice to give the same name to methods in different classes if these methods perform tasks that are similar.**

Names are discussed in more detail in Appendix A, ✻ *The 17 Bits of Style.*

5.4 Syntax vs. Style

> **Text within double quotes and end-of-line comments must be kept on one line.**

Aside from that, the compiler regards line breaks, spaces, and tabs only as separators between consecutive words, and one space works the same way as 100 spaces. All redundant white space (any combination of spaces, tabs, and line breaks) is ignored by the compiler. So our `HelloGui` class from Chapter 2 could be written as shown in Figure 5-3. It would still compile and execute correctly. But although some people might insist that it makes as much sense as before, most would agree that it has become somewhat less readable.

> **Arranging your code on separate lines, inserting spaces and blank lines, and indenting fragments of code is not required by the compiler — it is a matter of stylistic convention.**

More or less rigid stylistic conventions have evolved among Java professionals, and they must be followed to make programs readable and acceptable to the practitioners of the trade. But as we said before, the compiler doesn't care. What it does care about is every word and symbol in your program. And here programmers do not have much freedom. They can use comments as they like and they can name their classes, methods, and variables. The rest of the text is governed by the very strict rules of Java *syntax*.

```
import java.awt.*; import javax.swing.*; public
class HelloGui extends JFrame { public HelloGui() {
super("GUI Demo"); Container c=
getContentPane();c.setBackground(Color.CYAN);
c.setLayout(new FlowLayout()); c.add(new JTextField(
" Hello, GUI!",10)); } public static void main(String[]
args) {HelloGui window = new HelloGui();
    // Set this window's location and size:
    // upper-left corner at 300, 300; width 200, height 100
window.setBounds(300, 300, 200, 100);window.
setDefaultCloseOperation(JFrame.EXIT_ON_CLOSE);
window.setVisible(true); }}
```

Figure 5-3. `HelloGui.java`**: compiles with no errors**

As opposed to English or any other natural language, programming languages have virtually no *redundancy*. Redundancy is a term from information theory that refers to less-than-optimal expression or transmission of information; redundancy in language or code allows the reader to interpret a message correctly even if it has been somewhat garbled. Forgetting a parenthesis or putting a semicolon in the wrong place in an English sentence may hinder reading for a moment, but it does not usually affect the overall meaning. Anyone who has read a text written by a six-year-old can appreciate the tremendous redundancy in natural languages, which is so great that we can read a text with no capitalization or punctuation and most words misspelled.

Not so in Java or any other programming language, where almost every character is essential. We have already mentioned that in Java all names and reserved words have to be spelled exactly right with the correct rendition of the upper- and lowercase letters. Suppose we inadvertently misspelled `paintComponent`'s name in the `HelloGraphics` class:

```
public void painComponent(Graphics g)
{
  < ... code >
}
```

The class still compiles fine and the program runs, but instead of redefining the `paintComponent` method inherited from `JPanel`, as intended, it introduces another method with a strange name that will be never called. When you run your program, it does not crash, but you see an empty window.

Not only spelling, but also every punctuation mark and symbol in the program has a precise purpose; omitting or misplacing one symbol leads to an error. At first it is hard to get used to this rigidity of syntax.

> **Java syntax is not very forgiving and may frustrate a novice. The proper response is to pay closer attention to details!**

The compiler catches most syntax errors, but in some cases it has trouble diagnosing the problem precisely. Suppose we have accidentally omitted the phrase `implements ActionListener` on Line 8 in the `Banner` class (Figure 2.10 on page 36).

```
import java.awt.*;
import java.awt.event.*;
import javax.swing.*;
```

```
          . . .
  Line 7:  public class Banner extends JApplet
  Line 8:  // suppose we accidentally omitted implements ActionListener
          . . .
  Line 18:     Timer clock = new Timer(30, this);
```

When we compile the program, the compiler can tell that something is not right and reports an error on Line 18:

```
C:\Mywork\Banner.java:18: cannot find symbol
symbol  : constructor Timer(int,Banner)
location: class javax.swing.Timer
    Timer clock = new Timer(30, this);
                      ^
1 error
```

But it doesn't know what exactly we meant to do or what exactly we did wrong (in this call to `Timer`'s constructor, `this` is supposed to be an `ActionListener`, and we haven't defined it as one).

Appendix B⁕ lists a few common compiler error messages and their causes.

> **Notwithstanding the compiler's somewhat limited capacity to pinpoint your syntax errors, you can never blame the compiler for errors. You may be sure that there is <u>something</u> wrong with your code or a required class is missing if your class does not compile correctly.**

Unfortunately, the converse is not always true: the program may compile correctly but still contain errors ("bugs"). Just as a spell-check program will not notice if you type "wad" instead of "was" or "you" instead of "your," a compiler will not find errors that it can mistake for something else. So it is easy to make a minor punctuation or spelling error that conforms to all the syntax rules but happens to change the meaning of your code. For instance, in Java a semicolon marks the end of a statement. Suppose you wrote a method

```
public static int addSquares(int n)
{
  int i, sum = 0;
  for (i = 1; i <= n; i++);
    sum += i * i;
  return sum;
}
```

but, as above, you accidentally put an extraneous semicolon on the `for` line after the closing parentheses:

```
      for (i = 1; i <= n; i++);
```

The compiler doesn't care about your intentions or indentation; it would interpret your code as

```
public static int addSquares(int n)
{
  int i, sum = 0;
  for (i = 1; i <= n; i++);
  sum += i * i;
  return sum;
}
```

You <u>think</u> your code will iterate n times through the `sum += ...` statement. Guess what: instead it will iterate n times through nothing, an empty statement. As a result, `addSquares(5)` will return 36, rather than 55.

> **Beginners can usually save a lot of time by carefully reading their code a couple of times <u>before</u> running it through the compiler. Get in the habit of checking that nothing is misspelled and that all semicolons, braces, and other punctuation marks are where they should be.**

5.5 Statements, Blocks, Indentation

Java code consists mainly of declarations and control statements. Declarations describe objects and methods; control statements describe actions.

> **Declarations and other statements in Java are terminated with a semicolon. Statements can be grouped into blocks using braces { }. Semicolons are not used after a closing brace (except in enum type declarations, explained in Chapter 7 and certain array declarations explained in Chapter 12).**

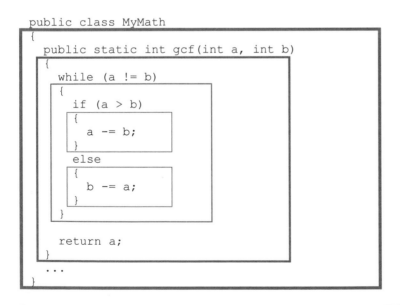

Figure 5-4. Nested blocks, marked by braces, within a class

Braces divide the code into *nested blocks* (Figure 5-4). Statements inside a block are usually indented by a fixed number of spaces or one tab. In this book we indent statements inside a block by two spaces, which is a common Java style. A braced-off block is used to indicate that a number of statements form one *compound statement* that belongs in the same control structure, for example a loop (for, while, etc.) or a *conditional* (if) statement. The outermost block is always the body of a class definition.

There are different styles of placing braces. One style is to place the opening brace at the end of the last line that precedes the block:

```
for (int i = 1; i <= n; i++) {
  sum += i * i;
}
```

Others (including us in this book) prefer braces aligned one above the other:

```
for (int i = 1; i <= n; i++)
{
  sum += i * i;
}
```

This makes it easier to see the opening brace. Just be sure you don't put, by mistake, an extra semicolon on the previous line.

Another important way to improve the readability of your code is by spacing lines vertically. Make generous use of special comment lines and blank lines to separate sections and procedural steps in your code.

5.6 *Lab:* Correcting Syntax Errors

Figure 5-5 shows a Java program that is supposed to display an orange disk moving across the "sky." However, the code in Figure 5-5 has several syntax errors. Find and fix them. Do not retype the program — just copy MovingDisk.java from JM\Ch05\Syntax into your current work folder.

You might wonder, "How am I going to fix syntax errors if I have no idea what the correct Java syntax is?" Well, consider it an adventure game.

```
 1   import java.awt.*;
 2   import java.awt.event*;
 3   import javax.swing.*;
 4
 5   public class MovingDisk extands JPanel
 6     implements ActionListener
 7   {
 8     private int time;
 9
10     public MovingDisk()
11     {
12       time = 0
13       Timer clock = new Timer(30, this);
14       clock.start;
15     }
16
17     public void paintComponent(Graphics g)
18     {
19       int x = 150 - (int)(100 * Math.cos(0.005 * Math.PI * time));
20       int y = 130 - (int)75 * Math.sin(0.005 * Math.PI * time));
21       int r = 20;
22
23       Color sky;
24       if (y > 130) sky = Color.BLACK
25       else sky = Color.CYAN;
26       setBackground(sky);
27       super.paintComponent(g);
28
29       g.setColor(Color.ORANGE);
30       g.fillOval(x - r, y - r, 2*r, 2*r);
31     }
32
33     public void actionPerformed(ActionEvent e)
34     {
35       time++;
36       repaint();
37     }
38
39     public static void main(String args)
40     {
41       JFrame w = new JFrame("Moving Disk);
42       w.setSize(300, 150);
43       w.setDefaultCloseOperation(JFrame.EXIT_ON_CLOSE);
44       Container c = w.getContentPane();
45       c.add(new movingDisk());
46       w.setResizable(false);
47       w.setVisible(true);
48     }
49   }
```

Figure 5-5. JM\Ch05\Syntax\MovingDisk.java (with syntax errors)

Add a comment at the top of `MovingDisk.java` stating the purpose of the `MovingDisk` class and your name. Read the source code carefully a couple of times to see if you can spot any errors. Then compile the code. Examine the error messages generated by the compiler carefully and look for clues in them. For example, if the compiler tells you that a certain name is undefined, check the spelling of the name.

Usually you should start working with the first error message. Do not panic if after fixing an error or two new errors pop up — this can happen if your compiler now understands your code better and sees other problems. Sometimes a compiler message may be misleading. For example, it may tell you "; expected" while in fact something else is wrong with your code.

When your program finally compiles, try to run it. If you get an "exception" error message, try to get some clues from it, look at the code again carefully, and fix the problem.

5.7 Summary

The text of a program is governed by rigid rules of *syntax* and *style*. The syntax is checked by the compiler, which does not allow a program with syntax errors to compile. The style is intended to make programs more readable and, even though the compiler does not check it, plays a very important role in producing readable, professional code.

Comments complement the program code, document classes and methods, and explain obscure places in the code. Comments can be also used to "comment out" (temporarily disable) statements in the program. Special "documentation" comments help the *Javadoc* program automatically generate documentation in the HTML format.

A program's text contains some *reserved words*, which are used for a particular purpose in the language, as well as some names given by the programmer. Java is case-sensitive, so all words must be spelled with the upper- and lowercase letters rendered correctly. Java reserved words use only lowercase letters.

A programmer gives names to classes, methods, variables, and constants, trying to choose names that make the program more readable. Names may contain letters, digits, and the underscore character. They cannot start with a digit.

Program code consists mostly of declarations and executable statements, which are normally terminated with a semicolon. The statements may be organized in *nested blocks* placed within braces. Inner blocks are indented in relation to the outer block by one tab or some fixed number of spaces.

Java syntax is not very forgiving and may frustrate a novice — there is no such thing as "just a missing semicolon."

Exercises

Sections 5.1-5.4

1. Name three good uses for comments. *comment out lines of code, Javadoc, explain what you've doing*

2. Add a *Javadoc*-style comment to the `paintComponent` method in the `MovingDisk` class from Section 5.6 (`JM\Ch05\Syntax\MovingDisk.java`).

3. Consider the *Moving Disk* program.

    (a) Find the sixteen different reserved words used in `MovingDisk.java`. ✓

    (b)▪ Identify the names of the packages, classes, methods, and constants that come from Java's libraries.

    (c)▪ Identify the twelve names chosen by the programmer of this program. ⋜ Hint: some of them are conventional, others rather unremarkable. ⋛ ✓

4. Identify the following statements as referring to required Java syntax or optional style:

    (a) A program begins with a comment. *Style*
    (b) The names of all methods begin with a lower case letter. *Syntax* ✓
    (c) Each opening brace has a matching closing brace. *Syntax*
    (d) All statements within a pair of matching braces are indented by 2 spaces. *Style*
    (e) A closing brace is placed on a separate line. *Style*
    (f) A class has a blank line before each method declaration. *Style*
    (g) The word IF is not used as a name for a variable. *Syntax* ✓

5.   Define "redundancy." *Stating same thing mult times*

6.   What happens if the name of the `main` method in the `MovingDisk` class is mistyped with a capital M? ✓

7.■   In

```
if (y > 150)
{
   sky = Color.PINK;
}
```

are the parentheses required by the Java syntax, or are they a matter of style? What about the braces? ✓

8.   Consider the *Banner* applet (with a "banner" moving across the screen) from Chapter 2 (JM\Ch02\HelloGui\Banner.java). Add an extra semicolon in the `if` statement in the `actionPerformed` method:

```
if (xPos < -100);
{
   xPos = c.getWidth();
}
```

Try to compile and run the applet and explain the result. Why does it compile with no errors? Why is the message not moving across the screen?

Sections 5.5-5.7

9.   Restore line spacing and proper indentation in the following code: ✓

```
public boolean badIndentation(int maxLines) {int lineCount = 3;
   while(lineCount < maxLines) {System.out.println
(lineCount); lineCount++;} return true;}
```

10.   Mark true or false and explain:

(a)   The Java compiler recognizes nested blocks through indentation. _____ ✓

(b)   Each line in a Java program ends with a semicolon. _____

(c)   Text within double quotes cannot be split between two lines. _____ ✓

(d)   Adding spaces around a + sign or a parenthesis (that is not inside quotes) is a matter of style. _____

(e)   The order of methods and fields in a class definition is a matter of style and the programmer's choice. _____

11.   (a)   Comment out the statement

```
super("GUI Demo");    // Set the title bar
```

in the *Hello GUI* program from Chapter 2
(JM\Ch02\HelloGui\HelloGui.java). Compile and run the
program. What happens? ✓

(b)   Keep `super` commented out and replace

```
public HelloGui()    // Constructor
```

with

```
public void HelloGui()    // Constructor
```

Does the program compile? If so, what does it do? Explain what
happens. ✓

12.   (a)   Find and fix three syntax errors in the program *Morning*
(JM\Ch05\Exercises\Morning.java). Compile and run the
program. Note that this program uses another class, EasySound,
whose source file, EasySound.java (from JM\Ch05\Exercises)
should be added to your project. Copy the file roost.wav into the
folder where your IDE places the compiled classes.

(b)♦   Using the *Moving Disk* program from this chapter as a prototype,
change the *Morning* program to play the sound every five seconds.

(c)♦   Find a free moo.wav file on the web. Change the program to alternate
the "rooster" sound with a "moo" sound and the white background
with a black background every five seconds.

```
int chapter = 6;
```

Data Types, Variables, and Arithmetic

6.1 Prologue

Java and other high-level languages let programmers refer to a memory location by name. These named "containers" for values are called *variables*. The programmer gives variables meaningful names that reflect their role in the program. The compiler/interpreter takes care of all the details — allocating memory space for the variables and representing data in the computer memory.

The term "variable" is borrowed from algebra because, as in algebra, variables can assume different values and can be used in *expressions*. The analogy ends there, however. In a computer program, variables are actively manipulated by the program. As we mentioned earlier, a variable is like a slate on which the program can write a new value when necessary and from which it can read the current value. For example, the statement

```
a = b + c;
```

does not mean that *a* is equal to *b* + *c*, but rather a set of instructions:

1. Get the current value of b;
2. Get the current value of c;
3. Add the two values;
4. Assign the result to a (write the result into a).

The same is true for

```
a = 4 - a;
```

It is <u>not</u> an equation, but a set of instructions for changing the value of a:

1. Get the current value of the variable a;
2. Subtract it from 4;
3. Assign the result back to a (write the new value into a).

In Java, a statement

```
someName = expression;
```

represents an *assignment* operation that <u>evaluates</u> (finds the value of) the expression on the right side of the = sign and <u>assigns</u> that value to (writes it into) the variable `someName` on the left side of =. The = sign is read "gets the value of": "`someName` gets the value of *expression*." (If you want to <u>compare</u> two values, use another operator, ==, to mean "is equal to.")

In Java, every variable has a *data type*. This can be either a *primitive data type* (such as `int`, `double`, and `char`) or a class type (such as `String`, `Foot`, `Walker`). The programmer specifies the variable's data type based on the kind of data it will contain.

> **A variable's data type determines the range of values that can be stored in the variable, the amount of space allocated for it in memory, and the kind of operations that can be performed with it.**

A variable of type `int`, for example, contains an integer value, which can be in the range from -2^{31} to $2^{31}-1$; a variable of type `double` represents a real number. A variable of type `String` refers to an object of the `String` class.

In Java, a variable that represents an object holds a *reference* to that object. A reference is basically the address of the object in memory. When an object is created with the `new` operator, that operator allocates memory space for the object and returns a reference to it. That reference can be saved in a variable and used to access the object. We'll explain references in more detail in Chapter 9.

In this chapter we explain the following concepts and elements of Java syntax:
- The syntax and placement of declarations for variables and constants
- Primitive data types
- Strings
- Literal and symbolic constants
- Conversion of values from one type to another (casts)
- The scope of variables and symbolic constants
- Java's arithmetic operators

6.2 Declaring Fields and Local Variables

Variables in Java fall into three main categories: *fields*, *local variables*, and *parameters* in constructors or methods. The fields are declared within the body of a class, outside of any constructor or method. They can be used in any constructor or method of the class. Local variables are declared and used inside a particular constructor or method. Parameters are described in the header for a constructor or method and act pretty much like local variables within that constructor or method.

The fragment of code in Figure 6-1 shows several declarations of fields in the `Walker` class and a constructor that sets their values.

```
public class Walker
{
  public static final int PIXELS_PER_INCH = 6;      ⎤
  private Foot leftFoot, rightFoot;                  ⎥___  Declarations
  private int stepLength;                            ⎥        of fields
  private int stepsCount;                            ⎦

  // Constructor
  public Walker(int x, int y, Image leftPic, Image rightPic)
  {
    leftFoot =  new Foot(x, y - PIXELS_PER_INCH * 4, leftPic);
    rightFoot = new Foot(x, y + PIXELS_PER_INCH * 4, rightPic);
    stepLength = PIXELS_PER_INCH * 12;
  }

  ...
}
```

Figure 6-1. A fragment from the `Walker` class

Fields are declared outside of any constructor or method, usually at the top of the class's body.

But regardless of where they are placed, they are "visible" in all the constructors and all the methods of the class.

Usually all fields are declared `private`, which means they can be used only by the constructors and methods of their class and are not directly accessible to methods of other classes.

However, some constants may be declared `public`.

The general format for a field declaration is

```
private sometype someName;
```

or

```
private sometype someName = expression;
```

If a field is not explicitly initialized, Java provides a default value, which is 0 for fields of numeric types and `null` for objects.

For example:

```
private int stepsCount;    // stepsCount is set to 0
private Foot leftFoot;     // leftFoot is set to null
```

Assigning a variable a `null` value indicates that it does not currently refer to any valid object. `null` is a Java reserved word.

Local variables are temporary variables that are declared <u>inside</u> a constructor or method. Once a method is finished, its local variables are discarded.

For example, the `setup` method in `WalkingGroup` uses local variables `width`, `height`, `x`, and `y`:

```
// Sets up this group of participants
public void setup(int floorDir, Dance steps1, Dance steps2)
{
  int width = danceFloor.getWidth();
  int height = danceFloor.getHeight();
  int x = width / 10;
  int y = height / 2;
  ...
}
```

The general format for a local variable declaration is similar to a field declaration:

```
sometype someName;
```

or

```
sometype someName = expression;
```

where `sometype` declares the type of the variable and `someName` is the name given by the programmer to this particular variable.

> **`public` or `private` cannot be used in declarations of local variables.**

A local variable must be declared and assigned a value before it can be used — local variables do not get default values.

> **Parameters in a constructor or method are sometimes called *formal parameters*. They get their initial values from the actual parameters that the caller passes to that constructor or method. They act like local variables within the constructor or method.**

Note the following features in the declarations of fields and local variables:

1. A declaration, like other Java statements, always ends with a semicolon.

2. A declaration must include the type of the variable and its name. For example:

   ```
   int stepLength;
   Foot leftFoot;
   Walker amy;
   ```

3. Several variables of the same type may be listed in one declaration, separated by commas. For example:

   ```
   Foot leftFoot, rightFoot;
   int stepLength, stepsCount;
   double x, y, z;
   ```

4. A declaration of a variable may include an initialization that sets its initial value. For example:

   ```
   int width = danceFloor.getWidth();
   EasySound beat = new EasySound("beat.wav");
   ```

5. A variable may be declared `final`, which means that its value, once assigned, cannot change. For example:

    ```
    public static final int PIXELS_PER_INCH = 6;
    ```

    So an initialized `final` "variable" is not actually a variable, but a constant. A constant's initial value is also its "final" value. A constant can be initialized in its declaration or later, in a constructor.

A variable can be declared only <u>once</u> within its *scope* ("scope" refers to the space in the program where the variable is "visible" — see Section 6.6).

For example, to have both

```
int sum;
...
int sum = m + n;
```

within the same method is a syntax error. Use either

```
int sum;
...
sum = m + n;
```

or

```
int sum = m + n;
```

> **Java allows you to use the same name for a field and a local variable. This may cause bugs that are sometimes hard to find.**

For example, if we inadvertently write

```
Walker person = new Walker (x, y, leftShoe, rightShoe);
```

instead of

```
person = new Walker (x, y, leftShoe, rightShoe);
```

in the `setup` method, the compiler will treat this statement as a declaration of a <u>local variable</u> person and leave the <u>field</u> person uninitialized (`null`). When later another method attempts to call one of `person`'s methods, the program will "throw" a `NullPointerException`.

You might wonder: Why do we need local variables? Why can't we make them all fields? Technically it would be possible to use only fields, but a class is much better organized if variables that are used locally are kept local. In a good design, a field is a variable that describes a truly important, "global" attribute of its object. You don't want to use global variables for your temporary needs — just like you don't carry your own plate and silverware to every fast-food restaurant you visit.

6.3 Primitive Data Types

In Java, values of primitive data types are <u>not</u> objects. This is a concession to more traditional programming languages, like C, from which Java borrows much of its syntax. Objects have data types, too: the data type of an object is its class. But `int`, `double`, and other primitive data types are not classes.

Java has the following eight *primitive data types*, designated by reserved words:

```
boolean     byte
char        short
int         long
double      float
```

Note that like other Java reserved words, the names of the primitive data types are spelled in lowercase letters. They are called *primitive* because variables of these types do not have the properties of objects (in particular, they do not have any methods). A `char` variable holds one character (in Unicode); an `int`, `byte`, `short`, or `long` variable holds an integer; a `float` or `double` variable holds a floating-point real number.

> **Because variables of different types occupy different numbers of bytes in memory, we say they have different *sizes*.**

In Java each data type has a fixed size, regardless of the particular computer model or brand of Java interpreter. Table 6-1 summarizes the primitive types, their sizes, and the ranges of their values.

Although `float` and `double` can represent a huge range of numbers, their precision is limited to only about seven significant digits for the `float` and about twice as many for the `double`.

> **In this book we will work primarily with the `int`, `double`, `char`, and `boolean` primitive data types.**

The `boolean` type is discussed in the next chapter.

> **It is a programmer's responsibility to make sure the values of variables and all the intermediate and final results in arithmetic expressions fit within the range of the chosen data types, and that these types satisfy the precision requirements for computations.**

Type	Size (bytes)	Range
boolean	1	true or false
char	2	Unicode character set (with ASCII subset)
byte	1	from $-2^7 = -128$ to $2^7 - 1 = 127$
short	2	from $-2^{15} = -32,768$ to $2^{15} - 1 = 32,767$
int	4	from -2^{31} to $2^{31} - 1$
long	8	from -2^{63} to $2^{63} - 1$
float	4	approx. from -3.4×10^{38} to 3.4×10^{38}
double	8	approx. from -1.8×10^{308} to 1.8×10^{308}

Table 6-1.   The primitive data types

6.4 Strings

In Java, character strings (short fragments of text) are represented by `String` objects. `String` is a library class from the `java.lang` package, which is built into Java. A `String` is an object, so `String` is <u>not</u> a primitive data type.

The `String` class mostly behaves like any other class: it has constructors and public methods, described in the Java API documentation. (The `String` class also has private methods and fields; we are not interested in them, because they are private.) We will discuss the most commonly used `String` methods in Chapter 10 and will also explain there why `String` constructors are rarely used.

There are two Java features, however, that make the String class special. First, the compiler recognizes strings of characters in double quotes as constant String objects — *literal strings*. You can write, for example,

```
String str = "Hello, World";
```

The compiler automatically creates a String object with the value "Hello, World" and assigns a reference to that object to the variable str. There is no need to use the new operator to create a literal string.

Second, Java allows you to apply the + operator to strings. In general, you cannot apply operators to objects. Strings are an exception: when + is applied to two strings, it concatenates them. For example,

```
String str = "Chapter" + "6";
```

is the same as

```
String str = "Chapter6";
```

6.5 Constants

A *constant* represents a "variable" whose value does not change while the program is running. Your source code may include *literal constants* and *symbolic constants*.

Examples of literal constants are decimal representations of integers and real numbers, characters in single quotes, and text in double quotes:

```
'y', 'H'                        (chars)
7, -3                           (ints)
1.19, .05, 12.0, 3.,0.4         (doubles)
"leftshoe.gif", "1776", "y"     (Strings)
```

It is possible for a literal character string to consist of only one character (for example, "y"). Java also allows an empty string — it is designated by two double quote characters next to each other, with nothing in between: "".

Character constants include a special set of non-printable characters designated by *escape sequences* (the term derives from printer control commands). In Java, an escape sequence is a pair of characters: a designated printable character preceded by the "escape character," a backslash. An escape pair is placed within single quotes to designate a one-character constant.

Escape sequences include:

\n	newline
\r	carriage return
\t	tab
\f	form feed
\'	single quote
\"	double quote
\\	backslash

The most commonly used one is \n — "newline."

Escape pairs can be used in literal string constants. For example:

```
System.out.print("\nDon\'t let me down\nDon\'t let me down\n");
```

"\n", for example, represents a string that consists of one newline character.

❖   ❖   ❖

Symbolic constants are usually represented by initialized final fields. For example:

```
public static final int PIXELS_PER_INCH = 6;
private final int stepLength = PIXELS_PER_INCH * 12;
```

(Sometimes, programmers write names of symbolic constants using all capital letters for better visibility.) final is a Java reserved words.

The general form of a symbolic constant's declaration is

```
[optional modifiers] final sometype someName = expression;
```

where sometype is a data type followed by a name of the constant and its value. A constant may also be initialized to the value of some expression.

> **A constant doesn't have to be initialized right away in its declaration — its "final" value can be set in a constructor.**

For example:

```
private final int stepLength;
...

// Constructor
public Walker(int x, int y, Image leftPic, Image rightPic)
{
  stepLength = PIXELS_PER_INCH * 12;
  ...
}
```

It may seem, at first, that symbolic constants are redundant and we can simply use their literal values throughout the program. Consider, for instance, the code that we put together for constructing a `Walker` object:

```
// Constructor
public Walker(int x, int y, Image leftPic, Image rightPic)
{
  leftFoot =  new Foot(x, y - PIXELS_PER_INCH * 4, leftPic);
  rightFoot = new Foot(x, y + PIXELS_PER_INCH * 4, rightPic);
  stepLength = PIXELS_PER_INCH * 12;
}
```

Surely we could write the same code with specific numbers plugged in:

```
  ...
  leftFoot =  new Foot(x, y - 24, leftPic);
  rightFoot = new Foot(x, y + 24, rightPic);
  stepLength = 72;
  ...
```

At a first glance it might seem simpler. However, there are several important reasons for using symbolic constants.

> **The most important reason for using symbolic constants is that it simplifies program maintenance. If the program is modified in the future and the value of a constant needs to be changed, a change to the constant's declaration will change the constant's value throughout the program (after the class that contains the constant is recompiled).**

In the above example, if we needed to adjust the scale of the dance floor, we would have to change all the numbers. A programmer making the change would have to figure out what all the numbers mean and recalculate them. The task is even harder if the numbers related to one constant are scattered throughout the program.

Another advantage of symbolic constants is that they make the code more readable and self-explanatory if their names are chosen well. The name can explain the role a constant plays in the program, making additional comments unnecessary.

It is also easier to change a symbolic constant into a variable if, down the road, a future version of the program requires it.

Symbolic constants, like variables, are declared with a particular data type and are defined only within their scope (explained in the next section). This introduces more order into the code and gives the compiler additional opportunities for error checking — one more reason for using symbolic constants.

On the other hand, there is no need to clutter the code with symbolic names assigned to universal constants such as 0 or 1, or

```
final int semiCircleDegrees = 180;
final int HOURS_IN_DAY = 24;
```

6.6 Scope of Variables

As we have discussed above, each constructor and method in a class can have its own local variables, while the fields of a class can be used in all its methods. The question of where a variable is visible and can be used relates to the subject of *scope*.

> **In Java a variable is defined only within a certain space in the program called the *scope* of the variable.**

Scope discipline helps the compiler perform important error checking. If you try to use a variable or constant outside its scope, the compiler detects the error and reports an undefined name. The compiler also reports an error if you declare the same name twice within the same scope.

> **The scope of a field extends throughout the class, including all its constructors and methods.**
>
> **The scope of a local variable extends from its declaration to the end of the block in which it is declared.**

A local variable exists only temporarily while the program is executing the block where that variable is declared. When a program passes control to a method, a special chunk of memory (a *frame* on the system *stack*) is allocated to hold that method's local variables. When the method is exited, that space is released and all local variables are destroyed.

Local variables in Java do not have to be declared at the top of a method but may be declared anywhere in the method's code. But declarations inside nested blocks can lead to elusive bugs. We recommend that at first you avoid declaring local variables inside nested blocks unless you know exactly what you are doing.

As we have mentioned earlier, Java allows you to use the same name for a field and a local variable, with the local variable taking precedence over the global one. This may lead to hard-to-catch errors if you inadvertently declare an identically named local variable that overrides the global one.

> **This possible overlap of names is a good reason to give a class's fields <u>conspicuous</u> names.**

x, y, or a are bad choices for field names — they should be saved for throwaway local variables. `person` and `stepsCount` are better names for fields.

> **It is perfectly acceptable to use the same name for local variables in different methods.**

In fact, this is a good practice when the variables represent similar quantities and are used in similar ways. But <u>never</u> try to economize on declarations of temporary local variables within methods by making them fields. Everything should be declared where it belongs.

6.7 Arithmetic Expressions

> **Arithmetic expressions are written the same way as in algebra and may include literal and symbolic constants, variables, the arithmetic operators +, −, ∗, and /, and parentheses.**

The order of operations is determined by parentheses and by the ranks of operators: multiplication and division are performed first (left to right), followed by addition and subtraction. Multiplication requires the ∗ sign — it cannot be omitted. You can also use the minus symbol for negation. For example:

```
x = -(y + 2*z) / 5;
a = -a;                   // Negate a
```

Java also has the % operator for integers:

```
a % b
```

which is read "a modulo b," and means the remainder when a is divided by b. For example, 31 % 7 is equal to 3; 365 % 7 is 1; 5 % 17 is 5. This operator is handy for computing values that change in a cyclic manner. For example:

```
int minsAfterHour = totalMins % 60;
int dayOfWeek = (dayOfWeekOnFirst - 1 + day) % 7;
int lastDigitBase10 = x % 10;
```

It is also used to check whether a number is evenly divisible by another number. For example:

```
if (k % 2 == 0) ... // if k is even ...
```

The % operator has the same rank as * and /.

Java allows programmers to mix variables of different data types in the same expression. Each operation in the expression is performed according to the types of its operands, and its result receives a certain type.

> **The type of the result depends only on the <u>types</u> of the operands, not their values. If the two operands have the same type, the result of the operation automatically gets the same type as the operands.**

This principle goes back to the C language and has serious consequences, especially for division of integers. If you write

```
int a = 7, b = 2;
System.out.println(a / b);
```

you will see 3, and not 3.5 as you might expect. The reason is that both a and b are integers and therefore the result of a / b must be also an integer. If it isn't, it is <u>truncated</u> to an integer (in the direction toward 0). So 7/2 is evaluated as 3 and −7/2 as −3.

> **If you want to get a true ratio of two int variables, you have to convert your ints into doubles. This can be done by using the *cast* operator, designated by the target type in parentheses.**

For example:

```
double ratio = (double)a / (double)b;
```

The above statement is basically equivalent to introducing two temporary variables:

```
double tempA, tempB;
tempA = a;
tempB = b;
double ratio = tempA / tempB;
```

But casts do it for you.

The general syntax for the cast operator is

```
(sometype)variable
```

or

```
(sometype)(expression)
```

> **Note that the "same type" rule applies to all intermediate results of all operations in an expression.**

If you write

```
int a = 7, b = 2;
double ratio = a / b;   // Too late!
```

`ratio` still gets the value of 3, because the result of `a / b` is truncated to an `int` before it is assigned to `ratio`. Similarly, if you write

```
int degreesCelsius = 5 / 9 * (degreesFahrenheit - 32);   // Error!
```

`degreesCelsius` will be always set to 0 (because `5 / 9` is evaluated first and its result is 0).

If the two operands have different types, the operand of the "smaller" type is *promoted* (that is, converted) to the "larger" type. (`long` is "larger" than `int`, `float` is "larger" than `long`, and `double` is the "largest"). Therefore, in the above example it would have sufficed to use only one cast:

```
        double ratio = (double)a / b;
```

or

```
        double ratio = a / (double)b;
```

The other operand would be promoted to a double. But trying to cast the resulting ratio would cause the same problem as above:

```
        double ratio = (double)(a / b);
                            // Error: the result of a / b is already
                            //   truncated!  The cast is too late!
```

Your code will be better documented if you indicate explicit type conversions using the cast operator, where necessary, rather than relying on implicit type conversions.

You don't need to use casts with literal constants — just choose a constant of the right type.

For example:

```
        double volume = 4.0 / 3.0 * Math.PI * Math.pow(r, 3.0);
```

computes the volume of a sphere with the radius *r* (which is equal to $\frac{4}{3}\pi r^3$).

Sometimes you may need to use a cast in the opposite direction: to convert a "larger" type into a "smaller" one, such as a double into an int. For example:

```
        int pointsOnDie = 1 + (int)(Math.random() * 6);
           // 0.0 <= Math.random() < 1.0
```

The (int) cast truncates the number in the direction of 0, so (int)1.99 is 1 and (int)(-1.99) is -1.

If you want to round a double value to the <u>nearest</u> integer, add 0.5 to a positive number or subtract 0.5 from a negative number first, and then cast it into an int. For example:

```
        int percent = (int)((double)count / totalCount * 100 + 0.5);
```

or

```
        int percent = (int)(100.0 * count / totalCount + 0.5);
```

> **The cast operator applies only to "compatible" data types. You cannot cast a number into a string or vice-versa.**

There are several ways to convert numbers and objects into strings. One of them is discussed in Section 6.9.

6.8 Compound Assignment and Increment Operators

Java has convenient shortcuts for combining arithmetic operations with assignment. The following table summarizes the *compound assignment* operators:

Compound assignment:	Is the same as:
a += b;	a = a + b;
a -= b;	a = a - b;
a *= b;	a = a * b;
a /= b;	a = a / b;
a %= b;	a = a % b;

For example, the following statement:

```
sum += i * i;
```

is the same as:

```
sum = sum + i * i;
```

The += form may seem cryptic at the beginning, but, once you get used to it, it becomes attractive — not only because it is more concise, but also because it emphasizes the fact that the same variable is being modified. The latter form immediately gives away an amateur.

❖   ❖   ❖

As we have seen, the + operator, when applied to two strings, concatenates them. `str1 += str2` also works for strings, creating a new string by concatenating `str1` and `str2` and assigning the result to `str1`. For example:

```
String fileName = "leftshoe";
fileName += ".gif";      // fileName now refers to "leftshoe.gif"
```

Another syntactic shortcut is the set of special *increment/decrement* operators. These operators are used for incrementing or decrementing an integer variable by one:

Increment/ decrement:	Is the same as:
a++	a = a + 1
a--	a = a - 1
++a	a = a + 1
--a	a = a - 1

Increment and decrement operators may be used in expressions. That is where the difference between the `a++` and `++a` forms and between the `a--` and `--a` forms becomes very important. When `a++` is used, the value of the variable `a` is incremented <u>after</u> it has been used in the expression; for the `++a` form, the value of the variable `a` is incremented <u>before</u> it has been used in the expression. This can get quite confusing and hard to read. For example:

```
a = b + c++;   // Too much!
```

Consider using `a++` and `a--` only as a separate statement. Avoid `++a` and `--a` altogether, and avoid using `++` and `--` in arithmetic expressions.

6.9 Converting Numbers and Objects into Strings

Java treats `String` objects in a special way: the + operator, when applied to two strings, concatenates them. This is simply a syntax shortcut that eliminates the need to call a method. (In fact, the `String` class has a method `concat` for concatenating a string to another, so `str1 + str2` is equivalent to `str1.concat(str2)`.)

Java also allows you to use the + operator for concatenation when one operand is a string and the other is a primitive data type or an object. In that case, the operand that is not a string is automatically converted into a string.

For example,

```
double v = 79.5;
System.out.print("Volume = " + v);
```

displays

```
Volume = 79.5
```

Here the + concatenates a string `"Volume = "` and a `double` value `79.5` to form a new string `"Volume = 79.5"`.

> **When the + operator is used for concatenation, at least one of its two operands must be a value or an expression of the `String` type.**

The non-string operand is then converted into a string according to a specific rule that depends on its type. A `char` value is converted into a string that consists of that one character; an `int` value is converted into a string of its digits, with a minus sign for a negative value; a `double` value is converted into a string that may include a minus sign, then one or more digits before the decimal point, and at least one digit after the decimal point; a `boolean` value is converted into `"true"` or `"false"`. For example,

```
                (+ converts)
    'A'           ===>        "A"
    123           ===>        "123"
    -1            ===>        "-1"
    3.14          ===>        "3.14"
    .1            ===>        "0.1"
    Math.PI       ===>        "3.141592653589793"
    false         ===>        "false"
```

The same conversion rules are used in

```
System.out.print(x);
```

for displaying the value of x for different types of x.

Note that if you have several + operators in a row without parentheses —

```
x + y + z
```

— they are evaluated from left to right. To concatenate x, y, and z, each + must have at least one String operand. For example,

```
System.out.print("***" + 2 + 2);
```

displays

```
***22
```

while

```
System.out.print(2 + 2 + "***");
```

displays

```
4***
```

Conversion also works for the += operator when the left-hand operand is a string. For example:

```
String str = "score: ";
int points = 90;
str += points;  // str now refers to "score: 90"
```

Sometimes you need to convert a value into a String without concatenating it with anything (for example, in order to pass it to a method that expects a String parameter).

The easiest way to convert a value into a String is to concatenate that value with an empty string.

For example:

```
JTextField scoreDisplay = new JTextField();
int score = 6;
...
scoreDisplay.setText("" + score);
```

Any <u>object</u> can be converted into a `String` by calling its `toString` method.

In Java, every object has a default `toString` method, which returns a `String`. The default `toString` method, however, is not very useful: it returns a string that is the object's class name followed by the object's address in memory in hexadecimal notation. Something like this: `"Foot@11a698a"`. Programmers often override the default and provide a more useful `toString` method for their class. For example:

```
public class Fraction
{
  private int num, denom;

  public Fraction(int n, int d)
  {
    num = n;
    denom = d;
  }

  ...

  public String toString()
  {
    return num + "/" + denom;
  }
}
```

With this `toString` method defined in `Fraction`, the statements

```
Fraction f = new Fraction(1, 2);
System.out.println(f);
```

display

```
1/2
```

As you can see, the `toString` method is used by `System.out`'s `print` and `println` methods for displaying an object. In other words, if `obj` is an object,

```
System.out.print(obj);
```

is equivalent to

```
System.out.print(obj.toString());
```

6.10 *Lab:* Pie Chart

Figure 6-2 shows a snapshot from the program *Poll* that helps to run a poll for the election of a school president. The results are shown as numbers for each of the three candidates and as slices on a pie chart.

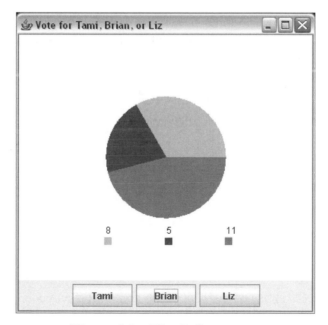

Figure 6-2.   The *Poll* program

The source code for this program consists of three classes: `Poll`, `PollControlPanel`, and `PollDisplayPanel`. `Poll` is the main class: it creates a program window and adds a control panel and a display panel to it.   A `PollControlPanel` object represents a control panel with the three buttons. It also handles the buttons' click events. A `PollDisplayPanel` object keeps track of the poll counts and displays them as numbers and as a pie chart.

Your task is to fill in the blanks in the `PollDisplayPanel` class. Collect the three files, `Poll.java`, `PollControlPanel.java`, and `PollDisplayPanel.java`, from JM\Ch06\Poll into one project. Then fill in the blanks in the `PollDisplayPanel`, following these steps:

1. Add a declaration for three `int` fields, `count1`, `count2`, `count3`, which hold the current poll counts.

2. Implement the `vote1`, `vote2`, and `vote3` methods, which increment the respective count.

3. Implement a `toString` method that returns a `String` containing the names of the candidates and their current vote counts. For example, the following method

   ```
   public static void main(String[] args)
   {
     PollDisplayPanel votingMachine =
                 new PollDisplayPanel("Tami", "Brian", "Liz");
     votingMachine.vote1();
     votingMachine.vote2();
     votingMachine.vote2();
     System.out.println(votingMachine);
   }
   ```

   should display

   ```
   Tami: 1  Brian: 2  Liz: 0
   ```

4. Compile the `PollDisplayPanel` class and fix the syntax errors, if any.

5. Write a simple test class with a `main` method similar to the one shown above. Compile and run it to test your progress so far.

6. Implement the `countToDegrees` method that converts the ratio of its two integer parameters, `count` and `total`, into the angle measure, in degrees, of a corresponding pie chart slice, <u>rounded to the nearest integer</u>.

7. Fill in the blanks in the `drawPieChart` and `drawLegend` methods.

8. Compile and test the *Poll* program.

6.11 Summary

Variables are memory locations, named by the programmer, that can hold values. *Fields* are variables declared outside of all constructors and methods of the class. Fields are "visible" in all the class's constructors and methods. *Local variables* are temporary variables declared inside a constructor or method and available only within the scope of that constructor or method.

Fields and local variables must be declared before they can be used. The declaration of a variable includes the data type of the variable, its name, and an optional initial value. Several variables of the same type may be declared in the same declaration:

```
[optional modifiers] sometype name1, name2, ...;
[optional modifiers] sometype name1 = expr1, name2 = expr2, ...;
```

Fields that never change their values are often declared with the keyword `final`, usually with initial values; they are actually not variables but constants. Declarations of *symbolic constants* have the form

```
[optional modifiers] final sometype someName = expression;
```

where the *optional modifiers* can be the reserved words `public` or `private`, and, if appropriate, `static` (Chapter 9).

Java has `byte`, `int`, `short`, and `long` *primitive data types* for representing integers of various sizes. We will always use `int`, which represents integers in the range from -2^{31} to $2^{31}-1$. Real numbers are represented by the `float` and `double` types. We will always use `double`. `char` represents single characters. A `String` object represents a fragment of text. The `boolean` type is discussed in Chapter 7.

Arithmetic expressions are written the same way as in algebra and may include literal constants, variables, the *arithmetic operators* +, -, *, /, and %, and parentheses. A multiplication sign * cannot be omitted.

The result of an arithmetic operation has the same type as the operands. If the operands have different types, the operand of the "smaller" type is automatically promoted to the "larger" type (for example, an `int` may be converted to a `double`). Java provides a cast operator that explicitly converts a variable or constant from one data type into another, compatible type.

It is a programmer's responsibility to make sure the values of variables and all the intermediate and final results in arithmetic expressions fit within the range of the chosen data types, and that these types satisfy the precision requirements for computations.

The + operator, when applied to two strings, concatenates them. It can also be used to concatenate a string with a value of another type. To convert a number or an object into a string, concatenate it with an empty string. A `toString` method in a class definition should specify a reasonable way for representing some information about the object of that class as a string. When an object is converted into a string, its `toString` method is called.

Exercises

Sections 6.1-6.6

1.   Which of the following lines are syntactically valid declarations of fields? Of local variables?

    (a)   `int hours, double pay;` _____ ✓
    (b)   `private double dollarsAndCents;` _____ ✓
    (c)   `char mi; int age;` _____
    (d)   `private final int year = 365, leapYear = year + 1;` _____

    (e)   `char tab = '\t', newline = '\n', a = 'a';` _____
    (f)   `public final double pi = 3.14159;` _____

2.   Mark true or false and explain:

    (a)   Each variable must be declared on a separate line. _____
    (b)   The scope of a variable is the largest range of its values. _____
    (c)   `i` is always a stylistically bad name for a variable because it is too short. _____
    (d)   Local variables in different methods of the same class are allowed to have the same name. _____ ✓
    (e)   If a local variable in a method and a field have the same name, the compiler reports a syntax error. _____ ✓

3.   Name three good reasons for using symbolic constants as opposed to literal constants.

4. (MC) Which one of the following statements prints a backslash on the screen?

    A.   `System.out.print("\b");`
    B.   `System.out.print("\\");`
    C.   `System.out.print(\bs);`
    D.   `System.out.print(\);`
    E.   `System.out.print(\\);`

5. Choose the right word: the scope of a variable is determined when the program is _____ (*compiled* / *executed*). ✓

Sections 6.7-6.11

6. What is the output from the following statements?

    (a)   `System.out.print(5 / 10);` ✓
    (b)   `System.out.print(1 / 2 * 10);`
    (c)   `System.out.print(1.0 / 2 * 10);` ✓
    (d)   `System.out.print(1 / 2.0 * 10);`
    (e)   `System.out.print(13 % 5);`

7. (a)   Assuming:

        ```
        double rate = 1.058;
        int balance0 = 100, balance = (int)(balance0 * rate);
        ```

        what is the value of `balance`? ✓

    (b)   Assuming:

        ```
        int miles = 98, gallons = 5;
        double gasMileage = miles / gallons;
        ```

        what is the value of `gasMileage`?

8. Remove as many parentheses as possible from the following statement without changing the result:

        ```
        count += (((total/pages) - 5) * words - 1);
        ```

9.   Find and fix a bug in the following statements:

```
final double g = 16.0;
double t = 35.5;
System.out.print ("The travel distance is ");
System.out.println(1 / 2 * (g * t * t));
```

10.   If `double` x has a negative value, write an expression that rounds x to the nearest integer.

11.   Given

```
int a, b, c;
```

write Java expressions that calculate the roots of the equation $ax^2 + bx + c = 0$ (assuming that the two real roots exist) and assign them to two `double` variables x1 and x2. Use a temporary variable to hold $\sqrt{b^2 - 4ac}$ in order not to compute it twice. ⸪ Hint: `Math.sqrt(d)` returns a square root of d as a `double`. ⸫ ✓

12.▪   Find a syntax error in the following code fragment:

```
double a, b;
int temp;

System.out.print("Enter two real numbers: ");
. . .
// Swap the numbers:
temp = a;
a = b;
b = temp;
. . .
```
✓

13.▪   Write an expression that, given a positive integer *n*, computes a new integer in which the units and tens digits have swapped places. For example, if *n* = 123, the result should be 132; if *n* = 3, the tens digit is zero and the result should be 30.

14. ■ An integer constant `dayOfWeek1` has a value from 0 to 6 and represents the day of the week for January 1st (0=Sunday, 1=Monday, etc.). A variable `day` has a value from 1 to 31 and represents a day in January. Write an expression that calculates the day of the week for any given value of `day`. For example, if `dayOfWeek1` = 0 (January 1st is a Sunday) and `day` = 13 (January 13th), then `dayOfWeek`, the day of the week for January 13th, should get a value of 5 (Friday).

15. ■ `curHour` and `curMin` represent the current time, and `depHour`, `depMin` represent the departure time of a bus. Suppose all these variables are initialized with some values; both times are between 1 p.m. and 11 p.m. of the same day. Fill in the blanks in the following statements that display the remaining waiting time in hours and minutes:

```
int _____ =

    _____ ;

System.out.println( _____ +

    " hours and " + _____ +

    " minutes.");
```

16. The *BMI* program computes a person's body mass index (BMI). BMI is defined as the weight, expressed in kilograms, divided by the square of the height expressed in meters. (One inch is 0.0254 meters; one pound is 0.454 kilograms.) The code of the `Bmi` class , with some omissions, is in `JM\Ch06\Exercises\Bmi.java`. Supply the missing code for the `calculateBmi` method, which takes a weight in pounds and height in inches as parameters and returns the body mass index.

17.■   A jar of jam weighs 1 lb. 5 oz. (One pound is 16 ounces). An empty
shipping carton weighs 1 lb. 9 oz. and can hold up to 12 jars. The shipping
costs include $1.44 for each full or partial carton plus $0.96 per pound or
fraction of a pound plus a $3.00 service charge.

Fill in the blanks in the following method that calculates the shipping cost for
a given number of jars:

```java
public double computeShippingCost(int nJars)
{
   int nCartons = (nJars + 11) / 12;

   int totalOunces = _____ ;

   int lbs = _____ ;

   return _____ ;
}
```

18.■   Write a method

```java
public int convertToHumanAge(int dogYears)
```

that converts a dog's age to the corresponding human age. Assume that a
dog's first year corresponds to a human age of 13, so
`convertToHumanAge(1)` should return 13. After that, every three years in
a dog's life correspond to sixteen years in human life. The method returns
the corresponding human age, rounded to the nearest integer. Write a
console Java application to test your method (or, if you prefer, recycle the
GUI from the *BMI* program in Question 16 into a dog-to-human-age
converter). ✓

19.♦   The figure below shows a window from the *Rainbow* program.

The "rainbow" is made of four overlapping semicircles. The outer ring is red
(`Color.RED`), the middle one is green (`Color.GREEN`), and the inner ring
has the magenta color (`Color.MAGENTA`). The innermost semicircle has the
same color as the background.

Follow the instructions below and fill in the blanks in `Rainbow.java` in
`JM\Ch06\Exercises`.

1. Copy `Rainbow.java` to your work folder.

2. Add a comment with your name at the top of the file.

3. Find and fix three syntax errors in `Rainbow.java` so that it compiles
    with no errors.

4. Add to the `Rainbow` class a declaration of a private final field
    `skyColor` of the type `Color`, initialized to `Color.CYAN` (the color of
    the sky). In `Rainbow`'s constructor, set the window's background to
    `skyColor` rather than `Color.WHITE`.

5. In the `paintComponent` method, declare <u>local</u> integer variables
    `xCenter` and `yCenter` that represent the coordinates of the center of the
    rings. Initialize them to 1/2 `width` and 3/4 `height` (down) of the panel,
    respectively. (Recall that the origin of graphics coordinates in Java is at
    the upper-left corner of the content pane with the *y*-axis pointing down.)
    Do not plug in fixed numbers from the window's dimensions.

Continued   ✍

6. Declare a local variable `largeRadius` that represents the radius of the largest (red) semicircle and initialize it to 1/4 of `width`.

7. A method call `g.fillArc(x, y, size, size, from, degrees)` (with all integer arguments) draws a sector of a circle. `x` and `y` are the coordinates of the upper-left corner of the rectangle (in this case a square) into which the oval is (logically) inscribed; `size` is the side of the square (and the diameter of the circle); `from` is the starting point of the arc in degrees (with 0 at the easternmost point of the horizontal diameter), and `degrees` (a positive number) is the measure of the arc, going counterclockwise. Add a statement to the `paintComponent` method to draw the largest (red) semicircle. Test your program.

8. Add statements to display the medium (green) and small (magenta) semicircles. The radius of the magenta semicircle should be 1/4 of `height`. The radius of the green one should be the geometric mean (the square root of the product) of the radius of the red semicircle and the radius of the magenta semicircle, rounded to the nearest integer. (A call to `Math.sqrt(x)` returns the value of square root of `x`, a `double`.) Retest your program.

9. Add statements to display the innermost semicircle of the background ("sky") color to complete the rainbow. Use the `skyColor` constant for this semicircle's color. Choose the radius of the sky-color semicircle in such a way that the width of the middle (green) ring is the arithmetic mean of the widths of the red and magenta rings. ⧽ Hint: you will need to do a little math to figure out a formula for the radius of the smallest semicircle in terms of the radii of the other three. ⧽

10. Test your program.

```
if (chapter == 7)
```

Boolean Expressions and `if-else` Statements

7.1 Prologue

Normally control flows sequentially from one statement to the next during program execution. This sequence is altered by several types of control mechanisms:

1. Calls to methods
2. Iterative statements (loops)
3. Conditional (if-else) statements
4. switch statements
5. Exceptions

In this chapter we will study the if-else statement, which tells the program to choose and execute one fragment of code or another depending on some condition. We will also take a look at the switch statement, which chooses a particular fragment of code out of several based on the value of a variable or expression.

The if-else control structure allows *conditional branching*. Suppose, for instance, that we want to find the absolute value of an integer. The method that returns an absolute value may look as follows:

```
public static int abs(int x)
{
   int ax;

   if (x >= 0)     // If x is greater or equal to 0
     ax = x;       //    do this;
   else            // otherwise
     ax = -x;      //    do this.
   return ax;
}          └─> What is this?
```

Or, more concisely:

```
public static int abs(int x)
{
   if (x >= 0)
     return x;
   else
     return -x;
}
```

There are special CPU instructions called *conditional jumps* that support conditional branching. The CPU always fetches the address of the next instruction from a special register, which in some systems is called the Instruction Pointer (IP). Normally, this register is incremented automatically after each instruction is executed so that it points to the next instruction. This makes the program execute consecutive instructions in order.

A conditional jump instruction tests a certain condition and tells the CPU to "jump" to a specified instruction depending on the result of the test. If the tested condition is satisfied, a new value is placed into the IP, which causes the program to skip to the specified instruction. For example, an instruction may test whether the result of the previous operation is greater than zero, and, if it is, tell the CPU to jump backward or forward to a specified address. If the condition is false, program execution continues with the next consecutive instruction.

In high-level languages, conditions for branching are written using *relational operators* such as "less than," "greater than," "equal to," and so on, and the *logical operators* "and," "or," and "not." Expressions combining these operators are called *Boolean* expressions. The value of a Boolean expression may be either true or false.

In the following sections we will discuss the syntax for coding `if-else` and `switch` statements, declaring `boolean` variables, and writing Boolean expressions with relational and logical operators. We will also briefly discuss two properties of formal logic, known as *De Morgan's Laws*, that are useful in programming. We will talk about *short-circuit evaluation* in handling multiple conditions connected with "and" and "or" operators. We also discuss enumerated data types.

In Sections 7.9 and 7.12 we use a case study to practice object-oriented design and implementation methodology: how to define the classes and objects needed in an application, how to divide work among team members, and how to test parts of a project independently from other parts. You will have to contribute code with a lot of `if-else` statements in it for one of the classes in this case study.

7.2 `if-else` Statements

The general form of the `if-else` statement in Java is:

```
if (condition)
{
   statementA1;
   statementA2;
   ...
}
else
{
   statementB1;
   statementB2;
   ...
}
```

where `condition` is a logical expression. The parentheses around `condition` are required. When an `if-else` statement is executed, the program evaluates the condition and then executes `statementA1`, etc. if the condition is true, and `statementB1`, etc. if the condition is false. If the compound block within braces consists of only one statement, then the braces can be dropped:

```
if (condition)
   statementA;
else
   statementB;
```

The `else` clause is optional, so the `if` statement can be used by itself:

```
if (condition)
{
   statement1;
   statement2;
   ...
}
```

When `if` is coded without `else`, the program evaluates the condition and executes `statement1`, etc. if the condition is true. If the condition is false, the program simply skips the block of statements under `if`.

7.3 `boolean` Data Type

Java has a primitive data type called `boolean`. `boolean` variables can hold only one of two values: `true` or `false`. `boolean`, `true`, and `false` are Java reserved words. You declare `boolean` variables like this:

```
boolean aVar;
```

There is not much sense in declaring `boolean` constants because you can just use `true` or `false`.

Boolean expressions are made up of `boolean` variables, relational operators, such as >=, and logical operators. You can assign the value of any Boolean expression to a `boolean` variable. For example:

```
boolean over21 = age > 21;  // or boolean over21 = (age > 21);
```

Here `over21` gets a value of `true` if `age` is greater than 21, `false` otherwise. This is essentially a more concise version of

```
int age = < some value >;
...

boolean over21;

if (age > 21)
  over21 = true;
else
  over21 = false;
```

7.4 Relational Operators

Java recognizes six relational operators:

Operator	Meaning
>	greater than
<	less than
>=	greater than or equal to
<=	less than or equal to
==	is equal to
!=	is not equal to

The result of a relational operator has the `boolean` type. It has a value equal to `true` if the comparison is true, `false` otherwise.

Relational operators are frequently used in conditions. For example:

```
if (x > y)
   max = x;
else
   max = y;
```

Note that in Java the "is equal to" condition is expressed by the == operator, while a single = sign means assignment. Be careful not to confuse the two.

Relational operators are applied mostly to variables of primitive numeric data types. The == and != operators can also be applied to characters. For example:

```
if (gender == 'F')
{
  System.out.print("Dear Ms. ");
}
else
{
  System.out.print("Dear Mr. ");
}
```

Avoid using == and != for double or float variables and expressions because floating-point arithmetic is imprecise. For example, in

```
15.0 / 3.0 == 5.0
```

the numbers on the left and right may be very close but not exactly equal due to rounding errors.

If you apply the == and != operators to <u>objects</u>, then instead of comparing the <u>values</u> of two objects you will be comparing two <u>references</u> to them (that is, their addresses). This is a potential source of bugs.

For example, in

```
String fileName;
...
if (fileName == "words.txt")
   ...
```

the == operator compares the addresses of the String object fileName and the String object that represents a literal string "words.txt". Their addresses are most likely different, even though their current <u>values</u> may be the same. As we'll explain in Chapter 10, you have to use String's equals method to compare string values, as in

```
if (fileName.equals("words.txt")) ...
```

or

```
if ("words.txt".equals(fileName)) ...
```

However, occasionally it is useful to compare references to objects, for example if you want to know which particular object (for example, a button) caused a particular event.

7.5 Logical Operators

Java has two binary logical operators, "and" and "or," and a unary logical operator, "not." They are represented by the following symbols:

Operator	Meaning
&&	and
||	or
!	not

> **The expression**
>
>   *condition1* && *condition2*
>
> **is true if and only if <u>both</u> *condition1* <u>and</u> *condition2* are true.**

> **The expression**
>
>   *condition1* || *condition2*
>
> **is true if *condition1* <u>or</u> *condition2* (or both) are true.**

> **The expression**
>
>   ! *condition1*
>
> **is true if and only if *condition1* is false.**

The following code:

```
boolean match = ...;
if (!match)
{
    ...
}
```

works the same way as:

```
boolean match = ...;
if (match == false)
{
   ...
}
```

The results of the logical operators `&&`, `||`, and `!` have the `boolean` data type, just like the results of relational operators.

The "and," "or," and "not" operations are related to each other in the following way:

Boolean expression	Has the same Boolean value as:
not (p and q)	not p or not q
not (p or q)	not p and not q

For example, "not (fun and games)" is the same as "not fun or not games."

These two properties of logic are called *De Morgan's Laws.* They come from formal logic, but they are useful in practical programming as well. In Java notation, De Morgan's Laws take the following form:

> **`! (p && q)` is the same as `!p || !q`**
>
> **`! (p || q)` is the same as `!p && !q`**

A programmer may choose either of the equivalent forms; the choice depends on which form is more readable. Usually it is better to distribute the `!` ("not"). For example:

```
if (x >= 0 && x < 5)
```

is much easier to read than:

```
if (!(x < 0 || x >= 5))
```

7.6 Order of Operators

In general, all unary operators have higher precedence than binary operators, so unary operators, including ! ("not"), are applied first. You have to use parentheses if you want to apply ! to the entire expression. For example:

```
if (!cond1 && cond2)
```

means

```
if ((!cond1) && cond2)
```

rather than

```
if (!(cond1 && cond2))
```

All binary arithmetic operators (+, *, etc.) have higher rank than all relational operators (>, < , ==, etc.), so arithmetic operators are applied first. For example, you can write simply:

```
if (a + b >= 2 * n)            // OK!
```

when you mean:

```
if ((a + b) >= (2 * n))        // The inside parentheses are
                               //   optional
```

Arithmetic and relational operators have higher rank than the binary logical operators && and ||, so arithmetic and relational operators are applied first. For example, you can write simply:

```
if (x + y > 0 && b != 0)       // OK!
```

instead of:

```
if ((x + y > 0) && (b != 0))   // The inside parentheses are
                               //   optional
```

When && and || operators are combined in one logical expression, && has higher rank than || (that is, && is performed before ||), but with these it is a good idea to always use parentheses to avoid confusion and make the code more readable. For example:

```
// Inside parentheses not required, but recommended for clarity:
if ((x > 2 && y > 5) || (x < -2 && y < -5))
{
    ...
}
```

The rules of precedence for the operators we have encountered so far are summarized in the table below:

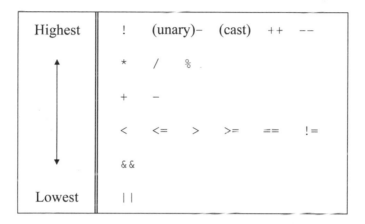

Highest	!	(unary)−	(cast)	++	−−
	*	/	%		
	+	−			
	<	<=	>	>=	==	!=
	&&				
Lowest	||				

> **In the absence of parentheses, binary operators of the same rank are performed left to right, and unary operators right to left.**

For example, `(double)(int)x` is the same as `(double)((int)x)`. If in doubt — use parentheses!

7.7 Short-Circuit Evaluation

In `&&` and `||` operations, the left operand is always evaluated first. There may be situations when its value predetermines the result of the operation. For example, if *condition1* is false, then the value of the expression *condition1 && condition2* is false, no matter what the value of *condition2* is. If *condition1* is true, then *condition1 || condition2* is true.

> **If the value of the first (left) operand in a binary logical operation is sufficient to determine the result of the operation, the second operand is <u>not</u> evaluated. This rule is called *short-circuit evaluation*.**

If the expression combines several `&&` operations at the same level, such as

```
condition1 && condition2 && condition3 ...
```

the evaluation of conditions proceeds from left to right. If a <u>false</u> condition is encountered, then the remaining conditions are <u>not</u> evaluated, because the value of the entire expression is false. Similarly, if the expression combines several `||` operations at the same level,

```
condition1 || condition2 || condition3 ...
```

the evaluation proceeds from left to right only until a <u>true</u> condition is encountered, because then the value of the entire expression is true.

The short-circuit evaluation rule not only saves program execution time but is also convenient in some situations. For example, it is safe to write:

```
if (y != 0 && x/y > 3)
   ...
```

because `x/y` is not calculated when `y` is equal to 0.

❖   ❖   ❖

Java also provides bit-wise "and" and "or" operators that normally work on <u>integers</u> and operate on individual bits. These operators are denoted as `&` and `|` (as opposed to `&&` and `||`). Unfortunately these operators also work on `booleans`, and they <u>do not</u> follow the short-circuit evaluation rule. This is really confusing and may lead to a nasty bug, if you inadvertently write `&` instead of `&&` or `|` instead of `||`. Make sure you use `&&` and `||` unless you are indeed working with individual bits. Bit-wise operators are explained in Chapter 17.

7.8 `if-else-if` and Nested `if-else`

Sometimes a program needs to branch three or more ways. Consider the *sign(x)* function:

$$sign(x) \;=\; \begin{cases} -1, & \text{if } x < 0 \\ 0, & \text{if } x = 0 \\ 1, & \text{if } x > 0 \end{cases}$$

The `sign(x)` method can be implemented in Java as follows:

```java
public static int sign(int x)     // Correct but clumsy code...
{
  int s;

  if (x < 0)
    s = -1;
  else
  {
    if (x == 0)
      s = 0;
    else
      s = 1;
  }
  return s;
}
```

This code is correct, but it looks cumbersome. The $x < 0$ case seems arbitrarily singled out and placed at a higher level than the $x == 0$ and $x > 0$ cases. Actually, the braces in the outer `else` can be removed, because the inner `if-else` is one complete statement. Without braces, the compiler always associates an `else` with the nearest `if` above it. The simplified code without braces looks as follows:

```java
public static int sign(int x)    // Correct but still clumsy...
{
  int s;

  if (x < 0)
    s = -1;
  else
    if (x == 0)
      s = 0;
    else
      s = 1;
  return s;
}
```

It is customary in such situations to arrange the statements differently: the second `if` is placed next to the first `else` and one level of indentation is removed, as follows:

```
public static int sign(int x)    // The way it should be...
{
  int s;

  if (x < 0)
    s = -1;
  else if (x == 0)    // This arrangement of if-else is a matter
    s = 0;            //    of style: structurally, the second
  else                //    if-else is still nested within the
    s = 1;            //    first else
  return s;
}
```

This format emphasizes the three-way branching that conceptually occurs at the same level in the program, even though technically the second if-else is *nested* in the first else.

A chain of if-else-if statements may be as long as necessary:

```
if (condition1)
{
   ...                   // 1st case
}
else if (condition2)
{
   ...                   // 2d case
}
else if (condition3)
{
   ...                   // 3d case
}

...
...

else if (conditionN)
{
   ...                   // N-th case
}
else  // the last "else" clause may be omitted
{
   ...                   // otherwise
}
```

This is a rather common structure in Java programs and usually quite readable. For example:

```
if (avg >= 90)
   grade = 'A';
else if (avg >= 80)
   grade = 'B';
else if (avg >= 70)
   grade = 'C';
else if (avg >= 60)
   grade = 'D';
else
   grade = 'F';
```

Or:

```
if (x < lowerLimit)
{
   x = lowerLimit;
}
else if (x > upperLimit)
{
   x = upperLimit;
}
```

❖   ❖   ❖

A different situation occurs when a program requires true hierarchical branching with nested if-else statements, as in a decision tree:

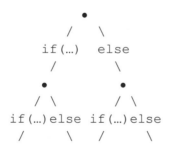

Consider, for example, the following code:

```
// Surcharge calculation:
if (age <= 25)
{
  if (accidents)
    surcharge = 1.4;  // Premium surcharge 40%
  else
    surcharge = 1.2;  // Surcharge 20%
}
else  // age > 25
{
  if (accidents)
    surcharge = 1.1;  // Surcharge 10%
  else
    surcharge = .9;   // Discount 10%
}
```

Here the use of nested if-else statements is justified by the logic of the task.

When if-else statements are nested in your code to three or four levels, the code becomes too complicated. This indicates that you probably need to restructure your code, perhaps using separate methods to handle individual cases.

Nested ifs can often be substituted with the && operation:

```
if (condition1)
  if (condition2)
    statement;
```

is exactly the same (due to short-circuit evaluation) as

```
if (condition1 && condition2)
  statement;
```

but the latter form is usually clearer.

Beware of the "dangling else" bug in nested if-else statements:

```
if (condition1)    // Compiled as: if (condition1)
  if (condition2)  //                {
    statement1;    //                  if (condition2)
else               //                    statement1;
  statement2;      //                  else
                   //                    statement2;
                   //                }
```

7.9 *Case Study and Lab:* **Rolling Dice**

In this section we will implement the *Craps* program. Craps is a game played with dice. In Craps, each die is a cube with numbers from 1 to 6 on its faces. The numbers are represented by dots (Figure 7-1).

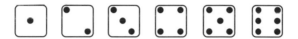

Figure 7-1. Dots configurations on a die

A player rolls two dice and adds the numbers of dots shown on them. If the total is 7 or 11, the player wins; if the total is 2, 3 or 12, the player loses. If the total is anything else, the player has to roll again. The total, called the "point," is remembered, and the objective now is to roll the same total as the "point." The player keeps rolling until he gets either "point" or 7. If he rolls "point" first, he wins, but if he rolls a 7 first, he loses. You can see why this game was chosen as a lab for if-else statements!

Our team has been asked to design and code a *Craps* program for our company's "Casino Night" charitable event. Three people will be working on this project. I am the project leader, responsible for the overall design and dividing the work between us. I will also help team members with detailed design and work on my own piece of code. The second person, Aisha, is a consultant; she specializes in GUI design and implementation.

The third person is you!

Run the executable *Craps* program by clicking on the Craps.jar file in JM\Ch07\Craps. When you click on the "Roll" button, red dice start rolling on a green "table." When they stop, the score is updated or the "point" is shown on the display panel (Figure 7-2). The program allows you to play as many games as you want.

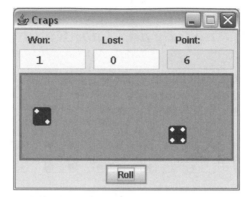

Figure 7-2. The *Craps* program

We begin the design phase by discussing which objects are needed for this application. One approach may be to try making objects in the program represent objects from the real world. Unfortunately, it is not always clear what exactly is a "real world" object. Some objects may simulate tangible machines or mechanisms, others may exist only in "cyberspace," and still others may be quite abstract and exist only in the designer's imagination.

Here we need one object that represents the program's window. Let us call this object `window` and its class `Craps`. As usual, we will derive this class from the `JFrame` class in Java's *Swing* package. The window (Figure 7-2) is divided into three "panels." The top panel displays the score and the current state of the game. Let's call it `display` and its class `DisplayPanel`. The middle panel represents the Craps table where the dice roll. Let's call it `table` and its class `CrapsTable`. The bottom panel holds the "Roll" button. Let's call it `controls` and its class `ControlPanel`. The control panel can also handle the "Roll" button's click events.

It makes sense that each of the `DisplayPanel`, the `CrapsTable`, and the `ControlPanel` classes extend the Java library class `JPanel`. For example:

```
public class DisplayPanel extends JPanel
{
   ...
}
```

The `table` object shows two "rolling dice," so we need a class that will represent a rolling die. Let's call it `RollingDie`.

These five classes, `Craps`, `DisplayPanel`, `CrapsTable`, `ControlPanel`, and `RollingDie`, form the GUI part of our *Craps* program (Figure 7-3).

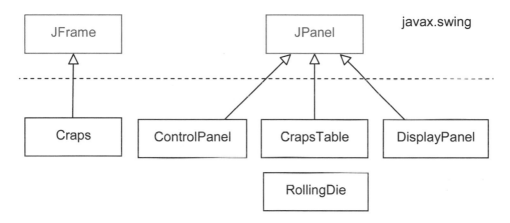

Figure 7-3. GUI classes in the *Craps* program

It makes sense to me to split the code for the visible and "numeric" aspects of a rolling die into two classes. The base class `Die` will represent a die as an abstract device that generates a random integer in the range from 1 to 6. The class `RollingDie` will <u>extend</u> `Die`, adding methods for moving and drawing the die:

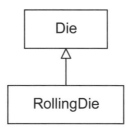

My rationale for this design decision is that we might reuse the `Die` class in another program, but the dice there might have a different appearance (or may remain invisible).

Last but not least, we need an "object" that will represent the logic and rules of Craps. This is a "conceptual" object, not something that can be touched. Of course that won't prevent us from implementing it in Java. Let's call this object `game` and its class `CrapsGame`. The `CrapsGame` class won't be derived from anything (except the default, `Object`), won't use any Java packages, and won't process any events.

There are many good reasons for separating the rules of the game from the GUI part. First, we might need to change the GUI (if our boss doesn't like its "look and feel") while leaving the game alone. Second, we can reuse the CrapsGame class in other applications. For example, we might use it in a statistical simulation of Craps that runs through the game many times quickly and doesn't need a fancy GUI at all. Third, we might have a future need for a program that implements a similar-looking dice game but with different rules. Fourth, Aisha and I know only the general concept of the game and are not really interested in learning the details. And finally, it is a natural division of labor. We have a beginner on our team (you) and we have to give you a manageable piece of work.

Now we need to decide how the objects interact with each other. Figure 7-4 shows the overall design for the *Craps* program that I have come up with.

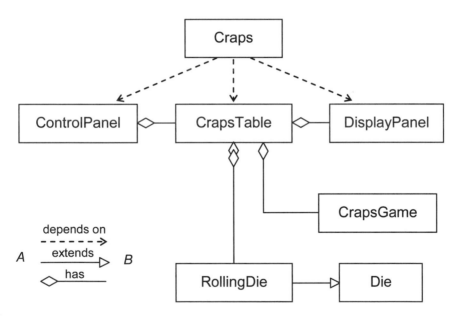

Figure 7-4. *Craps* classes and their relationships

There is no unique way, of course, of designing an application — a designer has a lot of freedom. But it is very helpful to follow some established *design patterns* and tested practices. We will talk about design patterns in Chapter 26. Here we want to emphasize two principles of sound design.

First, each class must represent a single concept, and all its constructors and public methods should be related to that concept. This principle is called *cohesion*.

> **In a good design, classes are <u>cohesive</u>.**

Second, dependencies between classes should be minimized. The reason we can draw a class diagram in Figure 7-4 without lines crisscrossing each other in all directions is that not all the classes depend on each other. OO designers use the term *coupling* to describe the degree of dependency between classes.

> **In a good design, coupling should be <u>minimized</u>.**

It is good when a class interacts with only few other classes and knows as little about them as possible. Low coupling makes it easier to split the work between programmers and to make changes to the code.

In our *Craps* program, for example, the `ControlPanel` class and the `DisplayPanel` class do not need to know about each other's existence at all. `ControlPanel` knows something about `CrapsTable` — after all, it needs to know what it controls. But `ControlPanel` knows about only a couple of simple methods from `CrapsTable`.

A reference to a `CrapsTable` object is passed to `ControlPanel`'s constructor, which saves it in its field `table`. The `ControlPanel` object calls `table`'s methods when the "roll" button is clicked:

```
// Called when the roll button is clicked
public void actionPerformed(ActionEvent e)
{
  if (!table.diceAreRolling())  // if dice are not rolling,
    table.rollDice();           //   start a new roll
}
```

Likewise, `table` has a reference to `display`, but it knows about only one of its methods, `update`. When the dice stop rolling, `table` consults `game` (the only class that knows the rules of the game) about the result of the roll and passes that result (and the resulting value of "point") to `DisplayPanel`'s `update` method:

```
display.update(result, point);
```

The `Craps` object creates a `ControlPanel`, a `DisplayPanel`, and a `CrapsTable` in its constructor —

```
public class Craps extends JFrame
{
  // Constructor
  public Craps()
  {
    ...
    DisplayPanel display = new DisplayPanel();
    CrapsTable table = new CrapsTable(display);
    ControlPanel controls = new ControlPanel(table);
    ...
  }
  ...
}
```

— so it knows how to invoke their respective constructors. But it does not know about any of the methods of other classes, nor does it know anything about the rules of the Craps game or dice in general. In fact, if we change Craps to, say, Soccer and replace CrapsTable with SoccerField, the same code can be used for a different game.

We are now ready to divide the work among the three of us. Aisha will do the Craps, ControlPanel, and DisplayPanel classes. I like animations, so I will work on the CrapsTable and RollingDie classes myself. You get the Die and CrapsGame classes. Figure 7-5 shows how we split the work.

Aisha and I have already agreed on how the GUI classes will interact with each other. But we still need to nail down the details for your Die class and the CrapsGame class.

From your Die class I need two methods:

```
public void roll() { ... }
```

and

```
public int getNumDots() { ... }
```

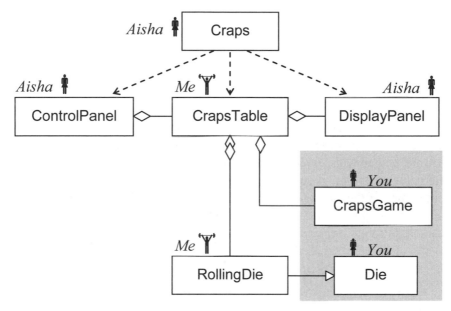

Figure 7-5. Task assignments in the *Craps* project

I will call these methods from `RollingDie`. The `roll` method simulates one roll of a die. It obtains a random integer in the range from 1 to 6 and saves it in a field. The `getNumDots` method returns the saved value from that field. Do not define any constructors in `Die`: the default no-args constructor will do. To get a random number, use a call to `Math.random()`. This method returns a "random" `double` x, such that $0 \leq x < 1$. Scale that number appropriately, then truncate it to an integer.

Now the `CrapsGame` class. My `CrapsTable` object creates a `CrapsGame` object called `game`:

```
private CrapsGame game;
...

// Constructor
public CrapsTable(DisplayPanel displ)
{
   ...
  game = new CrapsGame();
   ...
}
```

Again, no need to define a constructor in CrapsGame: we will rely on the default no-args constructor.

My CrapsTable object calls game's methods:

```
int result = game.processRoll(total);
int point = game.getPoint();
```

The processRoll method takes one int parameter — the sum of the dots on the two dice. processRoll should process that information and return the result of the roll: 1 if the player wins, –1 if he loses, and 0 if the game continues. In the latter case, the value of "point" is set equal to total. Define a private int field point to hold that value. If the current game is over, point should be set to 0. getPoint is an accessor method in your CrapsGame class. It lets me get the value of point, so that I can pass it on to display.

We are ready to start the work. The only problem is the time frame. Aisha's completion date is unpredictable: she is very busy, but once she gets to work she works very fast. My task can be rather time-consuming. I will try to arrange a field trip to Las Vegas to film some video footage of rolling dice. But most likely our boss won't approve that, and I'll have to settle for observing rolling dice on the carpet in my office. Meanwhile you are anxious to start your part.

Fortunately, Aisha has found an old test program to which you can feed integers as input. She added a few lines to make it call processRoll and getPoint and display their return values (Figure 7-6). She called her temporary class CrapsTest1. Now you don't have to wait for us: you can implement and test your CrapsGame class independently. You won't see any dice rolling for now, but you will be able to test your class thoroughly in a predictable setting.

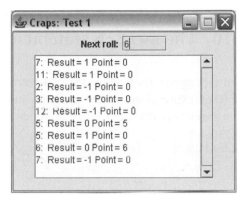

Figure 7-6. A preliminary program for testing `CrapsGame`

1. Copy `CrapsTest1.java` and `CrapsGame.java` from `JM\Ch07\Craps` to your work folder. Fill in the blanks in the `CrapsGame` class, combine it with the `CrapsTest1` class into one project, compile the classes, and test the program thoroughly.

2. Write the `Die` class and a small console application to test it by printing out the results of several "rolls." For example:

```
public static void main(String[] args)
{
  Die die = new Die();
  die.roll();
  System.out.println(die.getNumDots());
  die.roll();
  ...
}
```

3. After you get the `CrapsGame` and `Die` classes to work, test them with the *CrapsStats* application, which quickly runs the game multiple times and counts the number of wins. You will find `CrapsStats.java` in `JM\Ch07\Craps`. Note how we reuse for this task the `CrapsGame` and the `Die` classes that you have written for a different program.

   Compare your simulation result with the theoretical probability of winning in Craps, which is 244/495, or about 0.493. If you run 10,000 trial games, the number of wins should be somewhere between 4830 and 5030; 4930 on average.

7.10 The `switch` statement

There are situations when a program must take one of several actions depending on the value of some variable or expression. If the program has to handle just two or three possible actions, you can easily use if-else-if statements:

```
int x = expression;

if (x == valueA)
{
   // Take action A
   statementA1;
   statementA2;
   ...
}
else if (x == valueB)
{
   // Take action B
   statementB1;
   ...
}

...
...

else if (x == valueZ)
{
   // Take action Z
   statementZ1;
   ...
}
else
{
   // Take some default action
   ...
}
```

(*valueA*, *valueB*, ..., and *valueZ* are integer constants.)

When the number of possible actions is large, the use of if-else-if becomes cumbersome and inefficient. Java provides a special mechanism, the switch statement, for handling such situations. Its general form is:

```
switch (expression)
{
  case valueA:        // Take action A
    statementA1;
    statementA2;
    ...
    break;

  case valueB:        // Take action B
    statementB1;
    ...
    break;

  ...
  ...

  case valueZ:        // Take action Z
    statementZ1;
    ...
    break;

  default:            // Take some default action
    ...
    break;
}
```

valueA, *valueB*, ... , *valueZ* in a switch are integer or character literal or symbolic constants (or enum type constants — see Section 7.11).

When a switch statement is compiled, the compiler creates a table of these values and the associated addresses of the corresponding "cases" (code fragments). When the switch is executed, the program first evaluates *expression* to an integer. Then it finds it in the table and jumps to the corresponding case. If the value is not in the table, the program jumps to "default." The break statement at the end of a case tells the program to jump out of the switch and continue with the first statement after the switch. switch, case, default, and break are Java reserved words.

Note the following properties of the switch statement:

1. The expression evaluated in a switch must have an integral type (integer or char). In most programs it is really not an expression but simply one variable, as in switch(k).

2. Each case must be labeled by a literal or symbolic constant. A case cannot be labeled by a variable or an expression that is not constant.

3. The same action may be activated by more than one case label. For example:

```
case '/':            // both '/' and ':' signify division
case ':':
  < ... statements >
  break;
```

4. There may be a `break` in the <u>middle</u> of a case, but then it must be inside an `if` or `else`, otherwise some code in that case would be unreachable. Such a `break` tells the program to jump out of the switch immediately. For example:

```
case '/':
  ...
  if (y == 0)
  {
    System.out.println("*** Division by zero ***\n");
    break;     // Jump out of the switch
  }

  < ... other statements >

  break;          // Jump out of the switch
```

5. The `default` clause is optional. If not specified, the default action is "do nothing."

> **It is a common mistake to omit `break` at the end of a case. The `switch` syntax does not require that each case end with a `break`. Without a `break`, though, the program <u>falls through</u> and continues with the next case.**

This feature may lead to annoying bugs, and programmers usually take special care to put a `break` at the end of each case. Unusual situations, where a programmer intentionally allows the program to "fall through" from one case to the next, call for a special comment in the code.

7.11 Enumerated Data Types

An enumerated data type defines a list of symbolic values. For example:

```
private enum State {READY, SET, GO};
```

`enum` is a Java reserved word. In the above example, `State` is the name of the enum data type, given by the programmer, and `READY`, `SET`, and `GO` are the symbolic values in the enum list, also defined by the programmer. The name of the `enum` type usually starts with a capital letter; the enum values are often spelled in all caps to make them stand out more.

An enum definition is placed inside a class outside of any constructor or method. The keyword `private` in the enum definition indicates that this enum type is visible only within its class.

Once an enum type is defined, we can declare variables of that type and assign values to them. For example, we can declare a variable of the type `State` and assign to it one of the symbolic values from the enum list:

```
State currentState = State.READY;
```

Variables and constants of the type `State` can only hold one of the three values: `State.READY`, `State.SET`, or `State.GO`. We use the "type-dot" notation to refer to the symbolic values from the enum list.

The values in an enum list are defined only by their symbols. They are not literal strings and they have no numeric values.

We are not really interested in how the enum values are represented internally in Java. (If you really want to know, they are sort of like objects; they even have a `toString` method.) As far as we are concerned, the value of `State.READY` is just `State.READY`.

Since enum values cannot be used in arithmetic and do not represent characters or strings, what do we need them for? There are often situations in programs when an object's attribute or state can have only one of a small number of values. It makes sense to define an enum type for variables that describe such an attribute or state. For example:

```
private enum Speed {LOW, MEDIUM, HIGH};
private enum BoardColor {BLACK, WHITE};
private enum DayOfWeek {sunday, monday, tuesday,
              wednesday, thursday, friday, saturday};
```

Of course we could instead represent such values as strings or integers or symbolic constants of some type. But an enum type is more compact and convenient than several declarations of symbolic constants. It is also safer: the compiler won't let us accidentally refer to a value that is not in the enum list.

In `boolean` expressions, variables of an enum type are compared to each other or to values from the enum list using the `==` and `!=` operators. For example:

```
if (currentState == State.GO)
   ...
```

An enum variable and symbolic values can be also used in a switch statement. For example:

```
switch(currentState)
{
  case READY:
    ...
    break;

  case SET:
    ...
    break;

  case GO:
    ...
    break;
}
```

(The type-dot prefix is not used in case labels within a switch.)

You can also define a public enum type. If a public enum type SomeEnum is defined within a class MyClass, then <u>outside of MyClass</u> you refer to that enum type as MyClass.SomeEnum, and refer to a SomeEnum's symbolic value as MyClass.SomeEnum.*symbolicValue*. For instance:

```
public class Exam
{
  public enum LetterGrade {A, B, C, D, F};
  ...
}


public class Student
{
  private Exam.LetterGrade myGrade;
  ...
    if (myScore > 90)
      myGrade = Exam.LetterGrade.A;
    ...
}
```

7.12   *Case Study and Lab:* Rolling Dice Concluded

By this time you have finished your CrapsGame and Die classes and Aisha has found the time to put together her GUI classes. I myself have gotten bogged down with my CrapsTable and RollingDie classes, trying to perfect the animation effects. Meanwhile, not to stall Aisha's testing, I have written a *stub class* CrapsTable (Figure 7-7) to provide a temporary substitute for the actual class I am working on. A stub class has very simple versions of methods needed for testing other classes. This is a common technique when a programmer needs to test a part of the project while other parts are not yet ready.

```java
// A temporary stub class for testing Craps.

public class CrapsTable
{
  private DisplayPanel display;
  private CrapsGame game;
  private Die die1, die2;

  // Constructor
  public CrapsTable(DisplayPanel displ)
  {
    display = displ;
    game = new CrapsGame();
  }

  // Rolls the dice
  public void rollDice()
  {
    die1.roll();
    die2.roll();
    int total = die1.getNumDots() + die2.getNumDots();
    int result = game.processRoll(pts);
    int point = game.getPoint();
    display.update(result, point);
  }

  public boolean diceAreRolling()
  {
    return false;
  }
}
```

Figure 7-7.   Temporary "stub" class CrapsTable.java

My stub class includes a temporary version of the `rollDice` method that simply calls `game`'s `processRoll` method with a random sum of points and a version of `diceAreRolling` that always returns `false`.

You're certainly welcome to take a look at Aisha's GUI implementation (in $J_M\backslash Ch07\backslash Craps\backslash source.zip$), but no one has time right now to explain to you how it works.

Since you are done with your part, I thought you could help me out with my `RollingDie` class. I've made a lot of progress on it, but a couple of details remain unfinished.

I have coded the constructor, the `roll` method that starts the die rolling, and the `avoidCollision` method that keeps one die from overlapping with another. I have also provided the `boolean` method `isRolling`, which tells whether my die is moving or not. But I am still working on drawing a rolling and a stopped die. I took what is called *top-down* approach with *step-wise* refinement, moving from more general to more specific tasks. First I coded the `draw` method in general terms:

```
// Draws this die, rolling or stopped;
// also moves this die, when rolling
public void draw(Graphics g)
{
  if (xCenter < 0 || yCenter < 0)
    return;
  else if (isRolling())
  {
    move();
    drawRolling(g);
    xSpeed *= slowdown;
    ySpeed *= slowdown;
  }
  else
  {
    drawStopped(g);
  }
}
```

Note how I used the `if-else-if` structure to process three situations: my die is off the table, it is still moving, or it is stopped.

My `draw` method calls the more specialized methods `drawRolling` and `drawStopped`. I am still working on these, but I know that each of them will call an even lower-level method `drawDots` that will draw white dots on my die:

```java
// Draws this die when rolling with a random number of dots
private void drawRolling(Graphics g)
{
  ...
  Die die = new Die();
  die.roll();
  drawDots(g, x, y, die.getNumDots());
}

// Draws this die when stopped
private void drawStopped(Graphics g)
{
  ...
  drawDots(g, x, y, getNumDots());
}
```

I have started `drawDots` (Figure 7-8) and am counting on you to finish it. (Naturally, it involves a `switch` statement.) Meanwhile I will finish `CrapsTable`, and we should be able to put it all together.

```java
// Draws a given number of dots on this die
private void drawDots(Graphics g, int x, int y, int numDots)
{
  g.setColor(Color.WHITE);

  int dotSize = dieSize / 4;
  int step = dieSize / 8;
  int x1 = x + step - 1;
  int x2 = x + 3*step;
  int x3 = x + 5*step + 1;
  int y1 = y + step - 1;
  int y2 = y + 3*step;
  int y3 = y + 5*step + 1;

  switch (numDots)
  {
    case 1:
      g.fillOval(x2, y2, dotSize, dotSize);
      break;

    < missing code >

  }
}
```

Figure 7-8. A fragment from `JM\Ch07\Craps\RollingDie.java`

Copy `RollingDie.java` from J_M\Ch07\Craps into your work folder and fill in the blanks in its `drawDots` method. (Figure 7-1 shows the desired configurations of dots on a die.) Collect all the files for the *Craps* program together: `Craps.jar` (from J_M\Ch07\Craps); `CrapsGame.java` and `Die.java` (your solutions from the lab in Section 7.9); and `RollingDie.java`. Compile them, and run the program.

7.13 Summary

The general form of a *conditional statement* in Java is:

```
if (condition)
{
  statementA1;
  statementA2;
    ...
}
else
{
  statementB1;
  statementB2;
    ...
}
```

`condition` may be any Boolean expression.

Conditions are often written with the *relational operators*

<	less than
<=	less than or equal to
>	greater than
>=	greater than or equal to
==	equal to
!=	not equal to

and the *logical operators*

&&	and
||	or
!	not

It is useful for programmers to know two properties from formal logic called *De Morgan's Laws:*

```
! (p && q)  is the same as  !p || !q
! (p || q)  is the same as  !p && !q
```

Use the

```
if...
else if...
else if...
...
else ...
```

structure for multiway branching, and use nested `if-else` for hierarchical branching.

The general form of a `switch` statement is

```
switch (expression)
{
  case valueA:        // Take action A
    statementA1;
    statementA2;
    ...
    break;

  case valueB:        // Take action B
    statementB1;
    ...
    break;

  ...
  ...

  default:            // Take the default action
    ...
    break;
}
```

where *valueA*, *valueB*, etc., are integer or character literal or symbolic constants. The switch evaluates *expression* and jumps to the case labeled by the corresponding constant value, or to the default case if no match has been found. A switch can be used to replace a long `if-else-if` sequence.

Exercises

Sections 7.1-7.7

1. Write a method that returns the value of the larger of the integers x and y (or either one, if they are equal): ✓

    ```
    public static int max(int x, int y)
    {
       ...
    }
    ```

2. ∎ Fill in the missing code in the totalWages method, which calculates the total earnings for a week based on the number of hours worked and the hourly rate. The pay for overtime (hours worked over 40) is 1.5 times the regular rate. For example, totalWages(45, 12.50) should return 593.75.

    ```
    public double totalWages(double hours, double rate)
    {
      double wages;

      < ... missing code >

      return wages;
    }
    ```

    Add your code to the Wages.java program, available in JM\Ch07\Exercises, and test it.

3. ∎ Invent three ways to express the XOR ("exclusive OR") operation in Java (that is, write a Boolean expression that involves two boolean variables which is true if and only if exactly one of the two variables has the value true). ⸨ Hint: one of the possible solutions involves only one (relational) operator. ⸩ ✓

4. (MC) Which of the following expressions is equivalent to !(a || !b) (that is, has the same value for all possible values of the variables a and b)?

    A.   a || !b   B.   !a || b   C.   !a && b
    D.   !a && !b   E.   a && !b

5. Simplify the following expressions (remove as many parentheses as possible) using De Morgan's Laws:

(a)   `!((!x || !y) && (a || b))` ✓
(b)   `if (!(x == 7) && !(x > 7))` ...

6. Remove as many parentheses as possible without changing the meaning of the condition:

(a)   `if ((((x + 2) > a) || ((x - 2) < b)) && (y >= 0))` ✓
(b)   `if (((a >= b) && (a >= c)) && ((a % 2) == 0))`

7. Rewrite the following condition to avoid a possible arithmetic exception:

```
if (Math.sqrt(x) < 3 && x > 7) ...
```

8. Write a Boolean expression that evaluates to `true` if and only if the values of three integer variables *a*, *b*, and *c* form a geometric sequence (that is, *a*, *b*, *c* ≠ 0 and *a/b* = *b/c*). ⸓ Hint: recall that comparing `double` values for exact match may not work — use integer cross products instead. ⸓

9. Given an `int` variable *x*, write a Boolean expression that evaluates to `true` if and only if the decimal representation of the value of *x* ends with exactly two zeroes (no more and no less). ✓

10. Simplify the following statements:

(a)
```
boolean inside = !((x < left) || (x > right) ||
    (y < top) || (y > bottom));   ✓
```
(b)
```
boolean no = (ch[0] == 'N' && ch[1] == 'O') ||
             (ch[0] == 'n' && ch[1] == 'o') ||
             (ch[0] == 'N' && ch[1] == 'o') ||
             (ch[0] == 'n' && ch[1] == 'O');
```

11.▪ Write a `boolean` method `isLeapYear(int year)` that returns `true` if `year` is a leap year and `false` otherwise. A leap year is a year that is evenly divisible by 4 and either is not divisible by 100 or is divisible by 400. For example, 2000 and 2004 are leap years, but 2003 and 2100 are not.

12. ■   Write a method

```
public static boolean isLater(int month1, int day1, int year1,
                    int month2, int day2, int year2)
```

that returns true if the first date is later than the second and false otherwise. Test your method using the provided console application Dates (JM\Ch07\Exercises\Dates.java), which prompts the user to enter two dates, reads the input, and displays the result of the comparison. ✓

Section 7.8

13.   Rewrite the following code using < and no other relational operators.

```
if (avg >= 90)
   grade = 'A';
else if (avg >= 80)
   grade = 'B';
else if (avg >= 70)
   grade = 'C';
else if (avg >= 60)
   grade = 'D';
else
   grade = 'F';
```

14. ■   (a)   Restore appropriate indentation and optional braces in the following code fragment using if-else-if sequences and nested if-else statements as appropriate (this code is available in JM\Ch07\Exercises\WarmWeather.java):

```
boolean warm;
if(location.isNorthPole() || location.isSouthPole())
{warm = false;} else if(location.isTropics()) {warm
= true;} else if (time.getMonth()==4 || time.getMonth()==10)
{if (weather.isSunny()) {warm = true;}else{warm = false;}}
else if (location.isNorthernHemisphere()) {if(time.getMonth()
>=5 && time.getMonth() <= 9) {warm=true;} else{warm=false;}}
else if(location.isSouthernHemisphere()){if(time.getMonth()
>= 11 ||time.getMonth()<= 3) {warm = true;} else{warm=
false;}} else{warm = false;}
```

(b)   Simplify the statement from Part (a) by starting with warm = false; then setting warm to true under the appropriate conditions.

(c)   Rewrite the statement from Part (b) in the form

```
warm = < logical expression > ;
```

15.■ A "Be Prepared" test prep book costs $18.95; "Next Best" costs $21.95. A
      site called apzone.com offers a special deal: both for $37.95. If you buy
      three or more copies (in any mix of these two titles), they are $15.95 each. If
      you buy 12 or more copies, you pay only $14.00 for each.

   (a)   Write a method

```
public static double getOrderTotal(int bp, int nb)
{
    . . .
}
```

         that calculates the total for an order of bp copies of "Be Prepared" and
         nb copies of "Next Best," taking the above specials into account.

   (b)   Test your method in a class with a main method that prompts the user
         for two integers representing the quantities of "Be Prepared" and "Next
         Best" books desired, and displays the total cost.

16.■ Write a method

```
public Color bestMatch(int r, int g, int b)
```

      The method's arguments represent the red, green, and blue components of a
      color. If one of the components is greater than the other two, bestMatch
      returns that component's color (Color.RED, Color.GREEN, or
      Color.BLUE). If two components are equal and greater than the third, then
      bestMatch returns their "composite" color, Color.YELLOW,
      Color.MAGENTA, or Color.CYAN (for red-green, red-blue, and green-blue,
      respectively). If all three components are equal, bestMatch returns
      Color.GRAY.

17.■ size1 and size2 are the sizes of two files, and space is the amount of
      available space on a CD. Write a method that takes these integer numbers as
      parameters and figures out the largest combination of files that fits on a CD.
      The method should return 3 if both files fit together, the file number (1 or 2)
      corresponding to the largest file that fits by itself (1 if the files are the same
      size), or 0 if neither file fits on the CD. Your method must have only one
      return statement.

```
public int findBestFit(int size1, int size2, int space)
{
  < ... missing code >
}
```

Sections 7.9-7.13

18.   Generalize the `Die` class from Section 7.9 so that a die may have *n* faces with numbers from 1 to *n* on them. Provide a no-args constructor that initializes the number of faces to 6 and another constructor with one parameter, *n*.

19.   Finish the five-line poem:

> *One, two, buckle your shoe;*
> *Three, four, shut the door;*

and write a console Java application that displays the appropriate line of your poem:

```
Enter a number 1-10 (or 0 to quit): 1
Buckle your shoe

Enter a number 1-10 (or 0 to quit): 2
Buckle your shoe

Enter a number 1-10 (or 0 to quit): 6
Pick up sticks

Enter a number 1-10 (or 0 to quit): 0
Bye
```

Use a `switch` statement.

20.■   Finish the program in `JM\Ch07\Exercises\Rps.java` that plays the "Rock, Paper, Scissors" game. You need to supply code for the `nextPlay` method. Use nested `switch` statements.

21.◆   In your `CrapsGame` class, you probably have an `if-else` statement to process the roll correctly depending on the current state of the game:

```
if (point == 0)  // first roll
   ...
else   // subsequent rolls
   ...
```

Define instead a private enum type that would describe the two possible states of the game, `NEW_ROLL` and `KEEP_ROLLING`. Declare a field of that enum type that would represent the current state of the game and replace the `if-else` statement with a `switch` on the value of that field.

```
while (chapter < 8)
   chapter++;
```

Iterative Statements: `while`, `for`, `do-while`

193

8.1   Prologue

Loops or *iterative statements* tell the program to repeat a fragment of code several times for as long as a certain condition holds. Java provides three convenient iterative statements: while, for, and do-while. Strictly speaking, any iterative code can be implemented using only the while loop. But the other two add flexibility and make the code more concise and idiomatic.

Iterations are often used in conjunction with lists or files. We can use iterations to process all the elements of a list (useful for finding a particular element in a list or calculating the sum of all the elements) or read and process lines of text from a file. We will discuss how loops are used with lists later, in Chapters 12 and 19. Java has a convenient "for each" loop for traversing a collection of values.

In this chapter we will learn the Java syntax for while, for, and do-while loops and how to use break and return in loops.

8.2   The **while** and **for** Loops

The general form of the while statement is:

```
while (condition)
{
  statement1;
  statement2;
  ...
  statementN;
}
```

condition can be any logical expression; it is evaluated exactly as in an if statement.

Informally the while statement is often called a *while loop*. The statements within braces are called the *body* of the loop. If the body consists of only one statement, the braces surrounding the body can be dropped:

```
while (condition)
  statement1;
```

It is important <u>not</u> to put a semicolon after while(condition). With a semicolon, the loop would have no body, only an empty statement; *statement1* would be left completely out of the loop.

The following method of the `MyMath` class (`JM\Ch08\MyMath\MyMath.java`) returns the sum of all integers from 1 to *n*:

```
/**
 * Returns the sum of all integers from 1 to n, if n >= 1,
 * and 0 othorwioc.
 */
public static int sumUpTo(int n)
{
  int sum = 0;
  int i = 1;

  while (i <= n)
  {
    sum += i;
    i++;
  }

  return sum;
}
```

Three elements must be present with any while loop: an initialization, a test of the condition, and a change.

1. Initialization. The variables tested in *condition* must be initialized to some values before the loop. In the above example, `i` is initially set to `1` in the declaration `int i = 1`.

2. Testing. The condition is tested before each pass through the loop. If it is false, the body is not executed, the iterations end, and the program continues with the first statement after the loop. If the condition is false at the very beginning, the body of the `while` loop is not executed at all. In the `sumUpTo` example, the condition is `i <= n`. If `n` is zero or negative, the condition will be false on the very first test (since `i` is initially set to `1`). Then the body of the loop will be skipped and the method will return `0`.

3. Change. At least one of the variables tested in the condition must change within the body of the loop. Otherwise, the loop will be repeated over and over and never stop, and your program will "hang." The change of a variable is often implemented with increment or decrement operators, but it can come from any assignment or input statement. In any case, the tested variables must at some point get values that will make the condition false. Then the program jumps to the first statement after the body of the loop.

In the sumUpTo method, the change is achieved by incrementing i:

```
   ...
   i++;           // increment i
```

These three elements — initialization, testing, and change — must be present, explicitly or implicitly, in every while loop.

❖   ❖   ❖

The for loop is a shorthand for the while loop that combines the initialization, condition, and change in one statement. Its general form is:

```
for (initialization; condition; change)
{
  statement1;
  statement2;
  ...
}
```

where *initialization* is a statement that is <u>always executed once</u> before the first pass through the loop, *condition* is tested <u>before each pass</u> through the loop, and *change* is a statement executed <u>at the end of each pass</u> through the loop.

A typical for loop for repeating the same block of statements n times is:

```
for (int count = 1; count <= n; count++)
{
  < ... statements >
}
```

For instance, the following for loop prints *n* spaces:

```
for (int count = 1; count <= n; count++)
{
  System.out.print(" ");
}
```

The braces can be dropped if the body of the loop has only one statement, but many people like to have braces even around one statement because that makes it easier to add statements to the body of the loop. We don't feel strongly about either style, so we will use either, depending on the situation or our mood.

Note that a variable that controls the loop can be declared right in the `for` statement. For example:

```
for (int i = 1; i <= 100; i++)
{
    sum += i * i;
}
```

This is common style, but you have to be aware that the scope of a variable declared this way does <u>not</u> extend beyond the body of the loop. In the above example, if you add

```
System.out.println(i);
```

after the closing brace, you will get a syntax error: undefined variable `i`.

The `sumUpTo` method can be rewritten with a `for` loop as follows:

```
public static int sumUpTo(int n)
{
    int sum = 0;

    for (int i = 1; i <= n; i++)
        sum += i;

    return sum;
}
```

The following method (also in the `MyMath` class) calculates *n*! (*n factorial*), which is defined as the product of all integers from 1 to *n*:

```
/**
 *   Returns 1 * 2 * ... * n, if n >= 1; otherwise returns 1
 */
public static long factorial(int n)
{
    long f = 1;

    for (int k = 2; k <= n; k++)   // if n < 2, this loop is skipped
        f *= k;

    return f;
}
```

8.3 The `do-while` Loop

> The `do-while` loop differs from the `while` loop in that the condition is tested <u>after</u> the body of the loop. This ensures that the program goes through the loop at least once.

The `do-while` statement's general form is:

```
do
{
  ...
} while (condition);
```

The program repeats the body of the loop as long as *condition* remains true. It is better always to keep the braces, even if the body of the loop is just one statement, because the code is hard to read without them.

`do-while` loops are used less frequently than `while` and `for` loops. They are convenient when the variables tested in the condition are calculated or entered within the body of the loop. The following example comes from `main` in the `MyMath` class (J_M\Ch08\MyMath\MyMath.java):

```java
public static void main(String[] args)
{
  Scanner kb = new Scanner(System.in);
  int n;

  do
  {
    System.out.print("Enter an integer from 4 to 20: ");
    n = kb.nextInt();
  } while (n < 4 || n > 20);

  System.out.println();
  System.out.println("1 + ... + " + n + " = " + sumUpTo(n));
  System.out.println(n + "! = " + factorial(n));
}
```

In this code the `do-while` loop calls `Scanner`'s `nextInt` method to get the value of `n` from the user's input. The iterations continue until the user enters a number within the requested range.

If for some reason you do not like do-while loops, you can easily avoid them by using a while loop and initializing the variables in a way that makes the condition true before the first pass through the loop. The do-while loop in the above code, for example, can be rewritten as follows:

```
int n = -1;

while (n < 4 || n > 20)
{
   System.out.print("Enter an integer from 4 to 20: ");
   n = kb.nextInt();
}
```

8.4 return and break in Loops

We saw in Section 7.10 that break is used inside a switch statement to end a case and break out of the switch. break can be also used in the body of a loop. It instructs the program to break out of the loop immediately and go to the first statement after the body of the loop. break must always appear inside a conditional (if or else) statement — otherwise you will just break out of the loop on the very first iteration.

The following method checks whether a positive integer n is a prime. A prime is an integer that is greater than 1 and has no factors besides 1 and itself. Our algorithm has to check all potential factors m, but only as long as $m^2 \le n$ (because if m is a factor, then so is n/m, and one of the two must be less than or equal to the square root of n). The isPrime method below employs break to reduce the number of iterations:

```
/**
 *   Returns true if n is a prime, false otherwise.
 */
public static boolean isPrime(int n)
{
  boolean noFactors = true;

  if (n <= 1)
    return false;

  for (int m = 2; noFactors; m++)
  {
    if (m * m > n)
      break;

    if (n % m == 0)
      noFactors = false;
  }
  return noFactors;
}
```

Another way to break out of the loop (and out of the method) is to put a `return` statement inside the loop. A shorter version of `isPrime`, for example, uses `return`:

```
public static boolean isPrime(int n)
{
  if (n <= 1)
    return false;

  int m = 2;

  while (m * m <= n)
  {
    if (n % m == 0)
      return false;
    m++;
  }

  return true;
}
```

Either version is acceptable, but the latter may be clearer. You will find some programmers, though, who like to have only one `return` in each method and who find a `break` or `return` inside a loop objectionable.

8.5 Nested Loops

A nested loop is a loop within a loop. For example,

```
for (int i = 1; i <= n; i++)
{
  for (int j = 1; j <= i; j++)
    System.out.print("*");
  System.out.println();
}
```

prints a "triangle" made up of n rows of stars:

```
*
**
***
****
. . .
*******
```

Nested loops are convenient for traversing two-dimensional grids and arrays. For example:

```
for (int r = 0; r < grid.numRows(); r++)
{
  for (int c = 0; c < grid.numCols(); c++)
  {
    System.out.print(grid.getValue(r, c));
  }
  System.out.println();
}
```

Nested loops are also used for finding duplicates in a list. For example:

```
for (int i = 0; i < list.size(); i++)
{
  for (int j = i + 1; j < list.size(); j++)
  {
    if (list.get(i).equals(list.get(j)))
      System.out.println("Duplicates at " + i + ", " + j);
  }
}
```

We will talk about lists and arrays in Chapter 12.

The following method tests the so-called Goldbach conjecture that any even integer greater than or equal to 4 can be represented as a sum of two primes:[*]

```
/**
 *   Tests Goldbach conjecture for even numbers
 *   up to bigNum
 */
public static boolean testGoldbach(int bigNum)
{
  for (int n = 6; n <= bigNum; n += 2)   // obviously true for n = 4
  {
    boolean found2primes = false;

    for (int p = 3; p <= n/2; p += 2)
    {
      if (isPrime(p) && isPrime(n - p))
        found2primes = true;
    }

    if (!found2primes)
    {
      System.out.println(n + " is not a sum of two primes!");
      return false;
    }
  }

  return true;
}
```

This method can be made a little more efficient if we break out of the inner loop once a pair of primes is found:

```
for (int p = 3; p <= n/2; p += 2)
{
  if (isPrime(p) && isPrime(n - p))
  {
    found2primes = true;
    break;
  }
}
```

---

[*] In 1742, Christian Goldbach, an amateur mathematician, in a letter to Euler stated a hypothesis that any even number greater than or equal to 4 can be represented as a sum of two primes. For example, $18 = 5 + 13$; $20 = 7 + 13$; $22 = 11 + 11$. The Goldbach conjecture remains to this day neither proved nor disproved.

Note that `break` takes you out of the inner loop, but not the outer loop. But

```
if (isPrime(p) && isPrime(n - p))
{
   return true;
}
```

would be a mistake, because it would quit the method right away, before we had a chance to test the conjecture for all `n <= bigNum`.

You can have a loop within a loop within a loop — loops can be nested to any level. But once you go to more than two or three levels, your code may become intractable. Then you might consider moving the inner loop or two into a separate method. To be honest, our `testGoldbach` method would be simpler if we moved the inner loop into a separate method:

```
private static boolean found2Primes(int n)
{
   for (int p = 3; p <= n/2; p += 2)
   {
      if (isPrime(p) && isPrime(n - p))
         return true;
   }
   return false;
}
```

Then `testGoldbach` would become simply

```
public static boolean testGoldbach(int bigNum)
{
   for (int n = 6; n <= bigNum; n += 2)
   {
      if (!found2Primes(n))
      {
         System.out.println(n + " is not a sum of two primes!");
         return false;
      }
   }
   return true;
}
```

8.6 *Lab*: Perfect Numbers

A whole number is called *perfect* if it is equal to the sum of all of its divisors, including 1 (but excluding the number itself). For example, $28 = 1 + 2 + 4 + 7 + 14$. Perfect numbers were known in ancient Greece. In Book VII of *Elements*, Euclid (300 BC) defined a perfect number as one "which is equal to its own parts."

Nicomachus, a Greek mathematician of the first century, wrote in his *Introduction to Arithmetic* (around A.D. 100):

> *In the case of the too much, is produced excess, superfluity, exaggerations and abuse; in the case of too little, is produced wanting, defaults, privations and insufficiencies. And in the case of those that are found between the too much and the too little, that is, in equality, is produced virtue, just measure, propriety, beauty and things of that sort — of which the most exemplary form is that type of number which is called perfect.* perfectnumbers

Unfortunately, Nicomachus had many mistakes in his book. For example, he stated erroneously that the *n*-th perfect number has *n* digits and that perfect numbers end alternately in 6 and 8. He knew of only four perfect numbers and jumped to conclusions.

Write a program to find the first four perfect numbers.

❖   ❖   ❖

You might be tempted to use your program to find the fifth perfect number. Then you'd better be patient: on a relatively fast computer, it could take almost an hour. There is a better strategy. Euclid proved that if you find a number of the form $2^n - 1$ that is a prime, then $2^{n-1}(2^n - 1)$ is a perfect number! For example, $(2^3 - 1) = 7$ is a prime, so $28 = 2^2(2^3 - 1)$ is a perfect number. Many centuries later, Euler proved that any <u>even</u> perfect number must have this form. Therefore the search for even perfect numbers can be reduced to the search for primes that have the form $2^n - 1$. Such primes are called *Mersenne primes*, after the French math enthusiast Marin Mersenne (1588-1648) who made them popular.

In 1996, George Woltman, a software engineer, started The Great Internet Mersenne Prime Search project (GIMPS).✱mersenne   In this project, volunteers contribute idle CPU time on their personal computers for the search. The 42nd Mersenne prime, $2^{25,964,951} - 1$, was found on February 18, 2005. (It has 7,816,230 digits.)

Write a program to find the first six Mersenne primes, and use them to calculate the first six perfect numbers. Note that while the sixth Mersenne is still well within the Java `int` range, the sixth perfect number, 8,589,869,056, is not. Use a `long` variable to hold it.

❖   ❖   ❖

It is unknown to this day whether any odd perfect numbers exist. It has been shown that such a number must have at least 300 digits!

8.7 Summary

Java offers three iterative statements:

```
while (condition)
{
   ...
}

for (initialization; condition; change)
{
   ...
}

do
{
   ...
} while (condition);
```

In a `while` loop, the variables tested in *condition* must be initialized before the loop, and at least one of them has to change inside the body of the loop. The program tests *condition* before each pass through the loop. If *condition* is false on the very first test, the `while` loop is skipped, and the program jumps to the first statement after the body of the loop. Otherwise the program keeps iterating for as long as *condition* holds true.

The for loop combines *initialization*, *condition*, and *change* in one statement. The *initialization* statement is executed once, before the loop. *condition* is tested before each pass through the loop, and if it is false, the loop is skipped and the program jumps to the next statement after the body of the loop. The *change* statement is executed at the end of each pass through the loop.

The do-while loop is different from the while loop in that *condition* is tested <u>after</u> the body of the loop. Thus the body of a do-while loop is always executed at least once.

A break statement inside the body of a loop tells the program to jump immediately out of the loop to the first statement after the body of the loop. break should appear only inside an if or else statement; otherwise it will interrupt the loop on the very first iteration. A break statement inside a nested loop will only break out of the inner loop. However, a return statement inside a loop immediately quits the loop and the whole method, too.

Exercises

<u>Sections 8.1-8.4</u>

 1.   The population of Mexico in 2005 was 106.2 million. Write a program that calculates and prints out the year in which the population of Mexico will reach 120 million, assuming a constant growth rate of 1.7% per year. Use a while loop. ✓

2.   Each time Kevin re-reads his Java book (which happens every month), he learns 10% of whatever material he didn't know before. He needs to score at least 95% on the comprehensive exam to become a certified Java developer. When Kevin started, he knew nothing about Java. Write a method that simulates Kevin's learning progress and returns the number of months it will take him to get ready for the exam. Write a main method that displays the result (in years and months).

3.   Write a method int addOdds(int n) that calculates and returns the sum of all odd integers from 1 to *n*. Your method should use exactly one for loop and no other iterative or if-else statements. (Do not use the formula for the sum of odd numbers.) ✓

4.   Write a program to test the algorithms from Questions 1 and 2 in Chapter 4.

5.   Write a program that produces the following output (where the user may enter any positive integer under 10): ✓

```
Enter a positive integer under 10: 6
1 + 2 + 3 + 4 + 5 + 6 = 21
```

6.   (a)   Modify one of the versions of the `isPrime` method on page 200 so that if the argument is not 2 it tests only odd numbers as potential factors of *n*. ✓

   (b)   Make `isPrime` even more efficient by testing only potential factors that are relatively prime with 6 (that is, factors that are not evenly divisible by either 2 or 3). ✓

7.   Recall that $1 + 3 + ... + (2p - 1) = p^2$ for any integer $p \geq 1$. Write a "simple" method

```
public static boolean isPerfectSquare(int n)
```

that tests whether a given number is a perfect square. A "simple" method cannot use arrays, nested loops, Math functions, or arithmetic operations except addition (see Question 5 in Chapter 4). ✓

8.   (a)   Write a method `sumDigits` that calculates and returns the sum of all the digits of a given non-negative integer.

   (b)   Pretending that the modulo division operator does not exist in Java, write a `boolean` recursive method that tests whether a given number is evenly divisible by 3. A number is divisible by 3 if and only if the sum of its digits is divisible by 3. Use the `sumDigits` method from Part (a).

9.   Finish the program `GradeAvg.java` (in J_M\Ch08\Exercises), which reads integer scores from a file and prints out their average. ⸘ Hint: If `input` is a `Scanner` object associated with a file, `input.hasNextInt()` returns `true` if there is an integer value left unread in the file; otherwise it returns `false`; `input.nextInt()` returns the next integer read from the file. ⸘

10.■   Given a positive number a, the sequence of values

$$x_0 = \frac{a}{2}$$

$$x_{n+1} = \frac{1}{2}\left(x_n + \frac{a}{x_n}\right) \quad (n \ge 0)$$

converges to $\sqrt{a}$. Fill in the blanks in the following method, which uses iterations to estimate the square root of a number:

```
// Returns an estimate r of the square root of a,
// such that |r^2 - a| < 0.01
// Precondition: a is a positive number
public static double sqrtEst(double a)
{
  double r = a/2;
  double diff;

  do
  {
    . . .

  } while ( ... );

  return r;
}
```

Sections 8.5-8.7

11.   Write a method

```
public static void printStarTriangle(int n)
```

that displays n rows of stars, as follows:

```
    *
   ***
  *****
. . .
. . .
*************
```

The last row of stars should start at the first position on the line.

12.◆   Consider all fractions that have positive denominators between 1 and 100. Write a program that finds the two such fractions that are closest to 17 / 76: one from above and one from below.

13.■   Write a program that supports the following dialog with the user:

```
Enter quantity: 75
You have ordered 75 Ripples -- $19.50

Next customer (y/n): y

Enter quantity: 97
Ripples can be ordered only in packs of 25.

Next customer (y/n): t
Next customer (y/n): n

Thank you for using Ripple Systems.
```

If, in response to the "Next customer" prompt, the user presses <Enter> or enters anything other than a 'y' or an 'n', the program should repeat the question.

Define the unit price of a ripple as a <u>constant</u> equal to 26 cents.

⬚ Hints:

Use the following statement to display the quantity ordered and the total dollar amount of the order:

```
System.out.printf("You have ordered %d ripples -- $%.2f\n\n",
                        quantity, price * quantity);
```

Use the following statements to read the quantity ordered and the answer to the "Next customer?" question:

```
Scanner keyboard = new Scanner(System.in);
char answer;
...

  int quantity = keyboard.nextInt();
  keyboard.nextLine();  // skip the rest of the line
  ...

  String str = keyboard.nextLine().trim();
  if (str.length() == 1)
    answer = str.charAt(0);
  else
    answer = ' ';
```

14.❖   Write and test a method that takes an amount in cents and prints out all possible representations of that amount as a sum of several quarters, dimes, nickels, and pennies. For example:

```
30 cents = 0 quarters + 2 dimes + 1 nickels + 5 pennies
```

(There are 18 different representations for 30 cents and 242 for $1.00.)

15.■   Find and read a few informative websites dedicated to *Fibonacci numbers*. The following recursive method returns the *n*-th Fibonacci number:

```java
// Returns the n-th Fibonacci number.
// Precondition: n >= 1
public static long fibonacci(int n)
{
  if (n == 1 || n == 2)
    return 1;
  else
    return fibonacci(n - 1) + fibonacci(n - 2);
}
```

Rewrite it without recursion, using one loop. Add your method to the MyMath class in JM\Ch08\MyMath and test it.

Chapter chapter9 = new Chapter(9);

Implementing Classes and Using Objects

211

9.1 Prologue

In the previous chapters we took a rather general view of classes and objects and did not explain in detail how to write classes and how to invoke constructors and call methods. The time has come to fill in the gaps. Our example will be a simple class called Fraction, which has the common features that we are interested in. A Fraction object represents something very familiar: a fraction with an integer numerator and denominator.

Occasionally, a class has its own main method and works as a stand-alone program or as a "main" class in a program. More often, though, a class exists to be used by other classes. For example, our class Fraction provides a set of tools for dealing with fractions in various applications related to arithmetic. Our Fraction class provides several constructors (for creating fractions) and methods (for adding and multiplying fractions and for converting a Fraction into a double). It also includes a toString method that returns a description of a Fraction as a string.

> **A class that uses a given class *X* is called a *client* of *X*.**

The developer of a class looks at the class from a different perspective than its user (the author of client classes). The developer needs to know precisely how different features of the class are defined and implemented. A user is interested to know which features of the class are available and how to use them. In real life, the developer and the user can be the same programmer, just wearing different hats and switching between these points of view.

The developer's and the user's points of view must meet somewhere, of course: any usable feature of a class and the way to use it are defined by the developer, and the user must use it in just the right way. That is why we have invited Dave, the developer of Fraction, and Claire, who wrote a small client class TestFractions, to help us co-teach this chapter.

Claire: Hi!

Dave: That Fraction class — it wasn't a big deal. ⇐

Claire and Dave will help us present the following topics:

- Public and private features of a class

- The details of syntax for defining constructors and methods

- Syntax for invoking constructors and calling methods and the rules for passing parameters to them

- Returning values from methods using the `return` statement

Later in this chapter we will discuss two slightly more technical topics:

- Overloaded methods (giving different methods in a class the same name)

- Static (class) and non-static (instance) fields and methods.

By the end of this chapter, you should understand every feature of the `Fraction` class in Figure 9-1 and be able to use these features in client classes. You will then write your own class for the *Snack Bar* lab described in Section 9.9.

<u>Claire</u>: Wow, I didn't realize this `Fraction` class had so much stuff in it! ⇐

```
// Represents a fraction with an int numerator and int denominator
// and provides methods for adding and multiplying fractions.

public class Fraction
{
    // ****************  Instance variables  ******************

    private int num;
    private int denom;

    // ********************  Constructors  ********************

    public Fraction()        // no-args constructor
    {
        num = 0;
        denom = 1;
    }

    public Fraction(int n)
    {
        num = n;
        denom = 1;
    }
```

Figure 9-1 `Fraction.java` *Continued* ⇨

```java
public Fraction(int n, int d)
{
  if (d != 0)
  {
    num = n;
    denom = d;
    reduce();
  }
  else
  {
    throw new IllegalArgumentException(
        "Fraction construction error: denominator is 0");
  }
}


public Fraction(Fraction other)  // copy constructor
{
  num = other.num;
  denom = other.denom;
}

// ******************** Public methods ********************

// Returns the sum of this fraction and other
public Fraction add(Fraction other)
{
  int newNum = num * other.denom + denom * other.num;
  int newDenom = denom * other.denom;
  return new Fraction(newNum, newDenom);
}

// Returns the sum of this fraction and m
public Fraction add(int m)
{
  return new Fraction(num + m * denom, denom);
}

// Returns the product of this fraction and other
public Fraction multiply(Fraction other)
{
  int newNum = num * other.num;
  int newDenom = denom * other.denom;
  return new Fraction(newNum, newDenom);
}

// Returns the product of this fraction and m
public Fraction multiply(int m)
{
  return new Fraction(num * m, denom);
}
```

Figure 9-1 `Fraction.java` *Continued* ☞

```java
// Returns the value of this fraction as a double
public double getValue()
{
  return (double)num / (double)denom;
}

// Returns a string representation of this fraction
public String toString()
{
  return num + "/" + denom;
}

// ******************* Private methods  *******************

// Reduces this fraction by the gcf and makes denom > 0
private void reduce()
{
  if (num == 0)
  {
    denom = 1;
    return;
  }

  if (denom < 0)
  {
    num = -num;
    denom = -denom;
  }

  int q = gcf(Math.abs(num), denom);
  num /= q;
  denom /= q;
}

// Returns the greatest common factor of two positive integers
private int gcf(int n, int d)
{
  if (n <= 0 || d <= 0)
  {
    throw new IllegalArgumentException(
            "gcf precondition failed: " + n + ", " + d);
  }

  if (n % d == 0)
    return d;
  else if (d % n == 0)
    return n;
  else
    return gcf(n % d, d % n);
}
}
```

Figure 9-1. Jᴍ\Ch09\Fraction\Fraction.java

9.2 Public and Private Features of a Class

As you can see, every field, constructor, and method in the `Fraction` class is declared as either `public` or `private`. These keywords tell the compiler whether or not the code in other classes is allowed to access a field or call a constructor or method directly. These access rules are not complicated.

> **Private features of a class can be directly accessed only within the class's own code. Public features can be accessed in client classes (with an appropriate name-dot prefix).**

Dave: As you see, I have declared the `num` and `denom` fields `private`:

```
private int num;
private int denom;
```

I made them private because I don't want anyone to change them from the outside, and I want to be able to change their names or even data types without affecting client classes. I also made the `gcf` and `reduce` methods private.

Claire: Yes, I ran into a problem with that just the other day when I wrote

```
Fraction f = new Fraction(12, 20);
System.out.println("num = " + f.num + " denom = " + f.denom +
    " gcf = " + f.gcf(12, 20));
```

The compiler said:

```
num has private access in Fraction
denom has private access in Fraction
gcf(int, int) has private access in Fraction
```

You should have made at least the `gcf` method public. What if someone needs to find the GCF of two numbers?

Dave: I learned in school to provide as little information to clients as possible. This is called "information hiding." ⇐

The reason for making some of a class's features private is to control access to its fields by the class's *clients* and to "hide" its implementation details. That way the inner mechanics of the class (its private fields and private methods) can change without any changes to the rest of the program. This makes program maintenance easier.

> **In OOP, instance variables are almost always private. If necessary, the developer provides a special *accessor* method that returns the value of a particular private field. The developer may also define methods that update private fields. These are called *modifiers* or *mutators*.**

But some constants are declared public. For example, `Color.RED`, `Math.PI`, `Integer.MAX_VALUE`.

Some "helper methods" of a class may be useful only to the objects of this class, but not to the class's clients. It makes sense to declare such methods private, too. Making all of a class's fields private and making the helper methods private ensures that the class can be completely described to outsiders by its constructors and public methods. These constructors and public methods describe everything the class and its objects can do for clients. This concept is known in OOP as *encapsulation*.

Dave: I didn't provide any modifier methods for the private fields `num` and `denom` because I didn't want anyone to fiddle with their values outside the class. No need for accessor methods either. As to the `qcf` method, you're right: I should have made it `public static`. I'll change that later.

Claire: Good idea, whatever that "static" is.

Dave: But my `reduce` method will remain private. ⇐

> **The concepts of public and private apply to the class as a whole, not to individual objects of the class.**

For example, the compiler has no problem when `Fraction`'s `add` method refers directly to instance variables of `other Fraction`:

```
int newNum = num * other.denom + denom * other.num;
```

We mentioned earlier that a constructor can be declared private, too. You might be wondering: Why would one make a constructor private? This is indeed unusual. You might define a private constructor for one of two reasons. First, other constructors of the same class can call it. We will see the syntax for that in Section 9.3. Second, if a class has only one constructor and it is private, Java won't allow you to create objects of that class. This is used in such classes as `Math` or `System`, which are never instantiated.

9.3 Constructors

Constructors are procedures for creating objects of a class.

> **A constructor always has the same name as the class. Unlike methods, constructors do not return any values. They have no return type, not even void.**

All constructors are defined inside the class definition. Their main task is to initialize all or some of the new object's fields. Fields that are not explicitly initialized are set to default values: zero for numbers, `false` for `booleans`, `null` for objects.

> **A constructor may take parameters of specified types and use them for initializing the new object. If a class has more than one constructor, then they must differ in the number or types of their parameters.**

Dave: I have provided four constructors for my `Fraction` class:

```
public Fraction()        // no-args constructor
{
  num = 0;
  denom = 1;
}

public Fraction(int n)
{
  num = n;
  denom = 1;
}

public Fraction(int n, int d)
{
  if (d != 0)
  {
    num = n;
    denom = d;
    reduce();
  }
  else
  {
    throw new IllegalArgumentException(
        "Fraction construction error: denominator is 0");
  }
}
```

```java
public Fraction(Fraction other)    // copy constructor
{
  num = other.num;
  denom = other.denom;
}
```

The first one, the *no-args* constructor, takes no parameters (arguments) and just creates a fraction 0/1. The second one takes one `int` parameter *n* and creates a fraction *n*/1. The third one takes two `int` parameters, the numerator and the denominator. The last one is a *copy constructor*: it takes another `Fraction` object as a parameter and creates a fraction equal to it.

Claire: I have tested all the constructors and they seem to work:

```java
Fraction f1 = new Fraction();
Fraction f2 = new Fraction(7);
Fraction f3 = new Fraction(12, -20);
Fraction f4 = new Fraction(f3);

System.out.println("f1 = " + f1);
System.out.println("f2 = " + f2);
System.out.println("f3 = " + f3);
System.out.println("f4 = " + f4);
```

I got

```
f1 = 0/1
f2 = 7/1
f3 = -3/5
f4 = -3/5
```

⇦

> The number, types, and order of parameters passed to the new operator must match the number, types, and order of parameters expected by one of the constructors. That constructor will be invoked.

> You don't have to define any constructors for a class. If a class doesn't have any constructors, the compiler supplies a *default no-args constructor*. It allocates memory for the object and initializes its fields to default values. But if you define at least one constructor for your class, then the default no-args constructor is <u>not</u> supplied.

Normally constructors should prevent programs from creating invalid objects.

Dave: My constructor —

```
public Fraction(int n, int d)
{
  if (d != 0)
  {
    ...
  }
  else
  {
    throw new IllegalArgumentException(
        "Fraction construction error: denominator is 0");
  }
```

— throws an `IllegalArgumentException` if the parameter it receives for the denominator is 0. "Argument," as in math, and "parameter" is roughly the same thing.

Claire: What do I get if this "exception" happens?

Dave: Your program is aborted and the Java interpreter displays an error message, which shows the sequence of method and constructor calls, with their line numbers, that have led to the error. I am sure you've seen quite a few of those... ⇦

A constructor can call the object's other methods, even while the object is still "under construction."

Dave: One of my constructors, the one with two parameters, calls my `reduce` method. ⇦

A constructor can call another constructor of the same class by using the keyword `this`.

Dave: Sure, I could've written:

```
public Fraction()
{
  this(0, 1);
}

public Fraction(int n)
{
  this(n, 1);
}
```

And then those constructors would have called my two-parameter constructor. But I thought it'd be a little too fancy for these simple constructors. ⇐

If a constructor calls `this(...)`, the call must be the first statement in the constructor's body.

Unfortunately, Java allows you to use the class name for a method name. This is a potential source of bugs that are hard to catch.

Dave: Yep. I got burnt on this one many times. I'd accidentally write something like

```
public MyWindow extends JFrame
{
  public void MyWindow()
  {
    . . .
  }
  . . .
}
```

instead of

```
public MyWindow extends JFrame
{
  public MyWindow()
  {
    . . .
  }
  . . .
}
```

No calls to `this` or `super` in my "constructor," right? So the compiler thinks I've defined a `void` <u>method</u>, `MyWindow`, rather than a constructor. It supplies a default no-args constructor for my class. I compile, run, and all I see is a blank window! ⇐

9.4 References to Objects

Objects are created by using the `new` operator. When you declare a variable of a class type — as in

```
private JButton go;
private CrapsTable table;
private RollingDie die1, die2;
```

— such a variable holds a *reference* to an object of the corresponding type. You can think of a reference simply as the object's address in memory. In the above declarations the four references are not explicitly initialized: they do not yet refer to valid objects. If the value of a variable is `null`, it indicates that currently the variable does not refer to a valid object.

> **It is crucial to initialize a reference before using it. The `new` operator is one way of doing this.**

Another way is to set the variable to a reference returned from a method. With the exception of literal strings and initialized arrays, objects are always created with `new`, either in one of your methods or in one of the library methods that you call.

> **If you try to call a method or access a public field through a `null` reference, your program "throws" a `NullPointerException`.**

Sometimes you can create an anonymous temporary object "on the fly," without ever naming it. For example:

```
System.out.println(new Fraction(12, 20));
```

This is basically the same as:

```
Fraction temp = new Fraction(12, 20);
System.out.println(temp);
```

Dave: Like in my `add` method:

```
return new Fraction(newNum, newDenom);
```

⇐

In Java, several variables can hold references to the same object. The assignment operator, when applied to references, copies only the value of the reference (that is, the object's address), not the object itself. For example, after the statements

```
Fraction f1 = new Fraction(3, 7);
Fraction f2 = f1;
```

f2 refers to exactly the same `Fraction` object as f1 (Figure 9-2-a). This is not the same as

```
Fraction f1 = new Fraction(3, 7);
Fraction f2 = new Fraction(f1);
```

The latter creates a new `Fraction` object, a copy of f1 (Figure 9-2-b).

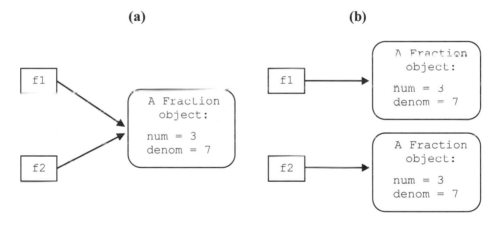

Figure 9-2. Copying references vs. copying objects

9.5 Defining Methods

A method is a segment of code that implements a certain task or calculation. Like a constructor, a method can take some parameters. For example, if the method's task is to calculate the GCF of two integers, it needs to know their values. A method either returns a value (for example, the GCF of two numbers) or completes a task (for example, reduces a fraction), or both.

From a pragmatic point of view, methods are self-contained fragments of code that can be called as often as needed from different places in your program. When a method is called, the caller places the parameters for the call in an agreed-upon place where the method can fetch them (for example, the system stack). The return address is also saved in a place accessible to the method (for example, the same system stack). When the method has finished, it returns control to the place in the program from which it was called. If the method returns a value, it places that value into an agreed-upon location where the caller can retrieve it (for example, a particular CPU register).

A method is always defined inside a class. When you define a method you need to give it a name, specify the types of its parameters, and assign them names so that you can refer to them in the method's code. You also specify the type of its return value:

```
public [or private] [static]
   returntype methodName(type1 paramName1, ..., typeN paramNameN)
```

This header is called the method's *signature*. *returntype* can be any primitive data type (such as `int`, `double`, `boolean`, `char`, etc.) or any type of object defined in Java or in your program (such as `String`, `Color`, `RollingDie`, `Fraction`, etc.). *returntype* can also be `void` (a reserved word) which means that this method performs some task but does not return any value. The parameters can be of any primitive type or any type of objects. Some methods have no parameters at all, only empty parentheses.

Common Java style for naming methods is to choose a name that sounds like a verb and to write it starting with a lowercase letter. If the name consists of several words, subsequent words are capitalized. If a method returns the value of a field, its name usually starts with `get...`, and if a method sets the value of a field, its name usually starts with `set...`, as in `getWidth()` or `setText(...)`. Following these conventions helps other programmers understand your code.

Even if a method's parameters have the same type, you still need to explicitly state the type for each parameter. For example, the following won't work:

```
    private int countToDegrees(int count, total)
                                        ^ Syntax error!
```

You need:

```
    private int countToDegrees(int count, int total)
```

Dave: I have defined the `add` and `multiply` methods in my `Fraction` class and also a `toString` method.

Claire: As far as I am concerned, your methods are black boxes to me. I don't really want to know how they do what they do.

Dave: You need to know how to call them. For example, one of my `add` methods takes one parameter of the type `Fraction` and returns a new `Fraction`, the sum of `this` and `other`:

```
// Returns the sum of this fraction and other
public Fraction add(Fraction other)
{
    ...
}
```

Claire: So I can write:

```
Fraction f1 = new Fraction(1, 2);
Fraction f2 = new Fraction(1, 3);
Fraction sum = f1.add(f2);
System.out.println(sum);
```

and see 5/6 displayed? By the way, how does `println` know to print 5/6, as opposed to [5, 6] or 0.833333333?

Dave: That's because I have defined the `toString` method in my `Fraction` class:

```
// Returns a string representation of this fraction
public String toString()
{
    return num + "/" + denom;
}
```

See the output string that I defined for a fraction: numerator, slash, denominator? My `toString` method overrides the default `toString`. Without it, `System.out.println(new Fraction(1, 3))` instead of 1/3 would print some garbage, something like `Fraction@126b249`.

When you call

```
System.out.println(obj);
```

it calls

```
System.out.println(obj.toString());
```

This version of overloaded `println` takes a parameter of the type `Object`, but due to polymorphism, the correct `toString` method is called automatically for any type of object passed to `println`.

Claire: Whoa, hold it! Overloaded? Polymorphism? I think I'm the one who is getting overloaded here! ⇐

Overloaded methods will be explained shortly, in Section 9.10. The `Object` class, class hierarchies, and polymorphism are discussed in Chapter 11.

After you specify the method's name, its return type, and its parameters with their types, you need to supply the code for your method, called its *body*. The body is placed within braces following the method's header. The code uses Java operators and control statements and can call other methods.

The names of parameters (such as `other` above) matter only inside the method's body. There they act pretty much as local variables. You cannot use these same names for local variables that you declare in that method.

9.6 Calling Methods and Accessing Fields

You have probably noticed from earlier code examples that the syntax for calling methods in Java is different in different situations. Sometimes a method name has a prefix that consists of an <u>object</u> name with a dot:

```
die1.roll();
result = game.processRoll(pts);
display.setText(str);
Fraction sum = f1.add(f2);
```

Sometimes the prefix is a <u>class</u> name with a dot:

```
y = Math.sqrt(x);
System.exit(1);
```

Sometimes there is no prefix at all:

```
degrees = countToDegrees(count1, total);
drawDots(g, x, y, getNumDots());
reduce();
```

To understand the difference we need to distinguish between *static* and *instance* methods. A static method is designated by the keyword `static` in its header. `static` is a Java reserved word. We will discuss static fields and methods in detail in Section 9.11. For now it is sufficient to understand how to call static methods.

A static method belongs to the class as a whole and doesn't deal with any instance variables. Such a method can be called by simply using the class's name and a dot as a prefix to the method's name, as in

```
x = Math.random();
ms = System.currentTimeMillis();
```

When we call a <u>non-static</u> (instance) method, we call it for a particular object:

```
obj.itsMethod(< parameters >);
```

> **In effect, the object for which the method is called becomes an implicit parameter passed to the call.**

This parameter is not in the list of regular parameters — it is specified by the object's name and a dot as a prefix to the method's name, as in

```
int total = die1.getNumDots() + die2.getNumDots();
int result = game.processRoll(total);
Fraction sum = f1.add(f2);
```

This syntax signifies the special status of the object whose method is called. While the method is running, the reference to this object becomes available to the method and all other methods of the same class under the special name `this`. `this` is a Java reserved word. `this` acts like an instance variable of sorts, and its value is set automatically when an instance method is called or a constructor is invoked.

When a constructor or an instance method calls another instance method <u>for the same object</u>, strictly speaking the latter should be called with the prefix `this`. Java made this prefix optional, and it is usually omitted.

<u>Dave</u>:   I could have written

    this.reduce();

  instead of

reduce();

  and some people do that all the time, but to me it's just a waste of keystrokes.
⇦

❖   ❖   ❖

Similar syntax rules apply to accessing <u>fields</u>. A non-static field of another object (of the same class) is accessed by adding the object's name and a dot as a prefix.

<u>Dave</u>:   For example, I wrote:

```
public Fraction multiply(Fraction other)
{
  int newNum = num * other.num;
  int newDenom = denom * other.denom;
  ...
}
```

⇦

An object's methods and constructors can refer to its own fields simply by their name. The prefix `this` is optional.

<u>Dave</u>:   I could've written:

```
public Fraction multiply(Fraction other)
{
  int newNum = this.num * other.num;
  int newDenom = this.denom * other.denom;
  ...
}
```

  More symmetrical, but, again, who wants to type extra stuff?

  Sometimes I use the prefix `this` to distinguish the names of a class's fields from the names of the parameters in methods or constructors. For example, in my code for the constructor —

```
public Fraction(int n, int d)
{
  ...
  num = n;
  denom = d;
}
```

I called the parameters n and d to avoid clashing with the field names num and denom. I could have written instead

```
public Fraction(int num, int denom)
{
  ...
  this.num = num;
  this.denom = denom;
}
```

Sometimes I find it easier to use this-dot than to think of good names for the parameters that are different from the names of the corresponding fields. Beware, though: if you misspell the parameter name in the method's header, the compiler won't complain. You can spend hours looking for a bug like this! ⇦

this is also used for passing "this" object (whose method is running) to another object's method or constructor as a parameter. For example,

```
clock = new Timer(delay, this);
```

invokes Timer's constructor with two parameters. The first parameter is the time interval between consecutive firings of the timer (in milliseconds); the second is an ActionListener object. this means that the same object that is creating a new Timer will serve as its "action listener": it will capture clock's events in its actionPerformed method.

9.7 Passing Parameters to Constructors and Methods

When a method is called or a constructor is invoked with a parameter of a primitive data type (int, double, etc.), the parameter can be any expression of the appropriate type: a literal or symbolic constant, a variable, or any expression that uses arithmetic operators, casts, and/or calls to other methods. For example,

```
game.processRoll(die1.getNumDots() + die2.getNumDots());
```

is equivalent to the sequence:

```
int dots1 = die1.getNumDots();
int dots2 = die2.getNumDots();
int total = dots1 + dots2;
game.processRoll(total);
```

The former form is preferable because it is shorter and just as readable. But when an expression gets too complicated, it is better to compute it in smaller steps.

Parameters of primitive data types are <u>always</u> passed "by value."

If a variable of a primitive type is passed to a constructor or method as a parameter, its value is <u>copied</u> into some location (for example, the system stack) that is accessible to the method.

Suppose you write a method to increment its parameter:

```
public static void increment(int n)
{
  n++;
}
```

You test it somewhere in your program —

```
int n = 0;
MyMath.increment(n);
System.out.println("n = " + n);
```

— but nothing happens: the value of n remains 0.

Claire: I know. I tried that when I first started learning Java. ⇐

The reason is that n in the method is not the same variable as n passed to increment as a parameter: it is a <u>copy</u> that has the same value (and happens to have the same name). You increment the copy, but the original remains unchanged.

Dave: In Pascal or C++, you can specify whether you want a parameter passed "by value" or "by reference." ⇐

These languages have special syntax that allows programmers to pass variables to functions "by reference." When you pass "by reference," a reference to (address of) the original variable is passed to the function and so there is a way to write a method similar to the one above that would work. But not in Java: <u>primitive types</u> are always passed to methods <u>by value</u>.

The situation is different when a parameter is an object of some class type (such as `String`, `RollingDie`, `Fraction`). When you pass an <u>object</u> to a method, <u>a copy of the reference</u> to the original object is passed. The method can reach and manipulate the data and methods of the original object through that reference. For example:

```
public void avoidCollision(RollingDie other)
{
  ...
  other.move();
}
```

Here `other` is a reference to another moving die that was passed to the method as a parameter. `other` holds the address <u>of the original</u>. Therefore `other.move()` will indeed move the other die.

Dave: In C++, you can pass a class-type variable by value: the whole object is copied and passed to a function. This is handy when the function needs to work with a temporary copy of the object and leave the original unchanged. ⇐

Not so in Java.

> **In Java, objects are always passed to methods and constructors as copies of references.**

❖   ❖   ❖

Claire: So, I take it, at any given time several variables can refer to the same object. Suppose I pass a reference to my object to someone's constructor or method, and it changes my object behind my back. This is unsafe!

Dave: That's why I made sure my `Fraction` objects are *immutable*. I provided no public methods that could change the instance variables of a `Fraction`. Once created, a `Fraction` object cannot change. You can pass your fraction safely to anyone and be sure they won't change it. Even my `add` method does not change either `this` fraction or `other`. Instead it creates a new one, equal to their sum, and returns a reference to it. ⇐

9.8 `return` Statement

A method that is not `void` returns something to the caller. The returned value is specified in the `return` statement in the method's body:

```
return <expression>;
```

What type of value is returned depends on the return type of the method. *expression* must be of the method's specified return type or something that can be readily converted into it.

If the return type is a primitive type (`int`, `double`, `boolean`, etc.), then the method returns a value of that type. The return expression in a `boolean` method can include a constant (`true` or `false`), a `boolean` variable, or a `boolean` expression. For example, you can write:

```java
public static boolean inRange(int x, int a, int b)
{
  return a <= x && x <= b;
}
```

This is more concise than

```java
public static boolean inRange(int x, int a, int b)
{
  if (a <= x && x <= b)
    return true;
  else
    return false;
}
```

<u>Dave</u>:   My `getValue` method returns the value of this fraction as a `double`:

```java
// Returns the value of this fraction as a double
public double getValue()
{
  return (double)num / (double)denom;
}
```

<u>Claire</u>: I can use the returned value in assignments and expressions. For example:

```
Fraction f = new Fraction(2, 3);
double x = f.getValue();    // x gets the value 0.6666...7
```

or

```
System.out.println(f.getValue());
```

❖   ❖   ❖

A method can also have a return type of some class. That means the method returns a <u>reference</u> to an object of that class.

Often such a method constructs and initializes a new object and sets its fields in a particular way and then returns a reference to the new object.

<u>Dave</u>:   My add and multiply do that:

```
// Returns the sum of this fraction and other
public Fraction add(Fraction other)
{
  int newNum = num * other.denom + denom * other.num;
  int newDenom = denom * other.denom;
  return new Fraction(newNum, newDenom);
}
```

Come to think of it, I could have made it shorter:

```
public Fraction add(Fraction other)
{
  return new Fraction(num * other.denom + denom * other.num,
                                    denom * other.denom);
}
```

<u>Claire</u>: I can assign the returned value to a variable or pass it to a method:

```
Fraction sum = f1.add(f2);
```

or

```
System.out.println(f1.add(f2));
```

Dave: You can even call its method right away:

```
double x = f1.add(f2).getValue();
        // first calls add, then calls getValue for the sum
```

⇐

We will encounter objects returned from methods again when we deal with `String` objects. For example, the `String` class has a method `toUpperCase` that returns a new string with all the letters converted to upper case. It also has a `trim` method that returns a new string with all whitespace characters removed from both ends. You can write, for example:

```
JTextField input = new JTextField();
...
String s = input.getText().trim().toUpperCase();
```

A `return` statement tells the method what value to return to the caller and immediately quits the method's code and passes control back to the caller.

A method can have several `return` statements, but all of them except one must be placed inside a conditional statement (or inside a case in a `switch`):

```
... returntype myMethod(...)
{
  ...
  if (...)
    return <expression1>;
  ...
  return <expression2>;
}
```

Otherwise a method will have some unreachable code that is never executed because it is positioned after an unconditional `return`.

A `void` method can also have a `return`, but without any value, just as a command to quit the method.

For example:

```
... void myMethod(...)
{
  ...
  if (...)
    return;
  ...
}
```

9.9 *Case Study and Lab:* Snack Bar

When Java was first conceived by James Gosling[gosling] at Sun Microsystems in the early 1990s, it was supposed to be a language for programming embedded microprocessors — chips that control coffee makers and washers and VCRs. As it turned out, that was not Java's destiny. The language might have been completely forgotten, but the advent of the Internet and the World Wide Web gave it another life.

In a tribute to Java's early history, let's implement a program that simulates a set of vending machines in an automatic snack bar. As you will see in this case study, Java is a very convenient tool for such a project. Our vending machines will be quite simple: each machine can sell only one product. The user "deposits" quarters, dimes, or nickels into a machine, then presses the red button and "receives" a soda or a snack and change. When one of the machines is empty, you can call "service." After a concession operator enters a password ("jinx"), all the machines are refilled with "merchandise" and emptied of "cash." Figure 9-3 shows a snapshot of this program. You can play with it by clicking on the `SnackBar.jar` file in `JM\Ch09\SnackBar`.

We begin, as usual, by identifying the classes involved in this project. One class, called `SnackBar`, is derived from `JFrame` and represents the program window. It constructs and displays a number of vending machines (in this case three) and handles service calls with a password login. The full source code for this class is in `JM\Ch09\SnackBar`.

The second class, called `VendingMachine`, represents a vending machine. `SnackBar`'s constructor creates three instances of this class — three machines. `VendingMachine` declares and creates the necessary display fields and buttons for a machine, handles events generated by these buttons, and displays the results of these events. This is where event-driven OOP is at its best: we can create three almost identical machines and let each of them process its own events automatically without any confusion. Several "customers" can "deposit coins" in random order into each of the three machines, and the Java run-time environment will sort out all the events correctly.

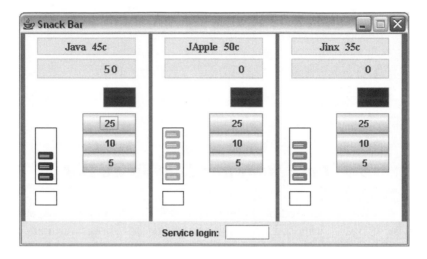

Figure 9-3. The *Snack Bar* program with three vending machines

Note that the `SnackBar` class actually knows very little about its vending machines: only how to construct them and that they need service or reloading once in a while (namely that `VendingMachine` has a constructor with three specific parameters and a `void` method `reload`). This is good OOP design: each object knows only what it really needs to know about other objects.

The complete `VendingMachine` class code is included in `JM\Ch09\SnackBar`. If you examine `VendingMachine`'s code, you will notice that a vending machine is really not the entire machine, but only its front panel, the GUI. One of the fields in this class is a `Vendor` object:

```
private Vendor vendor;
```

This object is created in `VendingMachine`'s constructor:

```
vendor = new Vendor(price, FULL_STOCK);
```

It is the machine's `vendor` that actually handles sales and keeps track of cash and stock (the remaining number of "snacks"). For example, when the user "deposits" 25 cents into a machine, the machine calls its `vendor`'s `addMoney` method:

```
vendor.addMoney(25);
```

If the user presses the red "sale" button, the machine calls its `vendor`'s `makeSale` and `getChange` methods:

```
trayFull = vendor.makeSale();
int change = vendor.getChange();
```

And when a machine needs to know whether there are any "snacks" left in the machine, it calls its vendor's `getStock` method:

```
if (vendor.getStock() > 0)
    . . .
```

As in our *Craps* program in Chapter 7 and for the same reasons, we have once again separated the GUI part from the number crunching. We try to define the `Vendor` class in rather general terms so we can reuse it in different situations: it can represent not only a mechanism of a vending machine, but a cash register, an online store, any kind of vendor. In fact, a `Vendor` is so general it doesn't even know what it sells, only the price of the items!

Figure 9-4 shows the objects involved in the *Snack Bar* program: a `SnackBar`, three `VendingMachines`, and three `Vendors`. The `SnackBar` object represents the main program window. It "knows" about the features of a vending machine and creates three of them, but it is not aware of "vendors" behind them. Each vending machine creates and utilizes its own vendor object. Even though all vendors have the same name, there is no confusion because each vending machine knows its own `vendor`.

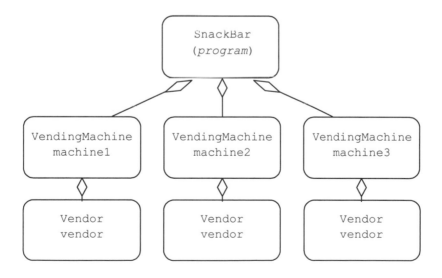

Figure 9-4. *Snack Bar* program's objects

As you have probably guessed, your job is to implement the `Vendor` class from the written specifications (Figure 9-5). Each `Vendor` object can sell only one kind of item at one specified price. The vendor operates by collecting payment from a buyer in several steps. `Vendor` has four fields, representing the available stock (the number of remaining items for sale), the price, the currently deposited amount, and the change due to the customer from the last sale. `Vendor`'s constructor sets the price and the initial stock and zeroes out the deposit and change fields.

```
/*
    This class implements a vendor that sells one kind of items.
    A vendor carries out sales transactions.
*/

public class Vendor
{
  < ... missing fields >

  //  Constructor
  //  Parameters:
  //     int price of a single item in cents
  //     int number of items to place in stock
  ... Vendor ...
  {
    < ... missing code >
  }

  //  Sets the quantity of items in stock.
  //  Parameters:
  //     int number of items to place in stock
  //  Return:
  //     None
  ... setStock ...
  {
    < ... missing code >
  }

  //  Returns the number of items currently in stock.
  //  Parameters:
  //     None
  //  Return:
  //     int number of items currently in stock
  ... getStock ...
  {
    < ... missing code >
  }
```

Figure 9-5 `Vendor.java` *Continued* ➔

```
//  Adds a specified amount (in cents) to the deposited amount.
//  Parameters:
//     int number of cents to add to the deposit
//  Return:
//     None
... addMoney ...
{
  < ... missing code >
}


//  Returns the currently deposited amount (in cents).
//  Parameters:
//     None
//  Return:
//     int number of cents in the current deposit
... getDeposit ...
{
  < ... missing code >
}


//  Implements a sale.  If there are items in stock and
//  the deposited amount is greater than or equal to
//  the single item price, then adjusts the stock
//  and calculates and sets change and returns true;
//  otherwise refunds the whole deposit (moves it into change)
//  and returns false.
//  Parameters:
//     None
//  Return:
//     boolean successful sale (true) or failure (false)
... makeSale ...
{
  < ... missing code >
}


//  Returns and zeroes out the amount of change (from the last
//  sale or refund).
//  Parameters:
//     None
//  Return:
//     int number of cents in the current change
... getChange ...
{
  < ... missing code >
}
}
```

Figure 9-5.   J_M\Ch09\SnackBar\Vendor.java

`Vendor`'s methods work as follows:

- The `addMoney` method adds a specified number of cents to the already deposited amount.

- The `makeSale` method is called when the buyer tries to complete the transaction. If the vendor is not out of stock and if the buyer has deposited enough money, then a sale takes place: the stock is decreased, the change is calculated, and `makeSale` returns true. Otherwise the sale fails: the stock remains unchanged, the whole deposit is returned to the buyer (by transferring it to the change amount), and `makeSale` returns false.

- The `getDeposit` accessor simply returns the value of the current deposit (not the money itself!) to the caller. A vending machine calls this method when it needs to display the deposited amount on its display panel.

- The `getChange` method completes the transaction: it returns the change due to the buyer after a sale and at the same time (well, almost at the same time) resets the change field to 0. You have to be a little careful here: save the return value in a temporary local variable before setting change to 0.

- The `getStock` accessor returns the current stock.

- The `setStock` method sets the new stock quantity.

Set up a project with the `SnackBar.java`, `VendingMachine.java`, and `Vendor.java` files from J_M\Ch09\SnackBar. Complete the `Vendor` class and test the program thoroughly.

9.10 Overloaded Methods

It is not surprising that methods in different classes may have exactly the same names. Since a method is always called for a particular object (or a particular class), there is no confusion. For example:

```
person.stop();    // calls stop in Walker class
t.stop();         // calls stop in Timer class

Fraction sum = f1.add(f2);
panel.add(button);
```

A more interesting fact is that several methods of <u>the same class</u> may also have the same name, as long as the number or the types of their parameters are different.

| Methods within the same class that have the same name but different numbers or types of parameters are called *overloaded* methods.

A method can have any number of overloaded versions as long as their parameter lists are different. For example, in

```
public class SomeClass
{
  ...
  public int fun(int a)
  {
    ...
  }

  public int fun(double b)
  {
    ...
  }

  public double fun(int a, double b)
  {
    ...
  }

  ...
}
```

`SomeClass` has three different methods, all called `fun`. The code may be completely different in each of these methods. Overloading allows you to use the same method name for tasks that are similar. For example, the same name `print` is used for the methods of the `System.out` object that display a `char`, an `int`, a `double`, a `String`, and an `Object`.

The compiler knows which one of the overloaded methods to call based on the types of the parameters passed to it. In the above example, if you call `fun(1)`, the first overloaded method will be called, because `1` is an integer, but if you call `fun(1.5)`, the second overloaded method will be called because `1.5` is a `double`. If you call `fun(1, .99)`, the third version, `fun(int, double)`, will be called.

If there is no exact match between the parameter types in a call and the available overloaded versions of a method, the compiler will make a reasonable effort to convert one or more parameters into something acceptable to one of the versions. For example, if you call `fun(1, 2)` the compiler will call `fun(1, 2.0)`. If an appropriate method is not found and a reasonable conversion is not possible, the compiler reports an error. For example, if `s` is a `String`, and you call `fun(s)`, the compiler reports something like "method `fun(String)` not defined in class

`SomeClass`." (The compiler also reports an error if there is no exact match for parameter types and more than one overloaded method can handle them.)

Note that the <u>names</u> of the formal parameters in the method definition do not distinguish overloaded methods. Only the <u>types</u> of the parameters matter. For example,

```
public int fun(int a, double b)
{
   ...
}
```

and

```
public int fun(int x, double y)
{
   ...
}
```

cannot be defined in the same class.

The return type alone cannot distinguish two methods either. For example,

```
public int fun(int a, double b)
{
   ...
}
```

and

```
public double fun(int a, double b)
{
   ...
}
```

cannot be defined in the same class.

> **When you are designing a class, be careful not to have too many overloaded versions of a method, because they may get confusing and cause bugs.**

Dave: I've defined two overloaded versions of the `add` method in my `Fraction` class: one takes another `Fraction` as a parameter, and the other takes an `int` as a parameter:

```
// Returns the sum of this fraction and other
public Fraction add(Fraction other)
{
  return new Fraction(num * other.denom + denom * other.num,
                                    denom * other.denom);
}



// Returns the sum of this fraction and m
public Fraction add(int m)
{
  return new Fraction(num + m * denom, denom);
}
```

Same for multiplication.

Claire: You mean I can write

```
Fraction f = new Fraction(1, 2);
Fraction f2 = new Fraction(1, 3);
Fraction sum1 = f.add(f2);
Fraction sum2 = f.add(3);
```

and the compiler will figure out which of your two `add` methods to call? That's very convenient. ⇦

All constructors in a class have the same name, so they are overloaded by definition.

9.11 Static Fields and Methods

In the previous chapters we said that an object's fields can be thought of as the "private memory" of the object. This is not the whole truth. A Java class may define two kinds of fields: non-static fields and *static* fields. Non-static fields are also called *instance variables*. They may have different values in different objects (instances of a class). Static fields are also called *class variables*. They are <u>shared</u> by all objects of the class. Static fields are declared with the keyword `static`.

When an object is created, a chunk of RAM is allocated to hold its <u>instance variables</u>. This is called *dynamic memory allocation*. But there is <u>only one</u> chunk of memory for the whole class that holds the values of static fields. Static fields are stored separately from all objects.

The word "static" may seem to imply that the values of static fields are constant. In fact it has nothing to do with constants. Static fields are called "static" because their memory is not dynamically allocated: memory for static fields is reserved even before any objects of the class have been created.

Why do we need static fields? Several reasons.

1. We might want to define a "universal" public constant. It makes sense to attribute it to the class as a whole, and not to waste memory space duplicating it in all objects. When we refer to such constants, we use the class name with a dot as a prefix, as opposed to a specific object's name. We have already seen many of these: `Color.BLUE`, `Math.PI`, and so on.

2. We might want to have all objects of the class share the same constants or settings. For example, in the `RollingDie` class, we have static fields that define the motion constants and the dimensions of the craps "table:"

```
private static final double slowdown = 0.97,
                            speedFactor = 0.04,
                            speedLimit = 2.0;

private static int tableLeft, tableRight, tableTop, tableBottom;
```

3. We may need to collect statistics or accumulate totals for all objects of the class that are in existence. Suppose, for example, we wanted to keep track of the total sales from <u>all</u> of the vending machines in the *Snack Bar* program. We need a common variable to which every vendor has access.

A class definition may also include *static methods*. Such methods do not access or manipulate any instance variables — they only work with static fields, or do not access any fields at all. Therefore, they are attributed to the class as a whole, not to individual instances. Static methods are also called *class methods*. They are declared with the keyword `static`.

There are two primary reasons for defining static methods:

1. A static method may provide a "public service" that has nothing to do with any particular object. For example, `Math.max(int a, int b)` returns the largest of the integers `a` and `b`. Or look at Dave's `gcf` method — it returns the GCF of two integers. Or `System`'s `exit` method that forces the program to quit.

2. A static method may work with static fields of the class. For example, it may be an accessor or a modifier for a static field.

Dave: While you were talking, I changed my `gcf` method in `Fraction` to make it
         `public` and `static`.

```
//  Returns the greatest common factor of two positive integers
public static int gcf(int n, int d)
```

Claire: That was my idea! But why is it static?

Dave: It does not need to deal with any fields at all — just calculates the GCF for
         two given numbers. If I didn't make it static, you'd have to create a
         `Fraction` object to call this method, even though the `gcf` method has
         nothing to do with any particular fraction (except that I call it from my
         `reduce` method). In fact, I could have placed it into another class or in a
         separate class. Too bad the folks at Sun didn't put a `gcf` method into their
         `Math` class.

Claire: You mean I can now write simply

```
int r = Fraction.gcf(a, b);
```

Dave: Yep. ⇦

> **`this` is undefined in static methods. A static method is not allowed to
> access or modify instance fields or to call instance methods (of the same
> class) without an object-dot prefix because such a call implies `this`-dot.**

Claire: I had this problem recently when I wrote

```
public class Test
{
  public void testConstructors()
  { ... }

  public void testArithmetic()
  { ... }

  public static void main(String[] args)
  {
    testConstructors();
    testArithmetic();
  }
}
```

I got

```
non-static method testConstructors() cannot be referenced from
a static context
non-static method testArithmetic() cannot be referenced from
a static context
```

I had to add `static` to the `testConstructors`'s and `testArithmetic`'s headers to make it work:

```
public static void testConstructors()
{ ... }

public static void testArithmetic()
{ ... }
```

Dave: That's because `main` is always static, so it can't call a non-static method without a reference to a particular object. You could've instead created one object of your `Test` class in `main` and then called that object's methods:

```
public class Test
{
  public void testConstructors()
  { ... }

  public void testArithmetic()
  { ... }

  public static void main(String[] args)
  {
    Test obj = new Test();
    obj.testConstructors();
    obj.testArithmetic();
  }
}
```

⇐

It is very common for `main` to create the first object in the program and then let it do the rest of the work.

Instance variables are initialized in constructors and used in instance (non-static) methods. Theoretically, a constructor is allowed to set static fields, too, but it doesn't make much sense to do that because normally you don't want to affect all class objects while constructing one of them.

Instance methods can access and modify both static and non-static fields and call both static and non-static methods.

Dave: Sure. My instance method `reduce`, for example, calls my static method `gcf`.

```
int q = gcf(Math.abs(num), denom);
```

I still call `gcf` without any dot prefix because it is in the same class. I could have written

```
int q = Fraction.gcf(Math.abs(num), denom);
```

but I am not a pedant.

Claire: I see that the `Math` class has another static method, `abs`. That must be for getting an absolute value of an integer. Are all `Math` methods static?

Dave: That's right. ⇐

Some classes have only static fields and methods and no public constructors. For example, the `Math` class doesn't have any non-static methods or fields, and `Math` objects are never created because all such objects would be identical! All `Math` methods — `sqrt`, `pow`, `random`, `abs`, `max`, `min`, `round`, `sin`, `cos`, etc. — are static. The `Math` class also defines the public static constants `PI` (for π) and `E` (for e, the base of the natural logarithm). But the `Math` class exists in name only: it is not really "a class of objects."

Claire: You mean I can't write

```
Math xyz = new Math();
```

?

Dave: Ha-ha. Try it. ⇐

Another example of such a class is `System`. It has a few static fields (such as `System.out`) and static methods, such as `exit`, which quits the application, and `currentTimeMillis`, which returns the current time in milliseconds, but you cannot create an object of the `System` class.

The `Math` and `System` examples are a little extreme — more typical classes have some instance variables and may also have some static fields. If a class has a mix of instance variables and *class variables* (static fields), it is also likely to have a mix of non-static methods and some static methods.

Now let us see how a static variable can be used to accumulate the total amount of sales for all `VendingMachine` objects in our *Snack Bar* program.

9.12 *Case Study:* Snack Bar Concluded

Suppose we want to modify our *Snack Bar* program so that it reports the total "day sales" from all of the machines. Suppose a "day" is the time from the start of the program to the first "service call" or between two service calls. How can we implement a mechanism to keep track of the total sales? Clearly each machine (or, more precisely, its vendor object) needs access to this mechanism.

One approach could be based on the following scenario:

1 We define a new class and create a special object, "bookkeeper," that will keep track of the total sales.

2. When we create a vendor, we pass a reference to the bookkeeper object to the vendor's constructor, and the vendor saves it in its instance variable `bookkeeper`.

3. The vendor reports each sale to `bookkeeper`, and `bookkeeper` adds it to the total.

4. At the time of a "service call," the `SnackBar` object gets the total from `bookkeeper`, and `bookkeeper` resets the total to zero.

This is doable, and it is elegant in a way. This is also a flexible solution: it allows different sets of vendors to have different bookkeepers, if necessary. However, it is a little too much work for a simple additional feature. (Besides, we are here to practice static fields and methods). So let us take a more practical approach.

1. Add a private static field `double totalSales` to the `Vendor` class. This class variable will hold the total amount of all sales (in dollars). Because `totalSales` is static, all `Vendor` objects share this field. Initially `totalSales` is set to zero by default. If you wish, for extra clarity add an explicit initialization to zero in the declaration of `totalSales`.

2. Add a public static method `getTotalSales` that returns the current value of `totalSales` and at the same time (well, almost at the same time) resets `totalSales` to zero.

3. Modify the `makeSale` method: if a sale is successful, add the amount of the sale to `totalSales`. (Don't forget to convert cents into dollars).

This way, each vendor updates the same `totalSales` field, so `totalSales` accumulates the total amount of sales from all vendors.

Meanwhile, we have modified the `SnackBar` class: we have added a call to Vendor's `getTotalSales` at the time of service:

```
double amt = Vendor.getTotalSales();
machine1.reload();
machine2.reload();
machine3.reload();
... etc.
```

Since the `getTotalSales` method is static in `Vendor`, we call it for the `Vendor` class as a whole and do not need access to any particular `Vendor` object. Still, we have inadvertently made the `SnackBar` class dependent on `Vendor` because `SnackBar`'s code now mentions `Vendor`. Perhaps a cleaner solution would be to add a static method `getTotalSales` to the `VendingMachine` class and call that method from `SnackBar`. `VendingMachine`'s `getTotalSales` in turn would call `Vendor`'s `getTotalSales`. That way we would keep `SnackBar` completely isolated from `Vendor`, reducing coupling.

9.13 Summary

Public fields, constructors, and methods can be referred to directly in the code of any other class. *Private* fields and methods are directly accessible only in the code of the same class. If necessary, the programmer provides public accessor "get" methods that return the values of private fields and/or modifier "set" methods that update private fields. In OOP, all instance variables are usually declared private. The only exception is public static constants.

Constructors are short procedures for creating objects of a class. A constructor always has the same name as the class. Constructors may take parameters of specified types. If a class has several constructors, they are by definition overloaded and must take different numbers and/or types of parameters. Constructors do not return a value of any type and should not have a return type, not even `void`. A constructor initializes instance variables and may perform additional validation to make sure that the fields are set to reasonable values.

Constructors are invoked by using the `new` operator:

```
SomeClass someVar = new SomeClass(<parameters>);
```

The parameters passed to `new` must match the number, types, and order of parameters expected by one of the constructors. The `new` operator returns a reference to the newly created object.

Methods are always defined within a class. A method can take a number of parameters of specific types (or no parameters at all) and return a value of a specified type. The syntax for defining a method is:

```
public [or private] [static]
   returntype methodName(type1 paramName1, ..., typeN paramNameN)
   {
     < method body (code) >
   }
```

The parameters and the return value can be of any primitive type (`int`, `double`, `boolean`, etc.) or any type of objects defined in the program. The return type can be `void`, which indicates that a method does not return any value.

Programmers often provide a `public String toString()` method for their classes. `toString` returns a reasonable representation of an object as a `String`. `toString` is called when the object is passed to `print` or `println` or concatenated with a string.

Methods and fields of an object are accessed using "dot" notation. Object `obj`'s `doSomething` method can be called as `obj.doSomething(<parameters>)`. However, an object can call its own methods without any prefix, using just `doSomethingElse(<parameters>)`. The same applies to fields.

All parameters of primitive data types are always passed to methods and constructors *by value*, which means a method or a constructor works with <u>copies</u> of the variables passed to it and cannot change the originals. Objects of class types, on the other hand, are always passed as <u>copies of references</u>. A method can change the original object through the supplied reference. *Immutable objects* have no modifier methods and, once created, can never change.

A method specifies its return value using the `return` statement. `return` tells the method what value to return to the caller. When a `return` statement is executed, the program immediately quits the method's code and returns control to the caller. A method can have several `return`s, but all of them must return a value or expression of the specified type, and all but one must be inside a conditional statement (or in a switch). All primitive types are returned by value, while objects (class types) are returned as references. A `void` method can also have a `return`, but without any value, just as a command to quit the method.

Several methods of the same class can have the same name as long as they differ in the numbers and/or types of their parameters. Such methods are called *overloaded* methods. Parameters passed to a method must match the number, types, and order of parameters in the method definition (or in one of the overloaded methods).

In addition to instance variables (non-static fields), a class definition may include *static fields* that are shared by all objects of the class. Likewise, a class may have static (class) methods that work for the class as a whole and do not touch any instance variables. Static fields are useful for sharing global settings among the objects of the class or for collecting statistics from all active objects of the class. Static methods cannot access non-static fields or call non-static methods. Static methods are called using the class's name as opposed to the individual object:

```
SomeClass.doSomething(<parameters>);
```

Exercises

Sections 9.1-9.8

1.   Write a header line for a public method `replace` that takes two parameters, a `String` and a `char`, and returns another `String`. ✓

2.   If a class `Complex` has two constructors, `Complex(double a)` and `Complex(double a, double b)`, which of the following statements are valid ways to construct a `Complex` object?

   (a)   `Complex z = new Complex();` _____ ✓
   (b)   `Complex z = new Complex(0);` _____ ✓
   (c)   `Complex z = new Complex(1, 2);` _____
   (d)   `Complex z = new Complex(0.0);` _____
   (e)   `Complex z = new Complex(1.0, 2);` _____
   (f)   `Complex z = new Complex(1.0, 2.0);` _____

3.   (MC) Which of the following constructors of a class `Date` are in conflict?

    I.   `Date(int month, int day, int year)`
   II. `Date(int julianDay)`
  III. `Date(int day, String month, int year)`
  IV. `Date(int day, int month, int year)`

    A.   I and II
    B.   II, III, and IV
    C.   I and IV
    D.   I, III, and IV
    E.   There is no conflict — all four can coexist

4.   Find out by looking it up in the Java API specifications whether the `String` and `Color` classes have copy constructors. ✓

5.   Java's class `Color` has a constructor that takes three integers as parameters: the red, green, and blue components of the color. A class `Balloon` has two fields: `double radius` and `Color color`. Write a constructor for the `Balloon` class that takes no parameters and sets the balloon's radius to 10 and its color to "sky blue" (with RGB values 135, 206, and 250).

6.   Add `subtract` and `divide` methods to the `Fraction` class and test them. If the parameter for the `divide` method is a zero fraction, `divide` should throw an `IllegalArgumentException`.

7.■   The program *Temperature* (`JM\Ch09\Exercises\Temperature.java`) converts degrees Celsius to Fahrenheit and vice-versa using the `FCConverter` class. Examine how this class is used in the `actionPerformed` method in the `Temperature` class. Now write and test the `FCConverter` class. ⸨ Hint: Recall that 0°C is 32°F; one degree Celsius is 5/9 degree Fahrenheit. For example, 68°F is 5/9·(68 – 32) = 20°C ⸩

8.■   Add an integer parameter `size` to `RollingDie`'s constructor (see Section 7.9) and set `dieSize` to `size` in the constructor. Change the `avoidCollision` method to compare the horizontal and vertical distances between the centers of `this` and `other` dice to the arithmetic mean of their sizes instead of `dieSize`. Change the `CrapsTable` class to roll two dice of different sizes in the program.

9.   (a)   A class `Point` has private fields `double x` and `double y`. Write a copy constructor for this class.

      (b)   A class `Disk` has private fields `Point center` and `double radius`. Write a copy constructor for this class. ✓

10.   (a)   Write a class `Rectangle` that represents a rectangle with integer width and height. Include a constructor that builds a rectangle with a given width and height and another constructor (with one parameter) that builds a rectangle that is actually a square of a given size. Make sure these constructors check that the width and height are positive. Add a constructor that takes no parameters and builds a square of size 1.

      (b)   Add a `boolean` method `isSquare` that returns `true` if and only if the rectangle is a square. Add a method `quadratize` that converts this rectangle into a square with approximately the same area — the closest possible for a square with an integer side.

      (c)   Test all your constructors and methods in a simple console application. Define several rectangles, check which ones among them are squares, and print appropriate messages. "Quadratize" one of the rectangles, verify that it becomes a square, and print an appropriate message.

11.   Examine the Java documentation and tell which of the following library classes define immutable objects:

              java.lang.Integer _____
              java.awt.Color _____
              java.awt.Point _____
              java.awt.Rectangle _____

12.■ A Java class can be declared `final`, which means that you cannot derive classes from it. For example, `Integer` and `String` are `final` classes. Why? ✓

13.   The class `Time` represents the time of day in hours and minutes using the "European" format (for example, 7:30 p.m. is 19:30, midnight is 00:00):

```
public class Time
{
  private int hours;
  private int mins;
  < ... etc. >
}
```

(a)   Write a constructor `Time(int h, int m)` that checks that its parameters are valid and sets `hours` and `mins` appropriately. If the parameters are invalid, the constructor should throw an exception.

(b)   Write a private method `toMins` that returns the time in minutes since the beginning of the day for this `Time` object.

(c)   Write a public `boolean` method `lessThan(Time t)` that returns `true` if this time is earlier than t and `false` otherwise.

(d)▪   Write a method `elapsedSince(Time t)` that returns the number of minutes elapsed from t to this time. Assume that t ≤ *this time* < t+24h. For example, if t is 22:45 and this time is 8:30, the method assumes that t is on the previous day and returns 585 (minutes). ⸜ Hint: use `toMins`. ⸝

(e)   Supply a reasonable `toString` method.

(f)   Test your `Time` class using the provided `TestTime` console application class (JM\Ch09\Exercises\TestTime.java).

14.   Write a class `Coins` with one constructor that takes a number of cents as a parameter. Supply four public methods, `getQuarters`, `getNickels`, `getDimes`, and `getPennies`, that return the number of corresponding coins that add up to the amount (in the optimal representation with the smallest possible number of coins). Make sure `Coins` objects are immutable (that is, none of the class's methods changes any fields). ⸘ Hint: It is easier to do all the work in the constructor and save the four coin counts in fields, making the four methods simple accessor methods. ⸘

  (a)   Test your class in a small console application that prompts the user for the change amount in cents and displays the number of quarters, dimes, nickels, and pennies.

  (b)■   Integrate your class into the *Snack Bar* program, so that the program reports the amount of change received by the customer in specific coin denominations (for example, `"Change 65c = 2q + 1d + 1n"`). ⸘ Hint: modify the statements in the `actionPerformed` method of the `VendingMachine` class after `vendor.getChange` is called. ⸘

Sections 9.9-9.13

15.   Will the class below compile? If not, suggest a way to fix it. ✓

```
public class Pair
{
  private double first, second;

  public Pair(double a, double b)
  {
    first = a;
    second = b;
  }

  public void swap()
  {
    double temp = first; first = second; second = temp;
  }

  public Pair swap()
  {
    return new Pair(second, first);
  }
}
```

16.   Figure out how to use the `Vendor` class from the *Snack Bar* program (without making any changes to it) for adding several integers. Write a console application that prompts the user to enter integers and adds the entered positive numbers separately and negative numbers separately. When the user enters a zero, the program displays both sums and exits. The + and − operators are not allowed in the program (except + for concatenating strings). Use `Scanner`'s `nextInt` method for entering numbers.

17.■   (a)   Implement a class `Complex` (which represents a complex number $a + b·i$) with two fields of the type `double` and two constructors described in Question 2. `Complex(a)` should make the same complex number as `Complex(a, 0.0)`.

(b)   Add a method `abs` to your class that returns $\sqrt{a^2 + b^2}$ for a complex number constructed as `Complex(a, b)`.

(c)   Recall that if $a + b·i$ and $c + d·i$ are two complex numbers, their sum is defined as $(a + c) + (b + d)·i$. Write the `Complex` class's `add` method, which builds and returns the sum of this number and `other`:

```
public Complex add(Complex other)
{
  < ... missing statements >
}
```

(d)   Add a `toString` method to your `Complex` class that returns a string representation of the number in the form *a+bi*.

(e)   Test your `abs`, `add`, and `toString` methods in a console application.

(f)   Find the rule for multiplying two complex numbers. ⦃ Hint: you can derive this rule yourself if you know that $i·i = -1$. ⦄ Implement and test a method `multiply` for multiplying this complex number by another complex number. As with the `add` method, the `multiply` method should not change this object; it should build and return a new complex number, the product. Can you pass a `double` rather than a `Complex` to this method as a parameter? Add an overloaded version of `add` that would allow you to do that.

18.   Find and fix a syntax error in the following program:

```
public class Puzzle
{
  private String message = "Hello, World";

  public void hello()
  {
    System.out.println(message);
  }

  public static void main(String[] args)
  {
    hello();
  }
}
```
✓

19.   Rewrite the `FCConverter` class from Question 6, eliminating the fields and all constructors and providing two static methods:

```
public static double cToF(double degrees)
public static double fToC(double degrees)
```

Adjust the `Temperature` class accordingly and retest the program.

20.■   Some of the Java library classes provide a static method `valueOf`. The `valueOf` method in a class usually converts its parameter into an object of that class and returns that object. For example, `String.valueOf(int x)` returns a string representation of x (the same as `"" + x`).

Add a static method `valueOf(double x)` to the `Fraction` class. This method should return a `Fraction` whose value is approximately equal to x. Define a public static symbolic constant `DFLT_DENOM` (for example, set to 10000) and use it as the denominator of the new fraction. Calculate its numerator as x * `DFLT_DENOM`, rounded to the nearest integer. Call `Math.round` to round the numerator. ⟨ Hint: `Math.round` returns a `long`; you need to cast it to an `int`. ⟩

21.✦ (a) Write a class `SoccerTeam` with fields that hold the number of wins, losses, and ties for this team in the current tournament.

Write a method

```
public void played(SoccerTeam other, int myScore,
                   int otherScore)
```

that compares the number of goals scored in a game by `this` team and `other` team and increments the appropriate fields (wins, losses, ties) for <u>both</u> teams.

(b) Write a method that returns this team's current number of points (each win is two points, each tie is one point). Write a `reset` method that zeroes out this team's wins, losses, and ties.

(c) Add fields to keep track of the total number of games played and the total number of goals scored by all teams in a tournament, combined. Modify the `played` method from Part (a) to update these fields. Add static accessor methods for these two fields and a static `startTournament` method to zero them out.

(d) Write a program that defines three teams, makes them "play" a few games with each other, and then reports each team's points as well as the total number of games played and the total number of goals scored by all teams in the tournament. The program should then repeat this for another tournament.

22.✦ Get rid of the static fields and methods in Part (c) of the previous question; instead, use an object of a separate class `TournamentOfficial` to keep track of the total number of games and the total number of goals scored in a tournament. Pass a reference to `official` to the `SoccerTeam` constructor and save it in an instance variable.

"Chapter 10"

Strings

10.1   Prologue

In Java, a string of characters is represented by an object of the `String` type. `String` objects are treated pretty much like any other type of objects: they have constructors and methods, and they can be passed to other methods (always as references) or returned from methods. But, they are different in two respects: the Java compiler knows how to deal with *literal string*s (represented by text in double quotes), and the + and += operators can be used to concatenate a string with another string, a number, or an object.

In this chapter we will cover some string properties and methods that help us use strings in our programs. In particular, we will discuss:

- `String` constructors

- The immutability property

- Commonly used `String` methods

- How to format numbers into strings and extract numbers from strings

- A few methods of the `Character` class that identify digits and letters

10.2   Literal Strings

Literal strings are written as text in double quotes. The text may contain escape characters (see Section 6.5). Recall that the backslash character '\' is used as the "escape" character: inside a literal string \n stands for "newline," \' represents a single quote, \" represents a double quote, and \\ represents a backslash. For example:

```
String hi = "T\'s up\n";
String pathName = "C:\\Ch10\\funny.txt";
                                // meaning C:\Ch10\funny.txt
```

A literal string can be empty, too, if there is nothing between the quotes.

```
String s = "";  // empty string
```

Literal strings act as `String` objects, but they do not have to be created — they are "just there" when you need them. The compiler basically treats a literal string as a reference to a `String` object with the specified value that is stored somewhere in memory. If you want, you can actually call that object's methods (for example, `"Internet".length()` returns 8). A declaration

```
String city = "Boston";
```

sets the reference `city` to a `String` object `"Boston"`. Note that `Boston` here is not the <u>name</u> of the variable (its name is `city`) but its <u>value</u>.

10.3 `String` Constructors and Immutability

The `String` class has nine constructors, but it is less common to use constructors for strings than for other types of objects. Instead, we can initialize `String` variables either to literal strings or to strings returned from `String`'s methods.

One of the constructors, `String()`, takes no parameters and builds an empty string; rather than invoking this constructor with the `new` operator, we can simply write:

```
String str = "";  // str is initialized to an empty string
```

Another constructor is a copy constructor `String(String s)`, which builds a copy of a string `s`. But in most cases we do not need to make copies of strings because, as we'll explain shortly, strings, once created, never change; so instead of copying a string we can just copy a reference. For example:

```
String str = "Foo Fighters";
```

This is not exactly the same as

```
String str = new String("Foo Fighters");
```

but, as far as your program is concerned, these two declarations of `str` act identically.

The other seven constructors create strings from character and byte arrays. They are potentially useful, but not before we learn about arrays (Chapter 12).

> **There is a big difference between an empty string and an uninitialized `String` reference.**

Empty strings are initialized to "" or created with the no-args constructor, as in

```
String s1 = "";           // s1 is set to an empty string
String s2 = new String(); // s2 is set to an empty string
```

A field of the `String` type is set to `null` by default:

```
private String s3;    // instance variable s3 is set to null
```

You can call methods for an empty string, and they will return the appropriate values. For example, `s1.length()` returns 0, and `s2.equals("")` returns `true`. But if a method is called for a reference that is equal to `null`, the program throws a `NullPointerException` and quits.

Once a string is constructed, it cannot be changed! If you look carefully at `String`'s methods, summarized in Figure 10-3, you will notice that none of these methods changes the content of a string.

> **A string is an *immutable* object: none of its methods can change the content of a `String` object.**

For example, you can get the value of a character at a given position in the string using the `charAt` method. But there is no method to <u>set or replace</u> one character in a string. If you want to change, say, the first character of a string from upper to lower case, you have to build a whole new string with a different first character. For example:

```
String bandName = "Foo Fighters";
char c = bandName.charAt(0);
bandName = Character.toLowerCase(c) + bandName.substring(1);
    // bandName now refers to a new string
    //   with the value "foo Fighters"
```

This code changes the <u>reference</u> — `bandName` now refers to your new string with the value "`foo Fighters`" (Figure 10-1).

The old string is thrown away (unless some other variable refers to it). Java's automatic garbage collector releases the memory from the old string and returns it to the free memory pool. This is a little wasteful — like pouring your coffee into a new mug and throwing away the old mug each time you add a spoonful of sugar or take a sip.

```
String bandName = "Foo Fighters";
char c = bandName.charAt(0);
bandName = Character.toLower(c) + bandName.substring(1);
```

```
                        ┌──────────────┐        ┌────────────────────┐
                        │              │ ·-·--▶ │  "Foo Fighters"    │
                        │   bandName   │◀·─·╟    └────────────────────┘
                        │              │         ┌────────────────────┐
                        └──────────────┘────────▶│  "foo Fighters"    │
                                                 └────────────────────┘
```

Figure 10-1. A new value assigned to a String variable

However, the immutability of strings makes it easier to avoid bugs. It allows us to have two String variables refer to the same string (Figure 10-2-a) without the danger of changing the string contents through one variable without the knowledge of the other. In some cases it also helps avoid copying strings unnecessarily. Instead of creating several copies of the same string —

```
String s2 = new String(s1); // s2 refers to a new copy of s1
```

as in Figure 10-2-b — you can use

```
String s2 = s1;   // s2 refers to the same string as s1
```

On the other hand, if you build a new string for every little change, a program that frequently changes long strings, represented by String objects, may become slow.

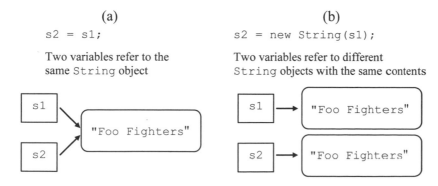

(a)	(b)
s2 = s1;	s2 = new String(s1);
Two variables refer to the same String object	Two variables refer to different String objects with the same contents

Figure 10-2. Assigning references vs. copying strings

Fortunately Java provides another class for representing character strings, called `StringBuffer`. `StringBuffer` objects are not immutable: they have the `setCharAt` method and other methods that change their contents. `String`s may be easier to understand, and they are considered safer in student projects. However, with the `StringBuffer` class we can easily change one letter in a string without moving the other characters around. For example:

```
StringBuffer bandName = new StringBuffer("Foo Fighters");
char c = bandName.charAt(0);
bandName.setCharAt(0, Character.toLowerCase(c));
  // bandName still refers to the same object, but its first
  //   character is now 'f';
```

If some text applications run rather slowly on your fast computer, it may be because the programmer was too lazy to use (or simply never learned about) the `StringBuffer` class. We have summarized `StringBuffer` constructors and methods in Section 10.9. Make sure you've read it before writing commercial applications!

10.4 `String` Methods

The more frequently used `String` methods are summarized in Figure 10-3. There are methods for returning the string's length, for getting the character at a specified position, for building substrings, for finding a specified character or substring in a string, for comparing strings alphabetically, and for converting strings to upper and lower case.

length **and** charAt

The `length` method returns the number of characters in the string. For example:

```
String s = "Internet";
int len = s.length();  // len gets the value 8
```

The `charAt` method returns the character at the specified position.

Character positions in strings are counted starting from 0.

```
int n       = s.length();
char ch     = s.charAt(pos);
String s2 = s.substring(fromPos);
String s2 = s.substring(fromPos, toPos);
String s2 = s.concat(str);
```

```
int result      = s.compareTo(s2);
int result      = s.compareToIgnoreCase(s2);
boolean match = s.equals(s2);
boolean match = s.equalsIgnoreCase(s2);
```

```
int k = s.indexOf(ch);
int k = s.indexOf(ch, fromPos);
int k = s.indexOf(str);
int k = s.indexOf(str, fromPos);
int k = s.lastIndexOf(ch);
int k = s.lastIndexOf(ch, fromPos);
int k = s.lastIndexOf(str);
int k = s.lastIndexOf(str, fromPos);
```

```
String s2 = s.trim();
String s2 = s.replace(oldChar, newChar);
String s2 = s.toUpperCase();
String s2 = s.toLowerCase();
```

Figure 10-3. Commonly used String methods

This convention goes back to C, where elements of arrays are counted from 0. So the first character of a string is at position (or index) 0, and the last one is at position `s.length()-1`. For example:

```
String s = "Internet";
char c1 = s.charAt(0);      // c1 gets the value 'I'
char c2 = s.charAt(7);      // c2 gets the value 't'
```

If you call `charAt(pos)` with `pos` less than 0 or `pos` greater than or equal to the string length, the method will throw a `StringIndexOutOfBoundsException`.

> **Always make sure that when you refer to the positions of characters in strings, they fall in the range from 0 to string length − 1.**

Substrings

The `String` class has two (overloaded) `substring` methods. The first one, `substring(fromPos)`, returns the tail of the string starting from `fromPos`. For example:

```
String s = "Internet";
String s2 = s.substring(5);  // s2 gets the value "net"
```

The second one, `substring(fromPos, toPos)` returns the segment of the string from `fromPos` to `toPos-1`. For example:

```
String s = "Internet";
String s2 = s.substring(0, 5);  // s2 gets the value "Inter"
String s3 = s.substring(2, 6);  // s3 gets the value "tern"
```

> **Note: the second parameter is the position of the character following the substring, and that character is <u>not</u> included into the returned substring. The length of the returned substring is always `toPos - fromPos`.**

Concatenation

The `concat` method concatenates strings; it works exactly the same way as the string version of the + operator. For example:

```
String s1 = "Sun";
String s2 = "shine";
String s3 = s1.concat(s2);  // s3 gets the value "Sunshine"
String s4 = s1 + s2;        // s4 gets the value "Sunshine"
```

The += operator concatenates the operand on the right to the string on the left. For example:

```
String s = "2*2 ";
s += "= 4";  // s gets the value "2*2 = 4"
```

It may appear at first that the += operator violates the immutability of strings. This is not so. The += first forms a new string concatenating the right-hand operand to the original s. Then it changes the reference s to point to the new string. The original string is left alone if some other variable refers to it, or thrown away. So `s += s2` may be as inefficient as `s = s + s2`.

As we said in Section 6.9, you can also concatenate characters and numbers to strings using the `+` and `+=` operators, as long as the compiler can figure out that you are working with strings, not numbers. For example:

```
String s = "Year: ";
s += 1776;    // s gets the value "Year: 1776";
```

But if you write

```
String s = "Year:";
s += ' ' + 1776;   // space in single quotes
```

it won't work as expected because neither `' '` nor `1776` is a `String`. Instead of concatenating them it will first add 1776 to the Unicode code for a space (32) and then append the sum to `s`. So `s` would get the value `"Year:1808"`. On the other hand,

```
String s = "Year:";
s += " " + 1776;        // space in double quotes
```

does work, because the result of the intermediate operation is a `String`.

Finding characters and substrings

The `indexOf(char c)` method returns the position of the first occurrence of the character `c` in the string. Recall that indices are counted from 0. If `c` is not found in the string, `indexOf` returns −1. For example:

```
String s = "Internet";
int pos1 = s.indexOf('e');  // pos1 gets the value 3
int pos2 = s.indexOf('x');  // pos2 gets the value -1
```

You can also start searching from a position other than the beginning of the string by using another (overloaded) version of `indexOf`. It has a second parameter, the position from which to start searching. For example:

```
String s = "Internet";
int pos = s.indexOf('e', 4);  // pos gets the value 6
```

You can search backward starting from the end of the string or from any other specified position using one of the two `lastIndexOf` methods for characters. For example:

```
String s = "Internet";
int pos1 = s.lastIndexOf('e');        // pos1 gets the value 6
int pos2 = s.lastIndexOf('e', 4);  // pos2 gets the value 3
int pos3 = s.lastIndexOf('e', 2);  // pos3 gets the value -1
```

`String` has four similar methods that search for a specified <u>substring</u> rather than a single character. For example:

```
String s = "Internet", s2 = "net";
int pos1 = s.indexOf("e");              // pos1 gets the value 3
int pos2 = s.indexOf("net");           // pos2 gets the value 5
int pos3 = s.indexOf(s2, 6);           // pos3 gets the value -1
int pos4 = s.lastIndexOf(s2);          // pos4 gets the value 5
int pos5 = s.lastIndexOf("net", 6);  // pos5 gets the value 5
```

<u>Comparisons</u>

You cannot use relational operators (==, !=, <, >, <=, >=) to compare strings.

Recall that relational operators `==` and `!=` when applied to objects compare the objects' <u>references</u> (that is, their addresses), <u>not their values</u>.   Strings are no exception.   The `String` class provides the `equals`, `equalsIgnoreCase`, and `compareTo` methods for comparing strings. `equals` and `equalsIgnoreCase` are `boolean` methods; they return `true` if the strings have the same length and the same characters (case-sensitive or case-blind, respectively), `false` otherwise.   For example:

```
String s = "OK!";
boolean same1 = s.equals("Ok!"); ·        // same1 is set to false
boolean same2 = s.equals("OK");           // same2 is set to false
boolean same3 = s.equalsIgnoreCase("Ok!"); // same3 is set to true
```

Occasionally the string in the comparison may not have been created yet. If you call its `equals` method (or any other method) you will get a `NullPointerException`. For example:

```
private String name;            // name is an instance variable
  ...
  boolean same = name.equals("Sunshine");
    // NullPointerException if name has not been initialized
```

To avoid errors of this kind you can write

```
boolean same = (name != null && name.equals("Sunshine"));
```

The above statement always works due to short-circuit evaluation (see Section 7.7). However, real Java pros may write

```
boolean same = "Sunshine".equals(name);
```

This always works, whether `name` is initialized or `null`, because you are not calling methods of an uninitialized object. The same applies to the `equalsIgnoreCase` method.

The `compareTo` method returns an integer that describes the result of a comparison. `s1.compareTo(s2)` returns a negative integer if `s1` lexicographically precedes `s2`, `0` if they are equal, and a positive integer if `s1` comes later than `s2`. (To remember the meaning of `compareTo`, you can mentally replace "compareTo" with a minus sign.) The comparison starts at the first character and proceeds until different characters are encountered in corresponding positions or until one of the strings ends. In the former case, `compareTo` returns the difference of the Unicode codes of the characters, so the string with the first "smaller" character (that is, the one with the smaller Unicode code) is deemed smaller; in the latter case `compareTo` returns the difference in lengths, so the shorter string is deemed smaller. This is called "lexicographic ordering," but it is not exactly the same as used in a dictionary because `compareTo` is case-sensitive, and uppercase letters in Unicode come <u>before</u> lowercase letters. For example:

```
String s = "ABC";
int result1 = s.compareTo("abc");
        // result1 is set to a negative number:
        //   "ABC" is "smaller" than "abc"

int result2 = s.compareTo("ABCD");
        // result2 is set to a negative number:
        //   "ABC" is "smaller" than "ABCD"
```

Naturally, there is also a `compareToIgnoreCase` method.

Conversions

Other useful `String` method calls include:

```
String s2 = s1.toUpperCase();
        // s2 is set to a string made up of the characters
        // in s1 with all letters converted to the upper case

String s2 = s1.toLowerCase();
        // Same for lower case

String s2 = s1.replace(c1, c2);
        // s2 is set to a string that has the same
        // characters as s1, except all occurrences of
        // c1 are replaced with c2.

String s2 = s1.trim();
        // s2 is set to the same string as s1, but with
        // the "whitespace" characters (spaces, tabs,
        // and newline characters) trimmed from the
        // beginning and end of the string.
```

For example:

```
String s1 = " <u>String Methods</u>  ";

String s2 = s1.trim();   // s2 becomes "<u>String Methods</u>"
                         // s1 remains " <u>String Methods</u>  "

String s3 = s2.toUpperCase();
                         // s3 becomes "<U>STRING METHODS</U>"
                         // s2 remains "<u>String Methods</u>"

String s4 = s3.replace('U', 'B')
                         // s4 becomes "<B>STRING METHODS</B>"
                         // s3 remains "<U>STRING METHODS</U>"
```

> **None of these methods (nor any other `String` methods) change the `String` object for which they are called. Instead, they build and return a new string.**

This is a potential source of tricky bugs. The names of these methods might imply that they change the string, and it is easy to call them but forget to put the result anywhere. For example:

```
String s1 = " <code>  ";
s1.trim();   // A useless call: s1 remains unchanged!
             // You probably meant s1 = s1.trim();
```

10.5 Formatting Numbers into Strings

As we discussed in Section 6.9, the easiest way to convert a number into a string is to concatenate that number with a string. For example:

```
int n = -123;
String s = "" + n; // s gets the value "-123"
s = "n = " + n;    // s gets the value "n = -123"
double x = -1.23;
s = "" + x;        // s gets the value "-1.23"
```

Java offers two other ways to convert an `int` into a string.

The first way is to use the static method `toString(int n)` of the `Integer` class:

```
int n = -123;
String s = Integer.toString(n);  // s gets the value "-123";
```

The `Integer` class belongs to the `java.lang` package, which is automatically imported into all programs. It is called a *wrapper class* because it "wraps" around a primitive data type `int`: you can take an `int` value and construct an `Integer` object from it. "Wrapping" allows you to convert a value of a primitive type into an object. For example, you might want to hold integer values in a list represented by the Java library class `ArrayList` (see Chapter 12), and `ArrayList` only works with objects. `java.lang` also has the `Double` wrapper class for `doubles` and the `Character` wrapper class for `chars`. `Integer` has a method `intValue`, which returns the "wrapped" `int` value, and a method `toString` that returns a string representation of this `Integer` object. For example,

```
Integer obj1 = new Integer(3);
Integer obj2 = new Integer(5);
Integer sum = new Integer(obj1.intValue() + obj2.intValue());
System.out.println(sum);
```

displays 8. Similarly, the `Double` class has a method `doubleValue` and the `Character` class has a method `charValue`.

For now, it is important to know that the `Integer`, `Double`, and `Character` classes offer several "public service" <u>static</u> methods. An overloaded version of `toString`, which takes one parameter, is one of them.

The second way is to use the static method `valueOf` of the `String` class. For example:

```
int n = -123;
String s = String.valueOf(n);     // s gets the value "-123";
```

Similar methods work for `double` values (using the `Double` wrapper class). For example:

```
double x = 1.5;
String s1 = Double.toString(x);   // s1 gets the value "1.5";
String s2 = String.valueOf(x);    // s2 gets the value "1.5";
```

For `doubles`, though, the number of digits in the resulting string may vary depending on the value, and a `double` may even be displayed in scientific notation.

It is often necessary to convert a `double` into a string according to a specified format. This can be accomplished by using an object of the `DecimalFormat` library class and its `format` method. First you need to create a new `DecimalFormat` object that describes the format. For example, passing the `"000.0000"` parameter to the `DecimalFormat` constructor indicates that you want a format with at least three digits before the decimal point (possibly with leading zeroes) and four digits after the decimal point. You use that format object to convert numbers into strings. We won't go too deeply into this here, but your programs can imitate the following examples:

```
import java.text.DecimalFormat;
...
    // Create a DecimalFormat object specifying at least one digit
    //   before the decimal point and 2 digits after the decimal point:
    DecimalFormat money1 = new DecimalFormat("0.00");

    // Create a DecimalFormat object specifying $ sign
    //   before the leading digit and comma separators:
    DecimalFormat money2 = new DecimalFormat("$#,##0");

    // Convert totalSales into a string using these formats:
    double totalSales = 12345678.9;
    String s1 = money1.format(totalSales);
        //   s1 gets the value "12345678.90"
    String s2 = money2.format(totalSales);
        //   s2 gets the value "$12,345,679" due to rounding

    // Create a DecimalFormat object specifying 2 digits
    //   (with a leading zero, if necessary):
    DecimalFormat twoDigits = new DecimalFormat("00");

    // Convert minutes into a string using twoDigits:
    int minutes = 7;
    String s3 = twoDigits.format(minutes);
        //   s3 gets the value "07"
```

If, for example, `totalSales` is 123.5 and you need to print something like

```
Total sales: 123.50
```

you could write

```
System.out.print("Total sales: " +
                        money1.format(totalSales));
```

If `hours` = 3 and `minutes` = 7 and you want the time to look like `3:07`, you could write

```
System.out.print(hours + ":" + twoDigits.format(minutes));
```

Starting with the Java 5.0 release, `PrintStream` and `PrintWriter` objects (including `System.out` and text files open for writing) have a convenient method `printf` for writing formatted output to the console screen and to files. `printf` is an unusual method: it can take a variable number of parameters. The first parameter is always a format string, usually a literal string. The format string may contain fixed text and one or more embedded *format specifiers*. The rest of the parameters correspond to the format specifiers in the string. For example:

```
int month = 5, day = 19, year = 2007;
double amount = 123.5;
System.out.printf("Date: %02d/%02d/%d  Amount: %7.2f\n",
                        month, day, year, amount);
```

displays

```
Date: 05/19/2007  Amount:  123.50
```

Here `%02d` indicates that the corresponding output parameter (`month`, then `day`) must be formatted with two digits including a leading zero if necessary; `%d` indicates that the next parameter (`year`) should be an integer in default representation (with whatever sign and number of digits it might have); `%7.2f` indicates that the next parameter (`amount`) should appear as a floating-point number, right-justified in a field of width 7, with two digits after the decimal point, rounded if necessary. `\n` at the end tells `printf` to advance to the next line. The details of `printf` formatting are rather involved — refer to the Java API documentation.

The Java 5.0 release has also added an equivalent of `printf` for "writing" into a string. The static method `format` of the `String` class arranges several inputs into a formatted string and returns that string. For example:

```
int month = 5, day = 19, year = 2007;
double amount = 123.5;
String msg = String.format("Date: %02d/%02d/%d  Amount: %7.2f",
                            month, day, year, amount);
```

The above statements set `msg` to `"Date: 05/19/2007  Amount:  123.50"`.

10.6 Extracting Numbers from Strings

The reverse operation — converting a string of digits (with a sign, if present) into an `int` value — can be accomplished by calling the static `parseInt` method of the `Integer` class. For example:

```
String s = "-123";
int n = Integer.parseInt(s);   // n gets the value -123
```

What happens if the string parameter passed to `parseInt` does not represent a valid integer? This question takes us briefly into the subject of Java *exception handling*.

If `parseInt` receives a bad parameter, it throws a `NumberFormatException`. You have already seen several occasions when a program "throws" a certain "exception" if it encounters some bug or unexpected situation. This exception, however, is different in nature from the other exceptions that we have experienced up to now, such as `NullPointerException`, `IllegalArgumentException`, or `StringIndexOutOfBoundsException`. Those exceptions are the programmer's fault: they are caused by mistakes in the program. When one of them is thrown, there is nothing to do but to terminate the program and report where the error occurred.

But a `NumberFormatException` may be caused simply by incorrect input from the user. The user will be very surprised if the program quits just because he types an 'o' instead of a '0'. The program should handle such situations gracefully, and Java provides a special tool for that: the `try-catch-finally` statement. You can call `parseInt` "tentatively," within a `try` block, and "catch" this particular type of exception within the `catch` block that follows. The `catch` block is executed only when an exception is thrown. It may be followed by the `finally` block that is always executed and therefore can perform the necessary clean-up. `try`, `catch`, and `finally` are Java reserved words. Figure 10-4 shows how all this may be coded.

```
Scanner input = new Scanner(System.in);
int n = 0;

while (n <= 0)
{
  System.out.print("Enter a positive integer: ");
  String str = input.next();   // read a token
  input.nextLine();  // skip the rest of the line
  try   // try to extract an int from str
  {
    n = Integer.parseInt(str);
  }
  catch (NumberFormatException ex)  // skip this if successful
  {
    System.out.println("*** Invalid input ***");
  }
  finally // either way execute this
  {
    if (n <= 0)
      System.out.println("Your input must be a positive integer");
  }
}

// Process n:
...
```

Figure 10-4. Converting input into an `int` with exception handling

A similar method, `parseDouble` of the `Double` class, can be used to extract a `double` value from a string. For example:

```
String s = "1.5";
double x = Double.parseDouble(s);   // x gets the value 1.5
```

10.7 Character Methods

When you work with characters and strings, you often need to find out whether a particular character is a digit, a letter, or something else. The `Character` wrapper class has several "public service" static `boolean` methods that test whether a character belongs to a particular category. All of these take one parameter, a `char`, and return `true` or `false`. For example:

```
        boolean result = Character.isDigit(c);
                        // result is set to true if c is a digit;
                        //    otherwise result is set to false
```

Other character "category" methods include `isLetter`, `isLetterOrDigit`, `isUpperCase`, `isLowerCase`, and `isWhitespace` (space, tab, newline, etc.).

There are also two methods that return the uppercase and lowercase versions of a character, if these are available. These are called `toUpperCase` and `toLowerCase`. For example:

```
        char c1 = Character.toUpperCase('a');   // c1 is set to 'A'
        char c2 = Character.toUpperCase('*');   // c2 is set to '*'

        Scanner input = new Scanner(System.in);
        String firstName = input.next();

        // Change the first letter in firstName to upper case:
        char c = firstName.charAt(0);
        firstName = Character.toUpperCase(c) + firstName.substring(1);
```

10.8 *Lab:* Lipograms

According to *Wikipedia* (the Internet encyclopedia),

a *lipogram* (from Greek lipagrammatos, "missing letter") is a kind of writing with constraints or word game consisting of writing paragraphs or longer works in which a particular letter or group of letters is missing, usually a common vowel, the most common in English being *e*.

"*Gadsby* is a notorious book by Californian author E. V. Wright, circa 1939. It was Wright's fourth book. It is famous for consisting only of words not containing any e's. Gadsby is thus a lipogram, or a display of constraint in writing. It is 50,100 words long. Wright informs us in Gadsby's introduction of having had to impair his own typing contraption to avoid slipups."

The *Lipogrammer* program, shown in Figure 10-5, helps to create and verify lipograms. It shows the original text, below it the same text with all letters *e* replaced with #, and to the right, the list of all 'offending' words (with an *e* in them). The user can load a lipogram text from a file or type it in or cut and paste it from another program. There is also a menu command to save the text. In this lab, you will write the `LipogramAnalyzer` class for this program.

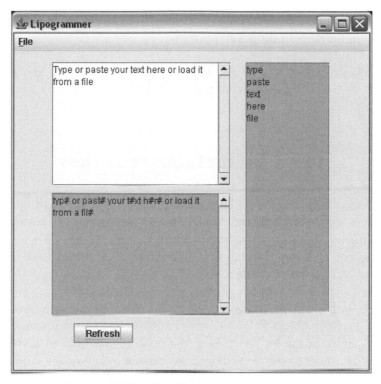

Figure 10-5. The *Lipogrammer* program

The `LipogramAnalyzer` should have the following constructor and two public methods:

```
// Constructor: saves the text string
public LipogramAnalyzer(String text)

// Returns the text string with all characters
// equal to letter replaced with '#'.
public String mark(char letter)

// Returns a String that concatenates all "offending"
// words from text that contain letter; the words are
// separated by '\n' characters; the returned string
// does not contain duplicate words: each word occurs
// only once; there are no punctuation or whitespace
// characters in the returned string.
public String allWordsWith(char letter)
```

Hint: write a private method to extract and return the word that contains the character at a specified position in `text`. Find the boundaries of the word by scanning the text to the left and to the right of the given position.

Combine in one project your `LipogramAnalyzer` class with the `Lipogrammer` and `LipogrammerMenu` GUI classes from the J_M\Ch10\Lipogrammer folder. Test the program.

10.9 The `StringBuffer` class

`StringBuffer` objects represent character strings that can be modified. Recall that `String` objects are immutable: you cannot change the contents of a string once it is created, so for every change you need to build a new string. To change one or several characters in a string or append characters to a string, it is usually more efficient to use `StringBuffer` objects.

This is especially true if you know in advance the maximum length of a string that a given `StringBuffer` object will hold. `StringBuffer` objects distinguish between the current <u>capacity</u> of the buffer (that is, the maximum length of a string that this buffer can hold without being resized) and the current <u>length</u> of the string held in the buffer. For instance, a buffer may have the capacity to hold 100 characters and be empty (that is, currently hold an empty string). As long as the length does not exceed the capacity, all the action takes place within the same buffer and there is no need to reallocate it. When the length exceeds the capacity, a larger buffer is allocated automatically and the contents of the current buffer are copied into the new buffer. This takes some time, so if you want your code to run efficiently, you have to arrange things in such a way that reallocation and copying do not happen often.

The `StringBuffer` class has three constructors:

```
StringBuffer()          // Constructs an empty string buffer with the
                        //   default capacity (16 characters)
StringBuffer(int n)     // Constructs an empty string buffer with the
                        //   capacity n characters
StringBuffer(String s)  // Constructs a string buffer that holds
                        //   a copy of s
```

Figure 10-6 shows some of `StringBuffer`'s more commonly used methods at work. As in the `String` class, the `length` method returns the length of the string currently held in the buffer. The `capacity` method returns the current capacity of the buffer.

In addition to the `charAt(int pos)` method that returns the character at a given position, `StringBuffer` has the `setCharAt(int pos, char ch)` method that sets the character at a given position to a given value.

`StringBuffer` has several overloaded `append(sometype x)` methods. Each of them takes one parameter of a particular type: `String`, `char`, `boolean`, `int`, and other primitive types, `Object`, or a character array (Chapter 12). `x` is converted into a string using the default conversion method, as in `String.valueOf(…)`. Then the string is appended at the end of the buffer. A larger buffer is automatically allocated if necessary. The overloaded `insert(int pos, sometype x)` methods insert characters at a given position.

The `substring(fromPos)` and `substring(fromPos, toPos)` methods work the same way as in the `String` class: the former returns a `String` equal to the substring starting at position `fromPos`, the latter returns a `String` made of the characters between `fromPos` and `toPos-1`, inclusive. `delete(fromPos, toPos)` removes a substring from the buffer and `replace(fromPos, toPos, str)` replaces the substring between `fromPos` and `toPos-1` with `str`. Finally, the `toString` method returns a `String` object equal to the string of characters in the buffer.

```
StringBuffer sb = new StringBuffer(10);   // sb is empty

int len = sb.length();                    // len is set to 0
int cap = sb.capacity();                  // cap is set to 10

sb.append("at");                          // sb holds "at"
sb.insert(0, 'b');                        // sb holds "bat"

char ch = sb.charAt(1);                   // ch is set to 'a'
sb.setCharAt(0, 'w');                     // sb holds "wat"

sb.append("er");                          // sb holds "water"
sb.replace(1, 3, "int");                  // sb holds "winter"

String s1 = sb.substring(1);              // s1 is set to "inter"
String s2 = sb.substring(1, 3);           // s2 is set to "in"
sb.delete(4, 6);                          // sb holds "wint"
sb.deleteCharAt(3);                       // sb holds "win"

sb.append(2009);                          // sb holds "win2009"
String str = sb.toString();               // str is set to "win2009"
```

Figure 10-6. Examples of common `StringBuffer` methods

10.10 Summary

Text in double quotes represents a *literal string*. Literal strings are treated as string objects, and you can assign them to `String` references without explicitly creating a string with the `new` operator. Literal strings may include *escape characters*, such as \n, \t, \\, and \".

Once a string is constructed, there is no way to change it because objects of the `String` class are *immutable*: no `String` method can change its object. However, you can reassign a `String` reference to another string. If no other variable refers to the old string, it will be released by Java's garbage collection mechanism. This may be quite inefficient; professional programmers often use the `StringBuffer` class instead of `String`.

Java supports the + and += operators for concatenating strings. If several + operators are combined in one expression for concatenation, you have to make sure that at least one of the operands in each intermediate operation is a string.

Figure 10-3 summarizes the most commonly used `String` methods. The positions of characters in strings are counted from 0, so the `charAt(0)` method returns the first character of a string.

The == or != operators are usually not useful for comparing strings because these operators compare the <u>references</u> to (addresses of) strings, not their contents. Use the `equals`, `equalsIgnoreCase`, and `compareTo` methods instead.

The `Integer` class is what is called a *wrapper class* for the primitive data type `int`. It provides a way to represent an integer value as an object. The static methods `Integer.toString(int n)` or `String.valueOf(int n)` return a string: a representation of n as a string of digits, possibly with a sign. The same can also be accomplished with "" + n. With `doubles` it is better to use a `DecimalFormat` object or the static method `format` in `String` for conversion into strings. For example:

```
DecimalFormat moneyFormat = new DecimalFormat("0.00");
. . .
String s1 = moneyFormat.format(totalSales);
String s2 = String.format("%.2f", totalSales);
```

To convert a string of decimal digits into an `int` value, call the static `parseInt` method of the `Integer` class. For example:

```
String s = "-123";
int n = Integer.parseInt(s);    // n gets the value -123
```

This method throws a `NumberFormatException` if s does not represent an integer. Your program should be able to catch the exception, alert the user, and keep running (see Figure 10-4).

The `Character` class (a wrapper class for `char`) has useful `boolean` static methods `isLetter`, `isDigit`, `isWhitespace`, and a few others that take a `char` as a parameter and return `true` or `false`. `Character`'s other two static methods, `toUpperCase(ch)` and `toLowerCase(ch)`, return a `char` value equal to ch converted to the appropriate case.

`StringBuffer` objects represent character strings that can be modified. In addition to `charAt`, `substring`, `indexOf`, and some other `String` methods, the `StringBuffer` class has `setCharAt`, `append`, and `insert` methods.

Exercises

Sections 10.1-10.4

1.   Find a bug in the following declaration: ✓

```
String fileName = "C:\dictionaries\words.txt";
```

2.   (a)   Write a method that returns `true` if a given string is not empty and ends with a star (`'*'`), `false` otherwise. ✓

(b)   Write a method that returns `true` if a given string has at least two characters and ends with two stars, `false` otherwise.

3.   Write a method that eliminates two dashes from a social security number in the format "ddd-dd-dddd" and returns a 9-character string of digits. For example, `removeDashes("987-65-4321")` returns a string equal to `"987654321"`.

4.   (a)   A string `dateStr` represents a date in the format "mm/dd/yyyy" (for example, `"05/31/2009"`). Write a statement or a fragment of code that changes `dateStr` to the format "dd-mm-yyyy" (for example, `"31-05-2009"`). ✓

(b)■   Make the method in Part (a) more general, so that it can handle dates written with or without leading zeroes (for example, it should convert `"5/3/2009"` into `"03-05-2009"`).

(c)   Use the program in `JM\Ch10\Exercises\StringTest.java` to test this code and for other exercises.

5.   A credit card number is represented as a `String ccNumber` that contains four groups of four digits. The groups are separated by one space. For example:

```
String ccNumber = "4111 1111 1111 1111";
```

(a)   Write a statement that declares a string `last4` and sets it to the last four digits in `ccNumber`. ✓

(b)   Write a statement that sets `String last5` to a string that holds the last five digits in `ccNumber`.

6.   Write a `scroll` method that takes a string as a parameter, moves the first character to the end of the string, and returns the new string.

7.   Suppose a string holds a person's last name and first name, separated by a comma. Write a method `convertName` that takes such a string and returns a string where the first name is placed first followed by one space and then the last name. For example:

```
String firstLast = convertName("von Neumann, John");
    // firstLast is set to "John von Neumann"
```

⧽ Hint: `trim` helps get rid of extra white space. ⧼

8.■   A string contains only `'0'` and `'1'` characters and spaces. Write a method that takes such a string and makes and returns a "negative" string in which all the 0s are replaced with 1s and all the 1s with 0s. Your method must rely only on `String`'s methods and not use any explicit iterations or recursion.

9.♦   Write a method that determines whether all the characters in a string are the same, using only library `String` methods, but no loops or recursion.

⸱ Hint: there are several approaches. For example, see Question 6 above. ⸱

10.   Write a method that tries to find opening and closing comment marks (`"/*"` and `"*/"`) in a string. If both are found, the method removes the first opening mark, the last closing mark, and all the characters between them from the string and returns the new string. If it fails to find both marks, the method returns the original string unchanged. Your method must rely only on `String`'s methods and not use any iterations explicitly.

11.   Write a method `cutOut` that removes the <u>first</u> occurrence of a given substring (if found) from a given string. For example:

```
String str = "Hi-ho, hi-ho";
String result = cutOut(str, "-ho");
  // result is set to "Hi, hi-ho"
```

    ✓

12.■   Write your own <u>recursive</u> implementation of `indexOf(ch, fromPos)`.

13.   The `String` class has `boolean` methods `startsWith(String prefix)` and `endsWith(String suffix)`. `startsWith` tests whether this string starts with a given substring; `endsWith` tests whether this string ends with a given substring. Pretending that these methods do not exist, write them using other string methods (but no iterations or recursion).

14.■   Web developers use HTML tags in angle brackets to format the text on web pages (see Appendix C). Write a method `removeTag` that checks whether a given string starts with an apparent HTML tag (a character or word in angle brackets) and ends with a matching closing HTML tag (the same character or word preceded by the '/' character, all in angle brackets). If yes, the method removes both tags and returns the result; otherwise the method returns the original string unchanged. For example, `removeTag("<b>Strings are immutable</b>")` should return a string equal to `"Strings are immutable"`.

---

15. Write a method that tests whether a given string contains only digits. ✓

16. If two strings, `s1` and `s2`, represent positive integers `n1` and `n2` in the usual way, as sequences of decimal digits, is it true that the sign of `s1.compareTo(s2)` is always the same as the sign of `(n1 - n2)`? Write a simple console application that prompts the user to enter two strings and tests this "hypothesis."

17. ∎ In *MS-DOS*, a file name consists of up to eight characters (excluding `'.'`, `':'`, backslash, `'?'`, and `'*'`), followed by an optional dot (`'.'` character) and extension. The extension may contain zero to three characters. For example: `1STFILE.TXT` is a valid file name. File names are case-blind. Write and test a method

```
private String validFileName(String fileName)
```

that validates the input, appends the default extension `".TXT"` if no extension is given (that is, no `'.'` appears in `fileName`), converts the name to the upper case, and returns the resulting string to the caller. If `fileName` ends with a dot, remove that dot and do not append the default extension. If the name is invalid, `validFileName` should return `null`.

18. ∎ (a) Write a method

```
public boolean isPalindrome(String word)
```

that tests whether `word` is a palindrome (the same when read forward or backward, as in "madam"). Test `isPalindrome` using the appropriately modified *String Test* program (`JM\Ch10\Exercises\StringTest.java`).

(b) Upgrade `isPalindrome` so that it can handle any phrase (as in "Madam, I'm Adam"). In testing for a palindrome, disregard all spaces, punctuation marks, apostrophes, and other non-alphanumeric characters and consider lower- and uppercase letters the same. ⸔ Hint: recall that the `Character` class has static methods `boolean isLetterOrDigit(ch)` and `char toUpperCase(ch)`. ⸕

19.■   The program *Cooney* (JM\Ch10\Exercises\Cooney.jar plays a game in which the player tries to guess which words Cooney "likes" and which ones Cooney "doesn't like." After five correct guesses in a row Cooney congratulates the player and the game stops. Play the game and guess the rule; then write the *Cooney* program. ⸗ Hint: write a console application or use JM\Ch10\Exercises\StringTest.java as a basis for your program. ⸗

20.■   An ISBN (International Standard Book Number) has ten digits. The first nine digits may have values from '0' to '9'; they identify the country in which the book was printed, the publisher, and the individual book. The tenth digit is a "check digit" assigned in such a way that the number $d_1d_2d_3d_4d_5d_6d_7d_8d_9d_{10}$ has the property:

$$(10d_1 + 9d_2 + 8d_3 + 7d_4 + 6d_5 + 5d_6 + 4d_7 + 3d_8 + 2d_9 + d_{10}) \mod 11 = 0$$

"mod" stands for modulo division (same as % in Java). If d_{10} needs the value 10 to balance the check digit equation, then the character 'X' is used. For example, 096548534X is a valid ISBN.

Note that if we simply took the sum of all the digits, the check digit would remain valid for any permutation of the digits. Different coefficients make the number invalid when any two digits are swapped, catching a common typo.

Write a method

```
public static boolean isValidISBN(String isbn)
```

that returns true if isbn represents a valid ISBN, false otherwise. Test your method in a simple program. ⸗ Hint: the Character class has the static int method digit(char ch, int base) that returns the numeric value of the digit in the specified base. For example, Character.digit('7', 10) returns 7. ⸗

21. ▪   Write a class `HangmanGame` that can help someone implement the *Hangman* game. (Do a web search for "Hangman" to find the rules and lots of versions of the program on the Internet.)

Provide three fields: a `String` to hold the answer word; a `StringBuffer` (of the same length as the word) to hold the partially filled string, with dashes for the letters that have not been guessed yet; and a `StringBuffer` to hold all the letters tried (with no duplicates), initially empty.

Provide a constructor that initializes the answer to a given string and all the other fields appropriately. Provide accessor methods: `String getWord()`, `String getGuessed()`, and `String getTried()` (note that accessors for the `StringBuffer` fields return `String`s). Finally, provide a method `int tryLetter(char letter)` that processes the player's next attempt. `tryLetter` should make the necessary adjustments to the current state of the game and return 0 if the letter has been tried before, –1 if it is not in the word, and 1 if the guess was successful.

Combine your `HangmanGame` class with a simple main class `Hangman`, provided in J<small>M</small>\Ch10\Exercises\Hangman.java, and test the program.

22. ◆   Write and test a method

```
public String shuffle(String abc)
```

that returns a new string with all the characters from `abc` rearranged in random order. Your method must first create a temporary `StringBuffer` object from `abc`, then shuffle the characters in that string buffer, then convert the string buffer back into a string and return the result. Read the Java API documentation for the `StringBuffer` class.

To shuffle the characters use the following algorithm:

> Set *n* to the total number of characters in the string buffer
> While *n* is greater than 1, repeat the following steps:
>> Pick a random character among the first *n*
>> Swap that character with the *n*-th character
>> Decrement *n* by 1

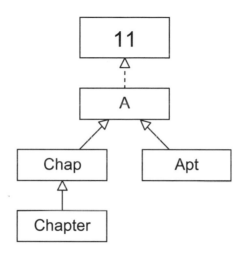

Class Hierarchies and Interfaces

11.1 Prologue

In the previous chapters we discussed the basics of OOP philosophy and design principles. We now continue with more advanced OOP concepts: class hierarchies, abstract classes, polymorphism, interfaces. But first, let us quickly review the basics.

As we know, a class can extend another class. This feature of OOP programming languages is called *inheritance*. The base class is called a *superclass*, and the derived class is called a *subclass* (Figure 11-1).

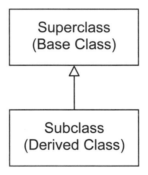

Figure 11-1. Inheritance terminology and notation in class diagrams

In Java, the keyword `extends` is used to declare that one class is derived from another class: a subclass `extends` a superclass. A subclass inherits all the fields and methods of its superclass (but not its constructors). An object of a subclass also inherits the type of the superclass as its own secondary, more generic type.

Inheritance represents the IS-A relationship between types of objects. A superclass defines more general features and properties of an object; its subclass defines more specific features and properties. In Figure 11-2, for example, `Walker` extends `Biped` (that is, `Walker` is a *subclass* of `Biped`). The class `Biped` is a generic class that represents any kind of "creature" that moves on two legs. (The term *biped* comes from Latin: *bi* means "two," and *ped* means "foot.") `Walker` represents a particular type of biped, a creature that alternates moving its left foot and right foot. We say that a `Walker` IS-A `Biped`.

As you can see in Figure 11-2, a class can have several subclasses. A subclass can have its own subclasses. And so on. Once the concept of inheritance is introduced into programming, it becomes possible to create a hierarchy of classes, with more general classes higher up in the hierarchy and more specific classes lower down.

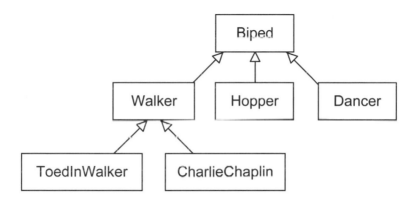

Figure 11-2. A hierarchy of classes

The concept of a hierarchy of types of objects in computer science can be traced to Artificial Intelligence (AI) research: in particular, to studies of models for representing knowledge using hierarchical *taxonomies*. Taxonomy is a system of classification in which an object can be defined as a special case, "a kind of" another object. In Linnaeus' zoological taxonomy, for example, a human being is a kind of primate, which is a kind of mammal, which is a kind of vertebrate, which is a kind of animal. Taxonomies have been one of the main ways of thinking in natural science for centuries, and they undoubtedly reflect an inclination of the human mind toward descriptive hierarchies.

In the rest of this chapter we will examine the use of class hierarchies and introduce *abstract classes* and *interfaces* — Java tools for managing different levels of abstraction.

11.2 Class Hierarchies and Polymorphism

In Chapter 3 we asked you in one of the exercises to "adapt" the class `Walker` into a new class, `Hopper`. The two classes have a lot in common. Like a `Walker`, a `Hopper` has a `leftFoot` and a `rightFoot`, but it hops (like a kangaroo) instead of walking. All you needed to do was to change the class name and revise a few lines of code in the `firstStep`, `nextStep`, and `stop` methods. The `draw` method —

```
public void draw(Graphics g)
{
  leftFoot.draw(g);
  rightFoot.draw(g);
}
```

— remained the same.

 Duplicate code in several classes is not only wasteful, but also bad for software maintenance.

This is because, if you ever need to change something in the code, you will spend a lot of time making the same change in several different classes.

So how can we avoid code duplication? One approach that comes to mind would be to derive `Hopper` from `Walker` as a subclass, redefining in `Hopper` only those methods that need to be different (`firstStep`, `nextStep`, `stop`). Technically this is possible. However, it would break down the logic of the IS-A relationship between classes: a `Hopper` <u>is not</u> a kind of `Walker`. Logically these classes belong at the same level: neither one should have "seniority" over the other.

A better solution is to introduce a common superclass, `Biped` (as shown in Figure 11-2) and define the `Walker`, `Hopper`, and `Dancer` classes as subclasses of `Biped`. Now it is fair to say that a `Walker` IS-A `Biped`, a `Hopper` IS-A `Biped`, and so on — every class is in the right place.

Such an arrangement has two advantages: (1) we can "factor out" the common code from all `Biped` subclasses into `Biped`'s code; (2) objects of `Biped`'s subclasses get a secondary, more generic type (`Biped`), which will come in handy in client classes.

1. "Factoring out" common code

In our example, the `leftFoot` and `rightFoot` fields, the `getLeftFoot` and `getRightFoot` accessor methods, and the `draw` method can all go into the `Biped` class (Figure 11-3), eliminating most of the duplicate code from its subclasses. We can also put into `Biped` other relevant methods, potentially useful to most bipeds, such as `turnAround`, `turnLeft`, and `turnRight`.

Remember the `Pacer` class? We derived it from `Walker`, adding the `turnAround`, `turnRight`, and `turnLeft` methods. As we can see now, the `Pacer` class does not fit into our new neat hierarchy. Its methods for turning belong in the superclass, so that different subclasses can inherit them.

```java
// This class represents a two-legged creature.

import java.awt.Image;
import java.awt.Graphics;

public class Biped
{
  public static final int PIXELS_PER_INCH = 6;
  private Foot leftFoot, rightFoot;

  // Constructor
  public Biped(int x, int y, Image leftPic, Image rightPic)
  {
    leftFoot =  new Foot(x, y - PIXELS_PER_INCH * 4, leftPic);
    rightFoot = new Foot(x, y + PIXELS_PER_INCH * 4, rightPic);
  }

  // Returns the left foot
  public Foot getLeftFoot()
  {
    return leftFoot;
  }

  // Returns the right foot
  public Foot getRightFoot()
  {
    return rightFoot;
  }

  < ... other methods >

  // Draws this Biped
  public void draw(Graphics g)
  {
    leftFoot.draw(g);
    rightFoot.draw(g);
  }
}
```

Figure 11-3.   A draft of the `Biped` class

In this case it makes sense to add such general-purpose useful methods to `Biped` itself. In general, however, it is not always possible to foresee all the methods that several subclasses will require. Nor is it practical to keep adding such methods to one superclass. It would be nice if a class could inherit methods from several superclasses. (For instance, a `Penguin` object might need the methods of both a `Biped` and a `Swimmer`; a `Pigeon` might need to be both a `Biped` and a `Flyer`.)

However, such *multiple inheritance* is not supported in Java. This looks like a serious limitation in OOP. There is a way around it: we can add the same functionality to different types of objects by defining a *wrapper class*. This solution is rather technical, though. Wrapper classes are discussed in Chapter 26.

2. Using more generic types of objects instead of specific types in client classes

Suppose, for example, we are working on a *client* class `Cartoon`, which manipulates `Walker`, `Hopper`, and other two-legged creatures. Suppose we need to write a method in `Cartoon` that moves a two-legged creature across a given distance. We could write:

```
public void moveAcross(Walker creature, int distance)
{
  creature.firstStep();
  while (creature.distanceTraveled() < distance)
    creature.nextStep();
  creature.stop();
}
```

This would work for a `Walker`. Then we would need an overloaded version with identical code to move a `Hopper`:

```
public void moveAcross(Hopper creature, int distance)
{
  creature.firstStep();
  while (creature.distanceTraveled() < distance)
    creature.nextStep();
  creature.stop();
}
```

Every time we added a different two-legged creature to our cartoon, we would need to add another `moveAcross` method for that particular type of creature. This solution is tedious and not very practical.

But with a common superclass `Biped`, the same method will work for all `Biped`s:

```
public void moveAcross(Biped creature, int distance)
{
  creature.firstStep();
  while (creature.distanceTraveled() < distance)
    creature.nextStep();
  creature.stop();
}
```

A caller of `moveAcross` passes to it as a parameter an object of some specific type. For example:

```
moveAcross(amy, 300);
```

`amy` is a particular type of `Biped`, say, a `Walker` or a `Hopper`. `amy`'s primary data type is `Walker` or `Hopper`, but `amy` also has a secondary, more generic data type, `Biped`. `amy` "knows" what particular type of `Biped` she is and what to do when her `firstStep` or `nextStep` or `stop` method is called (because the object `amy` holds a reference to the table of entry points to its own methods). `amy`'s correct method will be called automatically.

The feature of Java and other OOP languages that makes this possible is called *polymorphism* (from Greek: *poly* = many; *morph* = form).

> **Polymorphism ensures that the correct method is called for an object of a specific type, even when that object is disguised as a reference to a more generic type, that is, the type of the object's superclass or some ancestor higher up the inheritance line.**

To summarize, arranging classes in an inheritance hierarchy helps us avoid duplicate code by "factoring out" common code from subclasses into their common superclass. A class hierarchy also helps us avoid duplicate code in client classes by letting us write more general methods and take advantage of polymorphism.

For a polymorphic method like `moveAcross` to compile, however, Java requires that the `Biped` class have some kind of `firstStep`, `nextStep`, and `stop` methods. What do we put in them? Different `Biped`s of course redefine these methods. We could potentially just leave them empty. For example:

```
public class Biped
{
  ...

  public void nextStep()
  {
    // empty method: the method is defined, but does not do anything
  }

  ...
}
```

This works, but it is dangerous. If we forget to override one of the empty methods in a `Biped`'s subclass or if we do it incorrectly (for example, we misspell its name), the inherited empty method will be called, and our program won't work correctly. We could instead make these methods throw `UnsupportedOperationException`:

```
public void nextStep()
{
  throw new UnsupportedOperationException();
}
```

But Java offers us another solution: we can declare such methods *abstract*.

11.3 Abstract Classes

Java allows us to leave some of the methods in a class declared but undefined. Such methods are called *abstract*. The way to declare a method abstract is to use the keyword `abstract` in its header and to supply no code for it at all, not even empty braces. For example:

```
public abstract void nextStep();
```

An abstract method is better than an `UnsupportedOperationException` or an empty method, because when we declare a method `abstract`, the compiler checks whether each subclass properly defines this method before we even try to run our program.

> **If a class has at least one abstract method, it must be declared `abstract`.**

For example:

```
public abstract class Biped
{
  ...
}
```

Figure 11-4 shows `Biped` implemented as an abstract class; Figure 11-5 shows its subclass `Walker`. Note how the code is split between these two classes: `Biped` has feet and "knows" how to turn around and how to draw itself; `Walker` "knows" how to "walk" in a particular manner.

```java
// This abstract class represents a two-legged creature.

import java.awt.Image;
import java.awt.Graphics;

public abstract class Biped
{
  public static final int PIXELS_PER_INCH = 6;
  private Foot leftFoot;
  private Foot rightFoot;

  // Constructor
  public Biped(int x, int y, Image leftPic, Image rightPic)
  {
    leftFoot =  new Foot(x, y - PIXELS_PER_INCH * 4, leftPic);
    rightFoot = new Foot(x, y + PIXELS_PER_INCH * 4, rightPic);
  }

  // Returns the left foot
  public Foot getLeftFoot()
  {
    return leftFoot;
  }

  // Returns the right foot
  public Foot getRightFoot()
  {
    return rightFoot;
  }

  // Makes first step
  public abstract void firstStep();

  // Makes next step
  public abstract void nextStep();

  // Stops this Biped
  public abstract void stop();

  // Returns the distance traveled
  public abstract int distanceTraveled();

  < ... other methods >

  // Draws this Biped
  public void draw(Graphics g)
  {
    leftFoot.draw(g);
    rightFoot.draw(g);
  }
}
```

Figure 11-4. J~M~\Ch11\DanceStudio\Biped.java

```
// Represents a Biped that moves alternating the left and right foot

import java.awt.Image;

public class Walker extends Biped
{
  private int stepLength;
  private int stepsCount;

  // Constructor
  public Walker(int x, int y, Image leftPic, Image rightPic)
  {
    super(x, y, leftPic, rightPic);  // must be the first statement
    stepLength = PIXELS_PER_INCH * 12;
  }

  // Makes first step, starting with the left foot
  public void firstStep()
  {
    getLeftFoot().moveForward(stepLength);
    stepsCount = 1;
  }

  // Makes next step
  public void nextStep()
  {
    if (stepsCount % 2 == 0)  // if stepsCount is even
      getLeftFoot().moveForward(2 * stepLength);
    else
      getRightFoot().moveForward(2 * stepLength);

    stepsCount++;
  }

  // Stops this walker (brings its feet together)
  public void stop()
  {
    if (stepsCount % 2 == 0)  // if stepsCount is even
      getLeftFoot().moveForward(stepLength);
    else
      getRightFoot().moveForward(stepLength);
  }

  // Returns the distance walked
  public int distanceTraveled()
  {
    return stepsCount * stepLength;
  }
}
```

Figure 11-5. J_M\Ch11\DanceStudio\Walker.java

▌ **Java doesn't allow us to create objects of an abstract class.**

Note that our `Biped` class has a constructor. But if you try to use it to create a `Biped` object —

```
Biped amy = new Biped(x, y, leftShoe, rightShoe);
```

— the compiler will give you an error message, something like this:

```
Biped is abstract; cannot be instantiated.
```

This means you cannot create an *instance* (that is, an object) of an abstract class. (As explained in the next section, `Biped`'s constructor is provided so that it can be called from `Biped`'s subclasses).

▌ **A class with no abstract methods is called a *concrete class*.**

A concrete class supplies its own constructors and defines all the abstract methods inherited from its superclass and other ancestors higher up the inheritance line. Abstract and concrete classes can be intermixed in the same hierarchy at different levels as long as all classes at the bottom are concrete.

OO designers sometimes define rather elaborate hierarchies. Figure 11-6 shows a fragment of the hierarchy of Java library classes.

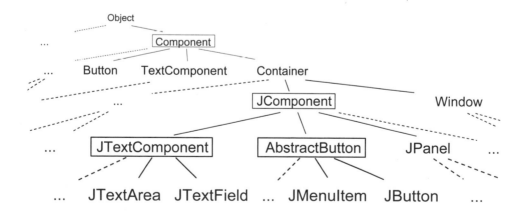

**Figure 11-6. A fragment of Java library GUI class hierarchy
(abstract classes are boxed)**

You can clearly see how the newer *Swing* GUI classes, starting with `JComponent`, were added (in the Java 2 release) under `Container`, while all the old *AWT* classes (`Button`, etc.) were left untouched. The hierarchy has the class `Object` at the very top.

> **In Java, if you do not explicitly specify a superclass for your class, your class automatically extends the class `Object`. So all Java classes fit into one giant hierarchical tree with `Object` at the root.**

In other words, every object IS-A(n) `Object`. `Object` is a concrete (not abstract) class that provides a few generic methods, such as `toString` and `equals`, but these methods are usually overridden in classes down the hierarchy.

11.4 Invoking Superclass's Constructors

In Section 3.6 we mentioned a paradox: a subclass inherits all the fields of its superclass but cannot access them directly if they are declared private. The solution is to provide public accessor methods for these fields. In the `Biped` class, for example, we have provided the methods `getLeftFoot` and `getRightFoot`. However, one question still remains: How do the private fields of the superclass get initialized?

The answer is to call a constructor of the superclass from the constructor of the subclass. Whenever an object of a subclass is created, the first thing Java does is to invoke a constructor of its superclass. A programmer specifies which of the superclass's constructors to call and what parameters to pass to it by using the keyword `super`. In a hierarchy of classes, the superclass's constructor in turn calls <u>its</u> superclass's constructor, and so on, up the inheritance line, all the way up to `Object` (Figure 11-7).

`Walker`'s constructor, for example, invokes `Biped`'s constructor:

```
// Constructor
public Walker(int x, int y, Image leftPic, Image rightPic)
{
  super(x, y, leftPic, rightPic);  // must be the first statement
  stepLength = PIXELS_PER_INCH * 12;
}
```

After that, the subclass's constructor initializes the subclass's own additional fields, if there are any.

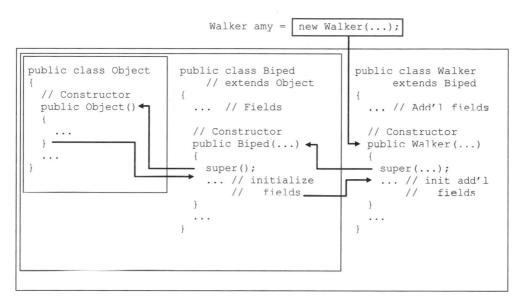

Figure 11-7.   A constructor invokes its superclass's constructor with `super`

In Java, the call `super()` is optional. If there is no explicit `super` statement, the no-args constructor of the superclass is invoked, and, in that case, the superclass must have one.

If it doesn't, an error message is displayed that a no-args constructor cannot be found. For example, if you temporarily comment out the statement `super(...)` in `Walker`'s constructor and try to compile `Walker`, you will get:

```
cannot find symbol
symbol  : constructor Biped()
```

The class `Object` obviously has a no-args constructor, and classes that "do not extend anything" (that is, classes that are derived directly from `Object`) rely on the default and do not need a `super()` statement in their constructors.

If your constructor has a `super(...)` statement, then it must be the first statement in the constructor.

11.5 Calling Superclass's Methods

Suppose we now want to create a biped that walks with its feet pointing out, like Charlie Chaplin[chaplin] (Figure 11-8). It makes sense to derive this class from `Walker`. Let's call this class `CharlieChaplin`.

Figure 11-8. Charlie Chaplin

Suppose `CharlieChaplin` objects use the same image for the left and right foot, so the `CharlieChaplin` constructor takes only three parameters: x, y, and `shoePic`.

```
public class CharlieChaplin extends Walker
{
  // Constructor
  public CharlieChaplin(int x, int y, Image shoePic)
  {
    super(x, y, shoePic, shoePic);
    turnFeetOut();
  }

  < other methods >

  private void turnFeetOut()
  {
    getLeftFoot().turn(-45);
    getRightFoot().turn(45);
  }
}
```

This constructor first invokes `Walker`'s constructor (which takes four parameters). The same image `shoePic` is passed to `Walker`'s constructor for both the left foot and right foot images. After that, `CharlieChaplin`'s constructor calls a method to make the feet point out.

So far, so good. Now we need to make `CharlieChaplin` walk. We could, of course, figure out how each foot should move and program that. But it might be easier to first restore the normal position of the feet, parallel to each other, then make a "regular" step, like a "normal" walker does, then turn the feet out again. (A walker is not displayed while a step is in progress, so all this turning of feet remains invisible.) Something like this:

```
public void nextStep()
{
  turnFeetIn();
  < make regular walker's step >
  turnFeetOut();
}
```

But how do we state "make regular walker's step" in the program? If we just call `nextStep` here, then `nextStep` will become a recursive method, and the program will go into infinite recursion and crash.

It turns out that Java has special syntax for explicitly calling a method of the superclass. This syntax uses the `super`-dot prefix in the method call. For example:

```
public void nextStep()
{
  turnFeetIn();
  super.nextStep();  // calls Walker's nextStep
  turnFeetOut();
}
```

The same idea works for the `firstStep` and `stop` methods. `CharlieChaplin` does not need to redefine `Walker`'s `distanceTraveled` method, because it works fine. But it does need to redefine the `turnAround`, `turnRight`, and `turnLeft` methods, and we can use the same technique. For example:

```
public void turnAround()
{
  turnFeetIn();
  super.turnAround();
  turnFeetOut();
}
```

Note that even though `turnAround` is defined in `Biped`, it is inherited by `Walker`, and the `super`-dot prefix works as usual: `super.turnAround()` calls `Walker`'s `turnAround`, which is simply `Biped`'s `turnAround`. In general, `super`-dot refers to the nearest explicitly defined method up the inheritance line.

11.6 *Case Study:* Dance Studio

If you have found our discussion in the previous sections a little, well... abstract, that's understandable. OOP has a complicated conceptual layer and a lot of terminology. Let us see how we can make it work in our project.

As we saw in Chapter 3, the *Dance Studio* program teaches a novice dancer basic ballroom dancing steps. Run the program by clicking on the `DanceStudio.jar` file in J_M\Ch11\DanceStudio. The user chooses a dance from the pull-down list, clicks on the "Go" button, and sees how the dancers' feet move (Figure 11-9).

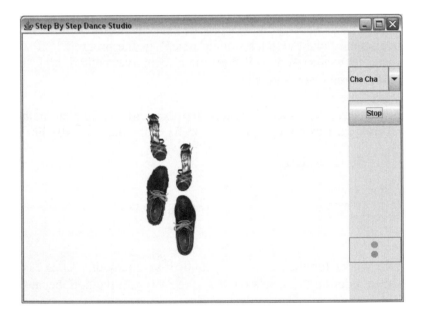

Figure 11-9. *Dance Studio* **program**

Luckily we are not starting this project from scratch. We already have the `Foot` and the `Biped` classes and a lot of usable GUI code. What is lacking is the dancing part.

Each of the dancers in the program performs a prerecorded sequence of steps for a particular dance. An obvious metaphor is that a dancer learns (gets a script for) a dance and then performs the appropriate steps for that dance. Our plan is to formalize this metaphor, to find software equivalents for "learn," "dance," and "dance step."

Let's start with "learn." We define a class Dancer, which is a kind of Biped, with an additional method learn. A Dancer has a field currentDance of the type Dance, and learn simply saves the parameter passed to it in the currentDance field (Figure 11-10).

```java
// Represents a dancer in the Dance Studio project.

import java.awt.Image;

public class Dancer extends Biped
{
  private Dance currentDance;
  private int stepsCount;

  // Constructor
  public Dancer(int x, int y, Image leftPic, Image rightPic)
  {
    super(x, y, leftPic, rightPic);
  }

  // Makes this dancer learn dance
  public void learn(Dance dance)
  {
    currentDance = dance;
  }

  < other methods >
}
```

Figure 11-10. A fragment from JM**\Ch11\DanceStudio\Dancer.java**

A "dance" is represented by a Dance object. At this point we don't know how it is implemented and really don't want to worry about that. All we need from Dance for now is that it can produce the next dance step for this dancer, when requested. Dance should have something like a getStep(i) method that returns the *i*-th dance step.

Finally, we can define a separate class, DanceStep, to represent a dance step. To keep things relatively simple, let us say that one dance step describes the move of both feet. For each foot four actions are defined: an initial turn, a move forward, a move sideways, and a final turn. (Some of these moves and turns are often not needed — then they are set to 0.) Accordingly, our DanceStep class has eight accessor methods, four for each foot:

```
getInitialTurnL              getInitialTurnR
getForwardDistanceL          getForwardDistanceR
getSidewaysDistanceL         getSidewaysDistanceR
getFinalTurnL                getFinalTurnR
```

Figure 11-11 shows how Dancer, Dance, and DanceStep interact.

A DanceStep is a very "passive" object: it is just a "data carrier." Its constructor stores the values of the parameters passed to it in the respective fields. Then it makes this data available via accessor methods. Objects like this are often needed in programs. If you are interested, you can find the complete code for this class in the DanceStep.java file in JM\Ch11\DanceStudio.

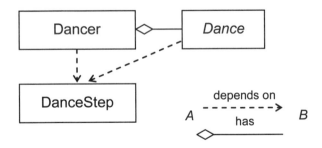

Figure 11-11. A Dancer first "learns" a Dance, then consults it about the next DanceStep.

Figure 11-12 shows the remaining code for Dancer. The nextStep method requests the *i*-th DanceStep from dance and moves the feet accordingly. The firstStep method does the same (it simply calls nextStep), stop does nothing, and distanceTraveled returns 0 (all this motion for nothing!).

```java
public class Dancer extends Biped
{
  private Dance currentDance;
  private int stepsCount;

  ...

  // Makes first step
  public void firstStep()
  {
    stepsCount = 0;
    nextStep();  // the first step is the same as next step
  }

  // Makes next step
  public void nextStep()
  {
    Foot lf = getLeftFoot();
    Foot rf = getRightFoot();

    DanceStep step = currentDance.gotStep(stepsCount);
    if (step != null)  // null means do not move
    {
      lf.turn(step. getInitialTurnL());
      lf.moveForward(step.getForwardDistanceL());
      lf.moveSideways(step.getSidewaysDistanceL());
      lf.turn(step.getFinalTurnL());

      rf.turn(step. getInitialTurnR());
      rf.moveForward(step.getForwardDistanceR());
      rf.moveSideways(step.getSidewaysDistanceR());
      rf.turn(step.getFinalTurnR());
    }

    stepsCount++;
  }

  // Stops this Dancer
  public void stop()
  {
    // do nothing
  }

  // Returns the distance traveled
  public int distanceTraveled()
  {
    return 0;
  }
}
```

Figure 11-12. JM\Ch11\DanceStudio\Dancer.java

Things have fallen into place rather nicely... But, where are the dances? Well, the dances are a whole different story. Maybe someone else is working on them? Perhaps someone has created a hierarchy of classes that represent different dances. Or perhaps there is one class that reads a dance description from a specified file. Maybe both. We don't know! The beauty of OOP design here is that we have two subsystems in our project, dancers and dances, which are virtually isolated from each other. The only piece of information that connects them is that every `Dance` has the `getStep` method.

In the computer world, the mechanism that connects two devices or entities and defines the rules for their interaction is often called an *interface*. We have to conclude that `Dance` acts as an interface between the dancers and the dances.

11.7 Interfaces

Not only does `Dance` "act as an interface," it actually <u>is</u> an `interface`:

```
public interface Dance
{
  DanceStep getStep(int i);
  int getTempo();
  int getBeat(int i);
}
```

> **A Java interface is similar to an abstract class: it has one or several abstract methods declared but left undefined. The difference is that <u>all</u> of an interface's methods are abstract: they have headers but no method bodies. Interfaces have no constructors and no other code, (except, perhaps, a few static constants).**

The keywords `public abstract` are omitted in the method headers because <u>every</u> method is public abstract.

> **Once an interface is defined, we can "officially" state that a class *implements* an interface. If the class is concrete, it must supply all the methods that are listed in the interface. If the class is abstract, it can leave some of the interface's methods abstract.**

`interface` and `implements` are Java reserved words.

Table 11-1 lists a few similarities and differences between classes and interfaces.

Classes	Interfaces
A superclass provides a secondary data type to objects of its subclasses.	**An interface provides a secondary data type to objects of classes that implement that interface.**
An abstract class cannot be instantiated.	**An interface cannot be instantiated.**
A concrete subclass of an abstract class must define all the inherited abstract methods. (An abstract subclass of an abstract class can leave some of the methods abstract.)	**A concrete class that implements an interface must define all the methods specified by the interface. (An abstract class that implements an interface can leave some of the interface's methods abstract.)**
A class can extend another class. A subclass can add methods and override some of its superclass's methods.	**An interface can extend another interface** (called its *superinterface*) by adding declarations of abstract methods. A *subinterface* cannot override methods of its *superinterface* (because there is nothing to override: all methods are abstract.)
A class can extend only one class.	A class can implement any number of interfaces.
A class can have fields.	An interface cannot have fields, except, possibly, some `public static final` constants.
A class defines its own constructors or is supplied with a default constructor by the compiler.	An interface has no constructors.
A concrete class has all its methods defined. An abstract class usually has one or more abstract methods.	All methods declared in an interface are abstract.
Every class is a part of a hierarchy of classes with `Object` at the top.	An interface may belong to a small hierarchy of interfaces, but this is not as common.

Table 11-1.   Similarities and differences between classes and interfaces (similarities are shown in bold)

The two main similarities are:

1. **A concrete class that extends an abstract class and/or implements an interface must supply code for all the abstract methods of its superclass and/or of the interface.**

2. **Like a superclass, an interface provides a secondary data type to the objects of classes that implement that interface, and polymorphism works for interface types.**

The `Dance` interface, for example, specifies three methods. A concrete class that implements `Dance` must have all three of these methods defined (Figure 11-13).

```
public class Waltz implements Dance
{
  < fields and constructors >

  public DanceStep getStep(int i) { < ... code not shown > }

  public int getTempo() { return 750; }

  public int getBeat(int i) { < ... code not shown > }

  < possibly other methods >
}
```

Figure 11-13.   A sketch of a concrete class that implements the `Dance` interface

You might ask: Why do we need interfaces? Why not just turn the interface into an abstract class? This has to do with the main difference between superclasses and interfaces: it is not possible for a class to have more than one superclass, but a class can implement <u>any number</u> of interfaces. Class hierarchies in Java have this limitation: Java assumes that each class neatly falls into <u>one</u> hierarchy. In real life, the situation is more complex. The same object may play different roles in different situations. For example, Natalie, a person, can be a high school student, an hourly employee, an online customer, a granddaughter, and a ballroom dancer. We would need five different class hierarchies to represent these aspects of Natalie: Natalie IS-A `Student`; Natalie IS-A(n) `Employee`; Natalie IS-A `Customer`; Natalie IS-A `FamilyMember`; Natalie IS-A `Dancer`.

We come across such situations frequently in OOP, and interfaces are the answer. If a class implements several interfaces, its objects can act out the functions of several different things at the same time.

If a class implements several interfaces, it must supply all the methods specified in each of them.

Polymorphism fully applies to interface data types.

For example, we can pass a Rumba object to a Dancer's learn method as a parameter. The statement that Rumba implements Dance tells the compiler that that this is allowed, even though learn expects a parameter of the Dance type. After all, a Rumba IS-A Dance. What's important is that a Rumba object has all the methods that any Dance is supposed to have, including the method getStep, called by the Dancer. (We can be also sure that a Rumba object has the getTempo and getBeat methods, called by the Band object.) If currentDance happens to refer to a Rumba, then Rumba's getStep will be called automatically when the call currentDance.getStep(stepsCount) is made.

Take another example:

```
public interface Edible
{
  String getFoodGroup();
  int getCaloriesPerServing();
}
```

The Edible interface serves as an interface between classes that represent different food items and client classes that work with food items. For example, we can write a class Breakfast with a general method eat:

```
public class Breakfast
{
  private int myTotalCalories = 0;
  ...
  public void eat(Edible obj, int servings)
  {
    myTotalCalories += obj.getCaloriesPerServing() * servings;
  }
  ...
}
```

The `eat` method takes an `Edible` object as a parameter. `eat` works properly whether the object passed to it is an `Apple`, a `Pancake`, or any other object of a class that implements `Edible`. The `getCaloriesPerServing` method will be called automatically for an `obj` of a particular type due to polymorphism.

Suppose `Apple` is defined as

```
public class Apple implements Edible
{
  < fields and constructors not shown >

  public String getFoodGroup() { return "Fruit"; }
  public int getCaloriesPerServing() { return 70; }

  < other methods not shown >
}
```

Then `eat` will add `70*servings` to `myTotalCalories`.

Names given to interfaces sometimes sound like adjectives because an interface supplies an additional characteristic to the object whose class implements that interface. If `Apple` implements `Edible`, it makes sense to say that an `Apple` is `Edible`.

11.8 *Case Study:* Dance Studio Concluded

Figure 11-14 shows the class diagram for the *Dance Studio* program. In OOP, a large number of classes is not considered a problem, as long as they are reasonably short and manageable and clearly define the responsibilities of their objects. An arrow with a dotted line and a triangular head from a class to an interface indicates that the class implements the interface.

> **In class diagrams, as in the API documentation, the names of interfaces are shown in italics.**

Note that the `ControlPanel` class is the only class in the program that "knows" about specific dances. The rest of the classes communicate with the dances through the `Dance` interface.

There is another interface in the program: `StudentGroup`. This interface isolates `DanceGroup` from the GUI classes and makes it possible to easily replace the `DanceGroup` with a `WalkingGroup` or a `PacingGroup`, as we did in Chapter 3.

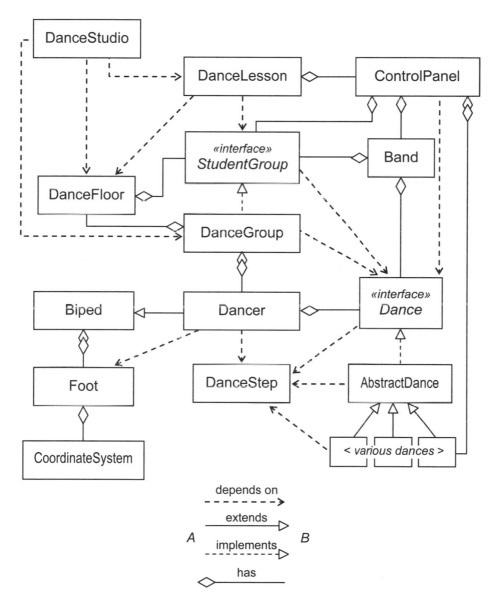

Figure 11-14. *Dance Studio* classes and interfaces

Several "dance" classes can be programmed in a similar manner. If several "dance" classes share some code, it makes sense to "factor out" their common code into an abstract superclass. Lets call it `AbstractDance`:

```
public abstract class AbstractDance implements Dance
{
   . . .
}
```

> **IS-A is a transitive relationship: if *X* IS-A *Y* and *Y* IS-A *Z*, then *X* IS-A *Z*. Objects of a class accumulate all their ancestors' IS-A relationships and secondary data types up the inheritance line, all the way up to `Object`, and also from all of the interfaces that this class and all its ancestors implement.**

In particular, if a class *C* implements interface *I*, there is no need to repeat `implements I` explicitly in subclasses of *C* — it is understood.

For example, if `Waltz` is a subclass of `AbstractDance` —

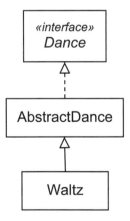

— we can write

```
public class Waltz extends AbstractDance
   // "implements Dance" is implied and usually is not written
{
   . . .
}
```

In simple ballroom dances, the "woman's" steps are the same as the "man's," but in the opposite direction. (The convention of ballroom dance instructors, which we'll follow here, is to describe one part as "male" and the other as "female," regardless of who is actually dancing. In practice, of course, skilled dancers are able to perform either set of steps, as needed.) For example, if the man moves his left foot forward, the woman moves her right foot backward. It is useful to have a mechanism that takes a `Dance` object describing the man's steps and converts it into a `Dance` object describing the woman's steps, or vice-versa. Your task is to create such a mechanism, by using a *wrapper class*. A wrapper class adds functionality to an object at run time or converts an object (or an item of a primitive data type) into a different form. (We already got a glimpse of wrapper classes in Chapter 10. The Decorator design pattern and wrapper classes are explained in more detail in Chapter 26.)

You will write a wrapper class called `ReversedDance`. This class should implement the `Dance` interface. It also has a constructor that takes a `Dance` as a parameter. A `ReversedDance` object "wraps around" a dance object passed to its constructor and becomes its "reversed" dance. This is a little unusual: `ReversedDance` both IS-A `Dance` and HAS-A `Dance`:

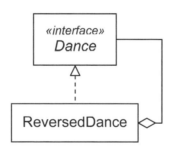

`ReversedDance` has to <u>be</u> a `Dance` because we want to be able to pass a `ReversedDance` type of parameter to our `Dancer`'s `learn` method. It has to <u>have</u> a `Dance` field because it needs to know what it is reversing.

Here is what you have to do. Provide a constructor that takes one parameter of the `Dance` type. That way you will be able to write something like this:

```
Dance dance = new Waltz();
maleDancer.learn(dance);
femaleDancer.learn(new ReversedDance(dance));
```

The `ReversedDance` constructor saves the parameter passed to it in a field; let's call it `dance`. (If all dance objects are immutable, then different dancers can "read" steps from the same dance without confusion, so there is no need to make another copy of the `dance`: you can just save a reference to it.)

Now let's figure out the `getStep` method. Because the man and the woman move opposite feet, we can negate the step data for the man's left foot (reverse the sign) and use it as step data for the woman's right foot, and likewise negate the data for the man's right foot and use it for the woman's left. The algorithm is quite simple: get the *i*-th `DanceStep` from `dance`; if it is `null`, return `null`; otherwise create a new step with all the values negated and the left- and right-foot data swapped; return the new step.

The `getTempo` and `getBeat` methods in `ReversedDance` are, of course, the same as in `dance`, so they return the values obtained by calling the respective method of the `dance` object.

Set up a project with your `ReversedDance` class and the `DanceStudio.jar` file in `JM\Ch11\DanceStudio` to test your class. (Your class will override the one in the `jar` file.)

Note the level of abstraction that interfaces provide. You have written a wrapper class that works with any type of `Dance` objects without ever knowing what kind of dances may exist.

11.9 Summary

When classes *X* and *Y* share a lot of code, this is a clear indication that *X* and *Y* represent related types of objects. It then makes sense to "factor out" their shared code into a common superclass *B*. This helps avoid duplication of code in *X* and *Y* and, at the same time, provides a common secondary, more generic type *B* to the objects of *X* and *Y*. This common type *B* allows you to write more general methods in clients of *X* and *Y*: instead of having separate overloaded methods

```
... someMethod(X x) { ... }
```

and

```
... someMethod(Y y) { ... }
```

you can have one method

```
... someMethod(B b) { ... }
```

The latter will work when you pass either an *X* or *Y* type of object *b* to someMethod as a parameter. The parameter *b* appears as type *B* in the method, but *b* itself knows what exact type of object it is (*X* or *Y*), and the correct method (*X*'s or *Y*'s) will be called automatically. This feature is called *polymorphism*. Polymorphism ensures that the correct method is called for an object of a specific type, even when that object is disguised as a reference to a more generic type.

A subclass of a class can have its own subclasses, and so on, so a programmer can design an *inheritance hierarchy* of classes. Classes lower in the hierarchy inherit fields and methods from their ancestors (the classes higher up along the inheritance line) and can add or redefine some of the methods along the way. Objects of a class also accumulate the IS-A relationships and the secondary types from all of the ancestors of that class (and from all of the interfaces that the class and its ancestors implement).

Java allows you to leave some of the methods in a class declared but undefined. Such methods are called *abstract*. You "officially" declare a method abstract by using the keyword abstract in the method's header and supplying no code for the method, not even empty braces:

```
public abstract sometype someMethod(< parameters if any >);
```

If a class has at least one abstract method, it must be declared abstract. Abstract classes can have fields, constructors, and regular methods, but it is impossible to create objects of an abstract class (in other words, abstract classes cannot be *instantiated*). The purpose of abstract classes is to serve as a common superclass to two or several classes.

A class with no abstract methods is called a *concrete* class. A concrete class must define all of the abstract methods of its superclass (and all of the methods of the interfaces that that class and its ancestors implement). Abstract and concrete classes can be intermixed at different levels in the same inheritance hierarchy, as long as all the classes at the bottom are concrete.

In Java, if you do not explicitly specify a superclass for your class, your class automatically extends the class `Object`. So all Java classes fit into one giant hierarchy tree with `Object` at the root. `Object` is a concrete (not abstract) class. It provides a few generic methods, such as `toString` and `equals`, but these are usually overridden in classes lower in the hierarchy.

Whenever an object of a subclass is created, the first thing Java does is to invoke a constructor of its superclass. The programmer specifies which particular superclass constructor to call and what parameters to pass to it by using the keyword `super`. The call `super()` is optional. If there is no explicit `super(…)` statement, the no-args constructor of the superclass is invoked, and, in that case, the superclass must have one. If your constructor has a `super(…)` statement, then it must be the first statement in the constructor.

You can explicitly call a method defined in the superclass from a method defined in its subclass:

```
super.someMethod(...);
```

Such statement would typically be used in the code of the subclass's `someMethod`, the one that overrides the superclass's `someMethod`.

An *interface* is similar to an abstract class: it has one or several abstract methods declared but left undefined. The difference is that an interface does not have any code (except, perhaps, a few static constants): no constructors, no method bodies. In an interface, the keywords `public abstract` are not used in method headers because all methods are public and abstract.

Once an interface is defined, you can "officially" state that a class *implements* an interface. In that case, to be a concrete class, it must supply all the methods that are listed in the interface. An abstract class that implements an interface can leave some of the interface's methods abstract. The same class can implement several interfaces. In that case it should define all the methods specified in all of them.

An interface can serve to isolate different subsystems from each other, limiting their interaction to a small number of methods. An interface also provides a secondary type to objects of classes that implement that interface, and that secondary type can be used polymorphically the same way as the secondary type provided by a common superclass.

Exercises

1.   True or false?

    (a)   You can't create objects of an abstract class. _____   ✓
    (b)   You can derive concrete classes from an abstract class. _____
    (c)   You can derive abstract classes from an abstract class. _____
    (d)   An abstract class can be useful as a common type for parameters in methods. _____
    (e)   `Object` is an abstract class. _____   ✓

2.   True or false?

    (a)   In Java, constructors of a subclass are inherited from the superclass. _____

    (b)   A subclass's constructor can explicitly call a superclass's constructor and pass parameters to it. _____

    (c)   A subclass's method can explicitly call a superclass's method. _____

    (d)   `super` is a Java reserved word. _____

3.   Suppose we have

```
public abstract class Toy { ... }
public class Doll extends Toy { ... }
public class BarbieDoll extends Doll { ... }
```

Doll and BarbieDoll each have a no-args constructor. If an object `child` has a method `play(Doll doll)`, which of the following statements will compile with no errors?

    (a)   `child.play(new Object());` _____
    (b)   `child.play(new Toy());` _____
    (c)   `child.play(new Doll());` _____
    (d)   `child.play(new BarbieDoll());` _____

4. Define a class `Diploma` and its subclass `DiplomaWithHonors`, so that the statements

```
Diploma diploma1 = new Diploma("Murray Smith", "Gardening");
System.out.println(diploma1);
System.out.println();

Diploma diploma2 = new DiplomaWithHonors("Lisa Smith",
                                "Evolutionary Psychology");
System.out.println(diploma2);
System.out.println();
```

display

```
This certifies that
Murray Smith
has completed a course in Gardening

This certifies that
Lisa Smith
has completed a course in Evolutionary Psychology
*** with honors ***
```

Make your class definitions consistent with the information-hiding principle and avoid duplication of code. ✓

5. Define an abstract class `Poem` with the following methods:

`public abstract int numLines()` — returns the number of lines in the poem.

`public abstract int getSyllables(int k)` — returns the number of syllables in the *k*-th line.

`public void printRhythm()` — shows the rhythm of the poem. For example, a haiku has 3 lines of 5, 7, and 5 syllables, so for haiku the `printRhythm` method should print

```
ta-ta-ta-ta-ta
ta-ta-ta-ta-ta-ta-ta
ta-ta-ta-ta-ta
```

A limerick has 5 lines of 9, 9, 6, 6, and 9 syllables. Define `Haiku` and `Limerick` as subclasses of `Poem`, and make the `printRhythm` method in each of them work without duplicating any code.

6. ▪   The class `Triangle` (`JM\Ch11\Exercises\Triangle.java`) has methods for calculating the area, the perimeter, and their ratio. The class works for equilateral triangles and for right isosceles triangles; the type of the triangle is passed in a string to the constructor. The class also has a `main` method.

(a)   Restructure this program in the OOP style. Make the `Triangle` class abstract. Keep the `side` field, but eliminate the `type` field. Make the `getArea` and `getPerimeter` methods abstract. Derive the concrete classes `EquilateralTriangle` and `RightTriangle` from `Triangle`. Provide an appropriate constructor for each of the two derived classes and make them call the superclass's constructor. Redefine the abstract methods appropriately in the derived classes. Put `main` in a separate test class and modify it appropriately.

(b)   The area of a triangle is equal to one half of its perimeter times the radius of the inscribed circle. If the length of a side of an equilateral triangle is the same as the length of the legs in a right isosceles triangle, which of these triangles can hold a bigger circle inside? ✓

7. ▪   Recall the `Bystander` class from Question 12 in Chapter 3. It was defined as a subclass of `Walker`. Now make `Bystander` a subclass of `Biped`. Add a `Bystander` to the `DanceGroup` in the *Dance Studio* program.

Sections 11.7-11.9

8.   (a)   Define an abstract class `WelcomeMessage` with a method

```
public String getWelcomeMessage();
```

that returns a welcome message. Define three subclasses `WelcomeEnglish`, `WelcomeSpanish`, and `WelcomeFrench`, whose `getWelcomeMessage` method returns a welcome message in English, Spanish, and French, respectively. Write a test class with a method

```
public void print(WelcomeMessage msg)
```

that prints out `msg`. Add a `main` method that calls `print` three times, passing it welcome messages in different languages.

(b)   Modify the project, replacing the `WelcomeMessage` class with the `WelcomeMessage` interface. Explain the advantage of using an interface rather than an abstract class in this project.

9.   Consider the following interface:

```
public interface Place
{
  int distance(Place other);
}
```

Write a program that tests the following method: ✓

```
// Returns true if p1 is equidistant from p2 and p3
public boolean sameDistance(Place p1, Place p2, Place p3)
{
   return p1.distance(p2) == p1.distance(p3);
}
```

10.■   Explain why the `toString` method is never listed in any interface.

11.■   (a)   Make the `Hopper` class (from Question 10 in Chapter 3) a subclass of `Biped`.

(b)   Create a class `RandomHopper`, which extends `Hopper`. A `RandomHopper` hops like a `Hopper` but chooses its direction randomly after each step: continues in the same direction, makes a left turn, makes a right turn, or turns around with equal probabilities.

(c)   Create a `HoppingGroup` class, adapting it from `DanceGroup` and replacing the `Dancer`s with a `RandomHopper`. Replace `DanceGroup` with `HoppingGroup` in `DanceStudio.java` (provided in J_M\Ch11\DanceStudio folder). Set up a project with your `Hopper`, `RandomHopper`, `HoppingGroup`, and `DanceStudio` classes and the `DanceStudio.jar` file from J_M\Ch11\DanceStudio folder, and test the program.

12.♦   Add your own "dance" class (but don't spend too much time on choreography!). Add an entry for your dance to the dances listed in `ControlPanel.java` (included in the J_M\Ch11\Exercises folder).

```
Section[] chapter12 =
            new Section[12];
```

Arrays and **ArrayLists**

321

12.1 Prologue

Java programmers can declare several consecutive memory locations of the same data type under one name. Such memory blocks are called *arrays,* and the individual memory locations are called the *elements* of the array. The number of elements is called the *size* or *length* of the array. Your program can refer to an individual element of an array using the array name followed by the element's number (called its *index* or *subscript*) in brackets. An index can be any integer constant, variable, or expression.

There are many good reasons for using arrays. Suppose your program requires you to enter a number of integers, such as test scores, and calculate their average. Of course you could try to hold the entered values in separate variables, score1, score2, ... But this would not work very well. First, since you might not know in advance how many scores would be entered, you would have to declare as many variables as the maximum possible number of inputs. Then you would have to read each score individually:

```
score1 = input.nextInt();
score2 = input.nextInt();
...
```

This could get tedious. And then adding the scores up would require a separate statement for each addition:

```
int sum = 0;
sum += score1;
sum += score2;
...
```

Now suppose you wanted to see the *k*-th score. Imagine programming it like this:

```
if (k == 1)
  System.out.print(score1);
else if (k == 2)
  System.out.print(score2);
else if < ... etc. >
```

Fortunately, arrays make the coding of such tasks much easier. You can write

```
int sum = 0;
for (int k = 0; k < scores.length; k++)
  sum += scores[k];
```

and

```
System.out.print(scores[k]);
```

Here `scores[0]` refers to the first score, `scores[1]` to the second, and so on.

In this chapter we will discuss how to

- Declare and create arrays
- Access an array's elements using indices
- Access an array's length
- Pass arrays to methods
- Use the `java.util.ArrayList` class
- Traverse an array or an `ArrayList` using a "for each" loop
- Declare and create two-dimensional arrays

12.2 One-Dimensional Arrays

Java treats arrays as objects of the type "array of `ints`," "array of `doubles`," "array of `Strings`," and so on. You can have an array of elements of any type. Use empty brackets after the type name to indicate that a variable refers to an array, as follows:

```
sometype[] someName;
```

For example:

```
int[] scores;
```

▌ **Arrays in Java are similar to objects.**

In particular, you need to first declare an array-type variable, then create the array using the `new` operator. You can declare and create an array in the same statement. For example, the following statement declares an array of integers, called `scores`, and creates that array with 10 elements:

```
int[] scores = new int[10];
```

An array of 5000 strings and an array of 16 "colors" can be declared and created as follows:

```
String[] words = new String[5000];
Color[] colors = new Color[16];
```

Note that brackets, not parentheses, are used here with the `new` operator. The number in brackets, as in `new int[10]` or `new String[5000]`, indicates the size (length) of the array.

> **When an array is created, its elements are initialized to default values. Numeric elements are initialized to 0, `boolean` to `false`.**
>
> **If array elements are of a <u>class</u> type, then the array contains <u>references</u> to objects of that type; these are initialized to `null`.**

If the elements are object references, you have to initialize each element by setting it to a valid reference before that element's methods are called. For example:

```
colors[0] = new Color(207, 189, 250);
colors[1] = Color.BLUE;
```

and so on. Otherwise you will get a `NullPointerException`.

❖ ❖ ❖

> **Another way to declare and create an array is to list explicitly, between braces, the values of all its elements. The `new` operator is not used in this form.**

For example:

```
int[] scores = {95, 97, 79, 99, 100};
String[] names = {"Vikas", "Larisa", "Nick"};

Color[] rainbowColors =
{
  Color.RED, Color.ORANGE, Color.YELLOW, Color.GREEN,
  Color.CYAN, Color.BLUE, Color.MAGENTA
};
```

The first statement creates an array of five integers; the second creates an array of three strings; the third creates an array of seven colors. The initial values within braces can be any constants, initialized variables, or expressions of the same type as given in the array declaration.

> **In Java, once an array is declared and initialized, either with the new operator or with a list of values, it is not possible to change its size.**

To increase the size, you have to create a larger array, copy the values from the original array to the new one, reassign the name of the original array to the new array, and abandon the original array (to be picked up by the garbage collector).

> **A program can access individual elements of an array using *indices* (also called *subscripts*). An index is an integer value placed in square brackets after the array name to identify the element. The elements of an array are numbered starting from 0.**

The following statements declare an array of 100 integer elements:

```
final int MAXCOUNT = 100;
int[] a = new int[MAXCOUNT];
```

The elements of this array can be referred to as `a[0], a[1], ... , a[99]`.

The power of arrays lies in the fact that an index can be any integer variable or expression. A program can refer, for example, to `a[i]`, where `i` is an integer variable. When the program is running, it interprets `a[i]` as the element of the array whose index is equal to whatever value `i` currently has. For example, if the variable `i` gets the value 3 and the program accesses `a[i]` at that point, `a[i]` will refer to `a[3]`, which is the fourth element of the array (`a[0]` being the first element). The index can be any expression with an integer value. For example:

```
double[] coordinates = new double[12];
for (int i = 0; i < 6; i++)
{
  coordinates[2 * i] = i;
  coordinates[2 * i + 1] = Math.sqrt(i);
}
```

In Java, every array "knows" its own size (length). Java syntax allows you to access the length of an array by using the expression *arrayName*`.length`. In terms of syntax, `length` acts as a public field that holds the size of the array.

> **In arrays, `length` is not a method (as in the `String` class). It is accessed like a field, without parentheses.**

For example:

```
double[] samples = new double[10];
...
if (i >= 0 && i < samples.length)
  ...
```

All indices must fall in the range between 0 and *length* – 1, where *length* is the number of elements in the array. If an index happens to be out of this range, your program will throw an `ArrayIndexOutOfBoundsException`.

You can set any element in an array with a simple assignment statement:

```
a[k] = < constant, variable, or expression >;
```

Arrays are always passed to methods as references.

If an array is passed to a method, the method gets the address of the original array and works with the <u>original array</u>, not a copy. Therefore, a method can change an array passed to it. For example:

```
// Swaps a[i] and a[j]
public void swap(int[] a, int i, int j)
{
  int temp = a[i];
  a[i] = a[j];
  a[j] = temp;
}
```

A method can also create a new array and return it (as a reference). For example:

```
public int[] readScores()  // return type is an integer array
{
  int[] scores = new int[10];

  for (int k = 0; k < 10; k++)
    scores[k] = readOneScore();

  return scores;
}
```

12.3 *Lab:* Fortune Teller

The applet in Figure 12-1 is a "fortune teller." When the user presses the "Next" button, the applet displays a message randomly chosen from an array of messages. The applet is implemented in one class, `FortuneTeller`.

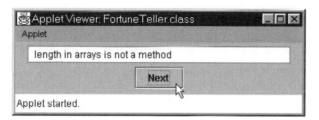

Figure 12-1. The *Fortune Teller* applet

Set up a project with the `FortuneTeller.java` and `TestFortune.html` files from `JM\Ch12\Fortunes`. (`TestFortune.html` describes a web page that holds the applet.) Fill in the blanks in the applet's code, adding an array of a few "fortunes" (strings) and the code to randomly choose and display one of them. Recall that the static `Math.random` method returns a random `double` value x such that $0 \le x < 1$. We have used it in earlier programs (for example, `JM\Ch07\Craps\Die.java`). Scale the value returned by `Math.random` appropriately to obtain a random value for an index within the range of your array. Use `display`'s `setText` method to show the chosen message.

12.4 The `ArrayList` Class

Java arrays are convenient and safe. However, they have one limitation: once an array is created, its size cannot change. If an array is full and you want to add an element, you have to create a new array of a larger size, copy all the values from the old array into the new array, then reassign the old name to the new array. For example:

```
Object[] arr = new Object[someSize];
...

Object[] temp = new Object[2 * arr.length]; // double the size

for (int i = 0; i < arr.length; i++)
  temp[i] = arr[i];

arr = temp;
```

The old array is eventually recycled by the Java garbage collector.

If you know in advance the maximum number of values that will be stored in an array, you can declare an array of that size from the start. But then you have to keep track of the actual number of values stored in the array and make sure you do not refer to an element that is beyond the last value currently stored in the array. The library class ArrayList from the java.util package provides that functionality.

As the name implies, an ArrayList allows you to keep a list of values in an array. The ArrayList keeps track of its *capacity* and *size* (Figure 12-2). The capacity is the length of the currently allocated array that holds the list values. The size is the number of elements currently stored in the list. When the size reaches ArrayList's capacity and you need to add an element, the ArrayList automatically increases its capacity by executing code similar to the fragment shown above.

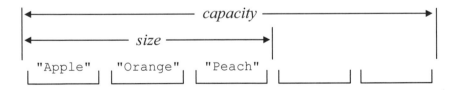

Figure 12-2. The capacity and size of an ArrayList

The ArrayList class provides the get and set methods, which access and set the *i*-th element, respectively. These methods check that $0 \leq i < size$. In addition, an ArrayList has convenient methods to add and remove an element.

From a more abstract point of view, an ArrayList represents a "list" of objects. A "list" holds several values arranged in a sequence and numbered. The ArrayList class is part of the Java *collections framework* and implements the java.util.List interface.

Another library class, `java.util.LinkedList`, also implements `java.util.List`:

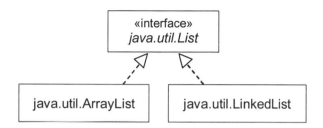

`LinkedList` has the same methods as `ArrayList`, but it uses a different data structure to store the list elements. This is explained in more detail in Chapter 19.

If your class uses `java.util.List` and `java.util.ArrayList`, add

```
import java.util.List;
import java.util.ArrayList;
```

or

```
import java.util.*;
```

at the top of your source file.

An `ArrayList` holds objects of a specified type.

Starting with Java 5.0, when you declare an `ArrayList`, you should specify the type of its elements. The type is placed in angle brackets after `ArrayList`. For example:

```
private ArrayList<String> names;
```

or

```
private ArrayList<Walker> family;
```

> Syntactically, the whole combination `ArrayList<`*`sometype`*`>` acts as one long class name, which is read "an ArrayList of sometypes." You need to use the whole thing whenever you use the `ArrayList` type: in declaring variables, method parameters, and return values, and when you create an `ArrayList`.

For example:

```
// Returns an ArrayList with the elements from names rearranged
// in random order
public ArrayList<String> scrambled(ArrayList<String> names)
{
  ArrayList<String> result = new ArrayList<String>();
  ...
  return result;
}
```

We hope you have good typing skills!

> An `ArrayList`, like other kinds of Java collections, can only hold objects. If you try to add a value of a primitive data type to a list, the compiler will convert that value into an object of a corresponding wrapper class (`Integer`, `Double`, etc.). For it to work, that wrapper type must match the declared type of the list elements.

For example,

```
ArrayList<Double> samples = new ArrayList<Double>();
samples.add(5.0);
```

works and is the same as

```
ArrayList<Double> samples = new ArrayList<Double>();
samples.add(new Double(5.0));
```

This is called *autoboxing*. But

```
samples.add(5);  // can't add an int to an ArrayList<Double>
```

won't work.

An `ArrayList` can also hold `null`s after calls to `add(null)` or `add(i, null)`. (We'll examine `add` and other `ArrayList` methods in the next section.)

12.5 `ArrayList`'s Constructors and Methods

`ArrayList`'s no-args constructor creates an empty list (`size() == 0`) of the default capacity (ten). Another constructor, `ArrayList(int capacity)`, creates an empty list with a given initial capacity. If you know in advance the maximum number of values that will be stored in your list, it is better to create an `ArrayList` of that capacity from the outset to avoid later reallocation and copying of the list. For example:

```
ArrayList<String> names = new ArrayList<String>(10000);
```

```
int size()                      // Returns the number of elements
                                //   currently stored in the list
boolean isEmpty()               // Returns true if the list is empty;
                                //   otherwise returns false
boolean add(E elmt)             // Appends elmt at the end of the list;
                                //   returns true
void add(int i, E elmt)         // Inserts elmt into the i-th position;
                                //   shifts the element currently at
                                //   that position and the subsequent
                                //   elements to the right (increments
                                //   their indices by one)
E get(int i)                    // Returns the value of the i-th
                                //   element
E set(int i, E elmt)            // Replaces the i-th element with elmt;
                                //   returns the old value
E remove(int i)                 // Removes the i-th element from the
                                //   list and returns its value;
                                //   shifts the subsequent elements
                                //   (if any) to the left (decrements
                                //   their indices by 1)
boolean contains(Object obj)    // Returns true if this list contains
                                //   an element equal to obj (the equals
                                //   method is used for comparison)
int indexOf(Object obj)         // Returns the index of the first
                                //   occurrence of obj in this list,
                                //   or -1 if obj is not found (the
                                //   equals method is used for comparison)
String toString()               // Returns a string representation of this
                                //   list as [elmt1, elmt2, ..., elmtN]
```

Figure 12-3. Commonly used `ArrayList<E>` methods

The `ArrayList` class implements over two dozen methods (specified in the `List` interface), but we will discuss only a subset of more commonly used methods. These are shown in Figure 12-3. (Java API docs use the letter *E* to refer to the type of `ArrayList` elements. So it would be more accurate to say that Figure 12-3 shows some of the methods of `ArrayList<E>`.)

As we've noted, the elements in an `ArrayList` are numbered by their indices from 0 to *list*.`size()` - 1. In the `get(i)` and `set(i, elmt)` methods, the parameter i must be in the range from 0 to *list*.`size()` - 1; otherwise these methods throw an `IndexOutOfBoundsException`.

The `add(E elmt)` method appends `elmt` at the end of the list and increments the size of the list by one. The `add` method is overloaded: the version with two parameters, `add(int i, E elmt)`, <u>inserts</u> `elmt` into the list, so that `elmt` becomes the *i*-th element. This method shifts the old *i*-th element and all the subsequent elements to the right and increments their indices by one. It also increments the size of the list by one. This method checks that $0 \le i \le list.size()$ and throws `IndexOutOfBoundsException` if it isn't. If called with $i = $ `list.size()`, then `add(int i, E elmt)` works the same as `add(E elmt)`.

The `remove(i)` method removes the *i*-th element from the list, shifts all the subsequent elements (if any) to the left by one, and decrements their indices. It also decrements the size of the list by one. `remove` returns the value of the removed element.

`ArrayList` implements the `get` and `set` methods very efficiently, because the elements are stored in an array, which gives direct access to the element with a given index. Inserting or removing an element at the beginning or somewhere in the middle of an `ArrayList` is less efficient, because it requires shifting the subsequent elements. Adding an element may occasionally require reallocation and copying of the array, which may be time-consuming for a long list.

The convenient `toString` method allows you to get a string representation of a list and to print the whole list in one statement. For example:

```
System.out.println(list);
```

The list will be displayed within square brackets with consecutive elements separated by a comma and a space.

The `indexOf(Object obj)` and `contains(Object obj)` methods are interesting. They need some way to compare `obj` to the elements of the list. This is accomplished by calling `obj`'s `equals` method, something like this:

```
if (list.get(i).equals(obj))
  ...
```

Therefore, you should make sure a reasonable `equals` method is defined for your objects if you plan to place them into an `ArrayList`. Appropriate `equals` methods are defined, of course, for `Integer`, `Double`, `String`. We will explain how to define `equals` for your own classes in Chapter 13.

12.6 ArrayList's Pitfalls

You have to be careful with the `add` and `remove` methods: keep in mind that they change the indices of the subsequent elements and the size of the list.

The following innocent-looking code, for example, intends to remove all occurrences of the word `"like"` from an `ArrayList<String>`:

```
ArrayList<String> words = new ArrayList<String>();
...

int n = words.size();

for (int i = 0; i < n; i++)
{
  if ("like".equals(words.get(i)))
    words.remove(i);
}
```

However, after the first `"like"` is found and removed, the size of the list `words` is decremented and becomes smaller than n. Once i goes past the new list size, the program will be aborted with an `IndexOutOfBoundsException`.

And that is not all. Even if we fix this bug by getting rid of n —

```
ArrayList<String> words = new ArrayList<String>();
...

for (int i = 0; i < words.size(); i++)
{
  if ("like".equals(words.get(i)))
    words.remove(i);
}
```

— another bug still remains. When an occurrence of "like" is removed, the subsequent words are shifted to the left. Then i is incremented in the for loop. As a result, the next word is skipped. If "like" occurs twice in a row, the second one will not be removed. The correct code should increment i only if the word is not removed. For example:

```
int i = 0;

while (i < words.size())
{
  if ("like".equals(words.get(i)))
    words.remove(i);
  else
    i++;
}
```

> An **ArrayList** holds references to objects. It can hold duplicate values — **not only equal objects (that is, `obj1.equals(obj2)`), but also several references to <u>the same</u> object (that is, `obj1 == obj2`).**

It is important to understand that an object can change <u>after</u> it has been added to a list (unless that object is immutable) and that the same object can belong to several ArrayLists.

Consider, for example, the following two versions of the method makeGuestList that builds a list of people (objects of the class Person) from a given array of names. Let's assume that the class Person has the constructors used in the code and a setName method, which sets the person's name.

Version 1:

```
public ArrayList<Person> makeGuestList(String[] names)
{
  ArrayList<Person> list = new ArrayList<Person>();
  for (int i = 0; i < names.length; i++)
    list.add(new Person(names[i]));
  return list;
}
```

Version 2:

```
public ArrayList<Person> makeGuestList(String[] names)
{
  ArrayList<Person> list = new ArrayList<Person>();
  Person p = new Person();
  for (int i = 0; i < names.length; i++)
  {
    p.setName(names[i]);
    list.add(p);
  }
  return list;
}
```

After the statements

```
String[] names = {"Alice", "Bob", "Claire"};
List<Person> guests = makeGuestList(names);
System.out.println(guests);
```

are executed, Version 1 displays

```
[Alice, Bob, Claire]
```

as expected (Figure 12-4-a). Version 2, however, displays

```
[Claire, Claire, Claire]
```

because the list contains three references to <u>the same</u> object (Figure 12-4-b). Adding this object to the list does not shield it from being modified by the subsequent setName calls.

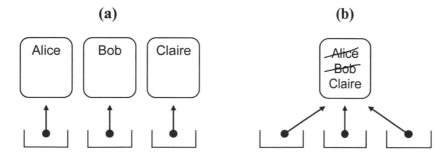

(a)   **(b)**

Figure 12-4. (a) A list with references to different objects;
(b) A list with references to the same object

12.7 Iterations and the "For Each" Loop

Iterations are indispensable for handling arrays and lists for two reasons. First, if a list is large and we want to access every element (for example, to find the sum of all the elements), it is not practical to repeat the same statement over and over again in the source code:

```
int sum = 0;
sum += a[0];
sum += a[1];
...
...
sum += a[999];
```

A simple `for` loop saves 998 lines of code:

```
int sum = 0;
for (int i = 0; i < 1000; i++)
   sum += a[i];
```

Second, a programmer may not know the exact size of a list in advance. The actual number of elements may become known only when the program is running. For example, a list may be filled with data read from a file, and we may not know in advance how many items are stored in the file. The only way to deal with such a "variable-length" list (such as an `ArrayList`) is through iterations.

Traversal is a procedure in which every element of a list is "visited" and processed once. An array or list is usually traversed in order of the indices (or in reverse order of the indices). Usually elements are not added or removed during traversal.

An array or list traversal can be accomplished easily with a simple `for` loop. For example:

```
String[] names = new String[numGuests];
...
for (int i = 0; i < names.length; i++)
{
  String str = names[i];
  ...  // process str
}
```

Or, for an `ArrayList`,

```
ArrayList<String> names = new ArrayList<String>();
...
for (int i = 0; i < names.size(); i++)
{
  String str = names.get(i);
  ... // process str
}
```

Starting with version 5.0, Java offers a convenient "for each" loop for traversing an array or a `List` (or another type of Java `Collection`). The above code fragments can be rewritten with a "for each" loop as follows:

```
for (String str : names)
{
  ... // process str
}
```

This works for both an array and an `ArrayList`. The "for each" syntax requires that the loop variable be declared inside the `for` statement, as in `String str`.

> **Note that if you use a "for each" loop to traverse an array with elements of a <u>primitive data type</u>, you <u>cannot</u> change their values because the loop variable holds a copy of the element, not a reference to the original.**

The "for each" loop does not give you access to the index of the "visited" element. For example, it will work fine in a method like `contains` —

```
public boolean contains (String[] names, String target)
{
  for (String name : names)
    if (name.equals(target))
      return true;
  return false;
}
```

— but not in a method like `indexOf`. Use a regular `for` loop if you need access to the indices.

❖   ❖   ❖

A frequent reason for traversing a list is looking for the list's largest or smallest element. To find the maximum value we can initialize a variable representing the maximum to, say, the value of the first element of the array, then compare it with all the other elements and update its value each time we encounter a larger element. For example:

```java
// Returns the value of the largest element in the array a
public static double findMax(double[] a)
{
  double aMax = a[0];

  for (int i = 1; i < a.length; i++)
  {
    if (a[i] > aMax)
      aMax = a[i];
  }

  return aMax;
}
```

Alternatively we can keep track of the <u>position</u> of the maximum:

```java
// Returns the position of the largest element in the array a
public static int findMaxPos(double[] a)
{
  int iMax = 0;

  for (int i = 1; i < a.length; i++)
  {
    if (a[i] > a[iMax])
      iMax = i;
  }

  return iMax;
}
```

To find the minimum we can proceed in a similar way but update the current minimum value (or its position) each time we encounter a smaller element. Similar code works for an `ArrayList<String>`:

```java
// Returns the position of the alphabetically first word in words
public static int findFirstWordPos(ArrayList<String> words)
{
  int iMin = 0;

  for (int i = 1; i < words.size(); i++)
  {
    String word = words.get(i);
    if (word.compareToCaseBlind(words.get(iMin)) < 0)
      iMin = i;
  }

  return iMin;
}
```

12.8 Inserting and Removing Elements

ArrayList's add and remove methods take care of inserting and removing elements. For regular arrays, you have to do it yourself. To insert an element, you have to first make sure that the array has room to hold one more element. When you create your array, you have to allocate sufficient space for the <u>maximum possible</u> number of elements. In this case, the array's length will refer to the maximum capacity of the array. You need a separate variable to keep count of the elements actually stored in it. For example:

```
final int maxCount = 5000;        // Maximum number of words
String[] dictionary = new String[maxCount];
int count = 0;                    // Start with an empty dictionary
< ... etc. >
```

To add an element at the end of an array you need to check that there is still room and, if so, store the element in the first vacant slot and increment the count. For example:

```
String word;

<... other statements >

if (count < maxCount)
{
  dictionary[count] = word;
  count++;
}
```

If you want to keep an array sorted in ascending or descending order, it may be necessary to insert a new element <u>in the middle </u>of the array. To do that, you first need to shift a few elements toward the end of the array to create a vacant slot in the desired position. You have to start shifting from the last element — otherwise you may overwrite an element before you get it out of the way. Figure 12-5 illustrates the process.

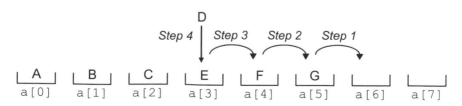

Figure 12-5. Inserting an element in the middle of an array

The following code serves as an example:

```
String word;
int insertPos;

<... other statements >

if (count < maxCount)  // count is the number of words already in
{                      //    dictionary
  for (int i = count; i > insertPos; i--)
  {
    dictionary[i] = dictionary[i-1];
  }
  dictionary[insertPos] = word;
  count++;
}
```

To remove an element you have to shift all the elements that follow it by one toward the beginning of the array. This time you have to start shifting at the position that follows the element that you are removing and proceed toward the end of the array.

12.9 *Lab:* Creating an Index for a Document

In this lab you will write a program that reads a text file and generates an index for it. All the words that occur in the text should be listed in the index in upper case in alphabetical order. Each word should be followed by a list of all the line numbers for lines that contain that word. Figure 12-6 shows an example.

The *Index Maker* program consists of three classes (Figure 12-7). It also uses ArrayList in two ways: IndexEntry <u>has</u> an ArrayList<Integer> field that holds the line numbers, and DocumentIndex <u>extends</u> ArrayList<IndexEntry>.

The IndexMaker class is the main class. We have provided this class for you in JM\Ch12\IndexMaker. Its main method prompts the user for the names of the input and output files (or obtains them from command-line arguments, if supplied), opens the input file, creates an output file, reads and processes all the lines from the input file, then saves the resulting document index in the output file.

Writing the DocumentIndex and IndexEntry classes is left to you (possibly in a team with another programmer). You don't have to deal with reading or writing files in this lab.

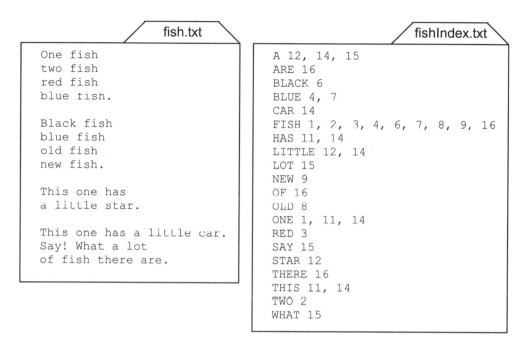

Figure 12-6.   A sample text file and its index

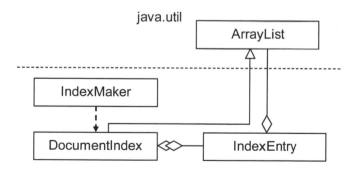

Figure 12-7.   IndexMaker classes

The `IndexEntry` class

An `IndexEntry` object represents one index entry. It has two fields:

```
private String word;
private ArrayList<Integer> numsList;
```

The numbers in `numsList` represent the line numbers where `word` occurs in the input file. (Note that the `IndexEntry` class is quite general and reusable: the numbers can represent line numbers, page numbers, etc., depending on the application.)

Provide a constructor for this class that takes a given word (a `String`), converts it into the upper case (by calling `toUpperCase`), and saves it in `word`. The constructor should also initialize `numsList` to an empty `ArrayList<Integer>`.

This class should have the following three methods:

1. `void add(int num)` — appends `num` to `numsList`, but only if it is not already in that list. You will need to convert `num` into an `Integer` to call `numsList`'s `contains` method.

2. `String getWord()` — this is an accessor method; it returns `word`.

3. `String toString()` — returns a string representation of this `IndexEntry` in the format used in each line of the output file (Figure 12-6).

The `DocumentIndex` class

A `DocumentIndex` object represents the entire index for a document: the list of all its index entries. The index entries should always be arranged in alphabetical order, as shown in Figure 12-6.

Make the `DocumentIndex` class <u>extend</u> `ArrayList<IndexEntry>`. Provide two constructors: one that creates a list with the default capacity, the other that creates a list with a given capacity. (These constructors simply call the respective constructors of the superclass, `ArrayList`.)

`DocumentIndex` should have the following two public methods:

1. `void addWord(String word, int num)` — adds `num` to the `IndexEntry` for `word` by calling that `IndexEntry`'s `add(num)` method. If `word` is not yet in this `DocumentIndex`, the method first creates a new `IndexEntry` for `word` and inserts it into this list in alphabetical order (ignoring the upper and lower case).

2. `void addAllWords(String str, int num)` — extracts all the words from `str` (skipping punctuation and whitespace) and for each word calls `addWord(word, num)`.

    You could code the word extractor yourself, of course, but it is much better to use the `String` class's `split` method. Look it up in the Java API. Use the one that takes one parameter, `regex`, that is, a *regular expression*☆regex. Regular expressions are not specific to Java: they are used in many languages and text parsers. `regex` describes the match pattern for all possible word separators. Use `"\\W+"` here. `\W` (with an uppercase 'W') stands for any "non-word" character, that is, any character that is not a digit or a letter. `+` means "occurs at least once." (Regular expressions use backslash as the escape character; hence the double backslash in the literal string.)

    `split` returns an array of `String`s. Use a "for each" loop to call `addWord` for each word in that array. Note, however, that `split` may put an empty string into the resulting array — when `str` starts with a separator or when `str` is empty. This is an unfortunate decision (or a bug). Make sure you skip empty strings and do not call `addWord` for them.

We recommend that you also define a private helper method

```
private int foundOrInserted(String word)
```

and call it from `addWord`. This method should traverse this `DocumentIndex` and compare `word` (case-blind) to the words in the `IndexEntry` objects in this list, looking for the position where `word` fits in alphabetically. If an `IndexEntry` with `word` is not already in that position, the method creates and inserts a new `IndexEntry` for `word` at that position. The method returns the position (we'd like to say "the index" but we have too many indices going already!) of the either found or inserted `IndexEntry`.

Test your program thoroughly on different text data files, including an empty file, a file with blank lines, a file with lines that have leading spaces or punctuation, a file with multiple occurrences of a word on the same line, and a file with the same word on different lines.

12.10 Two-Dimensional Arrays

Programmers use two-dimensional arrays to represent rectangular tables of elements of the same data type. For instance, a 2-D array may hold positions in a board game, a table of spreadsheet cells, elements of a matrix, or pixel values in an image.

The following example shows two ways to declare and initialize a 2-D array of doubles:

```
int rows = 2;
int cols = 3;

double[][] a = new double[rows][cols]; // Declares an array of doubles
                                       //    with 2 rows and 3 columns
                                       //    and sets them to 0.

double[][] b =                         // Declares a 2 by 3 array of
{                                      //    doubles initialized to
  {0.0, 0.1, 0.2},                     //    specified values
  {1.0, 1.1, 1.2}
};
```

> We access the elements of a 2-D array with a pair of indices, each placed in square brackets. We can think of the first index as a "row" and the second as a "column." Both indices start from 0.

In the above example,

```
b[0][0] = 0.0;    b[0][1] = 0.1;    b[0][2] = 0.2;
b[1][0] = 1.0;    b[1][1] = 1.1;    b[1][2] = 1.2;
```

In Java, a 2-D array is represented essentially as a 1-D array of 1-D arrays, its rows. Each row is an array. In the example above, b[0] is the first row, which contains the values 0.0, 0.1, and 0.2. b[1] is the second row of values: 1.0, 1.1, and 1.2. Strictly speaking, it is possible for different rows in a 2-D array to have different numbers of "columns." In this book, we will deal only with "rectangular" 2-D arrays that have the same number of elements in all rows.

> If m is a 2-D array, then m.length is the number of rows in the array, m[0] is the first row (a 1-D array), and m[0].length is the number of columns (in the first row). m[r][c] is the element in row r and column c.

If we want to traverse a two-dimensional array, it is convenient to use nested `for` loops. For example:

```
int rows = 12; cols = 7;
char[][] grid = new char[rows][cols];
    ...
// Set all elements in grid to '*':
for (int r = 0; r < rows; r++)
{
  for (int c = 0; c < cols; c++)
  {
    grid[r][c] = '*';
  }
}
```

Braces are optional here since the body of each loop consists of only one statement. You could just as well write:

```
for (r = 0; r < rows; r++)
  for (c = 0; c < cols; c++)
    grid[r][c] = '*';
```

(We find that `r` and `c` or `row` and `col` are often better choices for the names of the indices than, say, `i` and `j`.)

The following code fragment prints out the values of a 2-D array of `int`s m:

```
for (int r = 0; r < m.length; r++)
{
  for (int c = 0; c < m[r].length; c++)
  {
    System.out.printf("%5d ", m[r][c]);
  }
  System.out.println();
}
```

> **Be careful when using `break` in nested loops: a `break` statement inside a nested loop will only break out of the inner loop.**

For example, suppose you have a 2-D array of characters `grid` and you want to find the first occurrence of the letter 'A' in it (scanning the first row left to right, then the next row, etc.). You might be tempted to use the following code:

```
int rows = grid.length, cols = grid[0].length;
int r, c, firstArow, firstAcol;

for (r = 0; r < rows; r++)
{
  for (c = 0; c < cols; c++)
  {
    if (grid[r][c] == 'A')
      break;
  }
}
firstArow = r;
firstAcol = c;
```

Unfortunately, it will only find the first occurrence of 'A' in the <u>last</u> row (if any).

You can declare three-dimensional and multi-dimensional arrays in a manner similar to two-dimensional arrays. Arrays in three or more dimensions are not used very often. In this book we never go beyond two dimensions.

12.11   *Case Study and Lab:* Chomp

The game of Chomp can be played on a rectangular board of any size. The board is divided into squares (let's say the board represents a chocolate bar). The rules are quite simple: the two players alternate taking rectangular "bites" from the board. On each move, the player must take any one of the remaining squares as well as all the squares that lie below and to the right (Figure 12-8). The square in the upper-left corner of the board is "poison": whoever takes it loses the game. Click on the Chomp.jar file in the JM\Ch12\Chomp to run the *Chomp* program.

The number of all possible positions in Chomp is finite, and the players make steady progress from the initial position to the end, as the total number of remaining "edible" squares on the board decreases with each move. Games of this type always have a winning strategy either for the first or for the second player. But, despite its simple rules, Chomp turns out to be a tricky game: you can prove mathematically that the first player has a winning strategy, but the proof does not tell you what that strategy is.[*] You know you can win if you go first, but you don't know how! Frustrating...

---

[*] The proof looks like this. The first player can try to take the lower right corner on the first move. If this is the correct move in a winning strategy, the first player is all set. If it is not, the second player must have a winning move in response. But the first player could "steal"

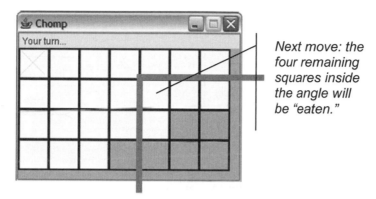

Next move: the four remaining squares inside the angle will be "eaten."

Figure 12-8.   The Chomp game program

As far as we know, at the time of this writing no one has been able to come up with a formula for the winning Chomp positions (except for two special cases, the 2 by *n* and *n* by *n* boards). There are computer programs that can backtrack from the final position (where only the "poison" square is left) and generate a list of all the winning positions. Our *Chomp* program uses such a list, so the computer has an unfair advantage. You could try to "steal" the winning moves from the computer, but the program's author has foreseen such a possibility and programmed the computer to intentionally make a few random moves before it settles into its winning strategy.

Luckily our goal here is not to beat the computer at Chomp, but to practice object-oriented software design and Java programming.

Let us begin by looking at the overall structure of this program (Figure 12-9). The program consists of eight classes and two interfaces, `Player` and `Strategy`. In designing this program we tried, as usual, to reduce *coupling* (dependencies between classes) and to separate the logic/calculations part from the GUI. `Chomp`, `HumanPlayer`, and `ComputerPlayer`, for instance, know very little about `BoardPanel`. `ComputerPlayer` is the only class that is aware of `Strategy` methods (but not of any particular Chomp strategy).

that winning response move and make it his own first move! In the theory of finite games, this argument is called "strategy stealing." Unfortunately, this proof gives no clue as to what the winning strategy might be.

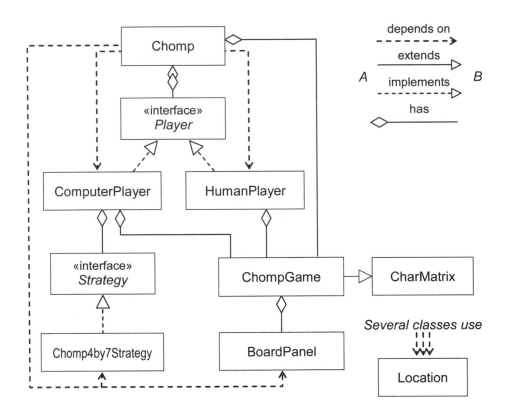

Figure 12-9. The classes in the *Chomp* program

The top class, `Chomp`, derived from `JFrame`, represents the main program window. Its constructor creates a `ChompGame`, a `BoardPanel` (the display panel for the board), and the human and computer "players." It also attaches a particular strategy to the computer player:

```
BoardPanel board = new BoardPanel();
...

game = new ChompGame(board);

HumanPlayer human = new HumanPlayer(this, game, board);
ComputerPlayer computer = new ComputerPlayer(this, game, board);
computer.setStrategy(new Chomp4by7Strategy());
```

A `ChompGame` object models Chomp in an abstract way. It knows the rules of the game, and, with the help of its superclass `CharMatrix`, keeps track of the current board position and implements the players' moves. But `ChompGame` does not display the board — that function is left to a separate "view" class, `BoardPanel`. `ChompGame` only represents the "model" of the game. This class and the `Chomp4by7Strategy` class are really the only classes that "know" and use the rules of Chomp.

The `ChompGame` class extends `CharMatrix`, a general-purpose class that represents a 2-D array of characters. A matrix of characters helps `ChompGame` to represent the current configuration of the board. We could potentially put all the code from `CharMatrix` directly into `ChompGame`. That would make the `ChompGame` class quite large. More importantly, general methods dealing with a character matrix would be mixed together in the same class with more specific methods that deal with the rules of Chomp. Such a class would be hardly reusable. By separating the more general functions from the more specific ones, we have created a reusable class `CharMatrix` without any extra effort.

`BoardPanel` is derived from the library class `JPanel`, and it knows how to display the current board position. `Chomp` adds the display to the main window's content pane and also attaches it to `ChompGame`. When the board situation changes, `ChompGame` calls `BoardPanel`'s `update` method to update the screen. `BoardPanel` is the longest class in this project. Its code has to deal with rendering different squares in different colors and to support the "flashing" feedback for computer moves.

The `HumanPlayer` and `ComputerPlayer` objects obviously represent the two players. The `HumanPlayer` captures and interprets mouse clicks on the board and tells `ChompGame` to make the corresponding move. The `ComputerPlayer` asks the `Strategy` given to it to supply the next move and tells `ChompGame` to make that move.

Finally, the `Location` class represents a (*row, col*) location on the board. `Location` objects are simple "data carriers": `Location` has one constructor, `Location(row, col)`, and two accessors, `getRow()` and `getCol()`. In the *Chomp* program, `Location` objects are passed from the board to the human player and from a `Strategy` object to the computer player.

Each of the two players implements the interface `Player`. However, the use of an interface here is different from the way we used the `Dance` interface in the *Dance Studio* project in Chapter 11. There we used `Dance` to isolate the "dance" subsystem from the rest of the program and to be able to pass different types of `Dance` parameters to a `Dancer`'s `learn` method. Here, as you can see in Figure 12-9, `Chomp` is well aware of both players, so `Player` does not isolate anything from anything. The reason we want both players to implement `Player` is that we want to hold them in the same array:

```
private Player[] players;
...

  players = new Player[2];
  players[0] = human;
  players[1] = computer;
```

This is convenient and adds flexibility: we can easily add other players in the future if we want.

> **A secondary common data type is useful for mixing different but related types of objects in the same array, list, or other collection.**

We could have made `Player` an abstract class rather than an interface, but the `HumanPlayer` and the `ComputerPlayer` do not share any code, so why waste the valuable "extends" slot in them? Eventually we might need it for something else.

But the `Strategy` interface works exactly the same way as `Dance` in *Dance Studio*: it isolates the subsystem that deals with different Chomp strategies from the rest of the program. A more advanced version of the *Chomp* program will need to support different strategies for different levels of play and board sizes. If all the strategy classes implement the same `Strategy` interface, we can pass any particular strategy as a parameter to the `ComputerPlayer`'s `setStrategy` method.

The `Strategy` interface is also useful for splitting the work among team members: more math-savvy developers can work on the strategy classes. The `Chomp4by7Strategy` class, for example, is rather cryptic. Luckily we don't really need to know much about it beyond the fact that it implements the `Strategy` interface and has a no-args constructor. Whoever wrote and tested this class is responsible for it! This is team development at its best.

You might have noticed that our designs of *Craps*, *Dance Studio*, and *Chomp* have some similarities. This is not a coincidence: we have followed established *design patterns*. Design patterns represent an attempt by experienced designers to formalize their experience and share it with novices. Design patterns help solve common design problems and avoid common mistakes.

In all three projects mentioned above, we used the *Model-View-Controller* (*MVC*) design pattern. The main idea of such a design is to clearly separate the "model" (a more abstract object that describes the situation) from the "controller" (the object that changes the state of the model) and from the "view" (the object that displays the model). The "view" is attached to the model and changes automatically (well, almost automatically) when the model changes. This way we isolate GUI from number crunching. Also, we can easily use several different controllers and attach several different views to the same model if we need to.

In the *Chomp* program, the ChompGame class is the "model," the BoardPanel object is the "view," and the "players" work as "controllers." In *Dance Studio*, DanceGroup is the "model," DanceFloor is the "view," and ControlPanel and Band are the "controllers."

Dance Studio and *Chomp* also follow the *Strategy* design pattern. This design pattern applies when a "player" needs to follow different "strategies" at different times. Rather than making the player itself create all the strategies and choose among them, we provide an interface or an abstract class to represent a strategy and a "setStrategy" method in the player object. A "strategy" and a "player" do not have to be interpreted literally, of course. For example, in *Dance Studio*, a particular dance is a "strategy" for a dancer and the Dancer's learn method is used to set the Dancer's "strategy."

We will explain several common design patterns in more detail in Chapter 26.

Your job in the *Chomp* project is to supply the missing code in the CharMatrix class, as described in the comments in CharMatrix.java. Then set up a project with the rest of the *Chomp's* classes provided in JM\Ch12\Chomp.

12.12 Summary

Java allows programmers to declare *arrays* — blocks of consecutive memory locations under one name. An array represents a collection of related values of the same data type.

You can refer to any specific element of an array by placing the element's *index* (*subscript*) in brackets after the array name. An index can be any integer constant, variable, or expression. In Java the index of the first element of an array is 0 and the index of the last element is *length* – 1, where *length* is the array's length. An index must always be in the range from 0 to *length* – 1; otherwise the program throws an `ArrayIndexOutOfBoundsException`.

In Java, arrays are objects. If `a` is an array, `a.length` acts as a public field of `a` that holds the number of elements in `a`. Arrays are passed to methods as references, so a method can change the contents of an array passed to it.

Programmers can also declare and use two-dimensional and multi-dimensional arrays. We can refer to an element in a 2-D array by placing two indices, each in brackets, after the array's name. Think of the first index as a "row" and the second as a "column." Both indices start from 0. In Java, a 2-D array is treated basically as a 1-D array of 1-D arrays, its rows. If `m` is a 2-D array, `m.length` is the number of rows and `m[0].length` is the number of columns (assuming that all rows have the same number of columns).

The `java.util.ArrayList` class helps implement "dynamic arrays" — arrays that can grow as needed. An `ArrayList` keeps track of the list's capacity (the length of the allocated array) and its size (the number of elements currently in the list). The no-args constructor creates an empty list of some small default capacity; another constructor creates an empty list of a specified capacity. When an `ArrayList` is full and we add a value, the `ArrayList` increases its capacity automatically by allocating a larger array and copying all the elements into it.

Starting with Java 5.0, `ArrayList` holds elements of a specified type. `ArrayList` doesn't work with values of a primitive data types — they are converted to objects of the corresponding wrapper class.

The most commonly used `ArrayList` methods are shown in Figure 12-3. The `add(obj)` method appends an element at the end of the list. The `get(i)`, `set(i, obj)`, `add(i, obj)`, and `remove(i)` methods check that `i` is from 0 to `size() - 1` (from 0 to `size()` in case of `add`) and throw an

IndexOutOfBoundsException if an index is out of the valid range. The add and remove methods adjust the indices of the subsequent elements and the size of the list. The contains method checks whether a given value is in the list, and the indexOf method returns the index of a given value (or –1 if not found).

ArrayList's get(i) and set(i, obj) methods are efficient because an array provides random access to its elements. The add(i, obj) and remove(i) methods are on average less efficient, because they require shifting of the elements that follow the *i*-th element. The add methods need to allocate more memory and copy the whole list when the list's capacity is exceeded.

An ArrayList holds references to objects. An object can be changed after it is added to the list (unless the object is immutable). A list is allowed to hold null references and multiple references to the same object.

Traversal is a procedure in which every element of a collection is "visited" and processed once. An array or a list is usually traversed in sequential order of its elements (or in reverse order). Elements are not added or removed during traversal.

The "for each" loop —

```
for (E elmt : list)
{
    ... // process elmt
}
```

provides a convenient way to traverse an array or a list from beginning to end. Use nested conventional for loops to traverse a 2-D array:

```
for (int r = 0; r < m.length; r++)
{
    for (int c = 0; c < m[0].length; c++)
    {
        ...
    }
}
```

Exercises

Sections 12.1-12.3

1.   (a)   Write a statement that declares an array of three integers, initialized to 1, 2, and 4. ✓

(b)   Write an expression that represents the sum of the three elements of the above array (regardless of their current values).

2.   Mark true or false and explain:

(a)   The following array has 101 elements:

```
int[] x = new int[100];  _____    ✓
```

(b)   Java syntax allows programmers to use any expression of the `int` data type as an array subscript. _____

(c)   The program, when running, verifies that all array subscripts fall into the valid range. _____ ✓

(d)   Any one-dimensional array object has a `length` method that returns the size of the array. _____ ✓

3.   Write a method that takes an array of integers as a parameter and swaps the first element with the last one. ✓

4.   An array of integers `scores` has at least two elements, and its elements are arranged in ascending order (that is, `scores[i]` ≤ `scores[i+1]`). Write a condition that tests whether all the elements in `scores` have the same values. ⸮ Hint: you do not need iterations. ⸮

5.   Write a method `getRandomRps` that returns a character `'r'`, `'p'`, or `'s'`, chosen randomly with odds of 3 : 5 : 6, respectively. ⸮ Hint: declare an array of `char`s and initialize it with values `'r'`, `'p'`, and `'s'`, with each value occurring a number of times proportional to its desired odds. Return a randomly chosen element of the array. ⸮ ✓

6.   What does the `mysteryCount` method count?

```
private int mysteryCount(int[] v)
{
  int count = 0;

  for (int i = 0; i < v.length; i++)
  {
    if (v[i] != 0) break;
    count++;
  }
  return count;
}
```

7.   If you take any two positive integers m and n ($m > n$), then the numbers a, b, and c, where

$$a = m^2 - n^2; \quad b = 2mn; \quad c = m^2 + n^2$$

form a Pythagorean triple:

$$a^2 + b^2 = c^2$$

You can use algebra to prove that this is always true.

Write a method `makePythagoreanTriple` that takes two integer parameters, m and n, swaps them if necessary to make m > n, calculates the Pythagorean triple using the above expressions, places the resulting values a, b, and c into a new array of three elements, and returns that array. Test your method in a simple program.

8.   Complete the following method:

```
// Returns an array filled with values
// 1, 2, ..., n-1, n, n-1, ..., 2, 1.
public static int[] createWedge(int n)
{
  ...
}
```

9.   In *SCRABBLE*,® different letters are assigned different numbers of points:

```
A – 1   E – 1   I – 1   M – 3   Q – 10   U – 1   X – 8
B – 3   F – 4   J – 8   N – 1   R – 1    V – 4   Y – 4
C – 3   G – 2   K – 5   O – 3   S – 1    W – 4   Z – 10
D – 2   H – 4   L – 1   P – 3   T – 1
```

Write a method `computeScore(String word)` that returns the score for a word without using either `if` or `switch` statements. ≷ Hint: find the position of a given letter in the alphabet string by calling `indexOf`; get the score for that letter from the array of point values, and add to the total. ≷

10.■   Change the `SnackBar` class from the lab in Chapter 9 (`JM\Ch09\SnackBar\SnackBar.java`) to be able to support any number of vending machines. Assume that the number of machines is passed to the program as a command-line argument. If not given, then the program should use the default number, three machines. Assign brand names and colors to the machines randomly from the three names and colors specified in the `SnackBar` class.

Sections 12.4-12.7

11.   Mark true or false and explain:

(a)   An `ArrayList` can contain multiple references to the same object. _____ ✓

(b)   The same object may belong to two different `ArrayLists`. _____

(c)   `ArrayList`'s `remove` method destroys the object after it has been removed from the list. _____ ✓

(d)   `ArrayList`'s `add` method makes a copy of the object and adds it to the list. _____

(e)   Two variables can refer to the same `ArrayList`. _____ ✓

12.   Write a method that takes an `ArrayList<String>` and returns a new `ArrayList<String>` in which the elements are stored in reverse order. The original list should remain unchanged. ✓

13.   Write a method that removes the smallest value from an `ArrayList<Integer>`. ≷ Hint: `Integer` has a method `compareTo(Integer other)` that returns a positive integer if `this` is greater than `other`, a negative integer if `this` is less than `other`, and 0 if `this` is equal to `other`. ≷

14. Write and test a method

```
public void filter(ArrayList<Object> list1,
                        ArrayList<Object> list2)
```

that removes from `list1` all objects that are also in `list2`. Your method should compare the objects using the == operator, <u>not</u> `equals`. ∈ Hint: the `contains` and `indexOf` methods cannot be used. ∋

15. Write and test a method

```
public void removeDuplicates(ArrayList<String> words)
```

that removes duplicate words (that is, for which `word1.equals(word2)`) from the list. ∈ Hint: start with the last element and use the `indexOf` and `remove` methods. ∋

16. Can an `ArrayList<Object>` be its own element? Test this hypothesis.

Sections 12.8-12.9

17. Find and fix the bug in the following code:

```
char[] hello = {' ', 'h', 'e', 'l', 'l', 'o'};

// Shift to the left and append '!':
int i = 0;
while (i < 6)
{
  hello[i-1] = hello[i];
  i++;
}
hello[5] = '!';
```

18. Write a method that determines whether a given number is a median for values stored in an array:

```
// Returns true if m is a median for values in the array
// sample, false otherwise. (Here we call m a median if
// the number of elements that are greater than m is the
// same as the number of elements that are less than m)
public boolean isMedian(double[] sample, double m)
```

19.■ (a)   Write methods `void rotateLeft(int[] a)` and
            `void rotateRight(int[] a)` that rotate the array a by one
            position in the respective direction.

    (b)   Write a method

          ```
          public static void rotate(int[] a, int d)
          ```

          that rotates an array by a given number of positions d. A positive d
          rotates the array to the right; a negative d, to the left. For example, if a
          holds elements 1, 4, 9, 16, 25, 36, after `rotate(a, -2)` the values in
          a are 9, 16, 25, 36, 1, 4.

20.■ Fill in the blanks in the following method that returns the average of the two
      largest elements of an array: ✓

```
// Finds the two largest elements in scores
// and returns their average.
// Precondition: scores.length >= 2.
public static double averageTopTwo(int[] scores)
{
  int i, n = scores.length;
  int iMax1 = 0;          // index of the largest element
  int iMax2 = 1;          // index of the second largest element

  // If scores[iMax2] is bigger than scores[iMax1] --
  //    swap iMax1 and iMax2
  if (scores[iMax2] > scores[iMax1])
  {
    i = iMax1;

    _____

    ...
  }

  for (i = 2; i < n; i++)
  {
    if (scores[i] > scores[iMax1])
    {
      _____
    }
    else if ( _____ )
    {
      _____
      ...
    }
  }
  return _____;
}
```

21.   (a)▪   Write and test a class `Polynomial` that represents a polynomial
$P(x) = a_0 + a_1 x + \ldots + a_n x^n$. Use an array of `doubles` of size $n + 1$ to
hold the coefficients. Provide a constructor

```
public Polynomial(double[] a)
```

that sets the coefficients by copying them from a given array. Make
sure the `Polynomial` class is fully encapsulated and its objects are
immutable. Provide a method `degree` that returns the degree of the
polynomial, n; provide a method `getValue(double x)` that
calculates and returns this polynomial's value for a given x. Also
include a reasonable `toString` method.

   (b)   The same polynomial can be rewritten as:

$$P(x) = a_0 + x(a_1 + x(a_2 + (\ldots + x(a_n))\ldots)$$

The latter representation is more efficient because it takes the same
number of additions but fewer multiplications to calculate $P(x)$.
Modify the `getValue` method from Part (a) using this formula.

   (c)◆   Write a method

```
public Polynomial multiply(Polynomial other)
```

that multiplies this polynomial by `other` and returns their product.

22.▪   A non-negative "large integer" is represented as an array of N digits. The
value of each digit is an integer from 0 to 9. The most significant digits are
at the beginning of the array; zero values at the beginning indicate leading
zeroes. Write the following method that calculates and returns the sum of
two "large integers" a and b: ✓

```
private final int N = 30;

    // Calculates the sum of two "large integers" a and b,
    // represented as arrays of digits, and returns their sum
    // as an array of N digits.
    // Precondition: the sum fits into N digits.
    private static int[] add(int[] a, int[] b)
    {
      ...
    }
```

23. A partition of a positive integer n is its representation as a sum of positive integers $n = p_1 + p_2 + ... + p_k$. Write a method that prints out all possible partitions of a given positive integer n. Consider only partitions where $p_1 \leq p_2 \leq ... \leq p_k$.

⸠ Hint: use an `ArrayList<Integer>` of capacity n to hold a partition; write a recursive helper method `displayPartitions(int n, ArrayList<Integer> list)`. If the sum of the values in `list` is n, just print these values. If the sum is less than n, try appending to the list another integer, in the range from the last value in the list (or 1, if the list was empty) to $n - sum$, and call `displayPartitions(n, list)` again. Don't forget to remove the last added value before trying the next one. ⸠

Sections 12.10-12.12

24. A two-dimensional array `matrix` represents a square matrix with the number of rows and the number of columns both equal to n. Write a condition to test that an element `matrix[i][j]` lies on one of the diagonals of the matrix. ✓

25. Write a method that returns the value of the largest positive element in a 2-D array, or 0 if all its elements are negative: ✓

```
// Returns the value of the largest positive element in
// the 2-D array m, or 0, if all its elements are negative.
private static double positiveMax(double[][] m)
```

26. Write a method

```
public void fillCheckerboard(Color[][] board)
```

that fills `board` with alternating black and white colors in a checkerboard pattern. For example:

27.   Let us say that a matrix (a 2-D array of numbers) m1 "covers" a matrix m2
       (with the same dimensions) if m1[i][j] > m2[i][j] for at least half of
       all the elements in m1. Write the following method: ✓

```
// Returns true if m1 "covers" m2, false otherwise.
// Precondition: m1 and m2 have the same dimensions.
private static boolean covers(double[][] m1, double[][] m2)
{
    ...
}
```

28.■   Pascal's Triangle, named after the French mathematician Blaise Pascal
       (1623-1662), holds binomial coefficients. All the numbers on the left and
       right sides are equal to 1, and each of the other numbers is equal to the sum
       of the two numbers above it. It looks like this:

```
              1
           1     1
        1     2     1
     1     3     3     1
  1     4     6     4     1
. . . . . . . . . . . . . . . . . . .
```

       Write a method

```
public int[][] pascalTriangle(int n)
```

       that generates the first *n* rows of Pascal's Triangle. The method should
       return a "jagged" 2-D array with *n* rows. The *k*-th row should be a 1-D array
       of length *k* that holds the values from the *k*-th row of Pascal's Triangle.

29.■   (a)   Modify the *Chomp* program so it can be played by two human players.

       (b)   Change the program further so that it displays different prompts for the
              two players (for example, "Your turn, Player 1" and "Your turn, Player
              2"). Accept the name of the player as a parameter in HumanPlayer's
              constructor and make getPrompt return a standard message
              concatenated with the player's name.

       (c)   Similar functionality can be achieved by deriving HumanPlayer1 and
              HumanPlayer2 from HumanPlayer and redefining the getPrompt
              method in them. Is this implementation more appropriate or less
              appropriate in an OOP program than the one suggested in Part (b)?
              Why? ✓

30.   Turn the *Chomp* program into a game for three players: two human players and one computer player.

31.▪   (a)   In the *Chomp* program, make the board scaleable. Eliminate the `CELLSIZE` constant in the `BoardPanel` class and obtain the cell's width and height from the current dimensions of the panel when you need them.

(b)   Add a constructor to the `BoardPanel` class that sets the row and column dimensions of the board. Make the program play on a 3 by 6 board. Which properties of the code make this change easy?

13ACEHPRT

Searching and Sorting

13.1 Prologue

Searching and *sorting* are vast and important subjects. At the practical level they are important because they are what many large computer systems do much of the time. At the theoretical level they help distill the general properties and interesting theoretical questions about algorithms and data structures and offer rich material on which to study and compare them. We will consider these topics in the context of working with arrays, along with other common algorithms that work with arrays.

Searching tasks in computer applications range from finding a particular character in a string of a dozen characters to finding a record in a database of 100 million records. In the abstract, searching is a task involving a set of data elements represented in some way in computer memory. Each element includes a *key* that can be tested against a target value for an exact match. A successful search finds the element with a matching key and returns its location or some information associated with it: a value, a record, or the address of a record.

Searching refers to tasks where matching the keys against a specified target is straightforward and unambiguous. If, by comparison, we had to deal with a database of fingerprints and needed to find the best match for a given specimen, that application would fall into the category of *pattern recognition* rather than searching. It would also be likely to require the intervention of some human experts.

To *sort* means to arrange a list of data elements in ascending or descending order. The data elements may be numeric values or some records ordered by keys. In addition to preparing a data set for easier access (for example, as required for Binary Search), sorting has many other applications. One example is matching two data sets. Suppose we want to merge two large mailing lists and eliminate the duplicates. This task is straightforward when the lists are alphabetically sorted by name and address but may be unmanageable otherwise. Another use may be simply presenting information to a user in an ordered manner. A list of the user's files on a personal computer, for example, may be sorted by name, date, or type. A word processor sorts information when it automatically creates an index or a bibliography for a book. In large business systems, millions of transactions (for example, bank checks or credit card charges) are sorted daily before they are posted to customer accounts or forwarded to other payers.

In this chapter we first consider different ways of comparing objects in Java. We then look at two searching algorithms, Sequential Search and Binary Search, and several common sorting algorithms: Selection Sort, Insertion Sort, and two faster ones: Mergesort and Quicksort.

13.2 `equals`, `compareTo`, and `compare`

Java offers three ways for comparing objects:

```
public boolean equals(Object other)
public int compareTo(T other)
public int compare(T obj1, T obj2)
```

where *T* is the name of your class. The `boolean` method `equals` compares `this` object to `other` for equality. The `int` method `compareTo` compares `this` object to another object of the same type and returns an integer that indicates whether `this` is greater than, equal to, or less than `other`. The `int` method `compare` compares two objects of the same type and returns an integer that indicates which of the two objects is greater than the other. Let us take a closer look at each of these methods: where they come from and how we can benefit from them.

1. `equals`

The `equals` method —

```
public boolean equals(Object other)
```

— is a method of the class `Object`. It compares the <u>addresses</u> of `this` and `other` and returns `true` if they are the same and `false` otherwise. Since every class has `Object` as an ancestor, every class inherits this method from `Object`. However, we are more often interested in comparing the <u>contents</u> of objects rather than their addresses (and we have the `==` operator to compare the addresses). So programmers often override `Object`'s `equals` method in their classes.

We have already seen `equals` in the `String` class. There strings are compared character by character for an exact match. Consider another example, the class `Country` in Figure 13-1. The `equals` method in `Country` compares `this` country to `other` based on their names: two countries with the same name are considered equal. It is common for an `equals` method in a class to employ calls to `equals` for one or several of its fields.

> In order to override `Object`'s `equals` method in your class, the signature of your `equals` method must be exactly the same as the signature of `equals` in `Object`. In particular, the declared type of the parameter `other` must be `Object`.

```java
public class Country implements Comparable<Country>
{
  private String name;
  private int population;

  public Country(String nm) { name = nm; population = 0; }
  public Country(String nm, int pop) { name = nm; population = pop; }
  public String getName() { return name; }
  public int getPopulation() { return population; }

  public boolean equals(Object other)
  {
    if (other != null)
      return name.equals(((Country)other).getName());
    else
      return false;
  }

  public int compareTo(Country other)
  {
    return name.compareTo(other.getName());
  }

  public String toString()
  {
    return name + ": " + population;
  }
}
```

Figure 13-1. J_M\Ch13\Compare\Country.java

That's why we had to cast `other` into `Country`. If you write

```java
public boolean equals(Country other)  // Error
{
  if (other != null)
    return name.equals(other.getName());
  else
    return false;
}
```

you will define a <u>different</u> `equals` method and not override the one from `Object`. You might say: "So what? I only intend to compare countries to each other, not to objects of other types." The problem is that certain library methods, such as `contains` and `indexOf` in `ArrayList`, call your `equals` method polymorphically when they need to compare objects for equality. So if you plan to store your objects in an `ArrayList` (or another Java collection), you have to override the `Object` class's `equals` properly in your class.

"Then," you might wonder, "What happens if I accidentally pass an incompatible type of parameter to `equals`?" For example,

```
Country country = new Country("USA");
...
if (country.equals("USA"))    // error!
  ...
```

Since `"USA"` is an object, this code compiles with no errors, but at run time the `equals` method throws a `ClassCastException`, because it cannot cast a `String` into a `Country`. It would be better to catch such errors at compile time, but better late than never. The correct comparison would be

```
if (country.getName().equals("USA"))
  ...
```

or

```
Country usa = new Country("USA");
if (country.equals(usa))
  ...
```

Some programmers make `equals` simply return `false` if the parameter is of an incompatible type. This may be necessary if a programmer plans to mix different types of objects in the same array or list or another collection. For example:

```
public boolean equals(Object other)
{
  if (other instanceof Country)
    return name.equals(((Country)other).getName());
  else
    return false;
}
```

Java's `boolean` operator

```
x instanceof T
```

returns `true` if and only if *x* IS-A *T*.   More precisely, if *x*'s class is *X*, *x* `instanceof` *T* returns `true` when *X* is exactly *T*, or *X* is a subclass of *T* or has *T* as an ancestor, or *T* is an interface and *X* implements *T*.

If you define `equals` this way, then you have to be extra careful when you use it because the program won't tell you when you pass a wrong type of parameter to equals — the call will just return `false`.

> Note that overriding the `Object`'s `equals` method does not change the meaning of the `==` operator for the objects of your class: it still compares <u>addresses</u> of objects.

2. `compareTo`

The `compareTo` method is an abstract method defined in the `java.util.Comparable<T>` (pronounced *com-'parable*) interface, so there is no default implementation for it. To implement `Comparable<T>` in your class, you need to supply the following method:

```
public int compareTo(T other)
```

where *T* is the name of your class. For example:

```
public class Country implements Comparable<Country>
{
  ...
  public int compareTo(Country other)
  {
    return name.compareTo(other.getName());
  }
  ...
}
```

> `compareTo` returns an `int`: a positive value indicates that `this` is "greater than" `other`; a zero indicates that they are "equal," and a negative value indicates that `this` is "less than" `other`.   So `x.compareTo(y)` is sort of like "x - y."

It is the programmer who decides what is "greater" and what is "less." `compareTo` is said to define a *natural ordering* among the objects of your class. In the above example, the "natural ordering" among countries is alphabetical, by name.

> Note that `compareTo` takes a parameter of your class type, not `Object`.

Why do we need the `Comparable` interface and why would we want our classes to implement it? The reason is the same as for the `equals` method: certain library methods expect objects passed to them to be `Comparable`. For example, the `java.util.Arrays` class has a `sort(Object[] arr)` method, which compares elements of `arr` by calling their `compareTo` method. So if there is a reasonable ordering among the objects of your class, and you plan to use library methods or classes that deal with `Comparable` objects, it makes sense to make the objects of your class `Comparable`.

> **String, Integer, Double, and several other library classes implement Comparable.**

> **If you do define a `compareTo` method in your class, don't forget to state in the header of your class**
>
>   **... implements Comparable<YourClass>**

If your class implements `Comparable`, then it is a good idea to define the `equals` method, too, and to make `compareTo` and `equals` agree with each other, so that `x.equals(y)` returns `true` if and only if `x.compareTo(y)` returns 0. Otherwise, some of the library methods (and you yourself) might get confused.

Very well. You've made `Countries` comparable. You can sort them by name using `Arrays.sort`. But suppose that sometimes you need to sort them by population. What can you do? Then you need a *comparator*.

3. compare

A *comparator* is an object that specifies a way to compare two objects of your class. Suppose the name of your class is *T*. A comparator is an object of a class that implements the `java.util.Comparator<T>` interface and has a method

```
public int compare(T obj1, T obj2)
```

> **If `compare` returns a positive integer, `obj1` is considered greater than `obj2`; if the returned value is 0, they are considered equal; if the returned value is negative, `obj1` is considered less than `obj2`. So `compare(obj1, obj2)` is sort of like "obj1 - obj2."**

The purpose of comparators is to be passed as parameters to constructors and methods of certain library classes (or your own classes). By creating different types of comparators, you can specify different ways of comparing objects of your class. You can create different comparators for ordering objects by different fields in ascending or descending order.

For example, the `PopulationComparator` class in Figure 13-2 defines comparators that compare countries by population. You can create an "ascending" comparator and a "descending" comparator by passing a `boolean` parameter to `PopulationComparator`'s constructor.

```java
// Comparator for Country objects based on population

import java.util.Comparator;

public class PopulationComparator implements Comparator<Country>
{
  private boolean ascending;

  // Constructors
  public PopulationComparator() { ascending = true; }
  public PopulationComparator(boolean ascend) { ascending = ascend; }

  public int compare(Country country1, Country country2)
  {
    int diff = country1.getPopulation() - country2.getPopulation();
    if (ascending)
      return diff;
    else
      return -diff;
  }
}
```

Figure 13-2. JM**\Ch13\Compare\PopulationComparator.java**

The `Arrays` class has an overloaded version of the `sort` method that takes a comparator as a parameter. Now we can either rely on the natural ordering or create different comparators and pass them to `Arrays.sort` (Figure 13-3). The output from the `main` method in Figure 13-3 is

```
[Brazil: 190, China: 1321, India: 1110, Indonesia: 249, USA: 301]
[Brazil: 190, Indonesia: 249, USA: 301, India: 1110, China: 1321]
[China: 1321, India: 1110, USA: 301, Indonesia: 249, Brazil: 190]
```

```
import java.util.Arrays;

public class ComparatorTest
{
  public static void main(String[] args)
  {
    Country[] countries =
      { // population is in millions
        new Country("China", 1321),
        new Country("India", 1110),
        new Country("USA", 301),
        new Country("Indonesia", 249),
        new Country("Brazil", 190),
      };

    // Sort by name:
    Arrays.sort(countries);
    System.out.println(Arrays.toString(countries));

    // Sort by population ascending:
    Arrays.sort(countries, new PopulationComparator(true));
    System.out.println(Arrays.toString(countries));

    // Sort by population descending:
    Arrays.sort(countries, new PopulationComparator(false));
    System.out.println(Arrays.toString(countries));
  }
}
```

Figure 13-3. J_M\Ch13\Compare\ComparatorTest.java

13.3 Sequential and Binary Search

Suppose we have an array of a certain size and we want to find the location of a given "target" value in that array (or ascertain that it is not there). If the elements of the array are in random order, we have no choice but to use *Sequential Search*, that is, to check the value of each consecutive element one by one until we find the target element (or finish scanning through the whole array). For example:

```
String[] words = { < ... some words> };
String target = < ... a word >;

for (int k = 0; k < words.length; k++)
{
  if (target.equals(words[k]))
    return k;
}
...
```

This may be time-consuming if the array is large. For an array of 1,000,000 elements, we will examine an average of 500,000 elements before finding the target (assuming that the target value is somewhere in the array). This algorithm is called an $O(n)$ ("order of *n*") algorithm because it takes an average number of operations roughly proportional to *n*, where *n* is the size of the array. ($O(...)$ is called the "big-O" notation; we explain it more formally in Chapter 18.)

In Chapter 4 we introduced a more efficient algorithm, called *Binary Search*, which can be used if the elements of the array are arranged in ascending or descending order (or, as we say, the array is *sorted*). Let's say our array is sorted in ascending order and we are looking for a target value *x*. Take the middle element of the array and compare it with *x*. If they are equal, the target element is found. If *x* is smaller, the target element must be in the left half of the array, and if *x* is larger, the target must be in the right half of the array. Each time we repeat this procedure, we divide the remaining range of search into two approximately equal halves and narrow the search to one of them (see Figure 4.10 on page 90). This sequence stops when we find the target or get down to just one element, which happens very quickly.

A binary search in an array of 3 elements requires at most 2 comparisons to find the target value or establish that it is not in the array. An array of 7 elements requires at most 3 comparisons. An array of 15 elements requires at most 4 comparisons, and so on. In general, an array of $2^n - 1$ (or fewer) elements requires at most *n* comparisons. So an array of 1,000,000 elements will require at most 20 comparisons ($2^{20} - 1 = 1,048,575$), which is much better than 500,000. That is why such methods are called "divide and conquer." Binary Search is an $O(\log n)$ algorithm because the number of operations it takes is roughly $\log_2 n$.

The `binarySearch` method in Figure 13-4 implements the Binary Search algorithm for an array of `Comparable` objects sorted in ascending order.

```java
/**
 * Uses Binary Search to look for target in an array a, sorted in
 * ascending order.  If found, returns the index of the matching
 * element; otherwise returns -1.
 */
public static <T> int binarySearch(T[] a,
                                   Comparable<? super T> target)

   // Wow!  We wanted to show you this bizarre syntax once!
   // <T> indicates that this method works for an array of
   // Comparable objects of any type T.  Comparable<? super T>
   // ensures that the method will work not only for a class T
   // that implements Comparable<T> but also for any subclass
   // of such a class.

{
  int left = 0, right = a.length - 1;

  while (left <= right)
  {
    // Take the index of the middle element between
    //   "left" and "right":

    int middle = (left + right) / 2;

    // Compare this element to the target value
    // and adjust the search range accordingly:

    int diff = target.compareTo(a[middle]);

    if (diff > 0)    // target > a[middle]
      left = middle + 1;
    else if (diff < 0)    // target < a[middle]
      right = middle - 1;
    else   // target is equal to a[middle]
      return middle;
  }

  return -1;
}
```

Figure 13-4. JM\Ch13\BinarySearch\BinarySearch.java

One way to understand and check code is to *trace* it manually on some representative examples. Let us take, for example:

```
Given:
    int[] a = {8, 13, 21, 34, 55, 89};
    // a[0] =  8; a[1] = 13; a[2] = 21; a[3] = 34;
    // a[4] = 55; a[5] = 89;
    target = 34

Initially:
    left = 0; right = a.length - 1 = 5

First iteration:
    middle = (0+5)/2 = 2;
    a[middle] = a[2] = 21;
    target > a[middle] (34 > 21)
        ==> Set left = middle + 1 = 3; (right remains 5)

Second iteration:
    middle = (3+5)/2 = 4;
    a[middle] = a[4] = 55;
    target < a[middle] (34 < 55)
        ==> Set right = middle - 1 = 3; (left remains 3)

Third iteration:
    middle = (3+3)/2 = 3;
    a[middle] = a[3] = 34;
    target == a[middle] (34 = 34)
        ==> return 3
```

A more comprehensive check should also include tracing special situations (such as when the target element is the first or the last element, or is not in the array) and "degenerate" cases, such as when a.length is equal to 0 or 1.

We also have to make sure that the method terminates — otherwise, the program may "hang." This is better accomplished by logical or mathematical reasoning than by tracing specific examples, because it is hard to foresee all the possible paths of an algorithm. Here we can reason as follows: our binarySearch method must terminate because on each iteration the difference right - left decreases by at least 1. So eventually we either quit the loop via return (when the target is found), or reach a point where right - left becomes negative and the condition in the while loop becomes false.

13.4 *Lab:* Keeping Things in Order

In this lab you will write a class `SortedWordList`, which represents a list of words, sorted alphabetically (case blind). `SortedWordList` should <u>extend</u> `ArrayList<String>`. You have to redefine several of `ArrayList`'s methods to keep the list always alphabetically sorted and with no duplicate words.

1. Provide a no-args constructor and a constructor with one `int` parameter, the initial capacity of the list.

2. Redefine the `contains` and `indexOf` methods: make them use Binary Search.

3. Redefine the `set(i, word)` method so that it first checks whether `word` fits alphabetically between the $(i-1)$-th and $(i+1)$-th elements and is not equal to either of them. If this is not so, `set` should throw an `IllegalArgumentException`, as follows:

   ```
   if (...)
      throw new IllegalArgumentException("word=" + word + " i=" + i);
   ```

4. Redefine the `add(i, word)` method so that it first checks whether `word` fits alphabetically between the $(i-1)$-th and i-th elements and is not equal to either of them. If this is not so, throw an `IllegalArgumentException`.

5. Redefine the `add(word)` method so that it inserts `word` into the list in alphabetical order. If `word` is already in the list, `add` should not insert it and should return `false`; otherwise, if successful, `add` should return `true`. Use Binary Search to locate the place where word should be inserted.

6. Define a new method `merge(SortedWordList additionalWords)`. This method should insert into this list in alphabetical order all the words from `additionalWords` that are not already in this list. `merge` should be efficient. You may not use any temporary arrays or lists. Each element from this list should move <u>at most once</u>, directly into its proper location. To achieve this while avoiding an `IndexOutOfBoundsException`, you first need to add some dummy elements to the list. Find the number of additional words to be inserted. To do that efficiently, do a "tentative merge" without moving any elements. Then save the current size of the list and append to it the required number of

arbitrary strings. Call `super.add("")` to append an empty string at the end of the list. Now merge the lists, starting at the end of each list and at the end of the added space. At each step decide which of the two lists should supply the next element for the next vacant location.

7.   Combine your class with `SortedListTest.java` from J_M\Ch13\SortedList and test the program.

13.5   Selection Sort

The task of rearranging the elements of an array in ascending or descending order is called *sorting*. We are looking for a general algorithm that works for an array of any size and for any values of its elements. There exist many sorting algorithms for accomplishing this task, but the most straightforward one is probably *Selection Sort*. We have already mentioned it in Chapter 4; we present it here again for convenience:

Selection Sort

1.   Initialize a variable *n* to the size of the array.
2.   Find the largest among the first *n* elements.
3.   Make it swap places with the *n*-th element.
4.   Decrement *n* by 1.
5.   Repeat steps 2 - 4 while $n \geq 2$.

On the first iteration we find the largest element of the array and swap it with the last element. The largest element is now in the correct place, from which it will never move again. We decrement *n*, pretending that the last element of the array does not exist anymore, and repeat the procedure until we have worked our way through the entire array. The iterations stop when there is only one element left, because it has already been compared with every other element and is guaranteed to be the smallest.

The `SelectionSort` class in Figure 13-5 implements this algorithm for an array of the type `double`. A similar procedure will sort the array in descending order; instead of finding the largest element on each iteration, we can simply find the smallest element among the first *n*.

Sorting is a common operation in computer applications and a favorite subject on which to study and compare algorithms. Selection Sort is an $O(n^2)$ algorithm because the number of comparisons in it is $n \cdot (n-1)/2$, which is roughly proportional to n^2. It is less efficient than other sorting algorithms considered in this chapter, but more predictable: it always takes the same number of comparisons, regardless of whether the array is almost sorted, randomly ordered, or sorted in reverse order.

```java
public class SelectionSort
{
  // Sorts a[0], ..., a[size-1] in ascending order
  //   using Selection Sort.
  public static void sort(double[] a)
  {
    for (int n = a.length; n > 1; n--)
    {
      // Find the index iMax of the largest element
      //   among a[0], ..., a[n-1]:

      int iMax = 0;
      for (int i = 1; i < n; i++)
      {
        if (a[i] > a[iMax])
          iMax = i;
      }

      // Swap a[iMax] with a[n-1]:

      double aTemp = a[iMax];
      a[iMax] = a[n-1];
      a[n-1] = aTemp;

      // Decrement n (accomplished by n-- in the for loop).
    }
  }
}
```

Figure 13-5. J_M\Ch13\Benchmarks\SelectionSort.java

13.6 Insertion Sort

The idea of the *Insertion Sort* algorithm is to keep the beginning part of the array sorted and insert each next element into the correct place in it. It involves the following steps:

Insertion Sort

1. Initialize a variable n to 1 (keep the first n elements sorted).
2. Save the next element and find the place to insert it among the first n so that the order is preserved.
3. Shift the elements as necessary to the right and insert the saved one in the created vacant slot.
4. Increment n by 1.
5. Repeat steps 2 - 4 while n < *array length*.

The `InsertionSort` class in Figure 13-6 implements this algorithm for an array of `doubles`.

```java
public class InsertionSort
{
  // Sorts a[0], ..., a[size-1] in ascending order
  //   using Insertion Sort.
  public static void sort(double[] a)
  {
    for (int n = 1; n < a.length; n++)
    {
      // Save the next element to be inserted:
      double aTemp = a[n];

      // Going backward from a[n-1], shift elements to the
      //   right until you find an element a[i] <= aTemp:

      int i = n;
      while (i > 0 && aTemp < a[i-1])
      {
        a[i] = a[i-1];
        i--;
      }

      // Insert the saved element into a[i]:
      a[i] = aTemp;

      // Increment n (accomplished by n++ in the for loop).
    }
  }
}
```

Figure 13-6. J_M\Ch13\Benchmarks\InsertionSort.java

Insertion Sort is also on average an $O(n^2)$ algorithm, but it can do better than Selection Sort when the array is already nearly sorted. In the best case, when the array is already sorted, Insertion Sort just verifies the order and becomes an $O(n)$ algorithm.

13.7 Mergesort

The tremendous difference in efficiency between Binary Search and Sequential Search hints at the possibility of faster sorting, too, if we could find a "divide and conquer" algorithm for sorting. Mergesort is one such algorithm. It works as follows:

<u>Mergesort</u>

    1. If the array has only one element, do nothing.
    2. (Optional) If the array has two elements, swap them if necessary.
    3. Split the array into two approximately equal halves.
    4. Sort the first half and the second half.
    5. Merge both halves into one sorted array.

This recursive algorithm allows us to practice our recursive reasoning. Step 4 tells us to sort half of the array. But how will we sort it? Shall we use Selection Sort or Insertion Sort for it? Potentially we could, but then we wouldn't get the full benefit of faster sorting. For best performance we should use Mergesort again!

Thus it is very convenient to implement Mergesort in a recursive method, which calls itself. This fact may seem odd at first, but there is nothing paradoxical about it. Java and other high-level languages use a *stack* mechanism for calling methods. When a method is called, a new frame is allocated on the stack to hold the return address, the parameters, and all the local variables of a method (see Section 21.4). With this mechanism there is really no difference whether a method calls itself or any other method.

Recall that any recursive method must recognize two possibilities: a *base case* and a *recursive case*. In the base case, the task is so simple that there is little or nothing to do, and no recursive calls are needed. In Mergesort, the base case occurs when the array has only one or two elements. The recursive case must reduce the task to similar but <u>smaller</u> tasks. In Mergesort, the task of sorting an array is reduced to sorting two smaller arrays. This ensures that after several recursive calls the task will fall into the base case and recursion will stop.

Figure 13-7 shows a `Mergesort` class that can sort an array of `doubles`. This straightforward implementation uses a temporary array into which the two sorted halves are merged. The `sort` method calls a recursive helper method that sorts a particular segment of the array.

```
public class Mergesort
{
  private static double[] temp;

  // Sorts a[0], ..., a[size-1] in ascending order
  //    using the Mergesort algorithm.
  public static void sort(double[] a)
  {
    int n = a.length;
    temp = new double[n];
    recursiveSort(a, 0, n-1);
  }

  // Recursive helper method: sorts a[from], ..., a[to]
  private static void recursiveSort(double[] a, int from, int to)
  {
    if (to - from < 2)        // Base case: 1 or 2 elements
    {
      if (to > from && a[to] < a[from])
      {
        // swap a[to] and a[from]
        double aTemp = a[to]; a[to] = a[from]; a[from] = aTemp;
      }
    }
    else                      // Recursive case
    {
      int middle = (from + to) / 2;
      recursiveSort(a, from, middle);
      recursiveSort(a, middle + 1, to);
      merge(a, from, middle, to);
    }
  }

  // Merges a[from] ... a[middle] and a[middle+1] ... a[to]
  //    into one sorted array a[from] ... a[to]
  private static void merge(double[] a, int from, int middle, int to)
  {
    int i = from, j = middle + 1, k = from;

    // While both arrays have elements left unprocessed:
    while (i <= middle && j <= to)
```

Figure 13-7 `Mergesort.java` *Continued* ➮

```
  {
    if (a[i] < a[j])
    {
      temp[k] = a[i];    // Or simply temp[k] = a[i++];
      i++;
    }
    else
    {
      temp[k] = a[j];
      j++;
    }
    k++;
  }

  // Copy the tail of the first half, if any, into temp:
  while (i <= middle)
  {
    temp[k] = a[i];      // Or simply temp[k++] = a[i++]
    i++;
    k++;
  }

  // Copy the tail of the second half, if any, into temp:
  while (j <= to)
  {
    temp[k] = a[j];      // Or simply temp[k++] = a[j++]
    j++;
    k++;
  }

  // Copy temp back into a
  for (k = from; k <= to; k++)
    a[k] = temp[k];
  }
}
```

Figure 13-7. J$_M$\Ch13\Benchmarks\Mergesort.java

The merge method is not recursive. To understand how it works, imagine two piles of cards, each sorted in ascending order and placed face up on the table. We want to merge them into the third, sorted, pile. On each step we take the smaller of the two exposed cards and place it face down on top of the destination pile. When one of the original piles is gone, we take all the remaining cards in the other one (the whole pile or one by one — it doesn't matter) and place them face down on top of the destination pile. We end up with the destination pile sorted in ascending order.

Mergesort is an $O(n \log n)$ algorithm — much better than the $O(n^2)$ performance of Selection Sort and Insertion Sort.

13.8 Quicksort

Quicksort is another $O(n \log n)$ sorting algorithm. The idea of Quicksort is to pick one element, called the pivot, then rearrange the elements of the array in such a way that all the elements to the left of the pivot are smaller than or equal to it, and all the elements to the right of the pivot are greater than or equal to it. The pivot element can be chosen arbitrarily among the elements of the array. This procedure is called *partitioning*. After partitioning, Quicksort is applied (recursively) to the left-of-pivot part and to the right-of-pivot part, which results in a sorted array (Figure 13-9).

Figure 13-8 illustrates the partitioning algorithm. You proceed from both ends of the array toward the meeting point comparing the elements with the pivot. If the element on the left is not greater than the pivot, you increment the index on the left side; if the element on the right is not less than the pivot, you decrement the index on the right side. When you reach a deadlock (the element on the left is greater than pivot and the element on the right is less than pivot), you swap them and advance both indices. When the left- and the right-side elements meet at a certain position, you swap the pivot with one of the elements that have met.

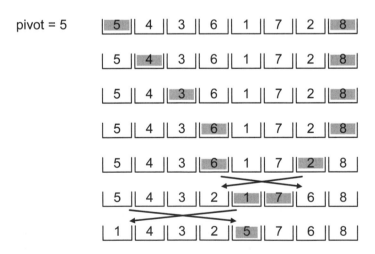

Figure 13-8. Array partitioning algorithm

The Quicksort algorithm was invented by C. A. R. Hoare in 1962. Although its performance is less predictable than Mergesort's, it averages a faster time for random arrays.

```java
public class Quicksort
{
  // Sorts a[0], ..., a[size-1] in ascending order
  //   using the Quicksort algorithm.
  public static void sort(double[] a)
  {
    recursiveSort(a, 0, a.length - 1);
  }

  // Recursive helper method: sorts a[from], ..., a[to]
  private static void recursiveSort(double[] a, int from, int to)
  {
    if (from >= to)
      return;

    // Choose pivot a[p]:
    int p = (from + to ) / 2;
      // The choice of the pivot location may vary:
      //   you can also use p = from or p = to or use
      //   a fancier method, say, the median of the above three.

    // Partition:
    int i = from;
    int j = to;
    while (i <= j)
    {
      if (a[i] <= a[p])
        i++;
      else if (a[j] >= a[p])
        j--;
      else
      {
        swap (a, i, j);
        i++;
        j--;
      }
    }

    // Finish partitioning:
    if (p < j)      // place the pivot in its correct position
    {
      swap (a, j, p);
      p = j;
    }
    else if (p > i)
    {
      swap (a, i, p);
      p = i;
    }
```

Figure 13-9 `Quicksort.java` *Continued* ⇗

```
    // Sort recursively:
    recursiveSort(a, from, p - 1);
    recursiveSort(a, p + 1, to);
  }

  private static void swap (double[] a, int i, int j)
  {
    double temp = a[i]; a[i] = a[j]; a[j] = temp;
  }
}
```

Figure 13-9. **JM\Ch13\Benchmarks\Quicksort.java**

13.9 *Lab:* Benchmarks

A benchmark is an empirical test of performance. The program in Figure 13-10 is designed to compare running times for several sorting methods. Enter the array size, select one of the four sorting methods in the "combo box" (pull-down list) and click the "Run" button. The program fills the array with random numbers and sorts them. This test is repeated many times for more accurate timing. (The default number of repetitions is set to 20, but you can enter that number as a command-line argument if you wish.) Then the program displays the average time it took to sort the array.

Figure 13-10. The *Benchmarks* program

Your task is to write the runSort method, which returns the total time spent sorting an array filled with random values the specified number of times.

First you need to learn how to generate a sequence of random numbers. To be precise, such numbers are called *pseudo-random*, because they are not entirely random: they are generated according to some algorithm. We have already used the `Math.random` method, but this time we won't use it because we want to have more control over how the sequence of random numbers is "seeded."

A "seed" is a value that is used to initialize the random number generator. If you seed the random number generator with the same seed, you will get exactly the same sequence of random numbers from it. Here we want to create a random number generator seeded each time the same way as we enter the `runSort` method, because we can call `runSort` for different sorting algorithms and want to compare them on exactly the same data.

To achieve that, use the `Random` class from the `java.util` package. `Random` has a no-args constructor that initializes the random number generator with an unpredictable seed, different each time. However, it has another constructor that takes a seed value as a parameter. This is the one you need to use. For example:

```
Random generator = new Random(seed);
```

Place this statement at the top of `runSort`.

Define `seed` as a `final` field in `Benchmarks`. The question remains, though, how to set its value. If we set it to a literal constant we will get exactly the same results each time we run *Benchmarks*. We do not want that: what if a particular seed value we picked produces a result that is not typical? We would never know. We will be more confident in our results if we use a different seed each time we run *Benchmarks* and the results are consistent. A common technique for obtaining a different seed value for different runs of a program is to set that value to the current system time in milliseconds. Thus, in `Benchmarks`'s constructor, we have

```
seed = System.currentTimeMillis();
```

Once you have created a random number generator (a `Random` object), you can generate the next random `double` by calling the generator's `nextDouble` method. For example:

```
a[k] = generator.nextDouble();    // 0.0 <= a[k] < 1.0
```

The `runSort` method should fill the array with random numbers and then sort it. This should be repeated `RUNS` times, and `runSort` should return the total time it took to sort the array in milliseconds. Call the system time before and after each sort and add the elapsed time to the total.

Set up a project with the files `SelectionSort.java`, `InsertionSort.java`, `Mergesort.java`, `Quicksort.java`, and `Benchmarks.java`, provided in JM\Ch13\Benchmarks. Fill in the blanks in the `Benchmarks` class. Once your program is working, collect benchmarks for each sorting algorithm for arrays of various sizes: ranging, say, from 10,000 to 50,000 elements (to 500,000 for Mergesort and Quicksort). Plot the running time vs. the array size for all four sorting methods. You can do this on your graphing calculator, manually, or by entering the results into a spreadsheet or another data analysis program. See how well your experimental results fit with parabolas for Selection Sort and Insertion Sort and with $n \log n$-shaped curves for Mergesort and Quicksort.

13.10 `java.util.Arrays` and `java.util.Collections`

No matter what you need to do in Java, chances are it has been done before. Sure enough, `java.util` package has a class `Arrays` and a class `Collections` with methods that implement Binary Search and sorting (using a fast version of the Mergesort algorithm). You will need to import `java.util.Arrays` or `java.util.Collections` in order to use their methods (unless you are willing to type in the full names every time). All of `Arrays`'s and `Collections`'s methods are static, and you cannot create objects of these classes.

`Arrays`'s `binarySearch` method is called as follows:

```
int pos = Arrays.binarySearch(a, target);
```

`Arrays` class has overloaded versions of `binarySearch` for arrays of `chars`, `ints`, and other primitive data types. There is also a version for any `Comparable` objects. In particular, it can be used with `Strings`.

`Arrays.sort` methods can sort an array of `chars`, `ints`, `doubles`, `Strings`, and so on, either the whole array or a segment within specified limits. For example:

```
String[] dictionary = new String[maxWords];
int wordsCount;
< ... other statements >

Arrays.sort(dictionary, 0, wordsCount - 1);
```

As we have seen, there is also a version that works with any `Comparable` objects and a version that takes a comparator as a parameter.

The `Arrays` class also offers a set of `fill` methods for different data types. A `fill` method fills an array or a portion of an array with a specified value. Another useful method is `toString`. For example,

```
String[] names = {"Apple", "Banana", "Kiwi"};
System.out.println(Arrays.toString(names));
```

produces the output

```
[Apple, Banana, Kiwi];
```

The `asList(T[] arr)` method returns a representation of the array `arr` as a fixed-length `List`. You can't add elements to this list, but you can call other methods and pass it as a parameter to library methods that expect a `List` or a `Collection`. For example, to shuffle the elements of the array `names` you can write

```
Collections.shuffle(Arrays.asList(names));
```

You can also print out the list:

```
System.out.println(Arrays.asList(names));
```

produces the same output as

```
System.out.println(Arrays.toString(names));
```

The `Collections` class works with Java collections, such as `ArrayList`. For example, to find a target word in `ArrayList<String>` words, you can call

```
Collections.binarySearch(words, target);
```

The `Collections` class also has methods to sort a `List` of `Comparable` objects (or to sort a `List` using a comparator), to shuffle a list, to copy a list, to fill a list with a given value, to find max or min, and other methods.

13.11 Summary

The `boolean` method `equals(Object other)` in the `Object` class compares the address of `this` object to `other`. The correct way to override the `equals` method in your class is:

```
public boolean equals(Object other)
{
  if (other != null)
    ...
  else
    return false;
}
```

The `int` method `compareTo` of the `java.util.Comparable<T>` interface has the following signature:

```
public int compareTo(T other)
```

`compareTo` returns an `int` value that indicates whether `this` is larger than, equal to, or less than `other`. It is like "`this` minus `other`." To implement the `Comparable` interface in `SomeClass`, state

```
public class SomeClass implements Comparable<SomeClass>
```

and provide a method

```
public int compareTo(SomeClass other) { ... }
```

that returns a positive integer if `this` is greater than `other`, 0 if they are equal, and a negative integer if `this` is less than `other`. The main reason for making objects of your class `Comparable` is that certain library methods and data structures work with `Comparable` objects. If provided, the `compareTo` method should agree with the `equals` method in your class.

A *comparator* is an object dedicated to comparing two objects of `SomeClass`. The comparator's class implements the `java.util.Comparator<SomeClass>` interface and provides a method

```
public int compare(SomeClass obj1, SomeClass obj2) { ... }
```

The `compare` method returns an integer, sort of like "`obj1 - obj2`." Comparators are passed as parameters to constructors and methods of library classes, telling them how to compare the objects of your class.

Sequential Search is used to find a target value in an array. If the array is sorted in ascending or descending order, *Binary Search* is a much more efficient searching method. It is called a "divide and conquer" method because on each step the size of the searching range is cut in half.

The four sorting algorithms discussed in this chapter work as follows:

Selection Sort

Set *n* to the size of the array. While *n* is greater than 2, repeat the following: find the largest element among the first *n*, swap it with the *n*-th element of the array, and decrement *n* by one.

Insertion Sort

Keep the first *n* elements sorted. Starting at *n* = 2, repeat the following: find the place for a[n] in order among the first *n* − 1 elements, shift the required number of elements to the right to make room, and insert a[n]. Increment *n* by one.

Mergesort

If the array size is less than or equal to 2, just swap the elements if necessary. Otherwise, split the array into two halves. Recursively sort the first half and the second half, then merge the two sorted halves.

Quicksort

Choose a pivot element and partition the array, so that all the elements on the left side of pivot are less than or equal to the pivot and all the elements on the right side of pivot are greater than or equal to the pivot; then recursively sort each part.

Selection Sort is the slowest and most predictable of the four: each element is always compared to every other element. Insertion Sort works quickly on arrays that are almost sorted. Mergesort and Quicksort are both "divide and conquer" algorithms. They work much faster than the other two algorithms on arrays with random values.

Java's `Arrays` and `Collections` classes from the `java.util` package have `binarySearch`, `sort`, and other useful methods. All `Arrays` and `Collections` methods are static. The `Arrays` methods work with arrays, with elements of primitive data types, as well as with `String`s and other `Comparable` objects. `Arrays` also offers the convenient methods `fill`, `toString(T[] arr)`, where *T* is a primitive or a class data type, and `asList(Object[] arr)`. The `Collections` class's methods work with `List`s, such as `ArrayList`, and other Java collections.

Exercises

1. Describe the difference between searching and pattern recognition.

2. Suppose a class `Person` implements `Comparable<Person>`. A `Person` has the `getFirstName()` and `getLastName()` methods; each of them returns a `String`. Write a `compareTo` method for this class. It should compare this person to another by comparing their last names; if they are equal, it should compare their first names. The resulting order should be alphabetical, as in a telephone directory. ✓

3. ▪ Make the `Fraction` objects, defined in Chapter 9, `Comparable`. The natural ordering for `Fraction`s should be the same as for the rational numbers that they represent. Also override the `equals` method to make it agree with this ordering.

4. (a) Write a class `QuadraticFunction` that represents a quadratic function $ax^2 + bx + c$, with integer coefficients a, b, and c. Provide a constructor with three `int` parameters for a, b, and c. Provide a method `double valueAt(double x)` that returns the value of this quadratic function at x. Also provide a `toString` method. For example,

    ```
    System.out.println(new QuadraticFunction(1, -5, 6));
    ```

    should display

    ```
    x^2-5x+6
    ```

    (b) Override the `equals` method in the `QuadraticFunction` class. Two `QuadraticFunctions` should be considered equal if their respective coefficients are equal.

    (c) Make the `QuadraticFunction` objects `Comparable`. The `compareTo` method should first compare the a-coefficients; if equal, then compare the b-coefficients; if also equal, compare the c-coefficients. (This ordering basically defines which function will have greater values for very large x.)

Continued   ⇗

(d)▪ Define a comparator class for comparing two QuadraticFunction objects. Provide two constructors: a no-args constructor and a constructor that takes one double parameter. When a comparator is created by the no-args constructor, it should compare two QuadraticFunctions based on their values at $x = 0$; when a comparator is created by the constructor with a parameter x, it should compare QuadraticFunctions based on their values at x.

Sections 13.3-13.4

5.   Describe a situation where the performance of Sequential Search on average is better than $O(n)$. ⸮ Hint: different target values in the array do not have to come with the same probability. ⸮ ✓

6.   Given a sorted array of 80 elements, what is the number of comparisons required by Binary Search in the worst case? Consider two scenarios:

(a)   We know for sure that the target value is always in the array; ✓
(b)   The target may be not in the array. ✓

7.▪   A string contains several X's followed by several O's. Devise a divide and conquer algorithm that finds the number of X's in the string in $\log_2 n$ steps, where n is the length of the string.

8.▪   Write a recursive method that tries to find target among the elements a[m], ..., a[n-1] of a given array (any array, not necessarily sorted).

```
public static int search(int[] a, int m, int n, int target)
```

If found, the method should return the position of the target value; otherwise it should return -1. The base case is when the searching range is empty or consists of one element ($m \geq n$). For the recursive case, split the searching range into two approximately equal halves and try to find the target in each of them. ✓

9.▪   Write a recursive implementation of Binary Search.

10.◆   An array originally contained different numbers in ascending order but may have been subsequently rotated by a few positions. For example, the resulting array may be:

         21 34 55 1 2 3 5 8 13

        Is it possible to adapt the Binary Search algorithm for such data?

Sections 13.5-13.11

11.   Mark true or false and explain:

        (a)   If the original array was already sorted, 190 comparisons would be performed in a Selection Sort of an array containing 20 elements. _____ ✓

        (b)   Mergesort works faster than Insertion Sort on any array. _____ ✓

12.   Write a method void shuffle(Object[] arr) that shuffles the objects in arr in random order. ⸘ Hint: the algorithm is very similar to Selection Sort, only on each iteration, instead of finding the largest element, you choose a random one. ⸮

13.   An array of six integers — 6, 9, 74, 10, 22, 81 — is being sorted in ascending order. Show the state of the array after two iterations through the outer for loop in Selection Sort (as shown in Figure 13-5).

14.   What are the values stored in an array a after five iterations in the for loop of the Insertion Sort (as shown in Figure 13-6) if the initial values are 3, 7, 5, 8, 2, 0, 1, 9, 4, 3? ✓

15.   What is the state of the array after the partitioning phase of the Quicksort algorithm, at the top level of recursion, if its initial values are

         int[] a = {6, 9, 74, 10, 22, 81, 2, 11, 54};

        and the middle element is chosen as a pivot? ✓

16.   Add Arrays's built-in sorting method to the *Benchmarks* program to see how it compares to our own sorting methods.

```
outputFile.printf
    ("Chapter %d", 14);
```

Streams and Files

14.1 Prologue

Any program that processes a considerable amount of data has to read the data from a file (or several files) and is likely to write data into a file. A file is a software entity supported by the operating system. The operating system provides commands for renaming, copying, moving, and deleting files, as well as low-level functions, callable from programs, for opening, reading, and writing files. A file has to be opened before it can be read. To open a file the program needs to know its *pathname* in the system (the path to the folder that holds the file and the name of the file). A new file has to be created before we can write into it. To create a new file, a program needs to know its path and what name to give it.

> **Data files are not a part of the program source code, and they are not compiled. The same executable program can work on different files as long as it can handle the particular format of the data in the files and knows the file pathnames (or receives them from the user at run time).**

A file can contain any kind of information: text, images, sound clips, binary numbers, or any other information that can be stored digitally. The size of a file is measured in bytes. The format of the data in a file is determined by the program that created that file. There are many standardized file formats that allow different programs to understand the same files. A standard format is usually designated by the file name's extension. For example, standard formats for representing compressed images may have the `.gif` or `.jpg` extensions, music files may have the `.mp3` extension, and so on. A text file often has the `.txt` extension. A Java source file with the extension `.java` is a text file, too.

A computer program may treat a file as either a *stream* or a *random-access file*. The term "stream" has its origins in operating systems, such as *UNIX* and *MS-DOS*. It refers to the abstract model of an input or output device in which an input device produces a stream of bytes and an output device receives a stream of bytes. Some input/output devices, such as a keyboard and a printer, are rather close to this abstract model. Ignoring the technical details, we can say that a keyboard produces an input stream of characters and a printer receives an output stream.

Other devices, such as graphics adapters, hard drives, or CD-ROM drives, are actually random-access devices rather than stream devices: software can transfer a whole block of bytes to or from any sector on a disk or set the values of pixels anywhere on a screen. Still, the operating system software lets us implement input/output from/to a disk file as a <u>logical</u> stream. For example, when we read from a disk file, the input is *buffered*: whole chunks of data are read into specially allocated memory space, called *buffer*, and the program takes bytes or characters from the buffer. Likewise, a console window on the screen can be thought of as a logical output stream of characters positioned line by line from left to right.

A stream can be opened for input (reading) or for output (writing), but not for both at the same time. Bytes are read sequentially from an input stream, although Java input streams have a method to skip several bytes. Bytes are written to an output stream sequentially, without gaps. If an output stream represents an existing file, a program can open it in the "create" mode and start writing from the beginning, destroying the old contents, or it can open it in the "append" mode and start adding data at the end of the file.

In a random-access file, the program can start reading or writing at any place. In fact, a random-access file can be opened for both input and output at the same time.

A program can work with several input and/or output files concurrently.

> **In a text file, each line is marked by a terminating end-of-line character or combination of such characters (for example, CR+LF, "carriage return" + "line feed").**

Files that do not hold text are often called *binary files*, because any byte in a file holds eight bits of binary data.

Most programming languages provide special functions for reading characters or a line of text from a text file or writing to a text file or to the screen.

> **It is more common to treat text files as streams. A binary file with fixed-length records can be opened as a random-access file.**

This is so because text lines may have different lengths, and it is hard to track where each line begins. Therefore random access is not useful for a text file. In a binary file, if all the records have the same length, we can easily calculate the position of the *n*-th record; then we can go directly to that place and read or write that record.

Programming languages usually include library functions or classes for opening, reading, creating, and writing files. These functions call low-level functions provided by the operating system. Programming languages and operating systems also support "standard input" and "standard output" streams for reading keyboard input and writing text to the screen. These streams are implemented in a manner similar to file streams, but they are automatically open when a program is running.

Java's classes for handling input and output streams and files are rich in functionality but confusing to a novice. Java's I/O package `java.io` offers two sets of classes: one for dealing with streams of bytes, the other for dealing with streams of characters. The <u>byte stream</u> input and output hierarchies are rooted in the abstract classes `InputStream` and `OutputStream`, respectively. The <u>character stream</u> input and output class hierarchies are rooted in the abstract classes `Reader` and `Writer`, respectively.

In the past, there was little difference between bytes and characters because each byte held the code for one character. With the internationalization of software and the introduction of Unicode, the situation has changed. As you know, in Unicode a character is represented by two bytes. "Native" files in many operating systems still use one byte per character, using a subset of Unicode. In the U.S. version of *Windows*, for example, text files use ASCII encoding. Java character streams provide conversion from the native or specified encoding to Unicode.

> **In this chapter we consider only reading from and writing to text files using some of Java's character stream classes. We won't deal with reading or writing to a file in a random-access manner.**

14.2 Pathnames and the `java.io.File` Class

In a typical operating system, such as *Unix* or *Windows*, files are arranged in a hierarchy of nested *directories* (or folders). Each file is identified by its *pathname*, which consists of the drive letter, a sequence of directories that lead to the file from the root directory, and the file name and extension. For example, the pathname for the file `words.txt` in the `Dictionary` subdirectory in the `Ch14` subdirectory in the `JM` directory (folder) on drive `C` is `C:/JM/Ch14/Dictionary/words.txt`. This is called *absolute pathname* because it traces the file's location all the way up to the root directory.

The class `File` in the `java.io` package represents an entry in the operating system's file management subsystem. (A `File` can refer to a file or the whole subdirectory.) `File` has a constructor with one `String` parameter, a pathname. The following statement, for example, creates a `File` object for the file named `words.txt`:

```
File wordsFile = new File("words.txt");
```

Note that we have not used the absolute pathname for the file in the above statement.

Programs almost never refer to a file's absolute pathname explicitly, because if the folders somewhere above the file are rearranged or renamed, the program won't be able to find the file.

Most programs refer to a file simply by its name or using a *relative pathname*, which starts at some folder but does not go all the way up to the root. The above declaration of `wordsFile`, for example, assumes that the file `words.txt` is located in the same directory (folder) as the program's compiled class files. If the class files were in `Ch14\Classes`, and `words.txt` were in `Ch14\Data`, we would write

```
File wordsFile = new File("../Data/words.txt");
```

`".."` means "go one directory level up."

Figure 14-1 shows a small subset of `File`'s methods.

```
String getName();              // Returns the name of this file.
String getAbsolutePath();      // Returns the absolute pathname
                               //    of this file.
long length();                 // Returns the size of this file
                               //    in bytes.
long lastModified();           // Returns the time when this file was
                               //    created or last modified.
boolean isDirectory();         // Returns true if this file represents
                               //    a subdirectory; otherwise
                               //    returns false.
File[] listFiles();            // Returns an array of files in the
                               //    subdirectory represented by this
                               //    file.
```

Figure 14-1. A subset of `java.io.File`'s methods

Note that a `File` object does not represent a file ready for reading or writing. In fact, a directory entry associated with a `File` object may not even exist yet. You need to construct a readable or writable stream associated with a file to read or write the data.

Another way to obtain a reference to a `File` in a Java program is to use a `JFileChooser` GUI component (from the `javax.swing` package). Figure 14-2 gives an example of that.

```
// Set the initial path for the file chooser:
private String pathname = System.getProperty("user.dir") + "/";
...

   ...
   JFileChooser fileChooser = new JFileChooser(pathname);

   // Allow choosing only files, but not subfolders:
   fileChooser.setFileSelectionMode(JFileChooser.FILES_ONLY);

   // Open a dialog box for choosing a file; locate it
   // in the middle of the JFrame window (or use null to
   // locate the dialog box in the middle of the screen):
   int result = fileChooser.showOpenDialog(window);

   // Check whether the "Cancel" button was clicked:
   if (result == JFileChooser.CANCEL_OPTION)
     return;

   // Get the chosen file:
   File file = fileChooser.getSelectedFile();

   // Save pathname to be used as a starting point for
   // the next JFileChooser:
   pathname = file.getAbsolutePath();
   ...
```

Figure 14-2. A `JFileChooser` example

14.3   Reading from a Text File

Java I/O classes provide many ways to accomplish the same task. Java developers have recognized the need to simplify the `java.io` package for novices, and in the 5.0 release of Java they have introduced a new class, `Scanner`, for reading numbers, words, and lines from a text file.

The `Scanner` class has been added to the `java.`<u>`util`</u> package.

To use this class, you first need to create a `Scanner` associated with a particular file. You can do this by using a constructor that takes a `File` object as a parameter.

> Be careful: `Scanner` also has a constructor that takes a parameter of the type `String`. However, that string is <u>not</u> a pathname, but rather a string to be used as an input stream.

If a `File file` does not exist, `new Scanner(file)` throws a `FileNotFoundException`, which you have to catch. For example:

```
String pathname = "words.txt";
File file = new File(pathname);
Scanner input = null;
try
{
  input = new Scanner(file);
}
catch (FileNotFoundException ex)
{
  System.out.println("*** Cannot open " + pathname + " ***");
  System.exit(1);  // quit the program
}
```

In general, Java I/O classes report errors by throwing "checked" exceptions. A checked exception is a type of event that can either be "caught" inside a method using the `try-catch` syntax or left unprocessed and passed up to the calling method (or to the Java run-time environment). In the latter case, you have to declare up front that your method might `throw` a particular type of exception. For example:

```
public StringBuffer loadFile(String pathname)
          throws IOException
  // this method doesn't have to catch I/O exceptions
{
  ...
}
```

The `Scanner` class is easier to use than other `java.io` classes because its methods do not throw checked exceptions — only its constructor does.

Some of the `Scanner` methods are summarized in Figure 14-3.

> **Don't forget**
>
> `import.java.io.*;`
> `import.java.util.Scanner;`
>
> when working with **`java.io` classes and `Scanner`**.

```
boolean hasNextLine();        // Returns true if this stream has another
                              //   line in it; otherwise returns false.
String nextLine();            // Reads all the characters from the
                              //   current position in the input stream
                              //   up to and including the next newline
                              //   character; removes these characters
                              //   from the stream and returns a string
                              //   that holds the read characters
                              //   (excluding newline).
boolean hasNext();            // Returns true if this stream has another
                              //   token (a contiguous block of
                              //   non-whitespace characters) in it.
String next();                // Reads the next token from this stream,
                              //   removes it from the stream, and
                              //   returns the read token.
boolean hasNextInt();         // Returns true if the next token in
                              //   this stream represents an integer.
int nextInt();                // Reads the next token from this stream,
                              //   removes it from the stream, and
                              //   returns its int value.
boolean hasNextDouble();      // Returns true if the next token in
                              //   this stream represents a double.
double nextDouble();          // Reads the next token from this stream,
                              //   removes it from the stream, and
                              //   returns its value as a double.
void close();                 // Closes this file.
```

Figure 14-3. A subset of `java.util.Scanner`'s methods

Once a `Scanner` object has been created, you can call its methods to read `int`s, `double`s, words, and lines. For example:

```
int sum = 0;
while(input.hasNextInt())
{
  int score = input.nextInt();
  sum += score;
}
```

A `Scanner` assumes that tokens (numbers, words) are separated by whitespace. `Scanner`'s `next`, `nextInt`, and `nextDouble` methods skip the white space between tokens. `Scanner` does not have a method to read a single character.

Note that if a token read by `next`, `nextInt`, or `nextDouble` is the last one on a line, then the newline character that follows the token remains in the stream. Before reading the next line, first get rid of the tail of the previous line (unless you will continue reading `int`s, `double`s, or individual words). For example:

```
int num = input.nextInt();
input.nextLine();                  // skip the rest of the line
                                   //   and newline
String str = input.nextLine();  // read the next line
```

❖   ❖   ❖

If you need to read a file character by character, use a `FileReader` with a `BufferedReader` "wrapped" around it. Figure 14-4 gives an example.

```
public static StringBuffer loadFile(String pathname)
      throws IOException
{
   File file = new File(pathname);
   StringBuffer strBuffer = new StringBuffer((int)file.length());
   BufferedReader input = new BufferedReader(new FileReader(file));

   int ch = 0;
   while ((ch = input.read()) != -1)
      strBuffer.append((char)ch);   // input.read returns an int

   input.close();
   return strBuffer;
}
```

Figure 14-4. Reading a file character by character using a `BufferedReader`

14.4 Writing to a Text File

Use the class `PrintWriter` to write to a text file. This class has two constructors: one creates an output character stream from a pathname string, the other from a `File` object. Each throws a `FileNotFoundException` if the file cannot be created. This exception has to be caught.

> **Be careful: if you try to write to a file and a file with the given pathname already exists, it is truncated to zero size and the information in the existing file is lost.**

The `PrintWriter` class has `println`, `print`, and `printf` methods similar to the ones we use with `System.out`. The `printf` method, added in Java 5.0, is used for writing formatted output (see Section 10.5).

> **It is important to close the file by calling its `close` method when you have finished writing. Otherwise some of the data that you sent to the output stream may end up not written to the file.**

Data is usually written not directly to disk, but into an intermediate buffer. When the file is closed, the data remaining in the buffer is written to the file.

Figure 14-5 gives an example of creating a text file.

```java
String pathname = "output.txt";
File file = new File(pathname);
PrintWriter output = null;
try
{
  output = new PrintWriter(file);
}
catch (FileNotFoundException ex)
{
  System.out.println("*** Cannot create " + pathname + " ***");
  System.exit(1);  // quit the program
}

output.println("Metric measures:");
output.printf("%2d kg = %5.3f lbs\n", 1, 2.2046226);
output.close();

/* output.txt will contain:
Metric measures:
 1 kg = 2.205 lbs    */
```

Figure 14-5. Creating a text file

If you want to append text to an existing file, use a `PrintWriter` "wrapped" around a `FileWriter` (Figure 14-6).

```
      String pathname = "output.txt";
      Writer writer = null;
      try
      {
        writer = new FileWriter(pathname, true);
            // "true" means open in the append mode
      }
      catch (IOException ex)  // Note: not FileNotFoundException!
      {
        System.out.println("*** Cannot create/open " + pathname + " ***");
        System.exit(1);  // quit the program
      }
      PrintWriter output = new PrintWriter(writer);
      output.printf("%2d km = %5.3f mile\n", 1, 0.6213712);
      output.close();

  /* output.txt will contain:
  Metric measures:
   1 kg = 2.205 lbs
   1 km = 0.621 mile     */
```

Figure 14-6. Appending data to a text file

14.5 *Lab:* Choosing Words

Suppose I am working on a program for a word game. (I call my game Ramblecs.) My game uses three-, four-, and five-letter words. In this lab you will help me create a dictionary for my program. You will start with a text file, words.txt, which contains about 20,000 English words. Your program (a simple console application) should choose the three-, four-, and five-letter words from words.txt, convert them into the upper case, and write them to an output file. Make the output file use the syntax of a Java class, as shown in Figure 14-7. Then I will be able to use this class in my program.

At first glance, this plan seems to contradict our earlier statement that data files are different from program source files. In fact there is no contradiction. In this lab, both the input file and the output file are data files. It just so happens that the output file uses Java syntax. The same thing happens when you create Java source using a program editor: for the editor, the resulting file is just some output text.

```
public class RamblecsDictionary
{
  private String[] words =
  {
    "ABACK",
    "ABASE",
    "ABASH",
    "ABATE",
    ...
    ...
    "ZIPPY",
    "ZLOTY",
    "ZONE",
    "ZOO",
    "ZOOM",
  };
}
```

Figure 14-7. The output file format in the *Dictionary Maker* program

Use a `Scanner` to read words from `words.txt` and a `PrintWriter` to create `RamblecsDictionary.java`. Review the output file and run it through the Java compiler to verify that the output of your program is correct.

14.6 Summary

Java's I/O classes are rich in functionality but are not very easy to use.

Use an object of the `java.util.Scanner` class to read a text file. `Scanner` has a constructor that takes a `File` object as a parameter and opens that file for reading. Some of `Scanner`'s methods are summarized in Figure 14-3.

Use an object of the `java.io.PrintWriter` class to write to a text file. `PrintWriter` has a constructor that takes a `File` as a parameter and another constructor that takes a `String pathname` as a parameter. It creates a new file and opens it for writing (or, if the file already exists, opens it and truncates it to zero size). `PrintWriter` has convenient `print`, `println`, and `printf` methods, which are similar to `System.out`'s methods.

Exercises

Sections 14.1-14.6

1. (MC) Which of the following is true? ✓

    A. Any file can be opened for reading either as a stream or as a random-access file.
    B. All files in *UNIX* are streams, while in *Windows* some may be random-access files.
    C. In both *Windows* and *UNIX*, all text files are streams and all binary (non-text) files are random-access files.
    D. When a file is first created, an attribute is set that designates this file as a stream or as a random-access file for all future applications.

2. Explain why random-access files usually contain fixed-length records.

3. Many methods in Java stream I/O classes throw an exception whenever an I/O error occurs. It would perhaps be more convenient for a programmer to handle certain errors by making the program check the return value or the stream status after the operation rather than letting it throw an exception. Which errors among the following would be good candidates for such no-exception treatment?

    (a) Failure to open a file because it does not exist _____ ✓
    (b) Failure to open a file that is already opened by another application _____ ✓
    (c) Failure to create a file because a read-only file with the same name already exists _____ ✓
    (d) Device is not ready for reading (for example, a CD-ROM drive is empty) _____
    (e) System error reading from a device (for example, a damaged sector on disk) _____
    (f) System write error (for example, disk full) _____
    (g) Device is not ready for writing (for example, a floppy disk is write-protected) _____
    (h) End of file is encountered while trying to read data _____

4.   Write a program that checks whether all the braces are balanced in a Java source file. ⋛ Hint: read the file one character at a time. When you encounter an opening brace, increment the count, and when you encounter a closing brace, decrement the count. The count should never be negative and should be zero at the end. ⋚ ✓

5.   Write a program that compares two files for exactly matching data. ✓

6.■   *grep* is an old utility program from *UNIX* that scans a file or several files for a given word (or a regular expression) and prints out all lines in which that word occurs. (The name "grep" comes from the "qed/ed" editor commands g/re/p — globally search for a regular expression and print the lines.)

Write a simplified version of *grep* that looks for a word in one file. A "word" is defined as a contiguous string of non-whitespace characters. For every line that contains the word, print out the line number and the text of the line in brackets. For example:

```
Line  5: [  private static PrintWriter output;]
```

Prompt the user for the target word and the file name or take them from the command-line arguments.

The search for a matching word can be accomplished by using `String`'s method `indexOf`. This method will find the target word even if it occurs as part of another word in the line. If you want to find only matches between complete words, write your own method. ⋛ Hint: search for all occurrences of the word in the line and then check that the matching substring is surrounded by not "isLetterOrDigit" characters wherever it doesn't touch the beginning or the end of the line. ⋚

7.■   Write a class that represents a picture: a 2-D array of characters set to either
'x' or '.'. Supply a constructor that loads the picture from a file with a
specified name. The first line of the file contains two integers, the number of
rows and the number of columns in the picture. The following lines, one for
each row, contain strings of x's and dots. The length of each string is equal
to the number of columns in the picture. For example:

```
3 4
x.xx
xx.x
..x.
```

Supply a `toString` method for your class and test your class. ✓

8.■   Write and test a program that merges two sorted files into one sorted file.
The files contain lines of text that are sorted lexicographically (the same
ordering used by `String`'s `compareTo` method). Your program should read
each file only once and should not use arrays or lists.

9.■   A word is said to be an *anagram* of another word if it is made up of the same
letters arranged in a different order. (For instance, "GARDEN" and
"DANGER" are anagrams.) Write a program that finds all anagrams of a
given target word in a file of words. Follow these steps:

(a)   Write a method that reads the words from a dictionary file into an array
of strings.

(b)   Write a method that creates an array of letter counts for a word. The
array should have 26 elements; the k-th element represents the number
of times the k-th letter of the alphabet occurs in the word.

(c)   Write a method that compares two letter count arrays for an exact
match.

(d)   For each word in the dictionary, generate a letter count array, compare
it with the letter count array for the target word, and print out the word
if they match.

(e)   See if you can find any anagrams for "RAMBLECS" in
`JM\Ch14\Dictionary\words.txt`.

Continued   ✍

(f)   There is another way to ascertain that two words are anagrams of each other: if we sort the letters in each word in ascending order, we should get equal strings. Implement this anagram searching algorithm instead of the one described in Parts (b) - (d). ⋛ Hints: (1) The `String` class has a convenient method `toCharArray`, which returns an array of `chars` from the string, in the same order. Use `Arrays.sort` to sort that array. (2) Convert the sorted `char` array back into a `String` by using the `String(char[])` constructor. ⋛

10.◆   In the Mad Libs™ party game, the leader has the text of a short story with a few missing words in it. The missing words are tagged by their part of speech or function: <noun>, <verb>, <place>, etc. For example:

```
It was a <adjective> summer day.
Jack was sitting in a <place>.
. . .
```

The leader examines the text and prompts the players for the missing words:

```
Please give me an/a:
adjective
place
. . .
```

She then reads the text with the supplied words inserted into their respective places.

Write a program that acts as a Mad Libs leader. It should prompt the user for a file name, read the text from the file, find the tags for the missing words (anything within <...>), prompt the user for these words, and save them in an `ArrayList`. It should then reopen the file and display the completed text, inserting the saved words in place of the corresponding tags. A sample file, `madlibs.txt`, is provided in `JM\Ch14\Exercises`. ⋛ Hint: you can read the text line by line and assume that tags are not split between lines, but it may be easier to read the text character by character. ⋛

Chapter 15

Height | Ascent | Baseline | Descent

Graphics

15.1 Prologue

What you see on your computer screen is ultimately determined by the contents of the video memory (*VRAM*) on the graphics adapter card. The video memory represents a rectangular array of *pixels* (picture elements). Each pixel has a particular color, which can be represented as a mix of red, green, and blue components, each with its own intensity. A typical graphics adapter may use eight bits to represent each of the red, green, and blue intensities (in the range from 0 to 255), so each color is represented in 24 bits (that is, three bytes). This allows for $2^{24} = 16,777,216$ different colors. With a typical screen resolution of 1024 by 768 pixels, your adapter needs $1024 \cdot 768 \cdot 3$ bytes — a little over 2 MB — to hold the picture for one screen. The picture is produced by setting the color of each pixel in VRAM. The video hardware scans the whole video memory continuously and refreshes the image on the screen.

A graphics adapter is what we call a *raster* device: each individual pixel is changed separately from other pixels. (This is different from a *vector* device, such as a plotter, which can draw a line directly from point *A* to point *B*.) To draw a red line or a circle on a raster device, you need to set just the right group of pixels to the red color. That's where a graphics package can help: you certainly don't want to program all those routines for setting pixels yourself.

A typical graphics package has functions for setting drawing attributes, such as color, line style and width, fill texture or pattern for filled shapes, and font for text, and another set of functions for drawing simple shapes: lines, arcs, circles and ovals, rectangles, polygons, text, and so on. Java's graphics capabilities are based on the `Graphics` class and the `Graphics2D` package. The `Graphics` class is pretty rudimentary: it lets you set the color and font attributes and draw lines, arcs, ovals (including circles), rectangles, rectangles with rounded corners, polygons, polylines (open polygons), images, and text. There are "draw" and "fill" methods for each basic shape (for example, `drawRect` and `fillRect`).

The `Graphics2D` class is derived from `Graphics` and inherits all its methods. It works with a number of related interfaces and classes:

- The `Shape` interface and classes that implement it (`Line2D`, `Rectangle2D`, `Ellipse2D`, etc.) define different geometric shapes.

- The `Stroke` interface and one implementation of it, `BasicStroke`, represent in a very general manner the line width and style for drawing lines.

- The `Paint` interface and its implementations `Color`, `GradientPaint`, and `TexturePaint` represent a color, a color gradient (gradually changing color), and a texture for filling in shapes, respectively.

`Graphics2D` also adds methods for various coordinate transformations, including rotations.

More importantly, `Graphics2D` adds a capability for treating shapes polymorphically. In the `Graphics` class, contrary to the OOP spirit, shapes are not represented by objects, and there is a separate special method for drawing each shape. Suppose you are working on a drawing editor program that allows you to add different shapes to a picture. You keep all the shapes already added to the picture in some kind of a list. To redraw the picture you need to draw all the shapes from the list. With `Graphics` you have to store each shape's identification (such as "circle," "rectangle," etc.) together with its dimensions and position and use a `switch` or an `if-else` statement to call the appropriate drawing method for each shape.

With `Graphics2D`, you can define different shapes (objects of classes that implement the `Shape` interface) and store references to them in your list. Each shape provides a "path iterator" which generates a sequence of points on that shape's contour. These points are used by `Graphics2D`'s `draw(Shape s)` and `fill(Shape s)` methods. Thus, shapes are treated in a polymorphic manner and at the same time are drawn using the currently selected `Paint` and `Stroke`. If your own class implements `Shape` and supplies a `getPathIterator` method for it, then your "shapes" will be drawn properly, too, due to polymorphism.

Like any package with very general capabilities, `Graphics2D` is not easy to use. We will stay mostly within the limits of the `Graphics` class, but, if you are adventurous, you can examine the `Graphics2D` API and learn to use some of its fancy features.

In the following sections we will examine Java's event-driven graphics model and review the basic drawing attributes and methods of the `Graphics` class. We will then use its capabilities to write a simple *Puzzle* program in which a player rearranges the pieces of a scrambled picture.

15.2 paint, paintComponent, and repaint

In Java, the hardest thing may be figuring out <u>when</u> and <u>where</u> to draw, rather than <u>how</u>. Java's graphics are necessarily event-driven because applets and applications run under multitasking operating systems. Suppose you are playing Solitaire when all of a sudden you decide to check your e-mail. You bring up your e-mail and its window overlaps a part of the Solitaire window. When you close or minimize your e-mail application, the operating system has to redisplay the Solitaire window. The operating system sends the *Solitaire* program a message that its window has been partially wiped out and now needs to be "repainted." *Solitaire* must be ready to dispatch a method in response to this "repaint" message.

In Java, this method is called `paint`. `paint` is a `void` method that receives one parameter of the type `Graphics`, usually named `g`:

```
public void paint(Graphics g)
{
  ...
}
```

`g` defines the graphics context: the size and position of the picture, the current attributes (color, font), the clipping area for the picture, and so on.

An object of the `JApplet` or `JFrame` type has a default `paint` method that calls the `paintComponent` method for each of the components (buttons, labels, text edit fields, etc.) in the object's "content pane" container. If you derive your main class from `JApplet` or `JFrame`, which is usually the case, and you want to do some drawing on your window, you can override the inherited `paint` method by defining your own. The first statement in your `paint` most likely will be a call to the base class's `paint`:

```
public void paint(Graphics g)
{
  super.paint(g);
  ...
}
```

After that you can add your own statements. That's exactly what we did in `JM\Ch02\HelloGui\HelloApplet.java`:

```
public void paint(Graphics g)
{
  super.paint(g);      // call JApplet's paint method
                       //  to paint the background
  g.setColor(Color.RED);
  g.drawRect(25, 40, 150, 45);  // draw a rectangle 150 by 45
  g.setColor(Color.BLUE);
  g.drawString("Hello, Applet!", 60, 65);
}
```

Naturally, paint does not have to define all the drawing work in its own code. It can call other methods, passing g to them as one of the parameters.

paint is called automatically in response to certain messages received from the operating system. But sometimes your program needs to repaint the window itself after changing its appearance. It can't call paint directly because it does not have a valid Graphics parameter, a g, to pass to it. Instead your program calls the repaint method, which does not take any parameters. repaint places a request to repaint the window into the event queue, and in due time the paint method is invoked.

paint is the central drawing method for your application window, where all drawing originates. Therefore, it must handle all the different drawing requirements for all the different situations in which the application might find itself. This is not easy. Fortunately, in Java's *Swing* GUI package, you can redefine the painting of individual GUI components. Each type of component (a JButton object, a JTextField object, etc.) has its own default paintComponent method. paintComponent also takes one parameter, Graphics g. You can derive a class from any of these classes and redefine paintComponent in it. It is not very common, though, to draw on top of buttons or text edit fields. But your class can extend JComponent or JPanel. The default paintComponent method in JPanel just paints its background. You can derive your own class from JPanel and add your drawing in your own paintComponent method. Again, it will usually start by calling the base class's paintComponent.

That is precisely what we did in *Hello Graphics*, *Craps*, *Snack Bar*, *Chomp*, *Dance Studio* and other programs. In *Craps*, for instance, we derived a class CrapsTable from JPanel (J_M\Ch07\Craps\CrapsTable.java):

```
public class CrapsTable extends JPanel
   . . .
```

We then provided our own `paintComponent` method for it:

```
public void paintComponent(Graphics g)
{
  super.paintComponent(g);
  die1.draw(g);
  die2.draw(g);
}
```

When you need to repaint a component, you call its `repaint` method. (A component's `repaint` is different from `JFrame`'s `repaint`: it calls `paintComponent` only for this particular component.) In *Craps*, when the dice roll, we adjust their positions and call `table`'s `repaint`:

```
// Processes timer events
public void actionPerformed(ActionEvent e)
{
  if (diceAreRolling())
  {
    ...
  }
  else
  {
    ...
  }

  repaint();
}
```

> Note that **repaint** just sends a request message to repaint the window or a component, and this request goes into the event queue. The actual painting may be postponed until your program finishes processing the current event and other events that are earlier in the event queue.

By painting individual components in *Swing* you can implement smoother animations. Without this capability you would have to repaint the whole window when just one small part of it has changed. We will return to the subject of using `JPanel` and see another example later in this chapter, in the Pieces of the Puzzle case study.

An insightful reader may wonder at this point: how can we call `Graphics2D` methods if all we get in `paint` or `paintComponent` is a reference to `Graphics g`? The truth is that `g` is a `Graphics2D` reference in disguise. It is presented as `Graphics` simply for compatibility with earlier versions of Java. To use it for calling `Graphics2D` methods you simply have to cast it into `Graphics2D`. For example:

```
Graphics2D g2D = (Graphics2D)g;
g2D.setPaint(new GradientPaint(0, 0, Color.RED,
                               100, 100, Color.BLUE, true));
< ... etc. >
```

15.3 Coordinates

The graphics context `g`, passed to `paint` and `paintComponent`, defines the coordinate system for the drawing. As in most computer graphics packages, the *y*-axis points down, not up as in math (Figure 15-1).

> **By default, the `Graphics` class places the origin at the <u>upper</u>-left corner of the content area of the application window (for `paint`) or in the upper-left corner of the component (for `paintComponent`). The coordinates are <u>integers</u>, and the units are pixels.**

The `translate(x, y)` method shifts the origin to the point (x, y). In the `Graphics2D` class, there are methods to scale and rotate the coordinates.

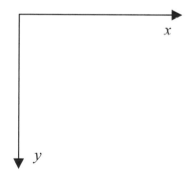

Figure 15-1. Graphics coordinates: *y*-axis points down

`Graphics` also sets the *clipping rectangle* to the window's drawing area or the component's drawing area. Anything outside the clipping rectangle does not show up on the screen. Therefore, one component's `paintComponent` method usually can't paint over other components that do not overlap with it. `Graphics` has a method `setClip` for redefining the clipping rectangle.

What about scaling? As a programmer, you decide what happens when the application window is resized. In some applications (like *Craps* or *Snack Bar*) you may want to simply disallow resizing the window (by calling `JFrame`'s method `setResizable(false)`). In other programs (like *Lipogrammer*) you may rely on Java's component layout manager to adjust the positions of the components on the window. You may choose to adjust the <u>positions</u> of some of the graphics elements in the picture, but not their sizes. Or you may want everything scaled, as in the *Puzzle* program later in this chapter.

You may lose some precision when scaling coordinates, but the high resolution (number of pixels per unit length) of modern graphics adapters makes these inaccuracies hardly visible.

Each component provides `getWidth` and `getHeight` methods that return the current width and height of the component in pixels. You can scale the coordinates based on these values.

Suppose you want to draw a filled red rectangle with its center at the center of the panel and its size equal to 75 percent of the panel's size. On top of it you want to draw a filled blue oval inscribed into the rectangle (Figure 15-2). This can be accomplished as follows:

```
public void paintComponent(Graphics g)
{
  super.paintComponent(g);   // call JPanel's paintComponent

  int width = getWidth();
  int height = getHeight();
  int xSize = (int)(.75 * width);
  int ySize = (int)(.75 * height);
  int x0 = width/2 - xSize/2;     // Coordinates of the
  int y0 = height/2 - ySize/2;    //   upper-left corner

  g.setColor(Color.RED);
  g.fillRect(x0, y0, xSize, ySize);
  g.setColor(Color.BLUE);
  g.fillOval(x0, y0, xSize, ySize);
}
```

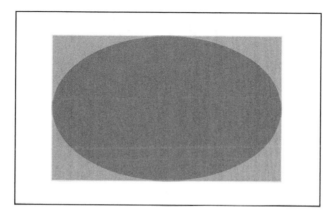

Figure 15-2.   A filled oval inscribed into a filled rectangle

The above example shows not only how a drawing can be scaled, but also how the positions of simple shapes (rectangles, ovals) are passed to drawing methods. The position and size of a rectangle are described by the x and y coordinates of its upper-left corner and by its width and height. In the above example we subtract half the size of the rectangle from the coordinates of the center of the panel to determine where the upper-left corner should be.

The position and size of a rounded rectangle, an oval, and even an arc are described by the position of the rectangle in which those shapes are inscribed (Figure 15-3).

In the above code the same parameters are passed to `fillRect` and `fillOval` because the oval is inscribed into the rectangle.

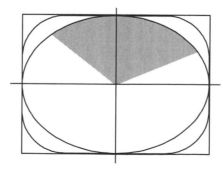

Figure 15-3.   Positioning of ovals, arcs, and rounded rectangles

15.4 Colors

We have already used the `setColor` method whose parameter is a `Color` object. The `Color` class has thirteen predefined constants for colors (`WHITE`, `BLACK`, `GRAY`, `LIGHT_GRAY`, `DARK_GRAY`, `BLUE`, `GREEN`, `CYAN`, `RED`, `MAGENTA`, `PINK`, `ORANGE`, and `YELLOW`). You can also construct your own color by specifying its red, green, and blue components:

```
int redValue = 18, greenValue = 50, blueValue = 255;
Color c = new Color(redValue, greenValue, blueValue);
g.setColor(c);
```

or simply:

```
g.setColor(new Color(18, 50, 255));
```

A `Color` object also has the methods `brighter` and `darker`, which return a new color made from the original color by adjusting its brightness. For example:

```
g.setColor(Color.ORANGE.darker().darker());
```

> **You can set the background color for a component by calling that component's `setBackground` method. This method only specifies the new background color but does not automatically repaint the component. If you set the background inside your `paintComponent` method, do it before calling `super.paintComponent`. If you do it elsewhere, call `repaint`.**

The Java default color for components is gray, and we often change it to white:

```
setBackground(Color.WHITE);
```

RGB numbers for different colors can be obtained from painting and imaging programs and color choosing tools on the web[rgbcolors] or from Java's own `JColorChooser` class.

15.5 Drawing Shapes

Figure 15-4 summarizes the drawing methods of the Graphics class.

```
g.drawLine(x1, y1, x2, y2);

g.clearRect(x, y, width, height);
g.drawRect(x, y, width, height);
g.fillRect(x, y, width, height);

g.drawOval(x, y, width, height);
g.fillOval(x, y, width, height);
g.drawRoundRect(x, y, width, height, horzDiam, vertDiam);
g.fillRoundRect(x, y, width, height, horzDiam, vertDiam);

g.draw3DRect(x, y, width, height, isRaised);
g.fill3DRect(x, y, width, height, isRaised);

g.drawArc(x, y, width, height, fromDegree, measureDegrees);
g.fillArc(x, y, width, height, fromDegree, measureDegrees);

g.drawPolygon(xCoords, yCoords, nPoints);
g.fillPolygon(xCoords, yCoords, nPoints);
g.drawPolyline(xCoords, yCoords, nPoints);

g.drawString(str, x, y);

g.drawImage(image, x, y, this);
```

Figure 15-4. The drawing methods of the Graphics class

The drawLine(x1, y1, x2, y2) method draws a straight line from (x1, y1) to (x2, y2).

There are eleven methods for drawing and filling rectangles, ovals, and arcs: clearRect, drawRect, fillRect, drawRoundRect, fillRoundRect, draw3DRect, fill3DRect, drawOval, fillOval, drawArc, and fillArc. We have already used most of them in one project or another, so they should look familiar. The first four parameters in each of these methods are the same: the *x* and *y* coordinates of the upper-left corner, and the width and height of the bounding rectangle (as explained in Section 15.3). The `clearRect` method fills the rectangle with the component's current background color. The `drawRoundRect` and `fillRoundRect` methods take two additional parameters: the horizontal and vertical diameters of the oval used to round the corners. The `draw3DRect` and `fill3DRect` methods add a shadow on two sides to hint at a 3-D effect. Their fifth parameter can be either `true` for a "raised" rectangle or `false` for a "lowered" rectangle.

The `drawArc` and `fillArc` methods, respectively, draw and fill a fragment of an oval inscribed into the bounding rectangle. `fillArc` fills a sector of the oval (a slice of the pie) bound by the arc. The fifth and sixth parameters in these methods are the beginning angle (with the 0 at the easternmost point) and the measure of the arc in degrees (going counterclockwise).

The `drawPolygon` and `fillPolygon` methods take three parameters: the array of *x*-coordinates of the vertices, the array of *y*-coordinates of the vertices, and the number of points:

```
drawPolygon(int[] xCoords, int[] yCoords, int n)
```

The number of points n should not exceed the smaller of `xCoords.length` and `yCoords.length`. As you can see, the `xCoords` and `yCoords` arrays do not have to be filled to capacity: they may hold fewer points than their size allows. This is convenient if you are adding points interactively or if you are reading them from a file and don't know in advance how many points you will end up with.

`drawPolygon` and `fillPolygon` automatically connect the last point to the first point and draw or fill a closed polygon, respectively. So

```
g.drawPolygon(xCoords, yCoords, n);
```

is basically the same as:

```
for (int i = 0; i < n - 1; i++)
{
  g.drawLine(xCoords[i], yCoords[i], xCoords[i+1]; yCoords[i+1]);
}
g.drawLine(xCoords[n-1], yCoords[n-1], xCoords[0]; yCoords[0]);
```

The `drawPolyline` method works the same way as `drawPolygon`, but it does not connect the last point to the first.

15.6 Fonts and Text

The `setFont` method lets you set the font for drawing text. Java uses an object of the `Font` class to describe a font. `Font` objects are used for graphics text displayed with `g.drawString` and for text in various GUI components (`JLabel`, `JTextField`, `JTextArea`, `JButton`, etc.). The `Graphics` method for setting a font and the methods for setting a font in Swing components share the same name, `setFont`.

 A font is described by its name, its style, and its size.

Font names are system-dependent, but Java guarantees that at least three font names are always recognized:

- `"Serif"`, a proportional font, in which letters may have different widths, with serifs, or little decorative strokes, like Times Roman: ABCabc

- `"SansSerif"`, a proportional font without serifs, like Arial: ABCabc

- `"Monospaced"`, a fixed-width font where all characters have the same width, like Courier: ABCabc

The `GraphicsEnvironment` class has a `getAllFonts()` method that returns an array of all the fonts available in the system. For example:

```
GraphicsEnvironment env =
            GraphicsEnvironment.getLocalGraphicsEnvironment();
Font[] allFonts = env.getAllFonts();
```

Each font can come in four styles: `Font.PLAIN`, `Font.BOLD`, `Font.ITALIC`, or `Font.BOLD | Font.ITALIC` (the bit-wise combination of the two attributes, meaning both bold and italic).

The font size is specified in *points*. In typography, a point is 1/72 of an inch, but this measure loses its meaning when the text is scaled to a computer screen. For default coordinates, Java assumes that one point is equal to one pixel.

You can create all the fonts you need ahead of time (possibly, in the constructor for your drawing panel). For example:

```
Font font1 = new Font("Monospaced", Font.PLAIN, 20);
Font font2 = new Font("Serif", Font.BOLD, 30);
```

Then you set the font with `setFont`. For example:

```
g.setFont(font2);
```

If you intend to use a font only once, you can create an anonymous font on the fly:

```
g.setFont(new Font("Serif", Font.BOLD, 30));
```

For very precise text positioning, `Graphics` has a method `getFontMetrics` that returns a `FontMetrics` object. This object, in turn, has `getAscent`, `getDescent`, and `getHeight` methods that return the font's vertical measurements (Figure 15-5).

Figure 15-5. Font metrics

The `Graphics` class's `drawString(text, x, y)` method draws the `text` string. This method positions the left end of the text's baseline at the point (*x*, *y*).

15.7 *Case Study and Lab:* **Pieces of the Puzzle**

In this section we will create a program *Puzzle* to implement a simple puzzle that involves rearranging pieces of a picture. The program first shows a picture made of nine pieces on a 3 by 3 grid. After two seconds, it scrambles the pieces randomly and shows the scrambled picture. The player has to restore the picture by moving the pieces around. There is an extra empty cell below the picture for holding a piece temporarily (Figure 15-6). The player can move a piece by "picking it up," then "dropping" it into the empty cell. To pick up a piece the player clicks on it. This is acknowledged by some feedback; for example, the picked piece gets a different background color. To "drop" the piece the player clicks on the empty cell.

Play with this program (click on JM\Ch15\Puzzle\Puzzle.jar) to get a feel for how it works. In this version the initial picture is not very creative: it simply shows a circle and the numbers of the pieces (numbered from left to right and top to bottom like a telephone keypad).   Examine the code for the Puzzle class in JM\Ch15\Puzzle. As you can see, the program processes one timer event and after that is driven by mouse events.   The Puzzle class implements a MouseListener interface by providing its five required methods. Of them only mousePressed is used.   There is a way to not include unused methods (using a so-called *adapter class*), but we just use empty methods.

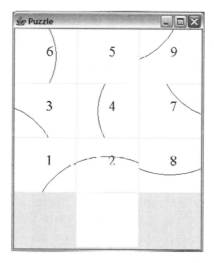

Figure 15-6. The *Puzzle* program

The pieces of the puzzle are numbered from 1 to 9, and the number 0 represents the empty cell. Before scrambling, the pieces are arranged as follows:

```
1 2 3
4 5 6
7 8 9
  0
```

The program uses an array of cells to hold the pieces. Each cell in the puzzle "knows" which piece it is currently holding. That number is returned by the cell's getPieceNumber method and can be set by the cell's setPieceNumber(k) method.   In the initial non-scrambled picture, the index of each cell in the array matches the number of the piece displayed in it.

The logic for moving the pieces is pretty straightforward. When a mouse clicks on the program's window, the `mousePressed` method is called:

```
public void mousePressed(MouseEvent e)
{
  int x = e.getX();
  int y = e.getY();

  // Figure out the index of the cell that was clicked:
  int col = 3 * x / getWidth();
  int row = 4 * y / getHeight();
  int i = 3 * row + col;
  if (i >= 0 && i < 9)
    i++;
  else if (i == 10)
    i = 0;
  else
    return;

  if (pickedIndex < 0)
    pickPiece(i);
  else
    dropPiece(i);
}
```

It gets the coordinates of the click and figures out in which cell i it occurred. Then it can go two different ways, depending whether there is already a picked-up piece "hanging in the air" or not. The `Puzzle` class has a field `pickedIndex` that holds the index of the cell whose piece has been picked up. If there is no picked piece, `pickedIndex` is equal to −1. Then if the player has clicked on a non-empty cell, the puzzle piece is (logically) "lifted" from that cell. The cell is highlighted, and its index i is saved in `pickedIndex` for future use. The `pickPiece` method implements this (Figure 15-7).

If, on the other hand, there is already a piece "in the air" (`pickedIndex` ≥ 0) and the player has clicked on the empty cell (the cell holding the 0 piece), then the piece that was picked up earlier is "dropped" into that cell. The cell is updated to reflect that it now holds a piece with a particular number while the previously picked cell is set to empty. This is implemented in the `dropPiece` method (Figure 15-7).

Figure 15-8 shows a little state machine with two states that represents this logic. A *state machine* is a model that uses nodes to represent different possible states (of a system or a program) and connecting arrows to represent the rules for changing states.

```
...

private void pickPiece(int i)
{
  if (cells[i].getPieceNumber() != 0) // pick only non-empty cells
  {
    pickedIndex = i;
    cells[i].setPicked(true);
    cells[i].repaint();
  }
  else
  {
    bzz.play();
  }
}

private void dropPiece(int i)
{
  if (cells[i].getPieceNumber() == 0) // drop only on the empty cell
  {
    // Set the empty cell's number to the picked piece
    int k = cells[pickedIndex].getPieceNumber();
    cells[i].setPieceNumber(k);
    cells[i].repaint();

    // Set the piece number for the source cell to "empty"
    cells[pickedIndex].setPieceNumber(0);
    cells[pickedIndex].setPicked(false);
    cells[pickedIndex].repaint();

    pickedIndex = -1;     // nothing picked now
    if (allSet())
      bells.play();
    else
      drop.play();
  }
  else
  {
    bzz.play();
  }
}

...
```

Figure 15-7. `pickPiece` and `dropPiece` methods in the `Puzzle` class
(J$_M$\Ch15\Puzzle\Puzzle.java)

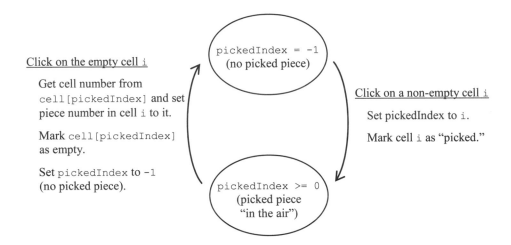

Figure 15-8. State machine diagram for moving pieces in the *Puzzle* program

The trickier part is to display different pieces of the puzzle in different cells. The question is: How can we show a particular piece in a cell? One approach would be to have a separate method draw each of the nine pieces of the puzzle. This might work, but only for very simple pictures. In the real puzzle we want to use drawings whose lines cut across the grid lines; to draw separate fragments of them would be a nightmare.

A better approach would be to use <u>one</u> method to draw the whole picture, but show only the appropriate piece of it in each cell. We use a separate panel for each of the ten cells. Each panel can be an object of the same class that we derive from `JPanel`. Each panel will use the same `paintComponent` method to draw the whole big picture, but only part of it will be visible on the panel. All we have to do is <u>shift the origin</u> of the coordinate system appropriately for each panel, depending on what puzzle piece it currently holds. For example (Figure 15-9), in order to draw piece number 6 correctly, no matter where it is currently located, the origin of its coordinate system should be shifted up by one cell height and to the left by two cell widths (with minor adjustments for the gaps between cells).

`JFrame`'s default `paint` method will automatically paint all the panels for us.

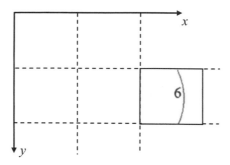

**Figure 15-9. The offset of relative coordinates
for a piece of the puzzle**

Now our plan of action is clear. Our program will use two classes. The first one,
`Puzzle`, is the main class derived from `JFrame`. The second class, let's call it
`PuzzleCell`, will be derived from `JPanel`. The program declares and initializes an
array of ten `PuzzleCell` objects, one for each cell on the 3 by 3 grid and an extra
empty cell. The cells are indexed 0, 1, 2, ..., 9. We first place cells 1 through 9 on
the puzzle grid starting from the upper-left corner, then we place cell 0 in the middle
of the fourth row (the program's layout actually uses a 4 by 3 grid).

Each `PuzzleCell` object holds a number representing the piece of the picture it
currently displays. When a cell is created, the piece number is passed as a parameter
to its constructor. At the beginning, before the picture is scrambled, the piece
number is set to that cell's index. The code in `Puzzle`'s constructor creates the cells
and adds them to the program's content pane:

```
public Puzzle()
{
  ...

  Container c = getContentPane();
  c.setLayout(new GridLayout(4, 3, 1, 1));
                    // 4 by 3; horz gap 1, vert gap 1
  cells = new PuzzleCell[10];

  for (int i = 1; i <= 9; i++)
  {
    cells[i] = new PuzzleCell(i);
    c.add(cells[i]);
  }

  ...
}
```

After showing the original picture we need to scramble it. To do that, we initialize a temporary array with values 1 through 9 and shuffle it, then assign the shuffled numbers to cells 1 through 9:

```
// Scramble the puzzle by setting shuffled numbers 1 through 9
//   to the puzzle cells:
int[] numbers = {1, 2, 3, 4, 5, 6, 7, 8, 9};

shuffle(numbers);
for (int i = 1; i <= 9; i++)
{
  int k = numbers[i-1];
  cells[i].setPieceNumber(k);
}
```

Set up a project with the `Puzzle.java`, `PuzzleCell.java`, and `EasySound.java` files from J$_M$\Ch15\Puzzle.

As a warm-up exercise, write the code for the `Puzzle` class's `shuffle` method (see Question 12 in the exercises for Chapter 13). This method should rearrange the elements of a given array in random order. The algorithm is very similar to Selection Sort, only instead of choosing the largest among the first *n* elements, you choose an element randomly among the first *n* elements and swap it with the *n*-th element. This algorithm produces all possible arrangements with equal probabilities.

As another little exercise, write the `Puzzle` class's `allSet` method, which returns `true` if all pieces have been returned to their proper places and `false` otherwise. Call the `getPieceNumber` method for each of the cells and compare its returned value with the cell number.

And now to the serious business. Fill in the blanks in the `PuzzleCell` class's `paintComponent` method. First set the background color — white for a non-picked piece and yellow for a picked piece — and call `super.paintComponent`. Then shift the origin appropriately, based on the value of `PuzzleCell`'s `pieceNumber` field, which represents the number of the piece this panel (cell) is supposed to show. Recall that the panel's `getWidth` and `getHeight` methods return the dimensions of the panel. You need to adjust them slightly to compensate for the gaps between panels. Finally, call a method that paints your picture.

Copy the three audio clip `.wav` files from J$_M$\Ch15\Puzzle to the folder that will hold your compiled class files. Test your code first with the simple picture (a circle d cell numbers) provided. It will also help you test your `shuffle` method and your coordinate offsets. The purpose of the circle is to test how the pieces fit together — make sure your circle looks smooth. After you get it working, create a different picture of your choice for the puzzle. For instance, you can draw circles, polygons, or letters of different sizes and colors that intersect the grid. Make sure your picture is <u>fully scalable</u>, so that if the program's window shrinks or stretches, the picture shrinks or stretches with it. Find several five- to seven-year-olds and test your working puzzle on them.

15.8 Summary

Java provides a straightforward but limited class `Graphics` for drawing simple shapes and graphics text. The `Graphics2D` package is much more powerful but harder to use.

Since Java applets and applications are event-driven, all drawing must originate either in the `paint` method of the applet or application window or in the `paintComponent` method of one of the *Swing* components (usually an object of a class derived from `JComponent` or `JPanel`). `paint` and `paintComponent` take one parameter, `Graphics g`, which defines the graphics context for this component. If the application needs to repaint its component, it calls `repaint`, which takes no parameters. The repaint request is added to the events queue and eventually `paintComponent` is called.

The Java coordinate system has the origin in the upper-left corner of the window or panel, with the *y*-axis pointing down. The coordinates are integers, and their units are pixels. The `drawLine` method draws a line segment described by the coordinates of its beginning and end. A rectangle is described by the *x, y* coordinates of its upper-left corner, width, and height. An oval, a rounded rectangle, and even an arc is defined by the position of the bounding rectangle into which it is inscribed. Besides filled or hollow rectangles, rounded rectangles, ovals, and arcs, `Graphics` can draw polygons and polylines.

You can set the current drawing color by calling `g.setColor(...)`, which takes a `Color` object as its parameter. To set the background color, call the component's `setBackground` method.

You can display graphics text by calling the `drawString` method; to choose a desired font, call `setFont`.

Exercises

Sections 15.1-15.8

1.   The program below (JM\Ch15\Exercises\Drawings.java) displays a
      red rectangle in the middle of the content pane:

```java
import java.awt.Graphics;
import java.awt.Color;
import javax.swing.JFrame;
import javax.swing.JPanel;

public class Drawings extends JPanel
{
  public void paintComponent(Graphics g)
  {
    super.paintComponent(g);
    int w = getWidth();
    int h = getHeight();
    g.setColor(Color.RED);
    g.drawRect(w/4, h/4, w/2, h/2);
  }

  public static void main(String[] args)
  {
    JFrame window = new JFrame("Drawings");
    window.setBounds(100, 100, 300, 200);
    window.setDefaultCloseOperation(JFrame.EXIT_ON_CLOSE);
    JPanel canvas = new Drawings();
    canvas.setBackground(Color.WHITE);
    window.getContentPane().add(canvas);
    window.setVisible(true);
  }
}
```

Add code to display a message inside the red rectangle. ✓

2.   Modify the program in Question 1 to display the following designs:

      (a) ✓   (b)   (c)   (d)

Continued   ☞

(e)   (f)   (g) ✓   (h)

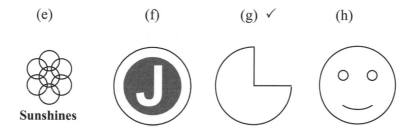

Sunshines

≋ Hint: (b) is a black rounded rectangle with four white circles; (c) is a polygon. ≋

Use any colors you want.

3. Define a class `Canvas` that extends `JPanel`. Make it show one of the designs from Question 2 (or your own design) by redefining its `paintComponent` method. Make your design centered approximately at the middle of the panel and make it scalable. Put the `main` method into a separate class.

4. (a) Adapt the program from Question 1 to show the logo of the American Association of Chomp Players:

(b)▪ Now take a different approach to showing the same logo. Create a class `LetterPanel` derived from `JPanel`. Supply a constructor that takes a letter and a background color as parameters and saves them. Make `LetterPanel`'s `paintComponent` method draw the letter on the specified background. Set the 2 by 2 grid layout for the program's content pane as follows:

```
Container c = getContentPane();
c.setLayout(new GridLayout(2, 2, 1, 1));
```

Add four `LetterPanel` objects to it, one for each letter in the logo.

5. ■   The program *Boxes* (`JM\Ch15\Exercises\Boxes.java`) can display
different types of boxes (rectangles) in different colors. The user chooses the
color of the box from a "combo box" that shows all 13 predefined colors
from the `Color` class. The user sets the box type by checking option boxes
for filled, rounded, and 3-D rectangles. The box type is represented as an
integer in which individual bits, when set to 1, indicate the attributes: bit 0
for filled, bit 1 for rounded, and bit 2 for 3-D. For example, the value 3
(binary 011) indicates a filled rounded box with no 3-D effect.

The *Boxes* program relies on a `BoxDrawer` class derived from `JPanel`. It
has the additional methods `setBoxType(int boxType)`,
`setBoxColor(Color color)`, and `drawBox(Graphics g)`.
`BoxDrawer` also redefines the `paintComponent` method to repaint the
background and call `drawBox`. Write the `BoxDrawer` class. Set the
background to gray or black in `paintComponent` if the white color is
chosen. Display an error message instead of a box if both rounded and 3-D
attributes are selected. ⧼ Hint: Use a `switch` on the box type in `drawBox`.
⧽

6.   (a)   Change the program from Question 4-b to display a checkerboard
pattern with 8 rows and 8 columns. Using an 8 by 8 grid layout, add
panels with alternating colors. ⧼ Hint: see Question 26 in exercises for
Chapter 12. ⧽

(b)   Create a class `ChessSquarePanel` derived from `JPanel`. Supply a
constructor that takes as parameters a background color and a
`boolean` flag indicating whether the square is empty or holds a picture
of a chess queen figure.

(c) ■   Find on the web a description and a solution to the "Eight Queens"
problem. Change the program to show the solution. ⧼ Hint: create an
8 by 8 array of appropriately colored `ChessSquarePanels` and set
the `hasQueen` flags appropriately in eight of them to show the queens;
set the content pane's layout to an 8 by 8 grid and add the panels to the
grid. ⧽

(d) ◆   Provide a method to find your own solution to the "Eight Queens"
problem. ⧼ Hint: make it a recursive method `addQueens` with one
parameter: a list of queens already placed. Start with an empty list. If
the list has eight queens, return `true` (the problem is solved). If not,
try to add one more queen to the list. If all such attempts fail, return
`false`. ⧽

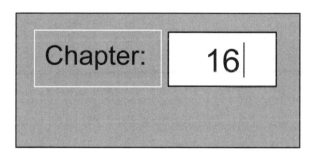

GUI Components and Events

16.1 Prologue

In this chapter we discuss the basics of *graphical user interfaces* and *event-driven programming* in Java. Event-driven GUI is what made the OOP concept popular, and it remains the area where it's most relevant. While you can write console applications in Java, such programs won't take full advantage of Java or OOP; in most cases such programs could just as well be written in C or Pascal. The style of modern user interfaces — with many different types of control components such as menus, buttons, pull-down lists, checkboxes, radio buttons, and text edit fields — provides an arena where OOP and event-driven programming naturally excel.

Our task in this chapter and the following one is to organize more formally the bits and pieces of the *Swing* package and multimedia that you have managed to grasp from our examples so far. Overall, the Java API lists hundreds of classes and interfaces, with thousands of constructors and methods. A sizable portion of the API — more than 100 classes — deals with *Swing* GUI components, events handlers, and multimedia. The online documentation in HTML format gives you convenient access to these detailed specifications. Still, it is not very easy to find what you need unless you know exactly what to look for. In many cases it may be easier to look up an example of how a particular type of object is used than to read about it in the API spec file. In most cases you need only the most standard uses of classes and their methods, and there are thousands of examples of these in JDK demos, books, online tutorials, and other sources.

This is the approach our book has taken, too. While introducing Java's fundamental concepts and basic syntax and control structures, we have sneaked in a variety of commonly used GUI methods and "widgets." We have added some bells and whistles here and there, just so you could see, if you cared to, how such things might be done. This chapter summarizes what you have already seen and fills in some gaps. Appendix D presents a synopsis and an index of the more commonly used GUI components that appear in the code examples in this book.

Knowing all the details of the latest GUI package still does not guarantee that the GUI in your application will "work." In addition to working the way you, the programmer, intend, it must also be intuitive and convenient for the user. Designing a good user interface is a matter of experience, good sense, trial and error, paying attention to the software users, developing prototypes, and in some cases, relying on more formal "human factors" research. To become a good user interface designer, one should gain experience with a wide range of applications, observe what works and what doesn't, and absorb the latest styles from cyberspace. Note that, strictly speaking, this skill may not be directly related to programming skills.

In this chapter we will discuss the "pluggable look and feel" and a few basic *Swing* components:

- `JLabel` — displays an icon or a line of text

- `JButton` — triggers an "action event" when pressed

- `JToggleButton` and `JCheckBox` — toggle an option

- `JComboBox` and `JRadioButton` — choose an option out of several possibilities

- `JSlider` — adjusts a setting

- `JTextField`, `JPasswordField`, and `JTextArea` — allow the user to enter and display or edit a line of text, a password, or a multi-line fragment of text, respectively

- `JMenuBar`, `JMenu`, `JMenuItem` — support pull-down menus.

We will discuss some of the methods of these GUI objects and the events they generate. We will also get familiar with four layout managers that help to arrange GUI components on the application's window.

 **16.2 - 16.7**

These sections are online at `http://www.skylit.com/javamethods`.

Exercises

Sections 16.1-16.7

1. For each the following Swing GUI components in Column One, mark the listeners from Column Two and the "status accessors" from Column Three that are commonly used with them. ✓

    (a) `JPanel`   *< none >*   *< none >*
    (b) `JLabel`   `ActionListener`   `isSelected`
    (c) `JButton`   `ItemListener`   `getSelectedIndex`
    (d) `JCheckBox`   `ChangeListener`   `getSelectedItem`
    (e) `JRadioButton`   `getText`
    (f) `JComboBox`   `getValue`
    (g) `JTextField`
    (h) `JSlider`
    (i) `JMenuItem`

2. Mark true or false and explain:

    (a) An object's `actionPerformed` method can be called directly in the program by other methods. _____ ✓

    (b) The same object can serve as an action listener for one component and an item listener for another component. _____ ✓

    (c) A button can have several different action listeners attached to it. _____ ✓

    (d) An object can serve as its own action listener. _____

3.▪ Write a program that serves as a GUI front end for the code you created for Question 11 in Chapter 6, the quadratic formula.

4.▪ Write a GUI application that adds several "large integers" as described in Chapter 12, Question 22.

5.   (a)   In the `Boxes` program (`JM\Ch15\Exercises\Boxes.java`) from
                   Question 5 in Chapter 15, add a menu bar with only one menu of two
                   items: "Increase size" and "Decrease size." When clicked, these items
                   should increase or decrease the current size of the box by 10%.
                   Modify the `BoxDrawer` class to support this functionality.

         (b)   Unite the `rounded` and `3-D` checkboxes in one group (a
                   `ButtonGroup` object), so that they cannot be both selected at the same
                   time. Usually such groups are used with radio buttons (see
                   Appendix D), but they can work for checkboxes as well.

6.▪   Create the following GUI layout:

‹ Hint: Put the two labels on a panel with a 2 by 1 grid layout. Use right-
justified labels `JLabel(<text>, null, JLabel.RIGHT)`. (Instead of
`null` you can put an icon showing the flag or an emblem of a country that
speaks the language.) Put input fields on another 2 by 1 panel. Put both
panels into a horizontal box with a strut between them; put this box and the
"Translate" button into a vertical box with struts around them. This is only
one way of doing it. ›

7.▪   (a)   Create the following GUI layout:

   ⸘ Hint: put all the radio buttons into a panel and all the checkboxes into another panel, each with a 3 by 1 grid layout. Add a border to each panel by calling its setBorder method. For example:

```
import javax.swing.border.*;
< ... other statements >
    CompoundBorder border = new CompoundBorder(
        new LineBorder(Color.BLACK, 1),
        new EmptyBorder(6, 6, 6, 6));
    // outside border: black, 1 pixel thick
    // inside border: empty, 6 pixels on
    //   top, left, bottom, right

    panel.setBorder(border);
```

Put both panels into a horizontal box with struts between them and on the left and right sides. Unite the radio buttons into a group (see Appendix D). ⸘ ✓

   (b)   Add a JToggleButton "To Go" on the right, initially set to "No." ✓

8.◆   Create a *Keypad* program. This program can serve as a basis for calculators of different models. First run a compiled version (JM\Ch16\Exercises\Keypad.jar). The program consists of two classes: Keypad and DigitalDisplay. Keypad is the main class. Its constructor creates an object display of the DigitalDisplay type. Write a class DigitalDisplay by extending JTextField. Make DigitalDisplay implement ActionListener and make display serve as an action listener for all the buttons. The "C" button clears the display; any other button appends the text from the button to the current display text. For example:

```
JButton b = (JButton)e.getSource();
String str = b.getText();
< ... etc. >
```

Let display's constructor configure the display: dark green background (for example, RGB 50, 200, 50), white or yellow foreground. Make it non-editable to prevent extraneous keyboard input. Set text alignment to the right:

```
setHorizontalAlignment(RIGHT);
```

Set the preferred size of the display in the program and add an empty border on the left and right to make it look better. For example:

```
import javax.swing.border.*;
< ... etc. >

    display.setPreferredSize(new Dimension(width, width/6));
    display.setBorder(new EmptyBorder(0, 10, 0, 10));
                            // top, left, bottom, right
```

Also set display's font to a fairly large fixed-pitch font (in proportion to width). Is it a good idea to set display's size, border, and font in DigitalDisplay's constructor? Explain.

In the Keypad class, place all the buttons on a 4 by 3 grid on a panel with some space between them. Add the display field above the buttons.
≶ Hint: place the display and the buttons panel into a vertical box. You can add the box directly to the content pane, or you can add it to a panel with a border, as we did. ≷

9.◆   Rewrite the *Madlibs* program described in Chapter 14 Question 10 as a GUI application. ⟨ Hint: use a `JTextArea` component to display the final text. ⟩

Chapter

Mouse, Keyboard, Sounds, and Images

17.1 Prologue

JVM (Java Virtual Machine) has a "virtual" mouse that rolls on an *x-y* plane and uses one button. Mouse coordinates are actually the graphics coordinates of the mouse cursor; they are in pixels, relative to the upper-left corner of the component that registers mouse events. Mouse events can be captured by any object designated as a `MouseListener` (that is, any object of a class that implements the `MouseListener` interface).

Keyboard events can be captured by any object designated as a `KeyListener`. Handling keyboard events in an object-oriented application is complicated by the fact that a computer has only one keyboard and different objects need to listen to it at different times. There is a fairly complicated system of passing the *focus* (the primary responsibility for processing keyboard events) from one component to another and of passing keyboard events from nested components up to their "parents." Handling mouse events is easier than handling keyboard events because the concept of "focus" does not apply.

In this chapter we will discuss the technical details of handling the mouse and the keyboard in a Java GUI application. We will also learn how to load and play audio clips and how to display images and icons.

✹ 17.2 - 17.7 ✹

These sections are online at `http://www.skylit.com/javamethods`.

Exercises

1. Write a *Four Seasons* program that changes the background color (from white to green to dark green to gold to white again, etc.) each time a mouse is clicked on it. ⸮ Hints: (1) Increment an index into an array of colors with wraparound. (2) Don't forget to repaint after each click. ⸮ ✓

2. Write a `DrawingPanel` class that extends `JPanel` and implements `MouseListener`. Redefine `paintComponent` to draw a filled circle or another shape. Make `mousePressed` change the shape's size or color when the mouse button is pressed anywhere on the panel and restore the shape when the button is released. Test your class with a simple program that creates one `DrawingPanel` object and makes it its own mouse listener. ✓

3. Adapt the `DrawingPanel` class from Question 2 to draw polygons. Each time the mouse is pressed, add the coordinates to a list of points. ⸮ Hints. (1) Use `mousePressed`, not `mouseClicked`, because a mouse "click" (in the Java definition) requires that pressed and released locations be the same, so "clicks" do not always register. (2) It is easier to hold the *x*- and *y*-coordinates in separate arrays for the sake of the `drawPolyline` method. (3) Don't forget to repaint after adding a point. ⸮

    Consider a polygon finished when the number of points reaches some maximum number (for example, 10) or when it has three or more points and the last one is close to (for example, is within 10 pixels of) the first one. ⸮ Hint: Java's `Point` class has a static method

    ```
    static double distance(int x1, int y1, int x2, int y2)
    ```

    that returns the distance between the points (x_1, y_1) and (x_2, y_2), and a method

    ```
    static double distanceSq(int x1, int y1, int x2, int y2)
    ```

    that returns the squared distance. The latter is more efficient because it does not need to calculate a square root. ⸮

    Draw an unfinished polygon as a polyline and a finished one as a filled polygon. Once a polygon is finished, mark that state and zero out the point count before starting a new polygon.

4.   Make the *Boxes* program from Question 5 in Chapter 16 respond to cursor keys: make the cursor keys move the box vertically or horizontally; make the cursor keys with the `Ctrl` key held down stretch or squeeze the box vertically or horizontally. Use `Boxes.java` from `JM\Ch15\Exercises` (or from your solution to Question 5 in Chapter 16) to test the updated `BoxDrawer` class. ⸶ Hints: make the `BoxDrawer` class implement `KeyListener`; make `canvas` its own key listener; request focus in the `BoxDrawer`'s `paintComponent` method. ⸜

5.   Write a program that displays the name of a key and its code in hex when that key is pressed. ⸶ Hint: the `KeyEvent` class has a static method `getKeyText(int keyCode)` that returns a string that describes the key. ⸜

6.   Write a class `ImagePanel`, derived from `JPanel`, that displays an image. Provide a constructor that takes the image file name as a parameter. Add `main` that prompts the user for an image file name (or takes it from the command-line argument), creates a window, adds an `ImagePanel` with the given image to the window's content pane, then opens the window on the screen. ✓

7.■   Create an applet that shows a series of images as a "slide show." Add a combo box for choosing an image. Also add "Forward" and "Back" buttons (with appropriate icons on them) for going to the next or previous slide. Find free left arrow and right arrow icons on the Internet. When the sequence reaches the end it should start over from the beginning. The same for the "Back" button: when the sequence reaches the beginning it should start over from the end. Place these controls on a control panel at the bottom and display the images on a separate panel located above the controls. Use the `TestSlides.html` file in `JM\Ch17\Exercises` and a few image files to test your applet.

⸶ Hint: the applet can retrieve image file names from a `param` tag. For example:

```
<param name="SLIDES" value="image1.gif image2.gif image3.gif">

    private String[] imageNames;
    ...
      imageNames = getParameter("SLIDES").split("\\s+");
        // extract tokens, separated by whitespace, from
        // the string in param.  "\\s+" is a regular expression
        // for "any number of whitespace characters."
⸜
```

Chapter 18

Big-O Analysis of Algorithms

18.1 Prologue

This chapter opens our discussion of a series of data structures that constitute a standard set of tools in software design and development. These include lists, stacks, queues, binary trees, priority queues, hash tables, and other structures.

> **A data structure combines data organization with methods of accessing and manipulating the data.**

For example, an array becomes a data structure for storing a list of values when we provide methods to insert, find, and remove a value. Similar functionality can be achieved with a *linked list* (we will explain linked lists in Chapter 20.) At a very abstract level, we can think of a general "list" data structure: a list contains a number of values arranged in sequence; we can add values to the list, find a target value in a list, and remove values from the list. Such a general abstract description of a structure for storing data and operations that can be performed on that data is called an *abstract data type* (ADT).

The data structures that we are going to study are not specific to Java — they can be implemented in any programming language. In Java, a data structure can be described as an interface and implemented as a class. There can be several implementations of the same abstract data type. `java.util.ArrayList` and `java.util.LinkedList`, for example, both implement the interface `java.util.List`.

Before we proceed with the data structures, though, we need to acquire some background knowledge of how to evaluate and compare the efficiency of different algorithms that work with these structures. Algorithms and data structures are often analyzed in terms of their time efficiency and space requirements. These are the concerns of a branch of computer science called *computational complexity* or *operations research*. In this book we concentrate on <u>time efficiency</u>.

As we saw in the *Benchmarks* program in Chapter 13, one obvious way to measure the time efficiency of an algorithm is to implement it in a computer program, run that program on various sets of input data, and measure the running time. It may seem that benchmarks leave little room for theory, but this first impression is incorrect. While benchmarks depend on the details of implementation (such as the actual code, the programming language, the optimizing capabilities of the compiler, and so on), as well as on the CPU speed and other hardware characteristics, it turns out it is possible to study the efficiency of algorithms excluding all these practical matters. The *big-O* concept serves this purpose. We already used it informally when we compared various searching and sorting algorithms. In this chapter we will discuss big-O in a more mathematically rigorous way.

The theoretical study of algorithms relies on an abstract model of a computer as a device with some defined capabilities, such as the capability to perform arithmetic operations and to store and retrieve data values in memory. The abstract model disregards all specific features of a particular computer system, such as the CPU speed and RAM size. The theoretical approach requires two simplifications. First, we have to stop measuring performance in real time (which depends on CPU speed, etc.). Nor do we measure it in terms of the number of required program instructions or statements (which depends on the language, compiler, implementation, etc.). Instead, we discuss performance in terms of some abstract "steps" that are necessary to complete the task.

What constitutes a "step" depends on the nature of the task. In a searching task, for example, we may define one step as one comparison between the target value and a data value in the list. In calculating a Fibonacci number iteratively, one step may be defined as one addition. The total number of required steps may depend on the size of the task, but it is assumed that each step takes the same amount of time. With this approach we cannot say how long a particular implementation of an algorithm might run on a particular computer system, but we can <u>compare</u> different algorithms that accomplish the same task.

The second simplification is that our theoretical analysis applies only when the task size is a large number. Let us denote the total number of steps that an algorithm requires to complete the task as $T(n)$. $T(n)$ is some function of the task size n. The theoretical approach focuses on the behavior of $T(n)$ for large n, which is called *asymptotic behavior*. In the following section we will see why knowing the asymptotic behavior of an algorithm is important and how it can be expressed in formal mathematical terms.

In the remainder of this chapter we will discuss a more formal definition of "big-O," consider some examples, and review the big-O performance of several sorting algorithms.

18.2 The Big-O Concept

As a starting point for our discussion, let us compare two familiar searching algorithms in an array, Sequential Search and Binary Search. We will assume that the elements in the array are arranged in ascending order.

Recall that in the Sequential Search algorithm we simply try to match the target value against each array value in turn until we find a match or finish scanning the whole array. Suppose this algorithm is implemented as follows:

```
for (int i = 0; i < n; i++)
{
  if (a[i] == target)
    return i;
}
```

The total running time includes the time it takes for the initialization and for the iterations through the loop. (In this example, the initialization is simply setting i equal to 0.) Assuming that the average number of iterations is $n/2$, the average time may be expressed as:

$$t(n) = t_{\text{init}} + t_{\text{iter}} \cdot \frac{n}{2}$$

where t_{init} is the initialization time and t_{iter} is the time required for each iteration. In other words, the average time is a linear function of n:

$$t(n) = An + B$$

As n increases, An also increases, and the relative contribution of the constant term B eventually becomes negligible as compared to the linear term An, even if A is small and B is large. Mathematically, this means that the ratio

$$\frac{t(n)}{An} = \frac{An + B}{An} = 1 + \frac{B}{An}$$

becomes very close to 1 as n increases without bound.

Therefore, <u>for a large n</u> we can drop the constant term B and say that the average time $t(n)$ is approximately equal to An. That means that the average time for the Sequential Search algorithm *grows linearly* with n (Figure 18-1-a).

Now let us consider the Binary Search algorithm applied to the same task. As we know from Chapter 13, the number of comparisons is approximately $\log_2 n$. Again, the total average time consists of the initialization time and the time for average number of iterations through the loop:

$$t(n) = t_{\text{init}} + t_{\text{iter}} \cdot \log_2 n$$

Following the same reasoning as for the sequential search, we conclude that the execution time of the binary search is, for large n, approximately proportional to the logarithm of n:

$$t(n) = C \log_2 n$$

The coefficient C is determined by the time spent in one iteration through the loop. Figure 18-1-b shows the general shape of this curve. $\log_2 n$ approaches infinity as n increases, but it does so <u>more slowly</u> than the linear growth of a straight line.

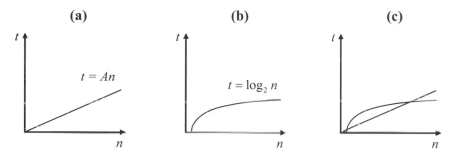

**Figure 18-1. (a) Linear growth   (b) Logarithmic growth
(c) Logarithmic growth is slower than linear**

Note that "one step" in the sequential search is not exactly the same as "one step" in the binary search, because besides comparing the values, we also need to modify some variables and control the iterations. Thus, the coefficients A and C may be different; for example, C may be larger than A. For some small n, a sequential search could potentially run faster than a binary search. But, no matter what the ratio of A to C, the linear curve eventually overtakes the logarithmic curve for large enough n (Figure 18-1-c).

In other words, <u>asymptotically</u>, binary search is faster than sequential search. Moreover, it is not just 5 times faster or 100 times faster. It is faster <u>in principle</u>: you can run sequential search on the fastest computer and binary search for the same task on the slowest computer, and still, <u>if n is large enough</u>, binary search will finish first.

This is an important theoretical result. The difference in the asymptotic behavior of these two searching algorithms provides an important new way of looking at their performance. Binary search time grows logarithmically and sequential search time linearly, so no matter what specific coefficients of the growth functions we use, linear time eventually surpasses logarithmic time.

In this context it makes sense to talk about the <u>order of growth</u> that characterizes the asymptotic behavior of a function, ignoring the particular constant coefficients. For example, $f(n) = n$ has a higher order of growth than $g(n) = \log_2 n$, which means that for any positive constant k, no matter how small,

$$k \cdot n > \log_2 n$$

when n is large enough. Two functions that differ only by a constant factor have the same order of growth.

The following definition of *big-O* (order of growth) helps us formalize this concept and refine our ideas about the order of growth. "Big-O" is defined as follows:

> **Given two positive functions $t(n)$ and $g(n)$, we say that**
>
> $$t(n) = O\big(g(n)\big)$$
>
> **if there exist a positive constant A and some number N such that**
>
> $$t(n) \le Ag(n)$$
>
> **for all $n > N$.**

The big-O definition basically means that $t(n)$ asymptotically (for large enough n) grows <u>not faster than</u> $g(n)$ (give or take a constant factor). In other words, the order of growth of $t(n)$ is not larger than $g(n)$.

Strictly speaking, $f = O(g)$ means "order of growth of f is less than or equal to g."

> **In practice, when the performance of algorithms is stated in terms of big-O, it usually refers to the lowest possible big-O bound. In this book, we have chosen to follow this widely accepted practice and use $f = O(g)$ to mean "order of growth of f is equal to g."**

For example, in our analysis of the two searching algorithms we can say that both the worst and average time is $O(n)$ for Sequential Search and $O(\log n)$ for Binary Search. We dropped 2 in the base of the logarithm because from the Change of Base Theorem, for any $b > 1$, $\log_b n = K \cdot \log n$, where $\log n$ is logarithm to the base 10, and $K = \dfrac{1}{\log b}$ is a positive constant. Since functions that differ only by a positive constant factor have the same order of growth, $O(\log_2 n)$ is the same as $O(\log n)$.

Therefore, when we talk about logarithmic growth, the base of the logarithm is not important, and we say simply $O(\log n)$.

One set of functions that are often used for describing the order of growth are, naturally, powers of n:

$$1, n, n^2, n^3, \ldots$$

The order of growth for n^k is higher than n^{k-1} .

If a function is a sum of several terms, its order of growth is determined by the fastest growing term. In particular, if we have a polynomial

$$p(n) = a_k n^k + a_{k-1} n^{k-1} + \ldots + a_0$$

its growth is of the order n^k :

$$p(n) = O(n^k)$$

Thus, any second-degree polynomial is $O(n^2)$. This is called *quadratic growth*.

> **No one uses such things as $O(3n)$ or $O(n^2 / 2)$ because they are the same as $O(n)$ or $O(n^2)$, respectively.**

Let us consider a common example of code that requires $O(n^2)$ operations. Suppose we have a nested loop:

```
// set up the outer loop
for (int i = 1;   i < n;   i++)
{
  // set up the inner loop
  for (int j = 0;   j < i;   j++)
  {
    ... // do something
  }
}
```

This kind of code may be used in a simple sorting method (Selection Sort), for finding duplicates in an array, or in some operations on matrices (such as transposing a matrix by flipping an n by n 2-D array symmetrically over its diagonal).

The outer loop runs for i from 1 to $n-1$, a total of $n-1$ times, and the inner loop runs for j from 0 to $i-1$, a total of i times. The code inside the inner loop will, therefore, execute a total of

$$1+2+...+(n-1)$$

times. Since 1, 2, 3, ... is an arithmetic sequence, its partial sum can be found by taking the number of terms and multiplying it by the average of the first and the last terms:

$$1+2+...+(n-1)=(n-1)\frac{1+(n-1)}{2}=\frac{(n-1)n}{2}$$

Even if we take into account the setup time for each loop, we still get a second-degree polynomial of n. Therefore, the above code runs in $O(n^2)$ time.

The time efficiency of almost all of the algorithms discussed in this book can be characterized by one of very few growth rate functions:

1. $O(1)$ — *constant time*. This means that the algorithm requires the same fixed number of steps regardless of the size of the task.

    Examples:
    (a) Finding a median value in a sorted array
    (b) Calculating $1+2+3+...+n$ using the formula for the sum of an arithmetic sequence
    (c) Push and pop operations in an efficiently implemented stack; add and remove operations in a queue (Chapter 21)
    (d) Finding a key in a lookup table or a sparsely populated hash table (Chapter 24)

2. $O(\log n)$ — *logarithmic time.*

    Examples:

    (a) Binary search in a sorted list of n elements
    (b) Finding a target value in a binary search tree with n nodes (Chapter 23)
    (c) *Add* and *remove* operations in a priority queue, implemented as a heap, with n nodes (Chapter 25)

3. $O(n)$ — *linear time.* This means that the algorithm requires a number of steps proportional to the size of the task.

    Examples:

    (a) Traversing a list of n elements (for example, finding max or min)
    (b) Calculating n-factorial or the n-th Fibonacci number iteratively
    (c) Traversing a binary tree with n nodes (Chapter 23)

4. $O(n \cdot \log n)$ — *"n log n" time.*

    Examples:

    (a) Mergesort and Quicksort of n elements
    (b) Heapsort (Chapter 25)

5. $O(n^2)$ — *quadratic time.* The number of operations is proportional to the size of the task squared.

    Examples:

    (a) More simplistic sorting algorithms, such as Selection Sort of n elements
    (b) Traversing an n by n 2-D array
    (c) Finding duplicates in an unsorted list of n elements (implemented with a nested loop)

6. $O(a^n)$ (with $a > 1$) — *exponential time.*

    Examples:

    (a) Recursive calculation of the n-th Fibonacci number ($a \geq 3/2$; see Chapter 22)
    (b) Solving the Tower of Hanoi puzzle ($a = 2$; see Section 22.5)
    (c) Generating all possible permutations of n symbols

The best time in the above list is obviously constant time, and the worst is exponential time, which overwhelms even the fastest computers even for relatively small *n*. *Polynomial* growth (linear, quadratic, cubic, etc.) is considered manageable as compared to exponential growth.

Figure 18-2 shows the asymptotic behavior of the functions from the above list.

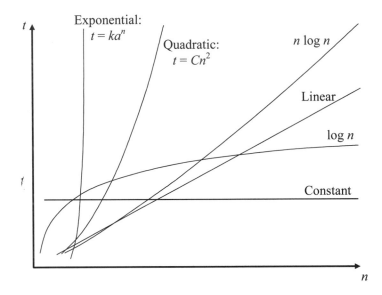

Figure 18-2. Rates of growth

Using the "<" sign informally, we can say that

$$O(1) < O(\log n) < O(n) < O(n \log n) < O\left(n^2\right) < O\left(n^3\right) < O\left(a^n\right)$$

The slow asymptotic growth of $\log_2 n$ (in comparison to linear growth) is especially dramatic: every thousand-fold increase in the size of a task results in only a fixed, fairly small increment in the required number of operations. Consider the following:

$$\log_2 1000 \approx 10; \ \log_2\left(10^6\right) \approx 20; \ \log_2\left(10^9\right) \approx 30; \ ...\text{etc.}$$

This property is used in many efficient "divide and conquer" algorithms such as Binary Search and is the basis for using binary search trees and heaps.

18.3 Big-O of Sorting Algorithms

In this section we quickly review the sorting algorithms we have studied and discuss their big-O properties more formally.

In general, the task of sorting is understood as rearranging the values of a list in ascending (or descending) order. The usual abstract formulation of this task assumes that we need to compare two values from the list to decide which one is smaller. What matters is the result of each comparison, not the values themselves. As we will see in Question 4 in Chapter 24, such methods as *Radix Sort* allow us to sort an array of values using some kind of lookup tables without any comparisons at all. These methods rely on information about the range and "composition" of values in the list. For example, if we know that the values in the list are in the range from 0 to 9, we can simply count the number of occurrences for each value and then recreate the list in order. The performance of such algorithms is $O(n)$. But here we deal with the algorithms that require actual comparisons.

Mathematically speaking, we assume that we have a list of objects, $X = \{x_0, ..., x_{n-1}\}$, and that an ordering relation $<$ is defined on X. This relation is called *total ordering* if for any two values a and b in X, exactly one of three possibilities is true: either $a < b$, or $b < a$, or $a = b$. An ordering relation must be *transitive*: if $a < b$ and $b < c$, then $a < c$. A sorting algorithm is a strategy for finding a permutation of the indices $p(0), p(1), ..., p(n-1)$ such that

$$x_{p(0)} \leq x_{p(1)} \leq ... \leq x_{p(n-1)}$$

(A permutation is a one-to-one mapping from the set of integers $\{0, 1, 2, ... n-1\}$ onto itself.)

The sorting strategy is based on pairwise comparisons of values. The decision as to which next pair of values to compare may be based on the results of all the previous comparisons. In these terms, how fast can we sort? Clearly if we compare each value with each other value, it will take n^2 comparisons. As we know, Mergesort and Quicksort can do the job in only $O(n \log n)$ comparisons. Can we do any better? The answer is no.

> **If you are limited to "honest" comparison sorting, any sorting algorithm in its worst case scenario takes at least $O(n \log n)$ steps.**

To prove this, envision our sorting algorithm as a decision tree: in each node we compare two values, then go left or right depending on the result (Figure 18-3). We will discuss tree structures and their properties in Chapter 23. Here we only need to know one simple fact: in a tree there is only one path from the root to any *leaf* (terminal node); if the length of the longest path from the root to a leaf is h, the total number of different paths does not exceed 2^h.

In our decision tree, the end of each path corresponds to a permutation of list values, and the number of comparisons in the worst case is the length of the longest path. For the algorithm to be complete, all possible permutations must be represented. Thus the number of all possible permutations, which is $n!$, should not exceed the number of leaves in the decision tree: $n! \le 2^h$, therefore $h \ge \log_2(n!)$.

For example, for $n = 4$, $n! = 24$, $\log_2 24 = 4.58...$ so the best algorithm needs 5 comparisons; for $n = 5$ it needs 7 comparisons. An algorithm with 7 comparisons for 5 values indeed does exist, but it is not at all obvious. Asymptotically, $\log_2(n!) = n \log n$,[*] so faster sorting is not possible.

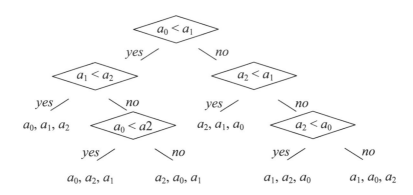

Figure 18-3. A sorting algorithm as a decision tree (for three values)

This is as far as we want to go with theory. Now let us review a few slower $O(n^2)$ algorithms and then a few more advanced $O(n \log n)$ algorithms.

---

[*] It is not hard to prove this fact using calculus. $\ln(n!) = \ln 1 + \ln 2 + ... + \ln n$, which can be viewed as a Riemann sum for $\int_1^n \ln x \, dx = (x \ln x - x)\big|_1^n = n \ln n - n + 1 = O(n \log n)$.

Sorting by Counting

In the most simplistic approach, we can compare each value in X to each other value. This means $n \cdot (n-1)$ or $O(n^2)$ comparisons. Indeed, for each x_i in X a computer program can simply count how many other values x_j do not exceed x_i. (If $x_j = x_i$ we only count it when $j < i$.) Then the position of x_i in the sorted list, $p(i)$, is set to the resulting count. This is called *sorting by counting*:

```
for (int i = 0; i < n; i++)
{
  int count = 0;
  for (int j = 0; j < n; j++)
  {
    if (a[j] < a[i] || (a[j] == a[i]  && j < i))
      count++;
  }
  b[count] = a[i];
}
```

This algorithm is inefficient because it makes a lot of redundant comparisons. If we have already compared x_i to x_j, there is no need to compare x_j to x_i.

Selection Sort

A slight improvement is achieved in Selection Sort. It cuts the number of comparisons in half, but the big-O for the Selection Sort algorithm is still $O(n^2)$.

The number of comparisons in Selection Sort does not depend on the initial arrangement of the values in the list. For example, if the list is already sorted, these algorithms still go through all the prescribed steps. There is no "best case" or "worst case" scenario: the number of comparisons is always the same: $\dfrac{n(n-1)}{2}$.

Insertion Sort

Slightly more sophisticated sorting algorithms may take advantage of a particular initial arrangement of values in the list to reduce the number of comparisons. For example, Insertion Sort keeps the beginning fragment of the list sorted and inserts each next element into it in order. On average, Insertion Sort takes half the number of comparisons of Selection Sort, but it is still an $O(n^2)$ algorithm. In the worst case, when the array is sorted in reverse order, the number of comparisons is the same as in Selection Sort, $n(n-1)/2$. But if the array is already sorted, the inner `for` loop performs only one comparison. If the array is nearly sorted, with only a couple of elements out of place, then Insertion Sort takes only $O(n)$ comparisons.

Mergesort

In Mergesort, we split the array into two equal (or almost equal) halves. We sort each half recursively, then merge the sorted halves into one sorted array. All the comparisons are actually performed at the merging stage — the sorting stage merely calls the method recursively for each half of the array (see Figure 13-7 on page 380).

This version of Mergesort predictably takes $O(n \log n)$ comparisons regardless of the initial configuration of the array. With a shortcut, discussed in Question 11 in the exercises to this chapter, it only takes n comparisons when the array is already sorted.

Quicksort

The idea of Quicksort is to choose one element, called the pivot, then partition the array in such a way that all the elements to the left of the pivot are smaller than or equal to it, and all the elements to the right of the pivot are greater than or equal to it. After partitioning, Quicksort is applied (recursively) to the left-of-pivot part and to the right-of-pivot part.

In general, you have to be careful with this type of recursion: you have to think not only about performance, but also about the required stack space. If everything goes smoothly, Quicksort partitions the array into approximately equal halves most of the time. Then the array length is divided roughly by two for each recursive call, recursion quickly converges to the base case, and the required stack space is only $O(\log n)$. But what happens if we always choose the first element of the array as the pivot and the array happens to be sorted? Then partitioning does not really work: one half is empty, while the other has all the elements except the pivot. In this case, the algorithm degenerates into a slow version of Selection Sort and takes $O(n^2)$ time.

What's worse, the depth of recursion becomes $O(n)$, and, for a large array, it may overflow the stack. (There is a version of Quicksort that overcomes the possible stack overflow problem by handling the shorter half of the array recursively and the longer half iteratively.)

Heapsort

We will consider this interesting algorithm in Chapter 25, after we learn about heaps.

18.4 Summary

The efficiency of algorithms is usually expressed in terms of asymptotic growth as the size of the task increases toward infinity. The size of a task is basically an intuitive notion: it reflects the number of elements involved or other similar parameters. The asymptotic growth may be expressed using big-O notation, which gives an upper bound for the order of growth. In practice, the big-O estimate is usually expressed in terms of the "tightest" possible upper bound.

The most common orders of growth (in increasing order) are

$O(1)$ — constant;

$O(\log n)$ — logarithmic;

$O(n)$ — linear;

$O(n \log n)$ — "n log n";

$O(n^2)$ — quadratic;

$O(a^n)$ — exponential.

Logarithmic growth is dramatically slower than linear growth. This explains the efficiency of "divide and conquer" algorithms, such as Binary Search, and of binary search trees and heaps (Chapters 23 and 25). Discovering an $O(\log n)$ algorithm instead of an $O(n)$ algorithm or an $O(n \log n)$ instead of an $O(n^2)$ algorithm for some task is justifiably viewed as a breakthrough in time efficiency. Exponential growth is unmanageable: it quickly puts the task out of reach of existing computers, even for tasks of rather small size.

Sorting algorithms provide a fertile field for formulating and studying general properties of algorithms and for comparing their efficiency. Simplistic sorting algorithms, such as Sorting by Counting, Selection Sort, and Insertion Sort, accomplish the task in $O(n^2)$ comparisons, although Insertion Sort may work much faster when applied to an array that is already sorted or almost sorted. More advanced algorithms, such as Mergesort, Quicksort, and Heapsort, accomplish the task in $O(n \log n)$ comparisons.

Sorting is a very well studied subject. There are hundreds of other algorithms and variations. There is no single "best" sorting algorithm. In the real world, the choice depends on specific properties of the target data and additional constraints and requirements.

Table 18-1 shows the average, best, and worst cases for the algorithms that we have discussed. The worst case, in general, assumes that the algorithm is running on the set of data that takes the longest time to process.

	Best case	**Average case**	**Worst case**
Sequential Search	$O(1)$ — found right away	$O(n)$ — found on average in the middle	$O(n)$
Binary Search	$O(1)$ — found right away	$O(\log n)$	$O(\log n)$
Selection Sort	$O(n^2)$	$O(n^2)$	$O(n^2)$
Insertion Sort	$O(n)$ — array already sorted	$O(n^2)$	$O(n^2)$
Mergesort	$O(n \log n)$, or $O(n)$ in a slightly modified version when the array is sorted	$O(n \log n)$	$O(n \log n)$
Quicksort	$O(n \log n)$	$O(n \log n)$	$O(n^2)$ — pivot is consistently chosen far from the median value, as when the array is already sorted and the first element is chosen as pivot
Heapsort	$O(n \log n)$	$O(n \log n)$	$O(n \log n)$

Table 18-1. Best, average, and worst case for sorting and searching

Exercises

1. Mark true or false and explain:

    (a) We often say $f = O(g)$ to indicate that the order of growth of f and g is the same. _____ ✓

    (b) $\log_2 n = O(\log_{10} n)$. _____ ✓

    (c) If $f(n) = 1 + 2 + \ldots + n$, then $f(n) = O(n^2)$. _____

2. What is the big-O of the number of operations required to perform the following tasks, assuming reasonably optimized implementations?

    (a) Transposing an n by n matrix (flipping an n by n 2-D array symmetrically over its diagonal) ✓

    (b) Reversing an array of n elements

    (c) Finding the number of pairs of consecutive double letters in a character string of length n ✓

3. What is the worst-case running time (big-O, in terms of n) of the following methods?

    (a)

```
public int maxCluster(double[] v, double d)
{
  int n = v.length, maxCount = 0;

  for (int i = 0; i < n; i++)
  {
    int count = 0;
    for (int j = 0; j < n; j++)
    {
      if (Math.abs(v[i] - v[j]) < d)
        count++;
    }
    if (count > maxCount)
      maxCount = count;
  }
  return maxCount;
}
```

Continued ➥

(b)

```
public boolean isPalindrome(String w)
{
  int n = w.length(), i = 0, j = n-1;
  while (i < j && w[i] == w[j])
  {
    i++;
    j--;
  }
  return i >= j;
}
```

(c) ✓

```
public double pow(double x, int n)
{
  double y = 1;

  if (n > 0)
  {
    y = pow(x, n/2);
    y *= y;
    if (n % 2 != 0)
      y *= x;
  }
  return y;
}
```

4. Indicate whether the specified task requires logarithmic (*L*), polynomial (*P*) or exponential (*E*) time (assuming an optimal implementation):

(a) Concatenating all the strings stored in a 2-D array —

```
private String[][] words = new String[n][n];
```

— assuming the length of the longest string does not exceed 10. ✓

(b) Finding the highest power of 2 that evenly divides a given positive integer *n*.

(c)◆◆ Finding among *n* people the largest group, such that any two people in that group know each other. ✓

5.▪   The code below calculates the sum of the elements in a 2-D array `matrix` that belong to a "cross" formed by an intersection of a given row and column:

```
int sum = 0;

for (int r = 0; r < matrix.length; r++)
{
  for (int c = 0; c < matrix[0].length; c++)
  {
    if (r == row || c == col)
      sum += matrix[r][c];
  }
}
```

Find the big-O for this code when `matrix` is an n by n array, and rewrite the code to improve its big-O.

6.◆   Suppose the array `s` contains a digitized seismogram recorded for 5 seconds during a remote earthquake. We want to find the time of the seismic wave's arrival. Suppose the seismogram is digitized at n samples per second and so the array contains $5n$ amplitudes of the signal. The code below averages the signal over one-second intervals and chooses the largest average to detect the arrival of the first wave:

```
// Find the sum starting at i = 0:
double sum = 0.0;
for (int i = 0; i < n; i++)
  sum += s[i];
double max = sum;
int kMax = 0;

for (int k = 1; k < 4*n; k++)
{
  // Find the sum starting at i = k:
  sum = 0.0;
  for (int i = k; i < k + n; i++)
    sum += s[i];

  if (sum > max)   // update max
  {
    max = sum;
    kMax = k;
  }
}
return kMax;
```

What is the big-O for this code in terms of n? Is there a way to improve it?

7.   Complete each sentence with the word *always*, *sometimes*, or *never*:

   (a)   Selection Sort in an array of *n* elements _____ works in $O(n^2)$ time. ✓

   (b)   Insertion Sort _____ works faster than Quicksort. ✓

   (c)   Quicksort is _____ slower than Mergesort.

8.   Suppose the Insertion Sort algorithm for sorting an array has been modified: instead of sequential search, binary search is used to find the position for inserting the next element into the already sorted initial segment of the list. What is the big-O for the average number of <u>comparisons</u> (in terms of the length of the array *n*)? What is the big-O for the best and worst cases?

9.   The Mergesort algorithm, as presented in Figure 13.7 on page 380, always takes $O(n \log n)$ comparisons. Add a shortcut —

```
if (...)
    return;
```

   — so that the algorithm works in $O(n)$ time when the array is already sorted.

10.   Mark true or false and explain:

   (a)   Quicksort is sensitive to data; the performance is $O(n \log n)$ only if most splits divide the array into two halves that are approximately equal in size. _____

   (b)   Quicksort requires a temporary array that is as large as the original array. _____ ✓

```
map.put(19,

       "Chapter");
```

The Java Collections Framework

19.1 Prologue

In software, a *framework* is a general system of components and architectural solutions that provides development tools to programmers for use with a relatively wide range of applications. A *collection* is... well, any collection of elements. The *Java collections framework* is a system of interfaces and classes in the `java.util` package that deal with different kinds of collections: lists, stacks, queues, priority queues, sets, and maps. Starting with Java 5.0, Java collections hold objects of a specified type. Java developers call them "*generic collections*" or "generics," because their code works for a collection with any specified type of elements. We would prefer to call them *type-specific collections*, because a collection holds elements of a specific type.

In this chapter we discuss the Java collections framework from the perspective of a user (that is, a software developer). We look at how each kind of collection can be used in a program, its efficiency in particular situations, and its API (Application Programming Interface), that is, its constructors and methods. We also show some coding examples. But we don't go into the implementation details of various kinds of collections. Data structures on which Java collections are based are discussed in the subsequent chapters.

The Java collections framework is vast. We will discuss only the more commonly used interfaces and classes, and only a subset of their constructors and methods. For further technical details, refer to the Java API.

Figure 19-1 shows what's in store. At the top of the collections framework lies the interface `Collection`. It defines a collection of elements in very abstract terms, with methods like `isEmpty`, `size`, `contains`, `add`, `remove`, and `iterator`. `Collection` has more specialized subinterfaces, `List` and `Set`. The `Map` interface defines maps. Strictly speaking, a map is not a collection but a *mapping* from one set of elements to another. For each interface `java.util` provides one or several classes that implement it. Different implementations are more suitable in different contexts. Some of the classes also refer to the `Iterator`, `Comparable`, and `Comparator` interfaces.

The `Stack` class seems to stand alone. In fact, we have deliberately omitted some of the connections in Figure 19-1 for reasons explained later in this chapter. `Stack` is a "legacy" class from the first release of Java. To be precise, `Stack` extends the class `Vector`, which is an ancient version of `ArrayList`, and `Stack` does implement `Collection`; also the `Queue` interface extends `Collection`.

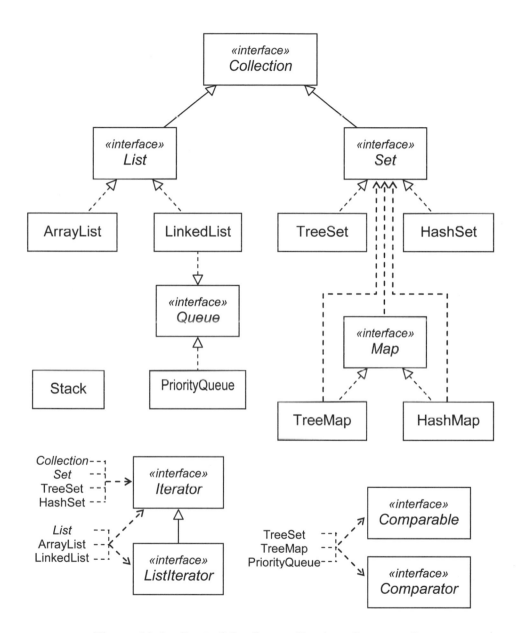

Figure 19-1. Part of the Java collections framework

> **If your class uses Java collections, add**
>
> `import java.util.*;`
>
> **at the top of the source file.**

19.2 Collection and Iterator

The `Collection<E>` interface represents any collection of elements of the type *E*. *E* is a type parameter — it can stand for any type of objects. Java API docs use the letter "E" for the name for this parameter, and so do we.

The commonly used `Collection<E>` methods are shown in Figure 19-2.

```
boolean isEmpty();              // Returns true if this collection is
                               //    empty; otherwise returns false.
int size();                     // Returns the number of elements in
                               //    this collection.
boolean contains(Object obj);
                               // Returns true if this collection contains
                               //    an element equal to obj; otherwise
                               //    returns false.
boolean add(E obj);             // Adds obj to this collection.  Returns
                               //    true if successful; otherwise
                               //    returns false.
boolean remove(E obj);          // Removes the first element that is
                               //    equal to obj, if any.*  Returns
                               //    true if successful; otherwise
                               //    returns false.
Iterator<E> iterator();         // Returns an iterator for this collection.
```

Figure 19-2. Some of the methods of `java.util.Collection<E>` interface

> **The `contains` and `remove` methods rely on whatever `equals` method is defined for objects of the type *E*.**

It is a programmer's responsibility to override the `Object` class's `equals` method with a reasonable version of it for the particular type *E*.

---

* First in the sequence produced by an iterator for a particular collection.

The add method adds an object of the type *E* to the collection.

Java collections work only with objects — they do not support primitive data types. If you want a collection to hold values of a primitive data type, you need to create a collection of objects of the corresponding wrapper class and create a wrapper object for each value before you add it to the collection.

For example, if you want to hold doubles in an ArrayList, you need to create an ArrayList<Double>:

```
ArrayList<Double> list = new ArrayList<Double>();
list.add(new Double(5.1));
...
```

Actually, if you don't do the wrapping explicitly, the compiler will do it for you. You can write simply

```
list.add(5.1);
```

Starting with Java 5.0, a value of a primitive data type is converted into an object of the corresponding wrapper type automatically, when appropriate. This feature is called *autoboxing* (or *autowrapping*).

The compiler does the reverse for you, too. For example, you can write

```
double x = list.get(i);
```

instead of

```
double x = list.get(i).doubleValue();
```

This is called *autounboxing*.

Autoboxing and autounboxing save a few keystrokes and make it easier to store numbers in collections, but converting a lot of numbers into objects will make your code less efficient.

An *iterator* is an object that helps to traverse a particular collection. Iterator<E> is an interface, because different collections implement different iterators with different rules, and the order of traversal can vary. Classes that implement the

`Iterator` interface are implemented as *private inner classes* in various collection classes. We give an example of this later, in Section 20.3. The programmer obtains an iterator from a particular collection by calling that collection's `iterator` method. You need to get a new iterator for every traversal.

At this point, all of this appears to be rather abstract, and in fact it is designed to be so. When we get to specific types of collections, we will see how their iterators work. In an `ArrayList`, for example, an iterator traverses the elements in order of their indices.

The `Iterator<E>` interface specifies three methods shown in Figure 19-3.

```
boolean hasNext();          // Returns true if there are more
                            //   elements to visit in this traversal;
                            //   otherwise returns false.
E next();                   // Returns the next element in
                            //   this traversal.
void remove();              // Removes the last visited element.
```

Figure 19-3. The methods of `java.util.Iterator<E>` interface

Traversal of an `ArrayList<String>`, for example, can be coded as follows:

```
ArrayList<String> words = new ArrayList<String>();
...
Iterator<String> iter = words.iterator();
while (iter.hasNext())
{
  String word = iter.next();
  < ... process word >
}
```

Since Java 5.0, iterators are used less frequently because a "for each" loop can replace an iterator (as long as the iterator's `remove` method is not needed). The above example can be rewritten more concisely with a "for each" loop:

```
ArrayList<String> words = new ArrayList<String>();
...
for (String word : words)
{
  < ... process word >
}
```

The compiler simply converts a "for each" loop into iterator calls. (That's why compiler error messages associated with "for each" loops sometimes mention iterators.)

Why do we need iterators? Why, for example, couldn't a Collection-type class itself have provided something like startIterations, next, and hasNext methods? The answer is, it could, as long as you used simple iterations. But when you tried <u>nested</u> loops, this approach would fall apart. Suppose, for example, you need to find duplicate titles in an ArrayList<String> movies. To do this you have to run nested loops on the same list, comparing every pair. The idea of a list serving as its own iterator would lead to an error, something like this:

```
movies.startIterations();
while (movies.hasNext())
{
  String movie1 = movies.next();
  movies.startIterations();  // Oops, a bug -- the outer loop's
                             //    position is lost
  while (movies.hasNext())
  {
    String movie2 = movies.next();
    if (movie2 != movie1 && movie2.equals(movie1))
      System.out.println("Duplicate name: " + movie2);
  }
}
```

What you need are <u>two separate iterators</u>, one for the outer loop and one for the inner loop:

```
Iterator<String> iter1 = movies.iterator();
while (iter1.hasNext())
{
  String movie1 = iter1.next();
  Iterator<String> iter2 = movies.iterator();

  while (iter2.hasNext())
  {
    String movie2 = iter2.next();
    if (movie2 != movie1 && movie2.equals(movie1))
      System.out.println("Duplicate name: " + movie2);
  }
}
```

This is similar to using nested "for each" loops:

```
for (String movie1 : movies)
{
  for (String movie2 : movies)
  {
    if (movie2 != movie1 && movie2.equals(movie1))
      System.out.println("Duplicate name: " + movie2);
  }
}
```

19.3 Lists and `ListIterator`

A list is a collection in which the elements are arranged in a sequence and numbered (indexed). The indices start from 0.

The `List<E>` interface extends the `Collection<E>` interface, adding methods that take advantage of indices; Figure 19-4 shows some of them.

```
boolean isEmpty();
int size();
boolean contains(Object obj);        ──────  Methods inherited from
boolean add(E obj);                          Collection<E>
boolean remove(E obj);
Iterator<E> iterator();

E get(int i);                 // Returns the i-th element.
E set(int i, E obj);          // Replaces the i-th element with obj and
                              //    returns the old value.
void add(int i, E obj);       // Inserts obj to become the i-th element.
                              //    Increments the size of the list by one.
E remove(int i);              // Removes the i-th element and returns its
                              //    value.  Decrements the size of the list
                              //    by one.
int indexOf(Object obj);      // Returns the index of the first element
                              //    equal to obj; if not found, returns -1.
ListIterator<E> listIterator();
                              // Returns a ListIterator for this list.

ListIterator<E> listIterator(int i);
                              // Returns a ListIterator, which starts
                              //    iterations at the i-th element.
```

Figure 19-4. Some of the methods of the `java.util.List<E>` interface

These methods should look very familiar. We already discussed them when we introduced the ArrayList class in Chapter 12. The only new methods are two overloaded versions of listIterator. These methods return a ListIterator<*E*> object, which is an enhanced iterator, specific to Lists (ListIterator<*E*> is a subinterface of Iterator<*E*>). ListIterator<*E*> methods are shown in Figure 19-5.

```
boolean hasNext();
E next();                                    Methods inherited from
void remove();                                  Iterator<E>

int nextIndex();               // Returns the index of the element
                               //    that would be returned by a
                               //    subsequent call to next().
boolean hasPrevious();         // Returns true if there are more
                               //    elements  to visit in reverse
                               //    direction; otherwise returns false.
E previous();                  // Returns the previous element in
                               //    the list.
int previousIndex();           // Returns the index of the element
                               //    that would be returned by a
                               //    subsequent call to previous().
void add(E obj);               // Inserts obj at the current position
                               //    of this iterator.
void set(E obj);               // Sets the element last returned
                               //    by next() or previous() to obj.
```

Figure 19-5. Methods of the `java.util.ListIterator<E>` interface

It may be useful to envision a list iterator as a logical "cursor" positioned before the list, after the list, or between two consecutive elements of the list (Figure 19-6). list.listIterator(0) positions the cursor before the first element of the list (the element with the index 0). list.listIterator(list.size()) positions the cursor after the end of the list. list.listIterator(i) positions the cursor between the elements with indices i-1 and i. The next method returns the element immediately after the cursor position, and the previous method returns the element immediately before the cursor position.

As you can see, ListIterator<*E*> can traverse the list either forward or backward. To traverse the list from the end backward, all you have to do is obtain a ListIterator that starts past the end of your list, then call previous. For example:

```
List<String> movies = new LinkedList<String>();
...
ListIterator<String> iter = movies.listIterator(movies.size());
while (iter.hasPrevious())
{
  String str = iter.previous();
  ...
}
```

The `ListIterator` interface also provides the `add` method, which inserts an element into the list at the current cursor position; and the `set` method, which sets the value of the element last returned by `next` or `previous`.

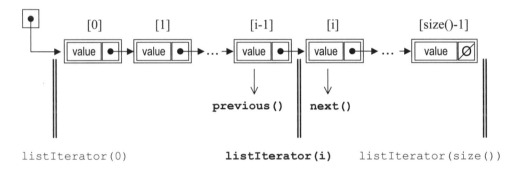

Figure 19-6. Logical "cursor" positioning for a `ListIterator`

The following example shows how the "remove duplicates" code from the earlier example can be rewritten more efficiently with `ListIterator`s:

```
ListIterator<String> iter1 = movies.listIterator();
while (iter1.hasNext())
{
  String movie1 = iter1.next();

  ListIterator<String> iter2 = movies.listIterator(iter1.nextIndex());
      // Start the inner loop at the current position
      //    of iter1

  while (iter2.hasNext())
  {
    String movie2 = iter2.next();
    if (movie1.equals(movie2))
      System.out.println("Duplicate name: " + movie1);
  }
}
```

As we know, a list can be implemented as an array — that's what the Java library class ArrayList does. In an ArrayList, the list elements are stored in consecutive memory locations. This provides direct access to the *i*-th element of the array. This property, called *random access*, is important in many algorithms. For example, the Binary Search algorithm requires direct access to the element precisely in the middle between two given elements.

ArrayList has two drawbacks, however. First, inserting or removing an element at the beginning or somewhere in the middle of an array is inefficient — a lot of bytes may need to be moved if the array is large. Second, if the list outgrows the allocated space, it has to allocate a bigger array and copy all the values into it, which takes time.

java.util offers another implementation of the List<*E*> interface: the LinkedList<*E*> class.

> **The LinkedList<*E*> class implements a list as a *doubly-linked* list.**

In a doubly-linked list, each element is held within a larger structure, called a *node*. In addition to holding a reference to the element, each node holds references ("links") to the previous node and the next node. Nodes can be scattered anywhere in memory, but each node "knows" where to find the next one and the previous one. A LinkedList keeps references to the first node (*head*) and the last node (*tail*) of the list (Figure 19-7). We will discuss the implementation of linked lists in detail in Chapter 20.

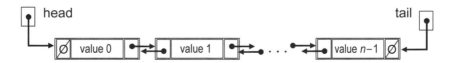

Figure 19-7. A doubly-linked list

A doubly-linked list makes it easy to insert or remove a node simply by rearranging a few links. This is a crucial property if we have a frequently updated list. Also, nodes of a linked list are allocated only when new values are added, so no memory is wasted for vacant nodes, and a list can grow as large as the total memory permits, without recopying. A drawback of a linked list, however, is that it is not a random-access collection: we have to traverse the list from the beginning or from the end to get to a particular element.

Table 19-1 compares the big-O running times for different methods in an `ArrayList` and a `LinkedList`. In an `ArrayList`, the `get(i)` and `set(i, obj)` methods work fast, $O(1)$, and they become the primary tools for handling the list. In a `LinkedList`, however, to get to the *i*-th element we have to start from the head or tail (whichever is closer to the *i*-th node) and traverse the nodes until we get to the *i*-th node. Thus, in a `LinkedList`, the `get` and `set` methods, take $O(n)$ time on average, where *n* is the size of the list. On the other hand, the `add(0, obj)` method takes $O(n)$ time in an `ArrayList`, because all the elements must shift to make room for the added first element. In a `LinkedList`, this method just rearranges a couple of links, so it takes constant time, $O(1)$. Appending an element at the end in both `ArrayList` and `LinkedList` takes $O(1)$ time (assuming the `ArrayList` has sufficient capacity and does not need to be reallocated).

	ArrayList	LinkedList
get(i) and set(i, obj)	$O(1)$	$O(n)$
add(i, obj) and remove(i)	$O(n)$	$O(n)$
add(0, obj)	$O(n)$	$O(1)$
add(obj)	$O(1)$	$O(1)$
contains(obj)	$O(n)$	$O(n)$

**Table 19-1. Average time big-O for some methods of
ArrayList and LinkedList**

One must be especially careful with `LinkedList` traversals: since `get(i)` takes $O(n)$ time, a simple traversal loop using indices —

```
List<E> list = new LinkedList<E>();
...
for (int i = 0; i < list.size(); i++)
{
  E obj = list.get(i);
  ...
}
```

— takes $O(n^2)$ time. (It starts over from the beginning or the end of the list on each pass through the loop.) But a traversal with an iterator or a "for each" loop —

```
for (E obj : list)
{
    ...
}
```

— runs in $O(n)$ time, because on each iteration the iterator simply proceeds from one node to the next.

For convenience, the `LinkedList` class provides six methods that are efficient for linked lists: `addFirst`, `addLast` (the same as `add(obj)`), `getFirst`, `getLast`, `removeFirst`, and `removeLast` (Figure 19-8). All of them take constant time, $O(1)$. `ArrayList` does not have these six methods.

```
void addFirst(E obj);       // The same as add(0, obj)
void addLast(E obj);        // The same as add(obj)
E getFirst();               // The same as get(0)
E getLast();                // The same as get(list.size() - 1)
E removeFirst();            // The same as remove(0)
E removeLast();             // The same as remove(list.size() - 1)
```

Figure 19-8. Additional methods in `java.util.LinkedList<E>`

In Chapter 12, we saw many examples of how `ArrayList`s are used. Each of these examples can be rewritten for a `LinkedList` by simply substituting "LinkedList" for "ArrayList" throughout. But in many cases the code will become much less efficient. As we said, a simple traversal loop

```
for (int i = 0; i < list.size(); i++)
    System.out.println(list.get(i));
```

runs in $O(n)$ time for an `ArrayList` and in $O(n^2)$ time for a `LinkedList`. You need to use a "for each" loop or an iterator for `LinkedList`s. To make your code more general, it is better to always use a "for each" loop or an iterator when traversing lists.

Figure 19-9 shows how `LinkedList`'s specific methods are used for merging two sorted `LinkedList`s into one.

```
// Merges two alphabetically sorted linked lists into one sorted list.
// Precondition: list1 and list2 are sorted alphabetically.
public static LinkedList<String> merge(
        LinkedList<String> list1, LinkedList<String> list2)
{
  LinkedList<String> result = new LinkedList<String>();

  while (!list1.isEmpty() && !list2.isEmpty())
  {
    if (list1.getFirst().compareTo(list2.getFirst()) < 0)
      result.addLast(list1.removeFirst());
    else
      result.addLast(list2.removeFirst());
  }

  // Copy the remaining elements of list1 or list2, if any
  while (!list1.isEmpty())
    result.addLast(list1.removeFirst());

  while (!list2.isEmpty())
    result.addLast(list2.removeFirst());

  return result;
}
```

Figure 19-9. Merging two sorted `LinkedLists`

19.4 The `Stack` Class

A *stack* stores data elements in such a way that the value stored last will be retrieved first. This method is sometimes called LIFO — Last-In-First-Out. A stack is controlled by two operations referred to as *push* and *pop*. Push adds an element to the top of the stack and pop removes the top element from the stack. Elements are said to be "on" the stack. You can only access the element on top of the stack.

The stack mechanism is useful for temporary storage, especially for dealing with nested structures and branching processes: expressions within expressions, methods calling other methods, pictures within pictures, GUI components within GUI components, and so on. The stack mechanism helps your program untangle the nested structure and trace all of its substructures in the correct order.

A stack can be easily implemented as an `ArrayList`: push adds an element at the end of the list, and pop removes the last element. These operations take constant time, $O(1)$, because no shifting of elements is necessary. A stack can be also implemented using a LinkedList: push would call addLast, and pop would call removeLast (or addFirst for push and removeFirst for pop).

> **In an efficiently implemented stack, both push and pop operations take constant time, $O(1)$.**

In the Java collections framework, a stack is implemented by the class Stack. Figure 19-10 shows some of its methods. Actually, as we noted in the prologue, Stack extends Vector, which is an older implementation of a dynamic array (a predecessor of ArrayList). Therefore, Stack inherits all of the Vector's methods. Stack also implements the Collection interface. So, in addition to the four stack-specific methods listed in Figure 19-10, the Stack class has many other methods. When you work with a stack, though, it is inappropriate to use iterators or methods outside of the four stack methods. If you feel you need other methods, don't call it a stack: use an ArrayList.

```
boolean isEmpty();          // Returns true if this stack is
                            //   empty; otherwise returns false.
E push (E obj)              // Pushes obj onto the stack.
                            //   (Returns obj.)
E pop()                     // Pops the top element from the stack
                            //   and returns it.
E peek();                   // Returns the top element on the stack
                            //   without removing it from the stack.
```

Figure 19-10. Methods of `java.util.Stack<E>` class

The stack methods themselves are straightforward, but algorithms that involve stacks may be harder to grasp. An example in Figure 19-11 is a simple kind: it shows how a stack is used to verify that parentheses and square brackets match in a given expression, represented as a string. It is not sufficient to count the opening and closing parentheses and brackets — they must come in the right order.

```
// Returns true if parentheses and square brackets
// match in expr; otherwise returns false
public static boolean matchParens(String expr)
{
  Stack<Character> stk = new Stack<Character>();

  for (int i = 0; i < expr.length(); i++)
  {
    char c = expr.charAt(i);

    if (c == '(' || c == '[')
    {
      stk.push(new Character(c));  // or simply stk.push(c);
    }                              //    due to autoboxing
    else if (c == ')' || c == ']')
    {
      char c0 = stk.pop().charValue(); // or simply char c0 = stk.pop();
                                       //    due to autounboxing
      if (c0 == '(' && c != ')')
        return false;
      if (c0 == '[' && c != ']')
        return false;
    }
  }

  if (!stk.isEmpty())  // or simply:
    return false;      //
                       //      return stk.isEmpty();
  return true;         //
}
```

Figure 19-11.   An example of a method that uses a stack

19.5 The Queue Interface

In a *queue* collection, data elements are retrieved in the same order as they were stored. This access method is called FIFO — First-In-First-Out (as opposed to LIFO — Last-In-First-Out, the access method of a stack). The queue is controlled by two operations: *add* and *remove*. *add* inserts a value at the rear of the queue, and *remove* removes a value from the front of the queue.

The queue structure is often used for processing events that are to be processed in the order of their arrival but not necessarily right away. The events are buffered in a queue while they await processing. One example is events handling in a Java program. Events generated by different objects (GUI components, timers, repaint requests, etc.) all go into the events queue. When the program is done with the previous event, it retrieves the next one from the queue and sends it to the appropriate "listener" for processing.

Queues are widely used at the system level for buffering commands or data between processes or devices. A personal computer has a keyboard queue implemented as a ring buffer (discussed in Chapter 21). When a key is pressed, its code does not go directly to the active program but is placed in the keyboard buffer until the program requests it. Printer output is also buffered: the characters are held in the output buffer until the printer is ready to receive them. An operating system maintains a queue of print jobs waiting to be sent to a printer while other programs are running.

In the Java collections framework, a queue is described by the `Queue` interface. Figure 19-12 shows a subset of its methods.

```
boolean isEmpty();          // Returns true if this queue is
                            //   empty; otherwise returns false.
boolean add (E obj)         // adds obj to the queue. Returns true
                            //   if successful, false otherwise.
E remove()                  // Removes the first element from the
                            //   queue and returns it.
E peek();                   // Returns the first element in the queue
                            //   without removing it from the queue.
```

Figure 19-12. Methods of `java.util.Queue<E>` interface

The Java collections framework has no separate implementations for a regular queue, because the `LinkedList` class, with its efficient `addLast` and `removeFirst` methods, serves as a fine implementation of a queue. The two methods `remove()` (with no parameters) and `peek` have been added to the `LinkedList` class to satisfy the requirements of the `Queue` interface. `remove` is simply an alias for `removeFirst`, and `peek` is an alias for `getFirst`.

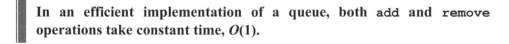 **In an efficient implementation of a queue, both `add` and `remove` operations take constant time, *O*(1).**

It is inappropriate to use any `LinkedList` methods outside the `Queue` subset or to use iterators when a `LinkedList` is used as a queue: when you work with a queue, you are supposed to only use the "pure" queue methods from Figure 19-12.

Figure 19-13 presents an example of code that involves queues.

```
// Uses Quicksort to sort the elements from q in ascending order;
// returns a new sorted queue
public static Queue<Integer> sort(Queue<Integer> q)
{
  if (q.isEmpty())  // base case
    return q;

  Queue<Integer> q1 = new LinkedList<Integer>();
  Queue<Integer> q2 = new LinkedList<Integer>();

  Integer pivot = q.remove();
  while (!q.isEmpty())
  {
    Integer num = q.remove();
    if (num.compareTo(pivot) < 0)
      q1.add(num);
    else
      q2.add(num);
  }
  q1 = sort(q1);    // recursive calls
  q2 = sort(q2);

  q1.add(pivot);

  while (!q2.isEmpty())
    q1.add(q2.remove());

  return q1;
}
```

Figure 19-13.   Quicksort algorithm implemented with queues

19.6 The `PriorityQueue` Class

A *priority queue* is a different kind of queue: elements are removed not in order of their arrival but in order of their <u>priority</u>. Consider, for example, a credit card authorization processing system in which pending transactions are transmitted from merchants to the bank's central office for authorization. In addition to checking available credit limits, the system may run all its transactions through a special fraud detection module that ranks them according to the likelihood of fraud. All the transactions that receive a significant fraud score may be inserted into a priority queue, ranked by their score, for review by specially trained operators.

It is assumed that any two elements in a priority queue can be compared with regard to their "priority." In the Java implementation, it is assumed that the elements of a priority queue are `Comparable` or a comparator is provided for them. By convention, a "smaller" element has a higher priority. Several elements can have the same priority.

It would be easy to implement a priority queue using a sorted linked list. The `add` method would insert a new element in the proper place to keep the list sorted, and the `remove` method would remove the first element. In this implementation, `remove` would take $O(1)$ time, but `add` would take $O(n)$ time (where n is the number of elements in the priority queue). Alternatively, we could keep a priority queue in an unsorted linked list, add an element at the end, and find and remove the smallest element in `remove`. Then `add` would be $O(1)$, but `remove` would be $O(n)$. Either way, one of the operations could become a bottleneck.

There is a way to implement a priority queue in such a way that both `add` and `remove` take $O(\log n)$ time. Such an implementation uses a *heap*, which is a particular kind of a binary tree. (We will discuss heaps in detail in Chapter 25.) The `PriorityQueue<E>` class in the Java collections framework is such an implementation.

As you can see in Figure 19-1, `PriorityQueue<E>` implements `Queue<E>`, so it has the same methods as `Queue<E>`: `isEmpty`, `peek`, `add`, and `remove` (Figure 19-12). But the meanings of the `peek` and `remove` methods are different: `peek` returns the smallest element, and `remove` removes and returns the smallest element (as opposed to the first element).

> **In the `PriorityQueue<E>` class, the `peek` operation takes $O(1)$ time and both the `add` and `remove` operations take $O(\log n)$ time.**

`PriorityQueue` has other methods, including `iterator` and `toString`, but it is better to stay away from them.

> **An `iterator` or a "for each" loop accesses the elements of a `PriorityQueue` in no particular order; nor does the `toString` method arrange the elements in order of priority.**

So if you print a `PriorityQueue` with `System.out.println`, you will see its elements listed in random order.

`PriorityQueue` has a no-args constructor, which assumes that the priority queue will hold `Comparable` objects. Another constructor —

```
public PriorityQueue(int initialCapacity, Comparator<E> comparator)
```

— takes a comparator as a parameter and uses it to compare the elements.

It is possible to use a priority queue to sort a list by first inserting all the elements into the priority queue, then removing them one by one (Figure 19-14). Actually, if the priority queue is based on a heap, this sorting method is not so bad: it runs in $O(n \log n)$. In Chapter 25, we will discuss a more elaborate implementation of the *Heapsort* algorithm, which does not require a separate heap.

```
// Sorts arr in ascending order
public static <E> void sort(E[] arr)
{
  PriorityQueue<E> q = new PriorityQueue<E>();

  for (E obj : arr)
    q.add(obj);

  for (int i = 0; i < arr.length; i++)
    arr[i] = q.remove();
}
```

Figure 19-14.   A simplistic version of Heapsort

19.7 Sets

A *set* is a collection that has no duplicate elements. More formally `x1.equals(x2)` returns `false` for any two elements `x1` and `x2` in a set. The `Set<E>` interface implements `Collection<E>` but it doesn't add any new methods: it just has a different name to emphasize the no duplicates rule. Figure 19-15 lists some of the `Set` (`Collection`) methods again, for convenience.

Since we want to avoid duplicate elements in a set, the `contains` method has to be efficient: we need to be able to search for a target element within a set quickly. The Java collections framework includes two classes that implement `Set<E>` with efficient searching: `TreeSet<E>` and `HashSet<E>`.

```
boolean isEmpty();
int size();
boolean contains(E obj);               Methods inherited from
boolean add(E obj);                    Collection<E>
boolean remove(E obj);
Iterator<E> iterator();
```

Figure 19-15. Some of the methods of `java.util.Set<E>` interface

`TreeSet<E>` implements a set as a binary search tree (BST). (BSTs are discussed in detail in Chapter 23.) BSTs combine the idea of Binary Search with the idea of a linked structure, such as linked list, where insertion and removal of elements is relatively fast.   The `TreeSet<E>` class assumes that objects of type *E* are `Comparable` or a comparator is provided for them and passed as a parameter to `TreeSet`'s constructor.

> **In a `TreeSet<E>`, the `contains`, `add`, and `remove` methods take, on average, $O(\log n)$ time, where *n* is the number of elements in the set.**

> **An iterator for a `TreeSet<E>` returns its elements in ascending order.**

In the second implementation, `HashSet<E>`, the elements of a set are held in a hash table. (We will discuss hash tables in detail in Chapter 24.) The basic idea is to assign all elements in the set to small subsets, called "buckets," based on the integer value returned by each element's `hashCode` method. The buckets are kept small, so it is easy to find a particular element in a bucket.

A `HashSet` does not make any demands on the comparability of the set elements, but it requires that the elements have a decent `hashCode` method that distributes them into buckets more or less evenly.

The `hashCode` method must agree with `equals`: if `x1.equals(x2)` is `true`, then it should be the case that `x1.hashCode() == x2.hashCode()`. In other words, equal elements should be consistently hashed into the same bucket in the table. `hashCode` is a method provided in `Object`, but classes whose objects are likely to be held in a `HashSet` usually override it.

> **In a `HashSet<E>`, the `contains`, `add`, and `remove` methods take constant time $O(1)$.**

▌ **An iterator for a `HashSet` returns the elements in no particular order.**

You may be wondering: Why would we ever use a `TreeSet` when we have a faster implementation in `HashSet`? The answer is that `TreeSet` is not really much slower (recall Binary Search — it takes only 20 comparisons for 1,000,000 elements), and it offers its own advantage: its iterator returns the elements in ascending order. Also, a `HashSet` may waste some space.

```
// Returns a set of all primes that do not exceed n
public static TreeSet<Integer> allPrimes(int n)
{
  TreeSet<Integer> primes = new TreeSet<Integer>();

  for (int k = 2; k <= n; k++)
  {
    boolean hasPrimeFactors = false;

    // Check whether one of the primes found so far
    //   is a factor of k:
    for (int p : primes)      // autounboxing
    {
      if (k % p == 0)
      {
        hasPrimeFactors = true;
        break;
      }

      if (p * p >= n)          // The values of p come from the TreeSet
      {                        //   in ascending order; there is no need
        break;                 //   to check beyond sqrt(n), because
      }                        //   if p is a factor, so is n/p
    }

    if (!hasPrimeFactors)
      primes.add(k);           // autoboxing
  }

  return primes;
}
```

Figure 19-16. An example of using a `TreeSet`

An example in Figure 19-16 shows how a `TreeSet<Integer>` is used to generate a set of all primes that do not exceed a given integer. The code relies on the fact that a "for each" loop for a <u>TreeSet</u> traverses the set in ascending order. For the same reason, when we print out a `TreeSet`, the elements are shown in ascending order.

19.8 Maps

A *map* is not a collection; rather, it represents a mapping from a set of "keys" to a set of "values." In a mapping, each key is mapped onto a single value, but different keys can be mapped onto the same value (Figure 19-17). Maps are very common: account numbers can be mapped onto customers, user names can be mapped onto passwords, index entries can be mapped onto lists of page numbers, people can be mapped onto their birthdays, and so on.

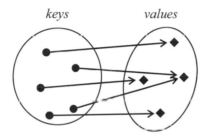

Figure 19-17. A mapping from a set of keys onto a set of values

In the Java collections framework, a map is represented by the Map<*K, V*> interface, where *K* is the type of key objects and *V* is the type of value objects. Map's methods are shown in Figure 19-18.

▌ **Note that a map <u>does not</u> have an `iterator` method.**

If you need to iterate over all the key-value pairs in a map, use an iterator for the set of keys. For example:

```
Map<String, Integer> map = new TreeMap<String, Integer>();
...
for (String key : map.keySet())
  System.out.println(key + " ==> " + map.get(key));
```

The Java collections framework offers two implementations of the Map<*K, V*> interface: TreeMap<*K, V*> and HashMap<*K, V*>. These implementations parallel the TreeSet<*K*> and HashSet<*K*> implementations for the set of keys: TreeMap is based on a binary search tree, and HashMap on a hash table.

```
boolean isEmpty();            // Returns true if this map is
                              //   empty; otherwise returns false.
int size();                   // Returns the number of key-value pairs
                              //   in this map.
V get(K key);                 // Returns the value associated with key.
V put(K key, V value);        // Associates value with key; returns the
                              //   value previously associated with key
                              //   (or null if there was none).
V remove(K key);              // Removes the key-value pair from this map;
                              //   returns the value previously associated
                              //   with key.
boolean containsKey(K key);   // Returns true if key is in the set of
                              //   keys; otherwise returns false.
Set<K> keySet();              // Returns the set of all the keys in
                              //   this map.
```

Figure 19-18. Some of the methods of `java.util.Map<K, V>` interface

The `get`, `put`, and `containsKey` methods take $O(\log n)$ time in a `TreeMap` and $O(1)$ time in a `HashMap`, where n is the number of key-value pairs in the map.

For a `TreeMap`, `keySet().iterator()` (or a "for each" loop for keys) will traverse the keys in ascending order.

If the truth be told, the `TreeMap` and `HashMap` implementations do not use separate sets for keys and for values. `TreeMap` uses a binary search tree of nodes; each node holds one (*key, value*) pair. `HashMap` uses a hash table of entries in which each entry holds a (*key, value*) pair. The `keySet` method returns a `Set` "view" of the keys, which is implemented as an inner class in `TreeMap` or `HashMap`, respectively. Any changes to the set of keys will affect the map.

To avoid duplication of code, Java developers actually implemented the `TreeSet` and `HashSet` classes as special cases of `TreeMap` and `HashMap`, respectively, in which all keys are mapped onto the same object. `TreeSet` and `HashSet` have a field `map`, and their methods are channeled through that field. For instance, `contains(obj)` is coded as `return map.containsKey(obj)`. This technical detail has no effect on your use of these classes.

Figure 19-19 shows an example of code that uses a `TreeMap`.

```
// The names of a few people and their birthdays are
// kept in two "parallel" arrays:
String[] names = {"Tom", "Lena", "Zoe", "Aaron"};
String[] bdays = {"Jun 11", "May 5", "Jun 11", "Oct 22"};

// The above representation is cumbersome and error prone. Let's
// put this data into a map instead, where a name is the key and
// the birthday is the value:
Map<String, String> map = new TreeMap<String, String>();
        // We chose a TreeMap because we want the names
        // to be printed in alphabetical order.

for (int i = 0; i < names.length; i++)
  map.put(names[i], bdays[i]);

// Let's print out the map:
System.out.println(map);
        // The output will be:
        // {Aaron=Oct 22, Lena=May 5, Tom=Jun 11, Zoe=Jun 11}

// Now let's see if any two people in this map have the same
// birthday.  To do that, let's put all birthdays into a set,
// then compare its size with the size of the map:
Set<String> bdaysSet = new HashSet<String>();
        // No particular reason for choosing a HashSet
        // over a TreeSet here.

for (String name : map.keySet())
  bdaysSet.add(map.get(name));

System.out.println("At least two people have the same birthday: " +
        (bdaysSet.size() < map.size()));

// A "random" fact: the probability that in any random group
// of 23 people at least two share the same birthday is greater
// than 0.5.
```

Figure 19-19.   An example of code that uses a map

This concludes our brief tour of the Java collections framework.   Table 19-2 summarizes what we have learned.

Collection<E>
boolean isEmpty()
int size()
boolean contains(E obj)
boolean add(E obj)
boolean remove(E obj)
Iterator<E> iterator()

List<E> extends Collection<E>	ArrayList<E>	LinkedList<E>
All Collection<E>'s methods, including:		
boolean add(E obj)	$O(1)$	$O(1)$
boolean remove(E obj)	$O(n)$	$O(n)$
boolean contains(E obj)	$O(n)$	$O(n)$
Methods specific to List<E>:		
E get(int i)	$O(1)$	$O(n)$
E set(int i, E obj)	$O(1)$	$O(n)$
void add(int i, E obj)	$O(n)$	$O(n)$
E remove(int i)	$O(n)$	$O(n)$
ListIterator<E> listIterator()		
ListIterator<E> listIterator(int i)		
Additional methods in LinkedList<E> only:		
E getFirst(E obj)		$O(1)$
E getLast(E obj)		$O(1)$
void addFirst(E obj)	n/a	$O(1)$
void addLast(E obj)		$O(1)$
E removeFirst(E obj)		$O(1)$
E removeLast(E obj)		$O(1)$

	Stack<E>
boolean isEmpty()	
E peek()	$O(1)$
E push(E obj)	$O(1)$
E pop()	$O(1)$

Table 19-2. The Java collections framework summary — continued

Queue<E>	LinkedList<E>	PriorityQueue<E> *E implements Comparable (or a comparator is provided).*
boolean isEmpty() E peek() boolean add(E obj) E remove()	$O(1)$ $O(1)$ $O(1)$	$O(1)$ $O(\log n)$ $O(\log n)$

Set<E>	TreeSet<E> *E implements Comparable (or a comparator is provided).* *Iterator traverses the set in order.*	HashSet<E> *equals and hashCode are redefined for E.* *Iterator traverses the set in no particular order.*

All Collection<E> methods, including:
    boolean add(E obj)
    boolean remove(E obj)
    boolean contains(E obj)
	$O(\log n)$
	$O(\log n)$
	$O(\log n)$
		$O(1)$
		$O(1)$
		$O(1)$

Map<K,V>	TreeMap<K,V> *K implements Comparable (or a comparator is provided).*	HashMap<K,V> *equals and hashCode are redefined for K.*
boolean isEmpty() int size() V get(K key) V put(K key, V value) V remove(K key) boolean containsKey() Set<K> keySet()	 $O(\log n)$ $O(\log n)$ $O(\log n)$ $O(\log n)$	 $O(1)$ $O(1)$ $O(1)$ $O(1)$

Table 19-2.   The Java collections framework summary

19.9   *Case Study and Lab:* Stock Exchange

In this section we consider a larger, more realistic case study: a miniature stock exchange. A stock exchange is an organization for trading shares in publicly owned companies. In the OTC (Over The Counter) system, stocks are traded electronically through a vast network of securities dealers connected to a computer network. There is no physical "stock exchange" location. In the past few years, thousands of investors have started trading stocks directly from their home computers through Internet-based online brokerage firms.

In this project we will program our own stock exchange and electronic brokerage, which we call *SafeTrade*. What do we mean by "safe"? Not too long ago, some unscrupulous online brokerage firms started encouraging a practice called "day trading," in which traders hold a stock for a few hours or even minutes rather than months or years. As a result, quite a few people lost all their savings and got into debt. Actually, this case study would be more appropriately placed in Chapter 11: in the U.S. code of bankruptcy laws,uscode "Chapter 11" deals with reorganization due to bankruptcy. With our *SafeTrade* program, you stay safely offline and out of trouble and don't pay commissions to a broker.

> **We picked this project because it illustrates appropriate uses of many of the interfaces and classes in the Java collections framework. This project is large enough to warrant a meaningful team development effort.**

❖   ❖   ❖

The stock exchange system keeps track of buy and sell orders placed by traders and automatically executes orders when the highest "bid" price to buy stock meets the lowest asking price for that stock. Orders to buy stock at a certain price (or lower) or to sell stock at a certain price (or higher) are called "limit" orders. There are also "market" orders: to buy at the currently offered lowest asking price or to sell at the currently offered highest bid price.

Each stock is identified by its trading symbol. For example, Sun Microsystems is "SUNW" and Microsoft is "MSFT." In the real world, very small stock prices may include fractions of cents, but in *SafeTrade* we only go to whole cents.

SafeTrade's brokerage maintains a list of registered traders and allows them to log in and trade stocks. The program keeps track of all active buy and sell orders for each stock. A trader can place buy and sell orders, specifying the price for a "limit" order or choosing a "market" order. Each order deals with only one stock. The order for a given stock holds six pieces of information: a reference to the trader who placed it, the stock symbol, the buy or sell indicator, the desired number of shares to be bought or sold, the market or limit indicator, and the price for a limit order. *SafeTrade* acknowledges a placed order by sending a message back to the trader.

When a new order comes in, *SafeTrade* checks if it can be executed and, if so, executes the trade and reports it to both parties by sending messages to both traders. In *SafeTrade*, all orders are "partial" orders. This means that if an order cannot be executed for the total number of shares requested in it, the maximum possible number of shares changes hands and an order for the remaining shares remains active.

A trader can also request a quote for a stock. The quote includes the last sale price, the price and number of shares offered in the current highest bid and lowest "ask" (sell order), the day's high and low price for the stock, and the volume, which is the total number of shares traded during the "day." (In our model, a "day" is one run of the program.)

> **The details of how orders are executed and at what price and the format for a stock quote are described in the *Javadoc* documentation for the `Stock` class.**

SafeTrade <u>does not</u> keep track of the availability of money or shares on the trader's account. If you want, you can add this functionality. For example, you can keep all transactions for a given trader in a list and have a separate field to hold his or her available "cash."

At a first glance, this appears to be a pretty large project. However, it turns out that with careful planning and an understanding of the requirements, the amount of code to be written is actually relatively small. The code is simple and consists of a number of small pieces, which can be handled either by one programmer or by a team of several programmers. We have contributed the main class and a couple of GUI classes.

One of the challenges of a project like this is testing. One of the team members should specialize in QA (Quality Assurance). While other team members are writing code, the QA person should develop a comprehensive test plan. He or she then tests the program thoroughly and works with programmers on fixing bugs.

To experiment with the executable program, set up a project in your IDE with the `SafeTrade.java` and `SafeTrade.jar` files from $J_M\backslash$Ch19$\backslash$SafeTrade. (Actually, `SafeTrade.jar` is a runnable jar file, so you can run *SafeTrade* by just double-clicking on `SafeTrade.jar`.)

`SafeTrade`'s `main` method creates a `StockExchange` and a `Brokerage` and opens a `LoginWindow`. To make program testing easier, `main` also lists several stocks on the `StockExchange` —

```
StockExchange exchange = new StockExchange();
server.listStock("DS", "DanceStudios.com", 12.33);
server.listStock("NSTL", "Nasty Loops Inc.", 0.25);
server.listStock("GGGL", "Giggle.com", 28.00);
server.listStock("MATI", "M and A Travel Inc.", 28.20);
server.listStock("DDLC", "Dulce De Leche Corp.", 57.50);
server.listStock("SAFT", "SafeTrade.com Inc.", 322.45);
```

— and registers and logs in a couple of traders at the `Brokerage`:

```
Brokerage safeTrade = new Brokerage(exchange);
safeTrade.addUser("stockman", "sesame");
safeTrade.login("stockman", "sesame");
safeTrade.addUser("mstrade", "bigsecret");
safeTrade.login("mstrade", "bigsecret");
```

Our design process for *SafeTrade* consists of four parts. The first part is structural design, which determines which data structures will be used in the program. The second part is object-oriented design, which determines the types of objects to be defined and the classes and interfaces to be written. The third part is detailed design, which determines the fields, constructors, and methods in all the classes. The fourth part is developing a test plan. We are going to discuss the structural design first, then the classes involved, and after that the detailed design and testing.

1. Structural design

Our structural design decisions are summarized in Table 19-3. We are lucky to have a chance to use many of the collections classes discussed in this chapter.

Data	*interface* => class
Registered traders	`Map => TreeMap<String, Trader>`
Logged-in traders	`Set => TreeSet<Trader>`
Mailbox for each trader	`Queue => LinkedList<String>`
Listed stocks	`Map => HashMap<String, Stock>`
"Sell" orders for each stock	`Queue => PriorityQueue<TradeOrder>` (with ascending price comparator)
"Buy" orders for each stock	`Queue => PriorityQueue<TradeOrder>` (with descending price comparator)

Table 19-3. Structural design decisions for *SafeTrade*

We have chosen to hold all registered traders in a `TreeMap`, keyed by the trader's login name. A `HashMap` could potentially work faster, but the response time for a new registration is not very important, as long as it takes seconds, not hours. A `HashMap` might waste some space, and we hope that thousands of traders will register, so we can't afford to waste any space in our database. For similar reasons, we have chosen a `TreeSet` over a `HashSet` to hold all currently logged-in traders.

A trader may log in, place a few orders, and log out. Meanwhile, *SafeTrade* may execute some of the trader's orders and send messages to the trader. But the trader may already not be there to read them. So the messages must be stored in the trader's "mailbox" until the trader logs in again and reads them. This is a perfect example of a queue. In *SafeTrade*, a mailbox for each trader is a `Queue<String>` (implemented as a `LinkedList<String>`).

SafeTrade also needs to maintain data for each listed stock. A stock is identified by its trading symbol, so it is convenient to use a map where the stock symbol serves as the key for a stock and the whole `Stock` object serves as the value. The number of all listed stocks is limited to two or three thousand, and the list does not change very often. *SafeTrade* must be able to find a stock immediately for real-time quotes and especially to execute orders. Traders will get upset if they lose money because their order was delayed. Therefore, a good choice for maintaining listed stocks is a hash table, a `HashMap`.

Finally, *SafeTrade* must store all the buy and sell orders placed for each stock in such a way that it has quick access to the highest bid and the lowest ask. Both adding and executing orders must be fast. This is a clear case for using priority queues. We need two of them for each stock: one for sell orders and one for buy orders. For <u>sell</u> orders the order with the <u>lowest</u> asking price has the highest priority, while for <u>buy</u> orders the order with the <u>highest</u> bid price has the highest priority. Therefore, we need to write a comparator class and provide two differently configured comparator objects — one for the buy priority queue and one for the sell priority queue.

<u>2. Object-oriented design</u>

Figure 19-20 shows a class diagram for *SafeTrade*. The project involves nine classes and one interface. We have provided three classes and the interface: the application launcher class `SafeTrade`, the GUI classes `LoginWindow` and `TraderWindow`, and the `Login` interface. Your team's task is to write the remaining six classes. The following briefly describes the responsibilities of different types of objects.

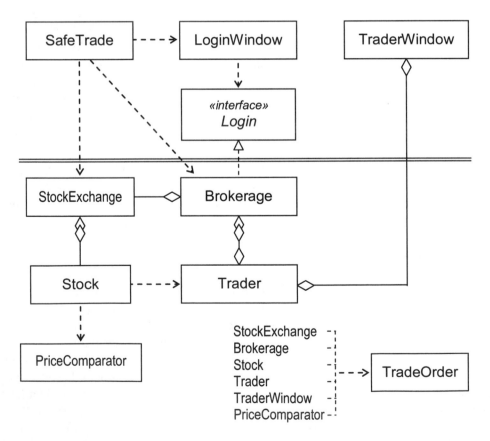

Figure 19-20. Class diagram for the *SafeTrade* program

_____ *Our classes:* _____

We have already mentioned `SafeTrade`, the class that has `main` and starts the program.

The `LoginWindow` accepts a user name and a password from a user and can register a new trader.

> **The `Login` interface isolates `LoginWindow` from `Brokerage`, because logging in is a common function: we want to keep the `LoginWindow` class general and reusable in other projects.**

The `TraderWindow` object is a GUI front end for a `Trader` (Figure 19-21). Each `Trader` creates one for itself. The `TraderWindow` collects the data about a quote request or a trade order and passes that data to the `Trader` by calling `Trader`'s methods.

Figure 19-21. A trader window

_____ *Your classes:* _____

The `StockExchange` keeps a `HashMap` of listed stocks, keyed by their symbols, and relays quote requests and trade orders to them.

The `Brokerage` keeps a `TreeMap` of registered traders and a `TreeSet` of logged-in traders. It receives quote requests and trade orders from traders and relays them to the `StockExchange`.

A `Stock` object holds the stock symbol, the company name, the lowest and highest sell prices, and the volume for the "day." It also has a priority queue for sell orders and another priority queue for buy orders for that stock.

> **The `Stock` class is more difficult than the other classes, because it includes an algorithm for executing orders.**

A `PriceComparator` compares two `TradeOrder` objects based on their prices; an ascending or a descending comparator is passed as a parameter to the respective priority queue of orders when the priority queue is created.

A `Trader` represents a trader; it can request quotes and place orders with the brokerage. It can also receive messages and store them in its mailbox (a `Queue<String>`) and tell its `TraderWindow` to display them.

A `TradeOrder` is a "data carrier" object used by other objects to pass the data about a trade order to each other. Since all the other classes depend on `TradeOrder`, it makes sense to write it first. This is a simple class with fields and accessor methods that correspond to the data entry fields in a `TraderWindow` (Figure 19-21).

3. Detailed design

The detailed specs for the *SafeTrade* classes have been generated from the Javadoc comments in the source files and are provided in the `SafeTradeDocs.zip` file in `JM\Ch19\SafeTrade`. Open `index.html` to see the documentation.

4. Testing

Proper testing for an application of this size is in many ways more challenging than writing the code. Entering and executing a couple of orders won't do. The QA specialist has to make a list of possible scenarios and to develop a strategy for testing them methodically. In addition, the tester must make a list of features to be tested. The most obvious are, for example: Do the "login" and "add user" screens work? Does the "Get quote" button work? When a trader logs out and then logs in again, are the messages preserved? And so on.

The `Stock` / `PriceComparator` subsystem can be tested separately. Write a simple console application for this. You will also need a *stub* class (a greatly simplified version of a class) for `Trader`, with a simple constructor, which sets the trader's name, and one method `receiveMessage(String msg)`, which prints out the trader's name and `msg`. Test the `StockExchange` class separately, using a stub class for `Stock`. Test the `Brokerage / Trader` subsystem separately using a stub class for `StockExchange`.

19.10   Summary

The commonly used features of the Java collections framework are summarized in Table 19-2. The collections framework provides developers with the necessary tools to implement a variety of data structures with ease.

While it is not possible to describe a large real-world project in a few pages, the *SafeTrade* case study gives you a glimpse of what it might be like. Careful structural design helps a software architect to choose the data structures appropriate for a software system. The object-oriented approach helps us split a fairly large project into smaller manageable pieces that we can code and test independently. With little additional effort, we have made one of the classes (`LoginWindow`) reusable for future projects.

Although it is possible to test individual software components in a project to some extent, a comprehensive test plan is needed for testing a software application as a whole. Developing and implementing such a test plan may actually be more challenging than writing the code.

Exercises

Sections 19.1-19.3

1.   Which of the following statements compile with no errors (assuming that the necessary library names are imported)?

(a)   `List<String> list = new List<String>();`
(b)   `List<String> list = new ArrayList<String>();`
(c)   `List<String> list = new LinkedList<String>();`
(d)   `ArrayList<String> list = new List<String>();`
(e)   `ArrayList<String> list = new ArrayList<String>();`
(f)   `LinkedList<String> list = new List<String>();`
(g)   `LinkedList<String> list = new ArrayList<String>();`
(h)▪   `LinkedList<Object> list = new LinkedList<String>();.`

2.   Write a method

```
public <E> void append(List<E> list1, List<E> list2)
```

that appends all the elements from `list2` to `list1` using indices. ⸨ Hint: Treat *E* within the method body as if it were a regular class. ⸩ ✓

3.   What is the primary reason for using iterators rather than indices with Java library classes that implement `java.util.List`?

4.   Rewrite the method in Question 2 using (a) an iterator; (b) a "for each" loop.

5.   Write a method

```
public LinkedList<String> mix(List<String> list1,
                              List<String> list2)
```

that takes two lists of equal size and makes and returns a new list, alternating values from `list1` and `list2`. For example, if `list1` refers to the list `["A", "B"]` and `list2` refers to the list `["1", "2"]`, the combined list should be `["A", "1", "B", "2"]`. Your code should work in $O(n)$ time, where *n* is the size of `list1` and `list2`.

6.■   A list contains *n*+1 `Double` values $a_0, ..., a_n$. Write a method

```
public double sum2(List<Double> list)
```

that calculates $a_0 a_1 + a_0 a_2 + ... + a_0 a_n + a_1 a_2 + ... + a_{n-1} a_n$ — the sum of products for all pairs of elements. <u>Do not</u> use indices. ✓

Section 19.4

7.   What is the output from the following code?

```
Stack<String> stack = new Stack<String>();

stack.push("A");
stack.push("B");
stack.push("C");
while (!stack.isEmpty())
{
  String s = stack.pop();
  System.out.print(s);
}
```

8.   What is the output from the following code? ✓

```
Stack<String> stk = new Stack<String>();

stk.push("One");
stk.push("Two");
stk.push("Three");

while (!stk.isEmpty())
{
  String s = stk.pop();
  if (!stk.isEmpty())
  {
    s += ("-" + stk.pop());
    stk.push(s);
  }
  System.out.println(s);
}
```

(handwritten annotations: "One" "Two" "Three")

(handwritten: "Three" — "Two")

9.   A Stack<Integer> stack **contains the values**

```
(top) -1  3  7  -2  4  -6
```

(handwritten annotations: "One" "Two" "Three-Two")

What is its content after the following code is executed?

(handwritten: "One" "Three-Two")

```
Stack<Integer> stackPos = new Stack<Integer>();
Stack<Integer> stackNeg = new Stack<Integer>();

while (!stack.isEmpty())
{
  Integer obj = stack.pop();
  if (obj.intValue() >= 0)
    stackPos.push(obj);
  else
    stackNeg.push(obj);
}

while (!stackPos.isEmpty())
  stack.push(stackPos.pop());

while (!stackNeg.isEmpty())
  stack.push(stackNeg.pop());
```

(handwritten: "Three-Two")

(handwritten: "Three-Two-One")

(handwritten: "Three-Two")

(handwritten calculations:
obj = -1
3 7 -2 4 -6
stackNeg: -6 -2 -1
stackPos: 4 7 3
stack: -1 -2 -6 3 7 4)

10.■   In the following code, `Point`'s `getX` and `getY` methods return `doubles`:

```
Point cursor;
Stack<Double> stk = new Stack<Double>();
...
// Save cursor position:
stk.push(cursor.getX());
stk.push(cursor.getY());

show(new LoginWindow());
...
// Restore cursor position:
double x = stk.pop();
double y = stk.pop();
cursor.move(x, y);
```

    (a) Find and fix a bug in the code.

    (b) Suggest a way to simplify the code. ✓

11.◆   A book's index contains entries and subentries nested to several levels. Subentries are indicated by deeper indentation. All the sub-entries of a given entry are preceded by the same number of spaces; that number is greater than the indentation at the previous level. For example (see `JM\Ch19\Exercises\bookindex.dat`):

```
class
    abstract
    accessors
    constructors
        overloaded
        no-args
    modifiers
method
    private
    public
    static
stack
    for handling nested structures
    methods
        push
        pop
        peek
```

Write a program that reads an index file and verifies that all the entries and subentries are in alphabetical order. Skip empty lines.

12.◆   Write a program in which Cookie Monster finds the optimal path from the upper-left corner (0, 0) to the lower-right corner (SIZE-1, SIZE-1) in a cookie grid (a 2-D array). Each element of the grid contains either some number of cookies (a non-negative number) or a barrel (-1). On each step Cookie Monster can only go down or to the right. He is not allowed to step on barrels. The optimal path contains the largest number of cookies.

The program reads the cookie grid from a file and reports the number of cookies on the optimal path. (The path itself is not reported.) A sample data file is provided in JM\Ch19\Exercises\cookies.dat.

⸙ Hints: Use a stack. If there is only one way to proceed from the current position, then go there and update the total accumulated number of cookies. If there are two ways to proceed, save one of the possible two points (and its total) on the stack and proceed to the other point. If you have reached the lower-right corner, update the maximum. If there is nowhere to go, examine the stack: pop a saved point, if any, and resume from there. ⸙

Sections 19.5-19.6

13.   What is the output from the following code? ✓

```
Queue<Integer> q = new LinkedList<Integer>();

for (int k = 1; k <= 3; k++)
{
  q.add(k-1);
  q.add(k+1);
}

while (!q.isEmpty())
  System.out.print(q.remove() + " ");
```

        0 2 1 3 2 4

        0   2   1   3   2   4

14.▪   Complete a class `Student`:

```
public class Student
{
  private String name;
  private double GPA;
  ...
}
```

Then write a method

```
public Queue<Student> cutAtGPA(Queue<Student> students,
                                        double minGPA)
```

that removes student records one by one from the `students` queue and adds those students whose GPA is not less than `minGPA` to a new "honors" queue. The method returns the "honors" queue. Test this method in a simple console application.

15.▪   A Morse code message is represented in a program as a queue of strings. Each string consists of dots and dashes. The message always ends with a special terminator string

```
private final String terminator = "END";
```

Write and test a method

```
public void replace(Queue<String> morseCode)
```

that replaces each question mark (represented by `"..--.."`) with a period (`".-.-.-"`), leaving all other codes unchanged. Do not use any temporary lists, queues, or other data structures.

16.▪   Write a method

```
public static <E> Queue<E> copy(Queue<E> q)
```

that builds and returns a copy of `q`, leaving the original unchanged. Assume that `q` does not hold duplicate objects. Use only `Queue` methods shown in Figure 19-12.

17.◆   A 6 by 6 game board contains arbitrarily arranged black and white squares. A path across this board may use only black squares and may move only down or to the right. Write and test a program that reads a board configuration from a file and finds and prints out all paths leading from the upper-left corner (0, 0) to the lower-right corner (5, 5). A sample data file is provided in J_M\Ch19\Exercises\board.dat. Use the `Location` class from the *Chomp* project in Chapter 12 to represent a location on the board, and a `Queue<Location>` to represent a path. Use a `Stack<Location>`, and a `Stack<Queue<Location>>` to hold the branching points and partial paths. ⸮ Hint: use the `copy` method from Question 16 to make a copy of a path. ⸮

Sections 19.7-19.10

18.   (a)   (MC) In a `TreeSet`, which of the following approaches is used to determine whether two objects are equal?

   A.   Only `==` operator
   B.   Only `equals`
   C.   `compareTo` (or `compare` if a `TreeSet` was created with a comparator)
   D.   Both `equals` and `compareTo` (the program throws an exception if the two disagree)

   (b)   (MC) In a `HashSet`, which of the following approaches is used to determine whether two objects are equal?

   A.   Only `==` operator
   B.   Only `equals`
   C.   Both `equals` and `hashCode` (a `HashSet` works properly only when the two agree)
   D.   Both `compareTo` and `hashCode`

19.■   Rewrite the *Index Maker* lab from Chapter 12 using sets and maps. Replace the `ArrayList` of numbers in an `IndexEntry` with a `TreeSet`. Derive `DocumentIndex` from `TreeMap<String, IndexEntry>` rather than from `ArrayList<IndexEntry>` (use word, converted to the upper case, as a key). Modify appropriately the "for each" loop in `IndexMaker` that writes all the entries from the `DocumentIndex` into the output file.

20.◆ (a) Define a class `Movie` that represents a movie record from the `movies.txt` file (in JM\Ch19\Exercises), with fields for the release year, title, director's name, and a list (`LinkedList`) of actors. Make `Movie` objects `Comparable`: the natural ordering should be alphabetical by title. Define a class `Person` to represent a movie actor or director with a first and last name. Make `Person` objects `Comparable`: the ordering should be alphabetical by last, then by first name.

     (b) Write a program that displays the list of movies from the `movies.txt` file, in the same format, but sorted by title. ⋛ Hint: read the movies into an `ArrayList<Movie>` and call `Collections.sort`. ⋛

     (c) Display the list of movies from `movies.txt`, sorted by director's last name. ⋛ Hint: define a `Comparator` that compares movies based on director's names. ⋛

     (d) Print out the total number of actors in `movies.txt` and all the actors in alphabetical order by last and first name, with no duplicates. ⋛ Hint: add all actors to a `Set<Person>`, then use an iterator (or a "for each" loop). ⋛

21.   What is the big-O of the running time in the following methods?

     (a) `addFirst` in a `LinkedList` with *n* elements ✓
     (b) `remove` in a `Queue` with *n* elements (implemented as a `LinkedList`)
     (c) traversal of a `TreeSet` with *n* elements ✓
     (d) `contains` in a `TreeSet` with *n* elements
     (e)■ `remove` in a `PriorityQueue` with *n* elements

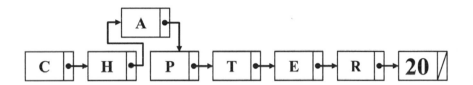

Lists and Iterators

20.1 Prologue

This chapter begins a series of chapters where we take a closer look at data structures. The Java collections framework provides a rich set of tools for incorporating various data structures into programs. In the previous chapter, we discussed a subset of these tools and when and how to use them. That's what most programmers need to know. However, we want to go a little beyond that and see how some of these data structures are implemented. We will proceed in a "do-it-yourself" manner, even though the Java library already has all the implementations. Of course we won't re-implement the library classes completely: we will just get a feel for how they work. We begin with lists.

The easiest implementation of a list is an array. As we've seen, the elements of an array are stored in consecutive locations in computer memory. We can calculate the address of each element from its index in the array. By contrast, the elements of a linked list are held in *nodes* that can be scattered in various locations in memory, but each node contains a reference to the next one. The last node in the list points to nothing, so instead of a reference to the next node it holds `null`.

Metaphorically, we can compare an array to a book: we can read its pages sequentially or we can open it to any page. A linked list is like a magazine article: at the end of the first installment it says, "continued on page 27." We read the second installment on page 27, and at the end it says, "continued on page 36," and so on, until we finally reach the □ symbol that marks the end of the article.

As we know from Chapter 19, the `java.util.LinkedList` class implements a list as a doubly-linked list. In this chapter we will learn the basics of implementing our own linked lists: a singly-linked list, a linked list with a tail, a doubly-linked list, and a circular list.

20.2 Singly-Linked List

> In a *singly-linked list*, each element is stored in a larger structure, called a *node*. In addition to the element's value, the node holds a reference to the next node.

Let us say that the information stored in a node is represented by an object called `value` and that the reference to the next node is called `next`. We can encapsulate these fields in a class `ListNode` with one constructor, two accessors, and two modifiers (Figure 20-1).

```java
// Represents a node of a singly-linked list.

public class ListNode
{
  private Object value;
  private ListNode next;

  // Constructor:
  public ListNode(Object initValue, ListNode initNext)
  {
    value = initValue;
    next = initNext;
  }

  public Object getValue() { return value; }
  public ListNode getNext() { return next; }

  public void setValue(Object theNewValue) { value = theNewValue; }
  public void setNext(ListNode theNewNext) { next = theNewNext; }
}
```

Figure 20-1.   A class that represents a node in a singly-linked list
(J_M\Ch20\Lists\ListNode.java)[*]

Note two things about `ListNode`'s definition. First, "next" is a name chosen by the programmer: it is not required by Java syntax. We could have called it "link" or "nextNode" or whatever name we wanted. The name of the class, "ListNode," is also chosen by the programmer.

Second, the definition is self-referential: it refers to the `ListNode` data type inside the `ListNode` data type definition! The compiler is able to untangle this because `next` is just a reference to an object, not the object itself. A reference takes a fixed number of bytes regardless of the data type, so the compiler can calculate the total size of a `ListNode` without paying much attention to what type of reference `next` is.

---

[*] Adapted from The College Board's *AP Computer Science AB: Implementation Classes and Interfaces.*

> We do not want to deal here with the rather complicated syntax for defining "generic" classes (which work with any specified type of objects). Therefore, the type of `value` in `ListNode` is `Object`, and we will use a cast to the appropriate type when we retrieve the value from a node.

As an example, let us consider a list of departing flights on an airport display. The flight information may be represented by an object of the type `Flight`:

```
public class Flight
{
  private int number;          // Flight number
  private String destination;  // Destination city
  ...                          // Other fields, constructors, methods
}
```

Suppose a program has to maintain a list of flights departing in the next few hours, and we have decided to implement it as a linked list. We can use the following statements to create a new node that holds information about a given flight:

```
Flight flt = new Flight(...);
...
ListNode node = new ListNode(flt, null);
```

To extract the flight info we need to cast the object returned by `getValue` back into the `Flight` type:

```
flt = (Flight)node.getValue();
```

A singly-linked list is accessed through a reference to its first node. This reference is held in a variable that we named `head`. When a program creates a linked list, it usually starts with an empty list — the `head` reference is `null`:

```
ListNode head = null;
```

To create the first node, we call `ListNode`'s constructor and store a reference to the new node in `head`:

```
head = new ListNode(value0, null);
```

This results in a list with one node (Figure 20-2).

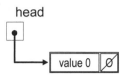

Figure 20-2.   A linked list with only one node

The first node in a non-empty linked list is called the head node. A second node may be appended to the first:

```
ListNode node1 = new ListNode(value1, null);
head.setNext(node1);
```

Or, combining the above two statements into one:

```
head.setNext(new ListNode(value1, null));
```

This statement changes the `next` field in the head node from `null` to a reference to the second node. This is illustrated in Figure 20-3.

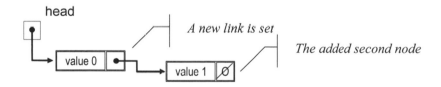

Figure 20-3.   The second node is appended to the list

> Now **head** refers to the first node of the list and **head.getNext()** returns a reference to the second node.

Diagrams like this one help us understand how links in a linked list are reassigned in various operations.

Figure 20-4 shows the field and constructors of the `SinglyLinkedList` class. (We are building this class just to learn how a linked list works; we will continue using the much more advanced `java.util.LinkedList` class in our projects.) `SinglyLinkedList` has two fields, `ListNode head` and `int nodeCount`, and two constructors. The no-args constructor creates an empty list. The constructor with one parameter, `Object[] values`, creates a list that contains all elements from the array `values` in the same order. When we build this list, we keep a reference to the last node, `tail`, append a new node to the tail node, then update `tail`.

```java
// Implements a singly-linked list.

import java.util.Iterator;

public class SinglyLinkedList
{
  private ListNode head;
  private int nodeCount;

  // Constructor: creates an empty list
  public SinglyLinkedList()
  {
    head = null;
    nodeCount = 0;
  }

  // Constructor: creates a list that contains
  // all elements from the array values, in the same order
  public SinglyLinkedList(Object[] values)
  {
    ListNode tail = null;
    for (Object value : values) // for each value to insert
    {
      ListNode node = new ListNode(value, null);
      if (head == null)
        head = node;
      else
        tail.setNext(node);
      tail = node;     // update tail
    }

    nodeCount = values.length;
  }
  ...
}
```

Figure 20-4. The constructors of the `SinglyLinkedList` class
(J_M\Ch20\Lists\SinglyLinkedList.java)

Figure 20-5 shows the resulting linked list.

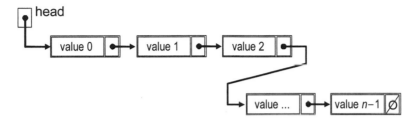

Figure 20-5. A singly-linked list

We can easily attach a new node at the head of the list. For example:

```
public void addFirst(Object value)
{
  ListNode node = new ListNode(value, null);
  node.setNext(head);
  head = node;
}
```

Or simply:

```
public void addFirst(Object value)
{
  head = new ListNode(value, head);
}
```

The above method creates a new node and sets its `next` field to the old value of `head`. It then sets `head` to refer to the newly created node (Figure 20-6).

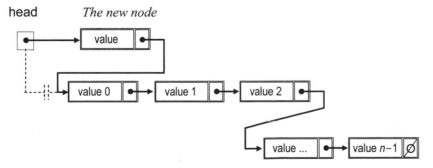

Figure 20-6. A new node inserted at the head of a linked list

But in an `addLast` method, you have to traverse the list to find the last node, then append the new node to the last one.

20.3 Traversals

It is easy to traverse a singly-linked list with a `for` loop that goes from one node to the next:

```
for (ListNode node = head; node != null; node = node.getNext())
{
  Object value = node.getValue();
  ...
}
```

It is also not very hard to make iterators and "for each" loops work with our `SinglyLinkedList` class. To achieve this, we need to make our linked lists "iterable." Here is a recipe:

1. State that `SinglyLinkedList` implements `Iterable<Object>`. `Iterable<T>` is an interface in the `java.lang` package (built into Java). It specifies only one method:

   ```
   Iterator<T> iterator();
   ```

2. Add a method `iterator` to the `SinglyLinkedList` class. This method constructs an iterator for a `SinglyLinkedList`, passing the `head` of the list to the iterator's constructor as a parameter:

   ```
   public Iterator<Object> iterator()
   {
     return new SinglyLinkedListIterator(head);
   }
   ```

   The method returns the newly constructed iterator object.

3. Write the `SinglyLinkedListIterator` class, which implements `java.util.Iterator<Object>`. A simplified version of this class is shown in Figure 20-7.

```java
// Implements an iterator for a SinglyLinkedList.

import java.util.Iterator;
import java.util.NoSuchElementException;

public class SinglyLinkedListIterator implements Iterator<Object>
{
  private ListNode nextNode;

  // Constructor
  public SinglyLinkedListIterator(ListNode head)
  {
    nextNode = head;
  }

  public boolean hasNext()
  {
    return nextNode != null;
  }

  public Object next()
  {
    if (nextNode == null)
      throw new NoSuchElementException();

    Object value = nextNode.getValue();
    nextNode = nextNode.getNext();
    return value;
  }

  // Not implemented.
  public void remove()
  {
    throw new UnsupportedOperationException();
  }
}
```

Figure 20-7. J_M\Ch20\Lists\SinglyLinkedListIterator.java

In Figure 20-7 the iterator class is implemented as a regular public class. It would be stylistically more appropriate to make `SinglyLinkedListIterator` a *private inner class* in `SinglyLinkedList`, because `SinglyLinkedList` is the only class that uses this type of iterator. We have avoided inner classes in this book, because, from the OOP standpoint, the relationship between an object of an inner class and an object of its embedding outer class is not well defined. In particular, the code in an inner class has access to the private fields and methods of the embedding class. But while inner classes are philosophically confusing, their syntax is straightforward. Here, just replace `public class` with `private class` and embed the whole definition of `SinglyLinkedListIterator` inside the `SinglyLinkedList` class body. Something like this:

```
import java.util.Iterator;
import java.util.NoSuchElementException;

public class SinglyLinkedList implements Iterable<Object>
{
  < ... fields, constructors, and methods >

  private class SinglyLinkedListIterator implements Iterator<Object>
  {
    ...
  }
}
```

A more elaborate iterator implementation would have the `remove` method implemented (which means keeping track of not just the current node but also the two previous ones). It would also check that the list has not been modified outside the iterator.

20.4 *Lab:* Implementing a Singly-Linked List

Finish the `SinglyLinkedList` class (`SinglyLinkedList.java` in `JM\Ch20\Lists`). Implement all of the `java.util.List` methods shown in Figure 19.4 on page 472 (for elements of the `Object` type only) except the two `listIterator` methods. Also implement a `toString` method: it should return a string in the same format as the library classes that implement `List`. Test your class thoroughly.

20.5 Linked List with a Tail

For a singly-linked list, adding an element at the beginning is an $O(1)$ operation, while adding an element at the end is an $O(n)$ operation (where n is the number of nodes), because you have to traverse the whole list to find the last node. (Incidentally, for arrays, it is exactly the opposite.)   With a small modification, however, we can make appending an element at the end efficient, too. All we have to do is keep track of a reference to the last node (Figure 20-8) and update it appropriately when we add or remove nodes. Such a structure is called a *linked list with a tail*.

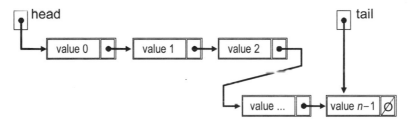

Figure 20-8.   A singly-linked list with a tail

Write a class `LinkedListWithTail`. Define two fields: `head` and `tail`. `tail` should refer to the last node of the list. Provide a no-args constructor that creates an empty list, setting both `head` and `tail` to null. Implement the `isEmpty`, `peek`, `add`, and `remove` methods specified by the `java.util.Queue<Object>` interface. (Make sure that all these methods run in $O(1)$ time.)

20.6 Doubly-Linked List and Circular List

We have already mentioned doubly-linked lists in Chapter 19 (Figure 19.6 on page 474). In a doubly-linked list, each node holds references to both the next node and the previous node (Figure 20-9).

The advantage of a doubly-linked list over a singly-linked list is that we can traverse it in both directions, and we have direct access to the last node. A disadvantage is that it takes more space than a singly-linked list.

Like a linked-list with a tail, a doubly-linked list can be implemented with two fields, head and tail, that would hold references to the first and last nodes of the list, respectively. In an empty list, both head and tail are null.

```java
// Represents a node of a doubly-linked list.
public class ListNode2
{
  private Object value;
  private ListNode2 previous;
  private ListNode2 next;

  // Constructor:
  public ListNode2(Object initValue, ListNode2 initPrevious,
                         ListNode2 initNext)
  {
    value = initValue;
    previous = initPrevious;
    next = initNext;
  }

  public Object getValue()  { return value; }
  public ListNode2 getPrevious() { return previous; }
  public ListNode2 getNext() { return next; }

  public void setValue(Object theNewValue) { value = theNewValue; }
  public void setPrevious(ListNode2 theNewPrev) { previous = theNewPrev; }
  public void setNext(ListNode2 theNewNext) { next = theNewNext; }
}
```

Figure 20-9.   A class that represents a node of a doubly-linked list
(J_M\Ch20\Lists\ListNode2.java)

To add a value at the end of the list, we have to write something like this:

```
public void addLast(Object value)
{
  ListNode2 newNode = new ListNode2(value, tail, null);
  if (head == null)
  {
    head = newNode;
    tail = newNode;
  }
  else
  {
    tail.setNext(newNode);
  }
  tail = newNode;
}
```

❖   ❖   ❖

In a *circular* doubly-linked list, the "next" link in the last node refers back to the first node, and the "previous" link in the first node refers to the last node (Figure 20-10).

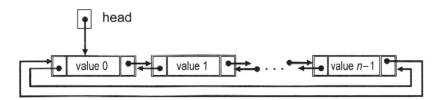

Figure 20-10. A doubly-linked circular list

In a circular list we do not need to keep a separate reference to the tail because we can access it as `head.getPrevious()`.

❖   ❖   ❖

In a doubly-linked list with separate references to the head and tail, we have to handle the case of an empty list separately. It is possible to streamline the code if we combine the `head` and `tail` references in one dummy node, which does not hold any valid value. Let's call this node `header`. Our list then becomes circular (Figure 20-11) and always has at least one node. This is how `java.util.LinkedList` is implemented.

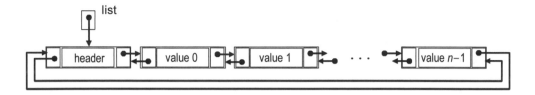

Figure 20-11. A circular doubly-linked list with a header node

In this implementation, an empty list has only one node, `header`, and its `next` and `previous` fields refer to `header` itself:

```
// Constructs an empty list:
public DoublyLinkedListWithHeader()
{
  header = new ListNode2(null, null, null);
  header.setPrevious(header);
  header.setNext(header);
}
```

With a header node, the code for methods that insert and remove elements is a little shorter, because we don't have to handle the case of an empty list separately. For example, we can write a method to insert an element after a given node:

```
// Inserts value after node.
public void addAfter(ListNode2 node, Object value)
{
  ListNode2 newNode = new ListNode2(value, node, node.getNext());
  node.getNext().setPrevious(newNode);
  node.setNext(newNode);
}
```

This code also works for inserting the first or the last node. For example:

```
// Appends value to the list.
public void addLast(Object value)
{
  addAfter(header.getPrevious(), value);
}
```

20.7 *Lab:* Teletext

Figure 20-12 shows a snapshot from the *Teletext* program. The program continuously scrolls up a list of headlines. The user can add a headline by typing it in the provided text input field. The line will be added after the blank line that follows "Today's headlines." The user can also delete a headline by entering d. The next headline after the top one will be deleted. Run *Teletext* by clicking on the Teletext.jar file in JM\Ch20\Teletext.

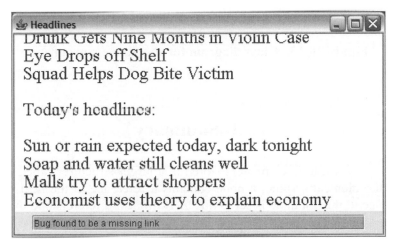

Figure 20-12. A snapshot from the *Teletext* program

Figure 20-13 shows the class diagram for the *Teletext* program. The program keeps the headlines in a doubly-linked circular list. (Circular lists are not used very often; this is a rare occasion where we can benefit from one.) The list is implemented in the TeletextList class. Your task is to fill in the missing code in that class. TeletextList.java is located in JM\Ch20\Teletext.

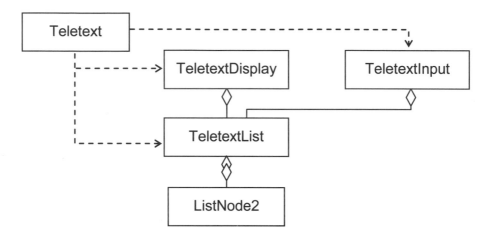

Figure 20-13. Class diagram for the *Teletext* program

20.8 Summary

In a *singly-linked list*, each element is stored in a larger structure, called a *node*. In addition to the element's value, a node contains a reference to the next node. The `next` reference in the last node is set to `null`. If `head` is a reference to the first node in the list, the statement

```
head = new ListNode(value, head);
```

appends a node holding `value` at the beginning of the list.

It is easy to traverse a linked list using a simple `for` loop:

```
for (ListNode node = head; node != null; node = node.getNext())
{
  Object value = node.getValue();
  ...
}
```

It is also not very hard to write a class that implements an "iterable" linked list for which iterators and "for each" loops work.

In a singly-linked list, inserting a node at the beginning takes $O(1)$ time, but appending a node at the end takes $O(n)$ time, where n is the number of nodes in the list. A *linked list with a tail* remedies this situation: it keeps a reference to the last node, so appending a node at the end takes $O(1)$ time. But removing the last node still takes $O(n)$ time because we need to traverse the whole list to properly update the tail reference.

In a *doubly-linked list*, each node, in addition to the list element, contains references to both the previous and the next node. A doubly-linked list can be traversed either forward or backward. Adding and removing elements at the beginning or at the end of such a list takes $O(1)$ time.

In a circular list, the last node is linked back to the first node.

The `java.util.LinkedList` class implements a list using a doubly-linked list (more precisely, a circular doubly-linked list with a header node).

Exercises

Sections 20.1-20.4

1. Fill in the blanks in the initialization of `node3`, `node2`, `node1` and `head`, so that `node1`, `node2`, and `node3` form a linked list (in that order) referred to by `head`. ✓

```
ListNode node3 = new ListNode("Node 3",_____);
ListNode node2 = new ListNode("Node 2",_____);
ListNode node1 = new ListNode("Node 1",_____);
ListNode head = _____;
```

2. Fill in the blanks in the following method:

```
// Returns true if the list referred to by head
// has at least two nodes; otherwise returns false
public boolean hasTwo(ListNode head)
{
    return _____;
}
```

3. Write a method

```
public ListNode removeFirst(ListNode head)
```

that unlinks the first node from the list and returns the head of the new list. Your method should throw a `NoSuchElementException` when the original list is empty. ✓

4.   Write a method

```
public int size(ListNode head)
```

that returns the number of nodes in the list referred to by `head`:

(a)   using a `for` loop
(b)   using recursion.

5.   `head` refers to the first node of a linked list (without a tail). Write a method

```
public ListNode add(ListNode head, Object value)
```

that appends a new node, holding `value`, at the end of the list and returns a reference to the first node of the modified list. ✓

6.   Fill in the blanks in the method below. This method takes the list referred to by `head`, builds a new list in which the nodes have the same information but are arranged in reverse order, and returns the head of the new list. The original list remains unchanged. Your solution must use a `for` loop (not recursion).

```
public ListNode reverseList(ListNode head)
{
  ListNode newHead = null;

  for ( _____ )
  {
     _____

     . . .
  }

  return newHead;
}
```

7.   Write a method

```
public ListNode concatenateStrings(ListNode head)
```

that takes the list referred to by `head`, builds a new list, and returns its head. The original list contains strings. The *k*-th node in the new list should contain the concatenation of all the strings from the original list from the first node up to and including the *k*-th node. For example, if the original list contains strings `"A"`, `"B"`, `"C"`, the new list should contain strings `"A"`, `"AB"`, `"ABC"`.

8. ▪ Write a method

```
public ListNode rotate(ListNode head)
```

that takes a linked list referred to by `head`, splits off the first node, and appends it at the end of the list. The method should accomplish this solely by rearranging links: do not allocate new nodes or move objects between nodes. The method should return the head of the rotated list.

9. ▪ A list referred to by `head` contains strings arranged alphabetically in ascending order. Write a method

```
public ListNode insertInOrder(ListNode head, String s)
```

that inserts `s` into the list, preserving the order. If `s` is already in the list, it is not inserted. The method should return the head of the updated list. ✓

10. ▪ Write a method

```
public ListNode middleNode(ListNode head)
```

that returns the middle node (or one of the two middle nodes) of a linked list. Design this method using no recursion and only one loop.

11. ◆ Let us say that a string matches an input pattern (another string) if the pattern is at least as long as the string and for every non-wildcard character in the pattern the string has the same character in the same position. (The wildcard character is `'?'`.) For example, both `"New York"` and `"New Jersey"` match the input pattern `"New ???????"`. Write a method

```
public ListNode moveToBack(ListNode head, String pattern)
```

that takes a list of strings referred to by `head` and moves all the strings that match `pattern` to the end of the list, preserving their order. Your method must work by rearranging links; do not allocate new nodes or use temporary arrays or lists. The method should return the head of the updated list.

12. Add a method

```
// Appends otherList at the end of this list.
public void append(LinkedListWithTail otherList)
```

to `LinkedListWithTail` that you wrote in Lab 20.5. `append` should work in $O(1)$ time, regardless of the list sizes, and it should work properly when either list is empty or both lists are empty.

13. Write a method

```
public static void sort(ListNode head)
```

that implements Selection Sort for a linked list, pointed to by `head`. Assume that the list holds `String` objects and sort them in alphabetical order. Your method should run in $O(n^2)$ time, where n is the number of nodes in the list. ⋜ Hint: set `firstNode` to `head`; find the smallest value in the list, starting from `firstNode`; swap that value with the value in `firstNode`; advance `firstNode`. ⋝

14. Write the following method:

```
// Removes the largest element from the doubly-linked list,
// pointed to by head, and returns the head of the modified list.
// Precondition: head refers to the first node of a
//               non-empty doubly-linked list with
//               Integer values.
public static ListNode2 removeMax(ListNode2 head)
```

15. Write a method

```
public void quicksort(ListNode2 fromNode, ListNode2 toNode)
```

that implements the Quicksort algorithm for a given segment of a doubly-linked list. `fromNode` refers to the first node of the segment, and `toNode` refers to the last node of the segment. (Assume that the list holds `Comparable` objects.) The links outside the segment should remain unchanged, and the segment should remain linked at the same place within the list. The method should run in $O(n \log n)$ time, where n is the number of nodes in the segment. Do not use any temporary arrays or lists.

Stacks and Queues

21.1 Prologue

A stack is useful for untangling nested structures and branching processes: when you jump to the next branch or level, you have to remember where you left off to be able to return there later. A stack is controlled by two operations referred to as *push* and *pop*. Push adds a value to the top of the stack; pop removes the value from the top of the stack.

One example of effective stack use is in a web browser. When you click on a link, the browser saves the current URL and your place in the document so that you can retrace your steps if necessary. When you follow another link, the current location is saved again. And so on. When you press the "Back" button, the browser needs to restore the location visited just before the current one. That is why a stack is appropriate for storing the sequence of visited locations.

In a *queue*, by contrast, data elements are retrieved in the same order as they were stored. The queue is controlled by two operations: *add* and *remove* (or *enqueue* and *dequeue)*. *Add* inserts a value at the rear of the queue, and *remove* removes a value from the front of the queue.

In this chapter we will discuss different implementations of the stack and queue data structures. The Line Cruiser lab in Section 21.3 illustrates the use of stacks in implementing "back" and "forward" buttons in a toy browser. The Actors World lab in Section 21.6 uses a queue of messages to simulate a world of active "actors."

21.2 Implementations of Stacks

As we saw in Chapter 19, the Java collections framework has a class `java.util.Stack<E>`, which implements a stack of objects of the type *E*. `Stack<E>` extends `Vector<E>`. (`Vector` is similar to `ArrayList`; it is a relic from the first release of Java.) In general it is not hard to implement a stack with the help of a list. Both the `ArrayList` and `LinkedList` classes provide methods that make programming a stack of objects very easy. One approach is to derive your stack class from one of them, similar to what `Stack<E>` does. However, in that case your stack will also inherit all of `List`'s methods. If you prefer to keep your stack's functionality pure, with only `push`, `pop`, `peek`, and `isEmpty` but no `List` methods or iterators, you can define your own `Stack` interface (Figure 21-1) and implement it using an `ArrayList<Object>` (Figure 21-2) or a `LinkedList<Object>` (Figure 21-3).

```
public interface Stack
{
  boolean isEmpty();
  Object peek();
  void push(Object obj);
  Object pop();
}
```

Figure 21-1. "Our own" Stack interface (J_M\Ch21\Stack.java)

```
import java.util.ArrayList;

public class ArrayStack implements Stack
{
  private ArrayList<Object> items;

  public ArrayStack()  { items = new ArrayList<Object>(); }
  public boolean isEmpty() { return items.isEmpty(); }
  public Object peek() { return items.get(items.size() - 1); }
  public void push(Object obj) { items.add(obj); }
  public Object pop() { return items.remove(items.size() - 1); }
}
```

Figure 21-2. An implementation of stack based on ArrayList
(J_M\Ch21\ArrayStack.java)

```
import java.util.LinkedList;

public class ListStack implements Stack
{
  private LinkedList<Object> items;

  public ListStack() { items = new LinkedList<Object>(); }
  public boolean isEmpty() { return items.isEmpty(); }
  public Object peek() { return items.getFirst(); }
  public void push(Object obj) { items.addFirst(obj); }
  public Object pop() { return items.removeFirst(); }
}
```

Figure 21-3. An implementation of stack based on LinkedList
(J_M\Ch21\ListStack.java)

In both implementations the `peek`, `push`, and `pop` methods run in $O(1)$ time.

> **When you implement a stack, the pop and peek methods are expected to throw an exception if the stack is empty.**

For example:

```
if (isEmpty())
    throw new NoSuchElementException();
```

In our `ArrayStack` and `ListStack` classes we don't throw exceptions, because `ArrayList` and `LinkedList` do it for us.

❖   ❖   ❖

It is also easy to program a specialized stack from scratch, using an array to hold the values. This may be useful for a stack of `ints` or `doubles`, so that you don't have to convert them into objects. This is one of the exercises at the end of this chapter. The array implementation maintains an integer index, called the stack pointer, which marks the current top of the stack. The stack usually grows toward the end of the array; the stack pointer is incremented when a new value is pushed onto the stack and decremented when a value is popped from the stack. In some implementations the stack pointer points to the top element of the stack; other programmers find it more convenient to point to the next available vacant slot on the stack. Figure 21-4 illustrates the latter implementation.

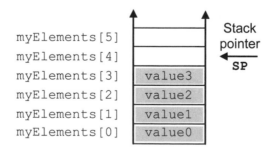

Figure 21-4. An array implementation of stack

> **In Java, a stack of objects holds <u>references</u> to objects. The objects potentially may change after they have been pushed on the stack (unless they are immutable). If you expect an object to change and you need to save its original state on a stack, create a copy of the object and <u>push a reference to that copy</u> onto the stack.**

21.3 *Lab:* Browsing

In this lab we will implement a toy browser called *Line Cruiser*. Rather than browsing web pages, our browser will "browse" several lines of text in the same file. Figure 21-5 shows the classes that we have to write for this project. As usual, this is a team effort: I'll provide the `LineCruiser`, `BrowserMouseListener`, `BrowserControlPanel`, and `BrowserView` classes, and you work on the `BrowserModel` class.

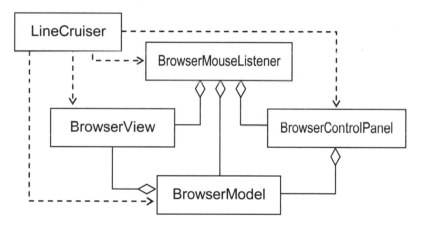

Figure 21-5. *Line Cruiser* **classes**

Our browser only understands two very basic HTML tags: `<a href="#`*name*`">` and `<a name="`*name*`">` (see Appendix C for an HTML tutorial). To avoid complicated parsing of strings, we'll assume that these tags are written exactly as shown, where *name* is any non-empty alphanumeric string. If a line contains an `<a href="#...">` tag, the whole line becomes a hyperlink. As usual, when such a hyperlink is clicked, our browser finds a line with a matching `<a name="...">` tag and brings that line to the top of the screen. Our browser ignores all other tags and preserves the actual line breaks in the file rather then interpreting `<p>`, `<br>`, or other tags.

All these details are handled in my `BrowserView` class; you only need to know them if you want to create your own test data file. Or just use the one provided by us: J_M\Ch21\Browser\lines.html.

Our browser has "Home," "Back," and "Forward" buttons, just like a real browser. <u>An important part of your task</u> is to figure out how exactly these buttons work in a real browser (such as *Firefox* or *Internet Explorer*). "Home," "Back," and "Forward" in our browser should work the same way.

Now let's agree on more formal specifications.

<u>My</u> `BrowserView` class provides one method of interest to you:

```
public void update(int n)
```

It displays several lines from the file, as many as fit in the display, with the *n*-th line at the top of the display. Your class, `BrowserModel`, should call `update` as necessary.

<u>Your</u> `BrowserModel` class should provide one constructor and six methods.

`BrowserModel`'s constructor takes one parameter:

```
BrowserModel(BrowserView view)
```

Your constructor should save `view` to be able to call `view`'s `update` method later. Don't forget to call `update` from `BrowserModel`'s constructor to initialize `view`.

Four of `BrowserModel`'s methods are used for navigation:

```
public void back();
public void forward();
public void home();
public void followLink(int n);
```

I call `home`, `back`, and `forward` methods when a corresponding button is clicked. I call `followLink(n)` when a hyperlink pointing to the *n*-th line is clicked.

`BrowserModel`'s two remaining methods let me know whether the "Back" and/or "Forward" buttons should be enabled or disabled:

```
public boolean hasBack();
public boolean hasForward();
```

The return `true` means enable; `false`, disable.

You'll find the *Line Cruiser* files in J~M~\Ch21\Browser. The `lines.html` data file for testing our browser is in the same folder. Use `java.util.Stack<Integer>` for the stacks. Write the `BrowserModel` class and test the program thoroughly.

21.4 The Hardware Stack

What happens when a method is called? When method `caller` calls method `task`, how does `task` know where to return control after it has finished? Obviously `caller` has to pass along some return address so that `task` can send the CPU to that address when it is through. Let us consider several possible locations where that return address can be stored.

The first guess is that it could be saved in some specially reserved memory location. This could work if `task` did not call any other methods. If, however, `task` called another method, `subTask`, then its return address would go into the same memory location and overwrite the first return address. In a more elaborate scheme, the return address could go into some special memory area attached to the method code, for instance just before the beginning of the method code. This would solve the problem of methods calling other methods, because every method has its own storage for the return address. This is, in fact, how some early models of computers worked. A problem arises, however, if `task` is allowed to call itself, or when there are circular calls: `task` calls `subTask`, `subTask` calls `anotherSubTask`, `anotherSubTask` calls `task`. Then `task` will get confused about whether to return control to `anotherSubTask` or to `caller`.

The notion of a method calling itself may at first seem absurd. But, as we know, such recursive calls are extremely useful for dealing with nested structures or branching processes where substructures or branches are similar to the whole. As we saw in Chapter 4, recursive methods can greatly simplify algorithms.

Practically the only solution remaining is a stack. When `caller` calls `task`, it pushes the return address on the stack. When `task` has finished, it pops the return address from the stack and passes control back to it. `task` can use the stack for its own purposes and for calling other methods: the only requirement is that it restore the stack pointer to its initial value before returning.

This way, methods can call each other without any conflict. In particular, a method can call itself or methods can call each other in a circular manner. In addition to the return address, though, the compiler or interpreter has to be careful with the parameters and local variables. If a method in the middle of its course calls itself, what becomes of its local variables? Again, the stack offers the solution. The method's parameters and local variables can all reside on the stack. The stack pointer is adjusted to reserve some space for them when the method is called, and the stack pointer is restored when the method has finished its processing. That way we can use only one copy of the method code but multiple copies of the method's return address, parameters, and local variables, one for every call currently in progress. The area of the stack that holds all the information for a particular method call is called a *frame*. Figure 21-6 illustrates the frames created on the stack after several method calls.

In modern computers the system stack is supported in hardware. The hardware stack does not require any special memory. It is implemented simply as a stack pointer *register* that can point to a desired memory location and can be modified either directly or by the `push` and `pop` CPU instructions. The CPU instruction `call` automatically pushes the address of the next instruction onto the stack before passing control to a subroutine. The CPU instruction `ret` (return) automatically pops the return address from the stack and passes control back to that address.

When method `caller` calls method `task`, `caller` pushes the parameters that it wants to pass to `task` onto the stack, then passes control to `task`. `task` allocates some space on the stack for its own local variables. When `task` has finished its job, it wipes out its local variables from the stack. Either the caller or the called method, depending on the convention in the compiler, performs the final clean-up by removing the parameters from the stack.

The hardware stack is also used for saving the system state when it is interrupted by an external event. Pressing any key on the keyboard, for example, generates a hardware interrupt, a situation that needs the CPU's immediate attention. When this happens, the address of the current CPU instruction is pushed on stack and control is passed to the special interrupt handling routine. This routine pushes all CPU registers on stack to save the current state. Then it receives and processes the pressed key and places its code into the keyboard buffer for later use by the running program. After that the keyboard routine pops all the registers from the stack (in reverse order) and returns control to the interrupted program. The stack helps to handle nested interrupts (when one interrupt comes in the middle of processing another interrupt) properly. People often use a similar method when their tasks or conversations are interrupted.

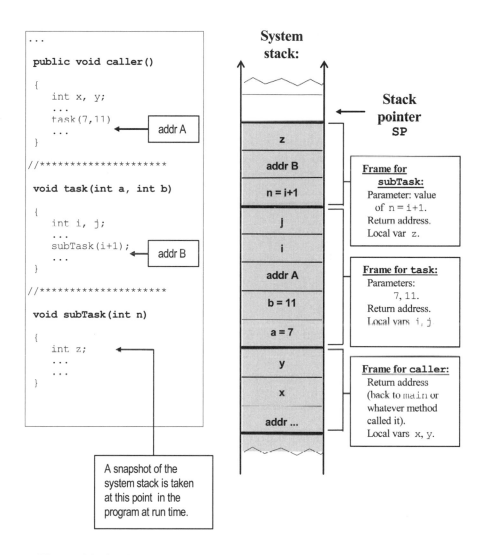

Figure 21-6.   Frames on the system stack after a few method calls

21.5 Implementations of Queues

As we saw in Chapter 19, the `java.util` package defines an interface `Queue<E>`; `LinkedList<E>` implements that interface. We will only use four methods from `Queue<E>`: `isEmpty`, `peek`, `add`, and `remove`. In this implementation, `peek`, `add`, and `remove` run in $O(1)$ time. As we know, `LinkedList` is implemented as a doubly-linked list. In Section 20.5 we saw that it is easy to implement a queue using a singly-linked list with a tail, and its methods will have the same $O(1)$ efficiency.

Another possible implementation uses a *ring buffer*, which is simply an array used in a circular manner. If we used an array in a regular linear manner, we would have to shift the whole array toward the front of the queue whenever we removed the first value. In a ring buffer we simply adjust a pointer that defines the "logical" first element. The state of the queue is maintained with the help of two indices, `front` and `rear`. `front` points to the first element in the queue, which will be returned by the next call to the `remove` method; `remove` also increments the `front` index. `rear` points to the empty slot following the last stored element. The `add` method stores the next value in the slot pointed to by `rear` and increments the `rear` index. Both `front` and `rear` wrap around the end of the array to the beginning (Figure 21-7). This mechanism helps to maintain a queue without shifting the whole array.

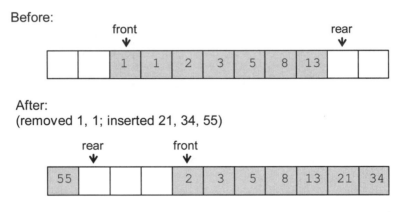

Figure 21-7. Ring-buffer implementation of a queue

21.6 *Case Study and Lab:* Actors World

After a skiing trip, Kitty, Tommy, and Lizzy discovered that they had misplaced some of their gloves. Some of their hats were missing, too. It turned out nothing was lost: they had simply been in a hurry and grabbed some random items that didn't belong to them. Kitty ended up with three right gloves and one hat; Tommy got only one left glove; Lizzy got two left gloves and two hats. (They all wear the same type and size of gloves and hats.) But, thanks to e-mail, they were quickly able to figure out who got what and swap, so that each ended up with a complete set.

In this case study we examine a program that simulates an *event-driven* world of "actors." The concept of *event-driven computations* is one of the two key OOP concepts (the other one is *inheritance*). The von Neumann computer architecture, with one CPU that controls all operations and has exclusive access to memory, imposes a particular view of programming: a program is thought of as a set of instructions to be performed in sequence. Research in artificial intelligence (or AI, a branch of computer science that strives to model intelligent systems and rational behaviors) and in cognitive science has drawn attention to models where many autonomous agents perform meaningful tasks by working together in parallel without rigid centralized control. Such models allow for the kind of parallelism and autonomy that scientists consider more typical of the cognitive activity in the human brain.

In event-driven models, independent agents can communicate with each other by sending signals or messages. Many things can be taking place at the same time without central synchronization of activities that do not have to be synchronized. In theory, this new model requires a new kind of computer. However, although research continues on various types of parallel computers and distributed systems, models based on active objects can run as <u>simulations</u> on conventional computers. One such model was implemented in the Simula programming language, developed in the mid-1960s by Ole-Johan Dhal and Kristen Nygaard at the Norwegian Computing Center (NCC) in Oslo. This model perhaps pioneered the OOP approach. Other well-known and influential models for concurrent OOP computations are known as *Actor* models. They originate from the work of Carl Hewitt at the Massachusetts Institute of Technology's AI Laboratory in the early 1970s.

A more recent metaphor for a distributed system of active agents is the Internet itself. It has millions of independent users exchanging messages and data asynchronously and without any centralized control. Yet things get done. The GIMPS (Great Internet Mersenne Prime Search)✸mersenne project, mentioned in Chapter 8, is one example.

In an actor model, each actor has a set of methods that allow it to recognize and process certain types of messages. An actor responds to a message by sending messages to other actors. Different mechanisms for distributing messages can be included in the model. For example, messages can be directed to one specific actor (somewhat like an e-mail message) or they can be broadcast to many actors at once (like newsgroups or e-mail lists). In the latter case, only those actors that can recognize a message and find it "relevant" respond to it.

When simulated on a conventional computer, the actors need a central mechanism for handling messages, a kind of a "message server." The server places all incoming messages into a queue. The whole program becomes one large loop that checks whether there are any messages waiting in the queue and dispatches them to the appropriate actors. This is quite similar to what happens with events in GUI operating systems, such as *Windows*. In Java, the keyboard, the mouse, and GUI components play the role of "actors," and the `EventQueue` class in the `java.awt` package handles the management of the event queue. It dispatches the events to objects designated as "listeners" (ActionListeners, KeyListeners, MouseListeners, etc.). All this normally happens behind the scenes. In this case study we made the management of the message queue explicit to show you how it might work.

Figure 21-8 shows the classes and objects involved in our *Actors World* program and their public methods. An actor is implemented as an object of the class Actor. Each actor has certain "possessions": a number of items out of a small list of items. In this example we have three actors and three types of items. The main method in the ActorsWorld class initializes the actors:

```
public static void main(String[] args)
{
  < ... window setup >

  String[] kittysPossessions = {"right glove", "right glove",
                                            "right glove", "hat"};
  String[] tommysPossessions = {"left glove"};
  String[] lizzysPossessions = {"left glove", "left glove",
                                            "hat", "hat"};

  List<Actor> actors = new ArrayList<Actor>();
  actors.add(new Actor("Kitty", Arrays.asList(kittysPossessions)));
  actors.add(new Actor("Tommy", Arrays.asList(tommysPossessions)));
  actors.add(new Actor("Lizzy", Arrays.asList(lizzysPossessions)));
  ...
}
```

Each actor can send or receive messages, either privately to another actor, or to the whole subscriber list. Messages do not have to be synchronized in any way. It is possible to envision a distributed computing environment in which our three actors would be implemented as three programs (or rather, three copies of the same program) running on computers in different cities; the programs would be connected to e-mail so that they could send and receive messages automatically. Each actor has its own "mailbox," which is a queue that holds the messages awaiting processing.

A message is an object of the class Message. It is a data-carrier kind of object with a constructor Message(Actor sender, Actor recipient, String text) and three accessor methods:

```
public Actor getSender()
public Actor getRecipient()
public String getText()
```

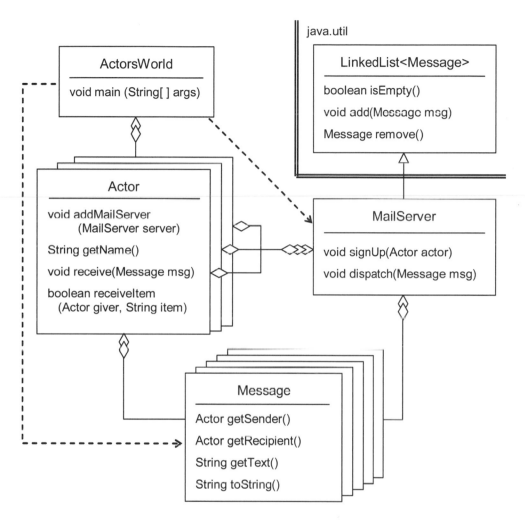

Figure 21-8. Classes, objects, and public methods in the *Actors World* program

If the `recipient` is `null`, the message is intended for the whole set of subscribers. A message also has a `toString` method that converts it into a readable message, such as

```
From: Kitty
To: Tommy
ship left glove
```

The `MailServer` class represents a mechanism for queuing and dispatching messages. A `MailServer` is a queue of messages (`MailServer` implements

`Queue<Message>`), and it has a method to dispatch a message to the appropriate recipient. A `MailServer` also keeps a set of all "registered" subscribers, implemented as a `TreeSet<Actor>`.

After `main` has created the actors and a `MailServer`, it notifies each actor who its `MailServer` is:

```
MailServer email = new MailServer();
for (Actor actor : actors)
  actor.addMailServer(email);
```

This is analogous to adding a listener to an object in Java.

After that, the program goes into an "infinite" loop. On each iteration the program checks whether the `MailServer` has any messages in its queue, retrieves them one by one, displays each message, and dispatches it to its recipient(s) by calling `MailServer`'s `dispatch` method. Then it gives each actor time to "read e-mail":

```
while (true)
{
  while (!email.isEmpty())
  {
    Message msg = email.remove();
    window.display.append(msg + "\n");
    email.dispatch(msg);
  }
  for (Actor actor : actors)
    actor.readMail();
}
```

Luckily Java does the same: it allocates CPU time to GUI components for processing their events, so when the "close window" button is clicked, our "infinite" `while` loop is interrupted and the program quits.

Your task in this project is to write the `MailServer` class and to supply two methods for the `Actor` class.

1. The `MailServer` class

This class should extend `LinkedList<Message>` (and, therefore, implement `Queue<Message>`). Only the `isEmpty`, `add`, and `remove` methods of `LinkedList` will be used.

A `MailServer` should maintain a set of "registered" subscribers (implemented as a `TreeSet<Actor>`).   A   `MailServer`   should   provide   a   method `signUp(Actor actor)`, which adds `actor` to the set of the registered subscribers.

Also provide a method `dispatch(Message msg)`, which either sends `msg` to the recipient indicated in `msg` (by calling the recipient's `receive(msg)`), or, if the recipient is `null`, to all registered subscribers (not including the sender).

2.   The `Actor` class

For this class, you have to fill in the blanks in the `receive` method and the `readMail` method in J_M\Ch21\Actors\Actors.java.

`receive` simply adds `msg` to the actor's mailbox.

The `readMail` method first checks this actor's possessions and sends requests to everyone for each missing item. After that, `readMail` "reads" all messages in this actor's mailbox and sends replies or takes appropriate actions. The proper responses to various messages are documented in `Actors.java` in the comment to the `readMail` method.

When you are done, set up a project with `ActorWorld.java` and `Message.java` (from J_M\Ch21\Actors) and your `MailServer` and `Actors` classes, and test your program to see if every actor has found all its possessions at the end. All three should post a "thanks, all set" message.

21.7 Summary

A *stack* is a data structure used for storing and retrieving data elements in the LIFO (Last-In-First-Out) manner. One possible implementation of a stack uses an array and an integer index, called the stack pointer, which marks the current top of the stack. The stack usually grows toward the end of the array; the stack pointer is incremented when a new value is pushed onto the stack and decremented when a value is popped from the stack.

A stack can also be easily implemented as a singly- or doubly-linked list with $O(1)$ running time for the `peek`, `push`, and `pop` methods. In the Java collections framework, a stack is implemented in the class `java.util.Stack<E>`, where E is the type of objects on the stack.

Stacks are used for temporary storage; they are especially useful when you are working with nested structures or branching processes.

The *queue* data structure is used for storing and retrieving values in the First-In-First-Out (FIFO) manner. A queue can be implemented as a *ring buffer*, which is simply an array used in a circular way. The `front` index marks the beginning of the queue, where the next value will be removed; the `rear` index marks the end of the queue (the first available slot), where the next value will be inserted. Both pointers wrap around the end of the array. Another queue implementation may use a linked list with a tail or a doubly-linked list. In all these implementations, the `peek`, `add`, and `remove` methods run in $O(1)$ time. In the Java collections framework, a queue is implemented as `LinkedList<E>`.

Queues are used for processing events that have to be handled in the order of their arrival but may have to wait for available resources or an appropriate time. Queues are widely used for system tasks such as scheduling jobs, processing events, passing data between processes, and input/output buffering for peripheral devices.

Exercises

Sections 21.1-21.4

1. Mark true or false and explain:

   (a) A stack is especially useful as temporary storage for events that have to be handled in the order of their arrival. _____ ✓

   (b) The *Queue* data structure is a special case of the *Stack* data structure. _____

   (c) A stack can be implemented efficiently (with constant time for `push` and `pop`) using either an array or a singly-linked list. _____

2. Write and test a class `IntStack` that implements a stack of integers with methods similar to the ones in the `Stack` class, but handling values of the type `int` rather than `Object`. Provide a no-args constructor that allocates an array of some default capacity to hold the values and another constructor that allocates an array of a specified capacity. Use a "stack pointer" to hold the index of the first empty slot. Reallocate the array, doubling its size, if the stack runs out of space.

3. Suppose a stack is implemented as a linked list. The nodes are represented by ListNode objects, and the field top refers to the top node:

```
public class ListNodeStack
{
  private ListNode top;
  ...
}
```

Given the code for the push method —

```
public void push(Object value)
{
  top = new ListNode(value, top);
}
```

— supply the code for the isEmpty, peek, and pop methods. (The peek and pop methods should throw a NoSuchElementException if the stack is empty.)

4.■ The following method takes a number represented as a string of binary digits and returns the number as an int:

```
public static int binToInt(String binNum)
{
  Stack<Character> stack = new Stack<Character>();

  for (int i = 0; i < binNum.length(); i++)
    stack.push(binNum.charAt(i));

  int result = 0, power2 = 1;

  while (!stack.isEmpty())
  {
    char ch = stack.pop();
    int dig = Character.digit(ch, 2);
    result += dig * power2;
    power2 *= 2;
  }

  return result;
}
```

Explain why the use of a stack here is overkill. Rewrite without the stack. ✓

5.   A stack of characters can be implemented using a `String`.

(a)   Does the following code correctly implement the `push` and `pop` methods?

```
private String stack = "";
              // Declare an empty stack of chars;
...
public void push(char ch)
{
  stack += ch;
}

public char pop()
{
  int n = stack.length() - 1;
  if (n >= 0)
  {
    char ch = stack.charAt(n);
    stack = stack.substring(0, n);
    return ch;
  }
  else
    throw new NoSuchElementException();
}
```

(b)   Discuss the merits of the above implementation of a stack. ✓

(c)   Rewrite the `push` and `pop` methods so that `pop` returns the first character in the string.

(d)▪   Rewrite the above code using a `StringBuffer` object and its `append` and `deleteCharAt` methods.

6.   A deck of cards is represented in a program as a stack of `Card` objects. Write a method

```
public boolean moveToTop(Stack<Card> deck, int n)
```

that takes the *n*-th card in the deck (counting the top card as the first one) and moves it to the top of the deck. The method returns `true` if the deck has *n* or more cards; otherwise it leaves the deck unchanged and returns `false`. Your method may use a temporary stack, but no other arrays or lists. ✓

7.   A class `RingBuffer` implements a queue of `char`s. It has a constructor that allocates a character array of a given size and initializes it to an empty state:

```
public RingBuffer(int capacity)
{
  items = new char[capacity + 1];
  front = 0;
  rear = 0;
  last = capacity;
}
```

(a)   Write a `void` method `flush()` that empties the queue.

(b)   Write a `boolean` method `isEmpty()`.

(c)▪   Write a `boolean` method `add(char ch)`. The method should return `true` if the operation is successful and `false` if the queue is full.

8.   Suppose a class `ListNodeQueue` implements a queue using a linked list of `ListNode` objects with references `front` and `rear` to the first and last nodes, respectively. Given the code for the `remove` method —

```
public Object remove()
{
  if (front != null)
  {
    Object obj = front.getValue();
    front = front.getNext();
    if (front == null)
      rear = null;
    return obj;
  }
  else
    throw new NoSuchElementException();
}
```

— supply the code for the `isEmpty`, `peek`, and `add` methods.

9.▪   The IBM PC BIOS (Basic IO System) uses a keyboard ring buffer of 16 bytes, starting at the address 40:1E. The two-byte locations 40:1A and 40:1C represent the front and the rear of the keyboard queue, respectively. These locations hold offsets from 40:00, stored with the least significant byte first. Each pressed keyboard key adds two bytes to the keyboard buffer: the ASCII code of the character followed by the so-called "scan code" that represents the location of the key on the keyboard. Examine the following hex memory dump and determine the current contents of the keyboard queue and the last eight characters typed. ✓

```
          _0 _1 _2 _3 _4 _5 _6 _7 _8 _9 _A _B _C _D _E _F
0040:0010                                  28 00 28 00 30 0B
0040:0020 3A 27 31 02 61 1E 0D 1C-64 20 20 39 34 05
```

10.   (MC) How are "actor" models usually implemented? ✓

A.   On parallel data flow computers
B.   Using neural networks hardware
C.   Through simulation on conventional von Neumann computers
D.   On the Internet

11.   If we add a call

```
Collections.shuffle(actors);  // shuffle the actors list
```

before

```
for (Actor actor : actors)
  actor.readMail();
```

in ActorsWorld's main method, will Kitty, Tommy, and Lizzy still be able to recover their possessions? Test this hypothesis.

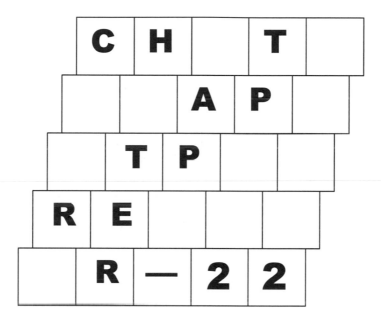

Recursion Revisited

22.1 Prologue

In this chapter we continue the discussion of recursion started in Chapter 4. Recursion is a powerful tool for handling branching processes and nested structures. Take a Java list, for example. It can contain any type of objects as values, including other lists. In an extreme case, a list even can be its own element! Java's documentation says: "While it is permissible for lists to contain themselves as elements, extreme caution is advised..." It is no coincidence that recursive structures and processes are especially common in the computer world. It is easier to implement and use a structure or a process when its substructures and subprocesses have the same form. The same function, for example, can deal with a picture and its graphics elements that are also pictures, or a list and its elements that are also lists. In Chapter 23 we will see how recursion can be used for handling binary trees, where each node is a root of a binary (sub)tree.

Recursion is not specific to Java: it works the same way with any language that allows functions to call themselves. In Java a method can call itself, or there can be a circular sequence of method calls. We saw in Section 21.4 that the hardware stack mechanism implements a method call in the same way whether the method calls itself or another method. All method parameters, the return address, and the local variables are kept in a separate frame on the system stack, so several methods, including several copies of the same method, can be waiting for control to be returned to them without any conflict. Multiple copies of the same method all share the same code but operate on different data.

In this chapter we will consider a few examples of recursion, discuss when the use of recursion is appropriate and when it is better to stay away from it, and learn how to debug and prove the correctness of recursive methods.

22.2 Three Examples

In Chapter 4, we discussed several recursive methods. Figure 4.9 on page 87, for example, shows a recursive implementation of a `gcf` method that finds the greatest common factor of two positive integers. In that example, however, a simple non-recursive implementation exists as well. In our first example here, we take a situation where a recursive implementation is short, while a non-recursive implementation is not at all obvious.

Suppose we want to write a method that evaluates the "degree of separation" between two people in a given set of people. The degree of separation between *A* and *B* is defined as the number of links in the smallest chain of people connecting *A* and *B*, in which neighbors know each other. If *A* knows *B*, the degree of separation between *A* and *B* is 1; if *A* knows *B* and *B* knows *C*, but *A* does not know *C*, the degree of separation between *A* and *C* is 2; and so on. Suppose a person is represented by an object of a class `Person`, which has a `boolean` method `knows`, so `Person p1` "knows" `Person p2` if and only if `p1.knows(p2)` returns `true`. We want to write the following method:

```
// Returns true if and only if the degree of separation between
// p1 and p2 in the set people is less than or equal to n
public boolean degreeOfSeparation(Set<Person> people,
                          Person p1, Person p2, int n)
```

If *n* = 1, we only need to check whether p1 and p2 "know" each other. If *n* > 1 we can try to find a `Person` in the set that can serve as an intermediate link in a chain that connects p1 and p2. It would be rather hard to implement this algorithm without recursion. But with recursion it is straightforward:

```
public boolean degreeOfSeparation(Set<Person> people,
                          Person p1, Person p2, int n)
{
  if (n == 1)                 // Base case
  {
    return p1.knows(p2);
  }
  else                        // Recursive case
  {
    for (Person p : people)
    {
      if (p1.knows(p) && degreeOfSeparation(people, p, p2, n-1))
        return true;
    }
    return false;
  }
}
```

As you know, a recursive method must have a base case (or several base cases), when no further recursion is necessary, and a recursive case (or several), where the same method is called recursively. For a recursive method to terminate properly, it must explicitly or implicitly handle the base case(s). When a method calls itself recursively, it must be applied to a similar but "smaller" task that eventually converges to one of the base cases; otherwise, the recursive calls will go deeper and deeper and eventually "blow the stack."

In our `degreeOfSeparation` method, the parameter *n* determines the "size" of the task. *n* == 1 is the base case. Since that parameter in the recursive call to `degreeOfSeparation` is reduced to `n-1`, the recursive calls eventually converge to the base case and recursion stops.

The above code is deceptively short, but it may become prohibitively time-consuming. For example, if the set is split into two groups of equal sizes such that everyone knows everyone else in each group but no one from the other group, and `p1` and `p2` belong to different groups, then the total number of calls to the `knows` method will be $\dfrac{3N^n - N^{n-1} - 2N}{N-1}$, where *N* is the number of people in each group. This is exponential growth, in terms of *n*. Also, each step deeper into recursion requires a separate frame on the system stack, so this method takes $O(n)$ space on the system stack.

There are actually more efficient algorithms for this task. Even a simple divide and conquer trick —

```
public boolean degreeOfSeparation(Set<Person> people,
                         Person p1, Person p2, int n)
{
  if (n == 1)                 // Base case
  {
    return p1.knows(p2);
  }
  else if (n == 2)            // Another base case
  {
    for (Person p : people)
    {
      if (p1.knows(p) && p.knows(p2))
        return true;
    }
    return false;
  }
  else                        // Recursive case
  {
    int m = n/2;
    for (Person p : people)
    {
      if (degreeOfSeparation(people, p1, p, m) &&
                degreeOfSeparation(people, p, p2, n-m))
        return true;
    }
    return false;
  }
}
```

— improves things. In this version `knows` will be called $\dfrac{n\left(3N^{k+1} - 2N^k - N\right)}{2\left(N-1\right)}$ times,

where $n = 2^k \Rightarrow k = \log_2 n$, which is better than exponential growth in terms of n, and the amount of stack space needed is only $O(\log n)$. There is a much more efficient solution that takes time proportional to N^2, regardless of n (see Question 5 in the end-of chapter exercises).

❖   ❖   ❖

In our second example, let us consider a method that implements "deep" traversal of a linked list that may contain strings and similar lists as elements. In effect, it is no longer a simple list, but a whole tree. For now, let's call such a list a "composite list" (Figure 22-1).

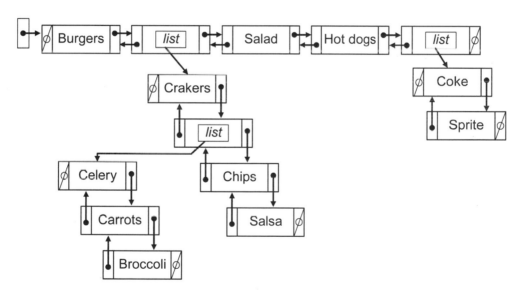

Figure 22-1. A "composite list": some nodes hold strings, others hold lists

A more formal definition of a "composite list" is recursive: a "composite list" is a list where each element is either a string or a "composite list..." Suppose our task is to print all the strings in the list, including all the strings in all the lists that are its elements, and in all the lists that are elements of elements, and so on. Without recursion, this would be a little tricky. With recursion, it's just a few lines of code:

```java
public void printAll(CompositeList list)
{
  String separator = "[";
  for (Object obj : list)
  {
    System.out.print(separator);
    if (obj instanceof String)
      System.out.print(obj);
    else  // if (obj instanceof CompositeList)
      printAll((CompositeList)obj);
    separator = ", ";
  }
  System.out.print("]");
}
```

Here the base case is when `list` contains only `String`s and no lists.

Given

```java
CompositeList veggies = new CompositeList();
veggies.add ("Celery");
veggies.add ("Carrots");
veggies.add ("Broccoli");
CompositeList munchies = new CompositeList();
munchies.add ("Crackers");
munchies.add (veggies);
munchies.add ("Chips");
munchies.add ("Salsa");
CompositeList drinks = new CompositeList();
drinks.add ("Coke");
drinks.add ("Sprite");
CompositeList partyFood = new CompositeList();
partyFood.add("Burgers");
partyFood.add(munchies);
partyFood.add("Salad");
partyFood.add("Hot dogs");
partyFood.add(drinks);

printAll(partyFood);
```

the output is

```
[Burgers, [Crackers, [Celery, Carrots, Broccoli], Chips, Salsa], Salad, Hot
dogs, [Coke, Sprite]]
```

— a recursive method generates the output with nested lists.

Actually, it would be more conventional to define a `toString` method in the `CompositeList` class itself, so that we could write

```
System.out.println(list);
```

rather than

```
printAll(list);
```

Here is how such method might look, assuming that `CompositeList` extends `ArrayList<Object>` or `LinkedList<Object>`:

```
public String toString()
{
  String s = "", separator = "[";
  for (Object obj : this)
  {
    s += separator;
    if (obj instanceof String)
      s += obj.toString();
    else  // if (obj instanceof CompositeList)
      s += ((CompositeList)obj).toString();
    separator = ", ";
  }
  s += "]";
  return s;
}
```

Now note that all this "`instanceof`" type checking is totally redundant: polymorphism takes care of it. We can just write:

```
public String toString()
{
  String s = "", separator = "[";
  for (Object obj : this)
  {
    s += separator;
    s += obj;
    separator = ", ";
  }
  s += "]";
  return s;
}
```

And this is roughly how `toString` is defined in `ArrayList` and `LinkedList`.

Now the recursion is hidden, but it kicks in when one of the elements of a list happens to be a list. It turns out an `ArrayList<Object>` or a

LinkedList<Object> can handle a composite list without any extra code. Later, in Chapter 26, we will see how we can use the Composite design pattern to properly define a more specific data type for the elements of a composite list.

It is possible, of course, to write the above toString method with no recursion, using a stack of iterators instead:

```java
public String toString()
{
  String s = "", separator = "[";

  Stack<Iterator<Object>> stk = new Stack<Iterator<Object>>();

  Iterator<Object> iter = iterator();
  while (iter.hasNext() || !stk.isEmpty())
  {
    if (iter.hasNext())
    {
      s += separator;
      Object obj = iter.next();
      if (obj instanceof String)
      {
        s += obj;
        separator = ", ";
      }
      else
      {
        CompositeList sublist = ((CompositeList)obj);
        stk.push(iter);
        iter = sublist.iterator();
        separator = "[";
      }
    }
    else
    {
      s += "]";
      iter = stk.pop();
    }
  }
  s += "]";
  return s;
}
```

This code will produce the same result. But it is much longer, harder to understand, more error prone, and does not take advantage of polymorphism.

Do not avoid using recursion where it simplifies code without significant loss of efficiency.

In our third example, we will generate all possible permutations of a string of characters. Suppose we are building a computer word game that tries to make a valid word out of a given set of letters. The program will require a method that generates all permutations of the letters and matches them against a dictionary of words. Suppose a string of n characters is stored in a `StringBuffer`. (We use the `StringBuffer` class rather than `String` to make rearranging characters more efficient — `Strings` are immutable objects.) Our strategy for generating all permutations is to place each character in turn in the last place in the string, then generate all permutations of the first $(n-1)$ characters. In other words, `permutations` is a recursive method. The method takes two arguments: a `StringBuffer` object and the number n of characters in the leading fragment that have to be permuted.

In this example, the process is branching and recursive in nature although there are no nested structures. The base case is when n is equal to 1 — there is nothing to do except to report the permutation.

The `permutations` method below is quite short and readable; still, it is hard to grasp why it works! We will return to it in Section 22.4, which explains the best way of understanding and debugging recursive methods.

```java
private void swap(StringBuffer str, int i, int j)
{
  char c1 = str.charAt(i);
  char c2 = str.charAt(j);
  str.setCharAt(i, c2);
  str.setCharAt(j, c1);
}

public void permutations(StringBuffer str, int n)
{
  if (n <= 1)                    // Base case
  {
    System.out.println(str);   // The permutation is completed
  }
  else                           // Recursive case
  {
    for (int i = 0; i < n; i++)
    {
      swap(str, i, n-1);
      permutations(str, n-1);
      swap(str, n-1, i);
    }
  }
}
```

22.3 When Not to Use Recursion

Any recursive method can be also implemented through iterations, using a stack if necessary. This raises a question: When is recursion appropriate, and when is it better avoided?

The most important rule is that recursion should be used only when it significantly simplifies the code without excessive performance loss. Recursion is especially useful for dealing with <u>nested</u> structures or <u>branching</u> processes. One typical example is algorithms for traversing tree structures, which are described in Chapter 23. On the other hand, when you are dealing with <u>linear</u> structures and processes, normally you can use simple iterations. The following test will help you decide when to use recursion and when iterations. If the method branches in two or more directions, calling itself recursively in each branch, it is justified to use recursion. If the method calls itself only once, you can probably do the same thing just as easily with iterations.

There are also some technical considerations that may restrict the use of recursive methods:

1. If a method allocates large local arrays, the program may run out of memory in recursive calls. A programmer has to have a feel for how deeply the recursive calls go; he may choose to implement his own stack and save only the relevant variables there, reusing the same temporary array.

2. When a method manipulates an object's fields, a recursive call may change their values in an unpredictable way unless the manipulation is done on purpose and thoroughly understood.

3. If efficiency is important, a method implemented without recursion may work faster.

As an example, let us consider the `factorial(n)` method that calculates the product of all numbers from 1 to *n*. This method has a simple recursive form:

```
// Precondition: n >= 0
public long factorial(int n)
{
  if (n <= 1)      // Base case
    return 1;
  else             // Recursive case
    return n * factorial(n - 1);
}
```

Our test shows that `factorial`'s code has only one recursive call. We are dealing with a linear process. It should be just as easy to accomplish the same thing with iterations, thus avoiding the overhead of recursive method calls:

```
public long factorial(int n)
{
    long product = 1;
    for (int k = 2; k <= n; k++)
    {
        product *= k;
    }
    return product;
}
```

Both versions are acceptable. The recursive version takes $O(n)$ amount of space on the system stack, but the factorial of large n is far too large, anyway.

A more pernicious example is offered by the famous Fibonacci Numbers. These are defined as a sequence where the first two numbers are equal to one, with each consecutive number equal to the sum of the two preceding numbers:

> 1, 1, 2, 3, 5, 8, 13, ...

Mathematically this is a recursive definition:

$F_1 = 1$; $F_2 = 1$;
$F_n = F_{n-1} + F_{n-2}$, if $n > 2$.

It can be easily converted into a recursive method:

```
// Computes and returns the n-th Fibonacci number.
// Precondition: n >= 1
public long fibonacci(int n)
{
    if (n == 1 || n == 2)    // Base case
        return 1;
    else                     // Recursive case
        return fibonacci(n-1) + fibonacci(n-2);
}
```

It may seem, at first, that this method meets our test of having more than one recursive call to `fibonacci`. But in fact, there is no branching here: `fibonacci` simply recalls two previous members in the same linear sequence. Don't be misled by the innocent look of this code. The first term, `fibonacci(n-1)`, will recursively call `fibonacci(n-2)` and `fibonacci(n-3)`. The second term, `fibonacci(n-2)`, will call (again) `fibonacci(n-3)` and `fibonacci(n-4)`. The fibonacci calls will start multiplying like rabbits.[*] To calculate the n-th Fibonacci number, F_n, fibonacci will actually make more than F_n recursive calls, which, as we will see in the following section, may be quite a large number.

On the other hand, the same method implemented iteratively will need only n iterations:

```java
public long fibonacci(int n)
{
  long f1 = 1, f2 = 1;
  while (n > 2)
  {
    long next = f1 + f2;
    f1 = f2;
    f2 = next;
    n--;
  }
  return f2;
}
```

For our final example of when recursion is inappropriate, let us consider Selection Sort of an array of n elements. As you know, the idea is to find the largest element and swap it with the last element, then apply the same method to the array of the first $n-1$ elements. This can be done recursively:

```java
public void selectionSort(int[] a, int n)
{
  if (n == 1)      // Base case: array of length 1 -- nothing to do
    return;
  else
  {
    // Find the index of the largest element:
    int iMax = 0;
    for (int i = 1; i < n; i++)
      if (a[iMax] < a[i])
        iMax = i;

    // Swap it with the last element:
    int aTemp = a[n-1]; a[n-1] = a[iMax]; a[iMax] = aTemp;

    // Call selectionSort for the first n-1 elements:
    selectionSort(a, n-1);
  }
}
```

---

[*] The numbers are named after Leonardo Pisano (Fibonacci) who invented the sequence in 1202, as part of an effort to develop a model for the growth of a population of rabbits.

This is a case of so-called *tail recursion*, where the recursive call is the last statement in the method: only the return from the method is executed after that call. Therefore, by the time of the recursive call, the local variables (except the parameters passed to the recursive call) are no longer needed. A good optimizing compiler will detect this situation and, instead of calling selectionSort recursively, will update the parameter n and pass control back to the beginning of the method. Or, we can easily do it ourselves:

```
public void selectionSort(int a[], int n)
{
  while (n > 1)
  {
    // Find the index of the largest element:
    int iMax = 0;
    for (int i = 1; i < n; i++)
      if (a[iMax] < a[i])
        iMax = i;

    // Swap it with the last element:
    int aTemp = a[n-1]; a[n-1] = a[iMax]; a[iMax] = aTemp;

    n--;
  }
}
```

To quote Niklaus Wirth, the inventor of the Pascal programming language,

> In fact, the explanation of the concept of recursive algorithm by such inappropriate examples has been a chief cause of creating widespread apprehension and antipathy toward the use of recursion in programming, and of equating recursion with inefficiency.[*]

22.4 Understanding and Debugging Recursive Methods

A common way of understanding and debugging non-recursive methods is to trace, either mentally or with a debugger, the sequence of statements and method calls in the code. Programmers may also insert some debugging print statements that will report to them the method's progress and the intermediate values of variables.

These conventional methods are very hard to apply to recursive methods, because it is difficult to keep track of your current location in the hierarchy of recursive calls. Getting to the bottom of the recursive process requires a detailed examination of the system stack — a tedious and useless activity. Instead of such futile attempts,

---

[*] Niklaus Wirth, *Algorithms + Data Structures = Programs*. Prentice Hall, 1976.

recursive methods can be more easily understood and analyzed with the help of a method known as *mathematical induction*.

In a nutshell, mathematical induction works as follows. Suppose we have a sequence of propositions (that is, statements that can be either true or false):

$$P_1, P_2, \dots, P_n, \dots$$

Suppose we can prove:

Base case: P_1 is true; and
Inductive step: for any $n \geq 2$, <u>if</u> P_1, ..., P_{n-1} are true (*induction hypothesis*), <u>then</u> P_n is also true.

Then we can conclude that P_n is true for any $n \geq 1$.

This is so because P_1 implies P_2, P_1 and P_2 imply P_3, and so on. However, we do not have to go through the entire logical sequence for every step. Instead, we can take a shortcut and just say that all propositions P_1, P_2, ... , P_n, ... are true by mathematical induction.

As an exercise in mathematical induction, let us estimate the running time for the recursive `fibonacci` method discussed in the previous section:

```
public long fibonacci(int n)
{
  if (n == 1 || n == 2)   // Base case
    return 1;
  else                    // Recursive case
    return fibonacci(n-1) + fibonacci(n-2);
}
```

We will prove that `fibonacci(n)` executes not less than $(3/2)^{n-2}$ total calls to the `fibonacci` method.

Base cases: This is true for $n = 1$ and $n = 2$, because both require just one call:

$$n = 1: \quad 1 \geq (3/2)^{1-2} = (3/2)^{-1} = 2/3$$
$$n = 2: \quad 1 \geq (3/2)^{2-2} = (3/2)^{0} = 1$$

Inductive step: For any $n > 2$, in addition to the initial call, the method calls `fibonacci(n-1)` and `fibonacci(n-2)`. <u>From the induction hypothesis,</u> the number of times `fibonacci` is called in `fibonacci(n-1)` is not less than $(3/2)^{n-3}$, and the number of times `fibonacci` is called in `fibonacci(n-2)` is not less than $(3/2)^{n-4}$. So the total number of `fibonacci` calls in `fibonacci(n)` is not less than:

$$1 + (3/2)^{n-3} + (3/2)^{n-4} > (3/2)^{n-3} + (3/2)^{n-4} = (3/2)^{n-4}(3/2 + 1) =$$
$$(3/2)^{n-4} \cdot (5/2) > (3/2)^{n-4} \cdot (9/4) = (3/2)^{n-4} \cdot (3/2)^2 = (3/2)^{n-2}$$

By mathematical induction, the number of calls to `fibonacci` in `fibonacci(n)` is not less than $(3/2)^{n-2}$, for any $n \geq 1$. QED.

Assuming that a reasonably fast computer can execute a hundred million calls per second (and that we somehow manage to represent very large Fibonacci numbers in memory), `fibonacci(100)` would run for over $(3/2)^{98} / 10^8$ seconds, or more than 57 years! The iterative implementation, by contrast, would run in a small fraction of a second.

You may notice a close conceptual link between recursion and mathematical induction. The key feature of mathematical induction is that we do not have to trace the sequence of statements to the bottom. We just have to first prove the base case and then, for an arbitrary n, show that <u>if</u> the induction hypothesis is true at all previous levels, <u>then</u> it is also true at the n-th level.

Let us see how mathematical induction applies to the analysis of code in recursive methods. As an example, let's take the `permutations` method from Section 22.2, which generates all permutations of a string of characters:

```java
public void permutations(StringBuffer str, int n)
{
  if (n <= 1)        // base case
  {
    System.out.println(str);    // the permutation is completed
  }
  else               // recursive case
  {
    for (int i = 0; i < n; i++)
    {
      swap(str, i, n-1);
      permutations(str, n-1);
      swap(str, n-1, i);
    }
  }
}
```

We will prove two facts about this code using mathematical induction:

1. `permutations` returns the string to its original order when it is finished.

2. `permutations(str, n)` generates all permutations of the first *n* characters.

In the base case, $n = 1$, the method just reports the string and does nothing else — so both statements are true. For the inductive step, let us <u>assume</u> that both statements are true for any level below *n* (induction hypothesis). <u>Based on that assumption</u> let us prove that both statements are also true at the level *n*.

In the recursive case, the method swaps `str[i]` and `str[n-1]`, then calls `permutations(str, n-1)`, then swaps back `str[n-1]` and `str[i]`. <u>By the induction hypothesis,</u> `permutations(str, n-1)` preserves the order of characters in `str`. The two swaps cancel each other. So the order of characters is not changed in `permutations(str, n)`. This proves Statement 1.

In the `for` loop we place every character of the string, in turn, at the end of the string. (This is true because the index `i` runs through all values from `0` to `n-1` and, as we have just shown, the order of characters does not change after each iteration through the loop.) With each character placed at the end of the string we call `permutations(str, n-1)`, which, <u>by the induction hypothesis,</u> generates all permutations of the first *n*-1 characters. Therefore, we combine each character placed at the end of the string with all permutations of the first *n*-1 characters, which generates all permutations of *n* characters. This proves Statement 2.

The above example demonstrates how mathematical induction helps us understand and, with almost mathematical rigor, prove the correctness of recursive methods. By comparison, conventional code tracing and debugging and attempts at unfolding recursive calls to the very bottom are seldom feasible or useful.

22.5   *Lab:* The Tower of Hanoi

The Tower of Hanoi puzzle is probably the most famous example of recursion in computer science courses. The puzzle has three pegs, with several disks on the first peg. The disks are arranged in order of decreasing diameter from the largest disk at the bottom to the smallest disk on top. The rules require that the disks be moved from peg to peg, one at a time, and that a larger disk never be placed on top of a smaller one. The objective is to move the whole tower from the first peg to the second peg.

The puzzle was invented by French mathematician François Edouard Anatole Lucas[lucas] and published in 1883. The "legend" that accompanied the game stated that in Benares, India, there was a temple with a dome that marked the center of the world. The Hindu priests in the temple moved golden disks between three diamond needles. God placed 64 gold disks on one needle at the time of creation and, according to the legend, the universe will come to an end when the priests have moved all 64 disks to another needle.

There are hundreds of Java applets on the Internet that move disks from peg to peg, either with animation or interactively.[hanoi] In this lab, fancy display is not required.

1. Write a program that solves the puzzle and prints out the required moves for a given number of disks.

2. Examine the number of moves required for 1, 2, 3, etc. disks, find the pattern, and come up with a formula for the minimum number of moves required for *n* disks. Prove the formula using the method of mathematical induction. Estimate how much time it will take your program to move a tower of 64 disks.

22.6 *Case Study and Lab:* the Game of Hex

The game of Hex was first invented in 1942 by Piet Hein, a Danish mathematician. (The same game was apparently reinvented independently a few years later by John Nash, then a graduate student at Princeton, who later won a Nobel prize in economics.) Martin Gardner made the game popular when he described it in his *Scientific American* article in the late 1950s and in a later book.

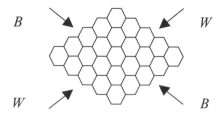

Figure 22-2. A 5 by 5 Hex board

Hex is played on a rhombic board with hexagonal fields, like a honeycomb. A common board size is 11 by 11; Figure 22-2 shows a smaller 5 by 5 board. The game starts with an empty board. Each of the two players, *B* and *W*, is assigned a pair of opposite sides of the board. For example, *B* gets northwest and southeast, and *W* gets northeast and southwest. *B* has a pile of black stones and *W* has a pile of white stones. Players take turns placing a stone of their color on an empty field. A player who first connects his sides of the board with a contiguous chain of his stones wins.

An interesting property of Hex is that a game can never end in a tie: when the board is filled, either *B* has his sides connected or *W* has his sides connected, always one or the other, but never both. Like all finite strategy games with no repeating positions, Hex has a winning strategy for one of the players. In this case it's the first player (it never hurts to have an extra stone of your color on the board). But this winning strategy is hard to find, because the number of all possible positions is large. For a smaller board, a computer can calculate it. It is not too difficult to write such a program, relying on a recursive algorithm. However (unless you have a lot of free time) in this lab our task is more modest: only to decide whether a given Hex position is a win for one of the players.

A human observer can glance at a Hex board and immediately tell whether one of the players has won. Not so in a computer program: it takes some computations to find out whether there is a chain of stones of a particular color connecting two opposite sides of the board. Our task is to develop an algorithm and write a method that does this.

But first we have to somehow represent a Hex board position in the computer. It is not very convenient to deal with rhombuses and hexagons in a program. Fortunately, an equivalent board configuration can be achieved on a regular square board, represented by a 2-D array. Each inner field on a Hex board has six neighbors; border fields have four, and corner fields have two or three. We can emulate the same configuration on a square board using the appropriate designation of "logical" neighbors. Figure 22-3 shows which squares are supposed to be "neighbors": the rows of a 2-D array are slightly shifted so that "neighbors" share a piece of border. Basically, a square at (*row*, *col*) has neighbors at (*row*-1, *col*-1), (*row*-1, *col*), (*row*, *col*-1), (*row*, *col*+1), (*row*+1, *col*), and (*row*+1, *col*+1), excluding those positions that fall outside the array.

Write a class `HexBoard` that represents a board position. You can represent stones of different colors using `chars`, `ints`, `Strings`, or `Colors`. If you use `chars` (for example, `'b'` for black, `'w'` for white, and space for an empty square), then you can conveniently derive your `HexBoard` class from the `CharMatrix` class that you wrote for the *Chomp* project in Chapter 12. To hide the implementation details, your `HexBoard` class should provide the modifiers `setBlack(row, col)` and `setWhite(row, col)` and the boolean accessors `isBlack(row, col)` and `isWhite(row, col)`. Also provide a `toString` method, which will allow us to print the board, each row on a separate line. It is convenient to use a private boolean method `isInBounds(row, col)` to determine whether (*row, col*) refers to a legal square on the board.

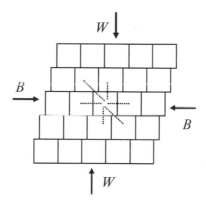

Figure 22-3. A Hex board represented as a 2-D array

It is probably easier to write a separate method that detects a win for each of the players. You need to implement only one of them. For example:

```
/**
 *   Returns true if there is a contiguous chain of black stones
 *   that starts in col 0 and ends in the last column of the board;
 *   otherwise returns false.
 */
public boolean blackHasWon()
```

At first, the task may appear trivial: just try starting at every black stone in the first column and follow a chain of black stones to the last column. But a closer look at the problem reveals that chains can branch in tricky ways (Figure 22-4), and there is no obvious way to trace all of them. What we really need is to find a "blob" of connected black stones that touches both the left and the right sides of the board.

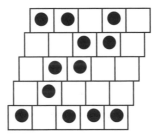

Figure 22-4.   Hex: detecting a win for black stones

The task of finding a connected "blob" is known as an "area fill" task. A very similar situation occurs when you need to flood a connected area in a picture, replacing one color with another, or to fill the area inside a given contour (see Question 14 in the exercises for this chapter). The only difference is that usually a pixel or a cell has four neighbors (or eight, if you count the diagonal neighbors), while in Hex a square on the board has six neighbors.

Since the black and white colors are taken, we will be filling the area in "gray," so add private `setGray(row, col)` and `isGray(row, col)` methods to your `HexBoard` class.

1. Write a method `areaFill(int row, int col)`. This method should check whether the (*row*, *col*) square is in bounds and holds a black stone. If both conditions are true, `areaFill` should color in gray the largest contiguous black area that contains the (*row*, *col*) square. To do that, set the color at (*row*, *col*) to gray, then call `areaFill` recursively for each of its six neighbors. Make the `areaFill` method public, so that you can test it from `main`.

2. In the `blackHasWon` method:

   • call `areaFill` for each square in the first column;

   • count the gray stones in the last column to see if any of the gray blobs touch the last column;

   • Restore all gray stones on the board back to black and return `true` or `false`, appropriately.

You might wonder whether there is a way to look for a win while doing `areaFill` and quit as soon as you reach the rightmost column. This is possible, of course. However, quitting a recursive method for good is not so easy: your original call may be buried under a whole stack of recursive calls and you need to properly quit all of them. Two approaches are possible.

First approach: make `areaFill` return a `boolean` value: `true` if it touched the rightmost column, `false` if it didn't. Then, if one of the recursive calls to `areaFill` returns `true`, skip the rest of the recursive calls and immediately return `true`. Something like this:

```
if (areaFill(row-1, col-1) == true)
  return true;
if (areaFill(row-1, col) == true)
  return true;
  . . .
```

Second approach: define a field in your class (a local variable won't do!) and set it to `true` as soon as `areaFill` touches the rightmost column. Something like:

```
if (col == numCols() - 1)
  won = true;
if (!won)
  areaFill(row-1, col-1);
if (!won)
  areaFill(row-1, col);
  . . .
```

Note how treacherous recursion may be: if you write what seems to be less redundant code —

```
if (col == numCols() - 1)
  won = true;
if (!won)
{
  areaFill(row-1, col-1);
  areaFill(row-1, col);
  . . .
}
. . .
```

— you will lose all the benefits of quitting early and your code will dramatically slow down!

"For extra credit," make `blackHasWon` work using one of the above two variations of a more efficient method that quits as soon as it detects a win. (Note that with this change, the `areaFill` method does not necessarily fill the area completely, so it might be a good idea to rename it into something more appropriate, say `findWin`.)

Test your class using a test program `Hex.java` and a sample data file `hex.dat` provided in $J_M\backslash Ch22\backslash Hex$. You will also need the `CharMatrix` class from $J_M\backslash Ch12\backslash Chomp$, if you used it.

22.7 Summary

Recursion is a programming technique based on methods calling themselves.

Recursive method calls are supported by the system stack, which keeps the method parameters, return address, and local variables in a separate frame for each call.

Recursion is useful for dealing with nested structures or branching processes where it helps to create short, readable, and elegant code that would otherwise be impossible.

Recursion is not essential in situations that deal with linear structures or processes, which can be as easily and more efficiently implemented with iterations.

The best way to understand and analyze recursive methods is by thinking about them along the lines of *mathematical induction*; attempts at unfolding and tracing recursive code "to the bottom" usually fail, except in simple exercises such as Question 1 below.

Exercises

Sections 22.1-22.3

1.   What is the output from the following method when called with $n = 3$? ✓

```
public void printX(int n)
{
  if (n <= 0)
    System.out.print(0);
  else
  {
    printX(n - 1);
    System.out.print(n);
    printX(n - 2);
  }
}
```

2. Consider

```
public void enigma(int n)
{
  for (int i = 0; i < n; i++)
    enigma(i);
  System.out.print(n);
}
```

Does the call `enigma(3)` terminate? If so, what is the output?

3. What is the output from the following method when called with the argument $x = 2009$? ✓

```
public void display(int x)
{
  if (x >= 10)
  {
    display(x/10);
    System.out.print(x % 10);
  }
}
```

4. Fill in the blanks in the following recursive method:

```
// Returns the value of the largest element among
// the first n elements in vector v.
// Precondition: 1 <= n <= v.length
public double max(double[] v, int n)
{
  double m = v[n-1], m2;

  if ( ________________________________ )
  {
    m2 = ________________________________________________ ;

    if (m2 > m)
      m = m2;
  }
  return m;
}
```

5.▪ Rewrite the `degreeOfSeparation` method from Section 22.2 without recursion. ⋚ Hint: start with a set that contains only `p1` and keep expanding it, adding on each iteration all the people who know anyone from that set. Iterate `n` times or until you find `p2` in the set of acquaintances. ⋛.

6.   A positive integer is evenly divisible by 9 if and only if the sum of all its digits is divisible by 9. Suppose you have a method `sumDigits` that returns the sum of the digits of a positive integer *n*. Fill in the blanks in the method `isDivisibleBy9(int n)` that returns `true` if n is divisible by 9 and `false` otherwise. Your method may use the assignment and relational operators and `sumDigits`, but no arithmetic operators (`*, /, %, *=, /=, %=`) are allowed. ✓

```
// Returns n % 9 == 0
// Precondition: n > 0
public boolean isDivisibleBy9(int n)
{
    if (_____)

        return _____ ;

    else if (_____)

        return _____ ;

    else

        return _____ ;
}
```

7.   (a)   The method below attempts to calculate x^n economically:

```
public double pow(double x, int n)
{
    double y;
    if (n == 1)
        y = x;
    else
        y = pow(x, n/2) * pow(x, n - n/2);    // Line 7
    return y;
}
```

How many multiplications will be executed when `pow(1.234, 5)` is called? ✓

(b)   How many multiplications will be executed if we replace Line 7 above with the following statements?

```
{ y = pow(x, n/2); y *= y; if (n % 2 != 0) y *= x; }
```

(c)   How many multiplications will Version (a) above take to calculate `pow(1.234, 9)`? Version (b)?

8.   A linked list has four nodes containing the values 10, 20, 30, and 40 (in that order) and is defined by a reference to its first node, head. The method doTheTrick below returns the head of the changed list. How many nodes will the changed list have and what values will be stored in them?

```
public ListNode doTheTrick(ListNode head)
{
  if (head == null || head.getNext() == null)
    return head;

  ListNode newHead = head.getNext();
  newHead = doTheTrick(newHead);

  head.setNext(newHead.getNext());
  newHead.setNext(head);
  return newHead;
}
```

Sections 22.4-22.7

9.   What is the return value of mysterySum(10), where

```
public int mysterySum(int n)
{
  if (n == 1)
    return 1;
  else
    return mysterySum(n - 1) + 2*n - 1;
}
```

Justify your answer by using mathematical induction. Explain why this is an inappropriate use of recursion. ✓

10.♦   In the degreeOfSeparation example in Section 22.2, prove the formula $\dfrac{3N^n - N^{n-1} - 2N}{N-1}$ for the number of calls to knows in the first version of the method. ⟨ Hint: use mathematical induction for n . ⟩ ✓

11.   Write a recursive method

```
public String removeDuplicateChars(String str)
```

that takes a string and returns a new string with all duplicate consecutive occurrences of the same character removed. For example, removeDuplicateChars("ABBCDDDEEFGG") should return "ABCDEFG". Do not use any iterative statements.

12. Fill in the blanks in the following method:

```
// Returns the number of all possible paths from the
// point(0,0) to the point(x,y), where x and y are
// any non-negative integers.  From any point the path
// may extend only down or to the right by one unit
// (that is, one of the current coordinates x or y can be
// incremented by one).
public long countPaths(int x, int y)
{
  if (x == 0 || y == 0)
    return _____;
  else
    return _____ ;
}
```

13. Rewrite the Cookie Monster program (Question 12 from Chapter 19) using recursion. For recursive handling, it often helps to restate the question in more general terms. Here we need to refer to the optimal path from (0,0) to any position (*row*, *col*). So our `optimalPath` method should now take two parameters: `row` and `col`. Note that since Cookie Monster can only move down and to the right, the maximum number of cookies accumulated at a position (*row*, *col*) is related to the previous positions as follows:

```
optimalPath(row, col) = cookies[row][col] +
    the larger of the two:
    {optimalPath(row-1, col), optimalPath(row, col-1)}
```

The only problem is invalid positions: either out of bounds or "barrels." How can we define `optimalPath` for an invalid position (*row*, *col*), so that the above formula still works? Identify the base case(s) and recursive case(s).

14. A "pool" is an irregularly shaped contiguous blob of cells with `Color.BLACK` values in a 2-D array. (Two cells in a 2-D array are considered neighbors if they share a side.) The pool is completely surrounded by a "white wall," a contour of cells with `Color.WHITE` values. Write a method

```
public void fillPool(Color[][] plane, int row,
                                int col, Color color)
```

that takes a location (`row, col`) inside a pool in `plane` and fills all the cells in that pool with `color`. Write a GUI program with mouse input to test your method.

15.■   On Beavis Island, the alphabet consists of three letters, A, B, and H — but no
word may have two A's in a row. Fill in the blanks in the following
recursive method `allWords`, which prints out all Beavis Island words of a
given length:

```
/**
 *   Prints all Beavis Island words that have
 *   length letters.  word contains the initial
 *   sequence of letters in a word that is being built
 *   (use an empty string buffer of capacity length
 *   when calling allWords from main).
 */
public void allWords(StringBuffer word, int length)
{
  if (length == word.length())  // base case
  {
    // Display the string:
    _____ ;

  }
  else  // recursive case
  {
    int k = word.length();
    word.append('*'); // reserve room for one char

    // Append 'A' only if last letter is not an 'A':
    if (k == 0 || word.charAt(k-1) != 'A')
    {
      word.setCharAt(k, 'A');
      _____ ;
    }
    _____ ; // append 'B'
    _____ ;

    _____ ; // append 'H'
    _____ ;

    _____ ;

  }
}
```

⧼ Hint: you might need `StringBuffer`'s `setLength` method, which
truncates the string in the buffer to a specified length. ⧽

16.◆   Suppose we have a list of positive integers. We want to choose several of
       them so that their sum is as large as possible but does not exceed a given
       limit. This type of problem is called a "Knapsack Problem." For example,
       we may want to choose several watermelons at the market so that their total
       weight is as large as possible but does not exceed the airline limit for one
       bag.

       (a)   Write a recursive method that solves a simplified Knapsack Problem: it
              only calculates the optimal sum but does not report the selected items:

```
/**
 *   w contains n positive integers (n <= w.length).
 *   Returns the sum of some of these integers such that
 *   it has the largest possible value without exceeding
 *   limit.
 */
public int knapsackSum(int[] w, int n, int limit)
```

              Use mathematical induction to prove that your code is correct.

       (b)   Write a more complete version —

```
public int knapsackSum(int[] w, int n, int limit,
                                    List<Integer> list)
```

              — that in addition builds a list of the values selected for the optimal
              sum. list is initially empty when the method is called from main (or
              from another method).

       (c)◆   Can you think of an alternative algorithm that uses neither recursion
              nor a stack?

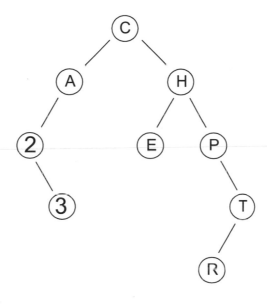

Binary Trees

23.1 Prologue

A *tree* is a branching hierarchical structure in which each element except the top one has a link to exactly one element higher in the hierarchy, called its *parent*. The elements of a tree structure are referred to as *nodes*. The top node in the structure is called the *root* of the tree. Any node in the tree may be connected to one or more nodes lower in the hierarchy, called its *children*. The nodes that have no children are called *leaves* (Figure 23-1). There is exactly one path from the root to any node. The nodes along this path (including the root) are referred to as the node's *ancestors* (that is, its parent, the parent of its parent, etc.). Trees do not have circular paths.

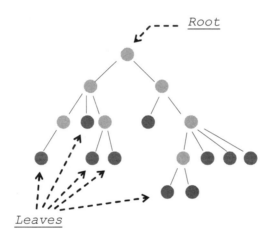

Figure 23-1.   A tree structure

As you can see, computer books normally show trees "growing" down, with the root shown on top. This convention probably reflects the fact that we read from the top of the page down, and we process trees starting from the root. Trees may be used for representing branching systems or processes, such as organizational charts or game strategies (Figure 23-2), decision charts, class hierarchies in Java, and other hierarchies of objects.

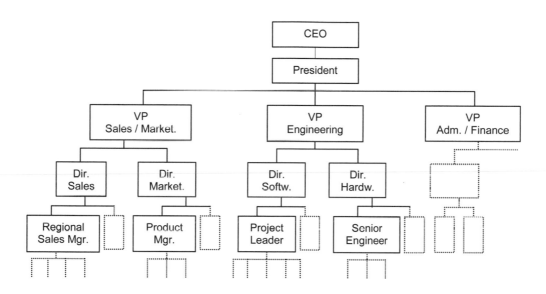

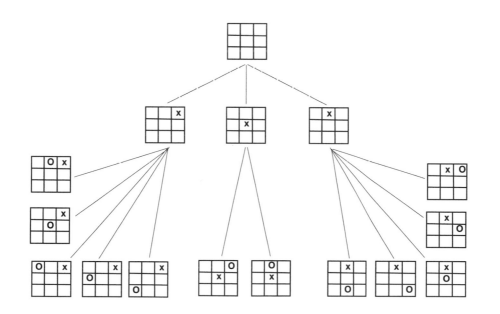

Figure 23-2.   Common uses of tree structures

All the nodes in a tree can be arranged in layers with the root at level 0, its children at level 1, their children at level 2, and so on. The level of a node is equal to the length of the path from the root to that node (Figure 23-3).

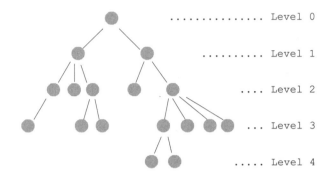

Figure 23-3. Arrangement of tree nodes in levels

One important property of trees is that we can arrange a relatively large number of elements in a relatively *shallow* tree (one with a small number of levels). For example, if each node in a tree (except the bottom level) has two children, a tree with h levels contains $2^h - 1$ nodes (Figure 23-4).

Tree Height	Total Nodes
1	1
2	3
3	7
4	15
...	...
h	$2^h - 1$

Figure 23-4. A shallow tree can hold many nodes

Such a tree with 20 levels contains over one million nodes. This property may be utilized for quick searching and data retrieval, decision trees, and similar applications where, instead of going through a whole list and examining all the elements, we can go down a tree and examine just a few. (In strategy games, this property works against us and becomes a major stumbling block: if we consider all the possible responses to a given move, then all the responses to those responses, etc., the tree of possible game paths grows so fast that it is not feasible to plan ahead beyond a few moves.)

A list can be viewed as a special case of a tree with only one node at each level: the first node is the root, the last node is the only leaf, and all other nodes have exactly one parent and one child. If a tree degenerates into a near-linear shape with only a few nodes at each level (Figure 23-5), its advantages for representing a large number of elements in a shallow structure are lost.

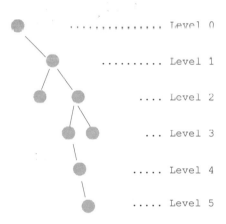

**Figure 23-5.   A tree with a nearly linear shape —
each level holds only a few nodes**

A tree is an inherently recursive structure, because each node in a tree can itself be viewed as the root of a smaller tree (Figure 23-6). In computer applications, trees are normally represented in such a way that each node "knows" where to find all its children. In the linked representation, for example, each node, in addition to some information, holds the list of references to its children. Knowing just the root, we can find all the elements of the tree; and given any node we can find all the nodes in its subtree.

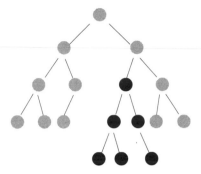

Figure 23-6.   Each node in a tree is the root of its own subtree

The recursive branching structure of trees suggests the use of recursive procedures for dealing with them. The following method, for example, allows us to traverse a tree:

```
public void traverse(TreeNode root)
{
  // Base case: root == null, the tree is empty -- do nothing
  // Recursive case: tree is not empty
  if (root != null)
  {
    visit(root);
    for (... <each child of the root>)
         traverse (<that child's subtree>);
  }
}
```

This method first "visits" the root of the tree, then, for each child of the root, calls itself recursively to traverse that child's tree. The recursion stops when it reaches a leaf: the subtrees rooted in leaf's children are empty. Due to the branching nature of the process, an iterative implementation of this method would require your own stack and would be rather cumbersome. In this example, therefore, the recursive implementation may actually be slightly more efficient in terms of the processing time, and it does not take too much space on the system stack because the depth of recursion is the same as the number of levels in the tree, which is normally a relatively small number. The major advantage of a recursive procedure is that it yields clear and concise code.

A tree in which each node has no more than two children is called a *binary tree*. The children of a node are referred to as the *left child* and the *right child*. In the following sections <u>we will deal exclusively with binary trees</u>. We will see how a binary tree can be used as a *binary search tree*. In Chapter 19, we learned that the `TreeSet` and `TreeMap` classes in the Java collections framework are based on binary search trees. In this chapter we will dig a little deeper and implement our own very simple binary search tree. In Chapter 25, we will look at another application of trees: priority queues and heaps.

23.2 Implementations of Binary Trees

A node of a binary tree can be represented as a class, `TreeNode` (Figure 23-7).

```
public class TreeNode
{
  private Object value;
  private TreeNode left;
  private TreeNode right;

  // Constructors:

  public TreeNode(Object initValue)
  { value = initValue; left = null; right = null; }

  public TreeNode(Object initValue, TreeNode initLeft, TreeNode initRight)
  { value = initValue; left = initLeft; right = initRight; }

  // Methods:

  public Object getValue() { return value; }
  public TreeNode getLeft() { return left; }
  public TreeNode getRight() { return right; }
  public void setValue(Object theNewValue) { value = theNewValue; }
  public void setLeft(TreeNode theNewLeft) { left = theNewLeft; }
  public void setRight(TreeNode theNewRight) { right = theNewRight; }
}
```

Figure 23-7. `TreeNode` represents a node in a binary tree[*]
(J_M\Ch23\TreeNode.java)

---

[*] Adapted from The College Board's *AP Computer Science AB: Implementation Classes and Interfaces*.

TreeNode is similar to ListNode, a node in a linked list, except that instead of one reference to the next element of the list, a TreeNode has two references, to the left and right child of that node. These references are called left and right, and the information held in a node is represented by an object called value. The TreeNode class has two constructors: one sets value to the specified value, and the left and right references to null; the other takes three parameters and sets value, left, and right to their respective values. The TreeNode class also has accessor and modifier methods for each of the three fields.

In a linked list each node refers to the next one — a setup suitable for iterations. If, for instance, you need to count the nodes in the list, a for loop can do the job:

```
public int countNodes(ListNode head)
{
  int count = 0;
  for (ListNode node = head; node != null; node = node.getNext())
    count++;
  return count;
}
```

The same task can be accomplished recursively, although some people may find this unnecessarily fancy:

```
public int countNodes(ListNode head)
{
  if (head == null)  // base case -- the list is empty
    return 0;
  else
    return 1 + countNodes(head.getNext());
}
```

But for binary trees, recursion is a perfect tool. For example:

```
public int countNodes(TreeNode root)
{
  if (root == null)  // base case -- the tree is empty
    return 0;
  else
    return 1 + countNodes(root.getLeft())
                        + countNodes(root.getRight());
}
```

As we will see in Section 23.5, those methods that follow a path in a tree and choose whether to go right or left in each node have simple iterative versions. But recursion is the rule when working with trees. The base case in recursive methods usually handles an empty tree. Sometimes a method may treat separately another base case, when the tree has only one node, the root. Recursive calls are applied to the left and/or right subtrees.

23.3 Traversals

A method that visits all nodes of a tree and processes or displays their values is called a *traversal*. It is possible to traverse a tree iteratively, using a stack, but recursion makes it really easy:

```
private void traversePreorder (TreeNode root)
{
  // Base case: root == null, the tree is empty -- do nothing
  if (root != null)  // Recursive case
  {
    process(root.getValue());
    traversePreorder(root.getLeft());
    traversePreorder(root.getRight());
  }
}
```

The above is called *preorder traversal* because the root is visited <u>before</u> the left and right subtrees. There are other ways to traverse a tree. In *postorder traversal*, the root is visited <u>after</u> the subtrees:

```
private void traversePostorder (TreeNode root)
{
  if (root != null)
  {
    traversePostorder(root.getLeft());
    traversePostorder(root.getRight());
    process(root.getValue());
  }
}
```

Finally, in *inorder traversal*, the root is visited <u>in the middle</u>, between subtrees:

```
private void traverseInorder (TreeNode root)
{
  if (root != null)
  {
    traverseInorder(root.getLeft());
    process(root.getValue());
    traverseInorder(root.getRight());
  }
}
```

If a tree is implemented as a class with the root of the tree hidden in a private field, then the task of visiting nodes becomes restricted to some predefined method or code within the class. If you want to traverse the tree from outside the class, then, just as in the case of linked lists, you need an iterator. It is harder to program an iterator for a tree than for a list: you need to use a stack. Java library classes that implement trees provide iterators for you.

23.4 Binary Search Trees

A *binary search tree* (*BST*) is a structure for holding a set of ordered data values in such a way that we can efficiently find any specified value and insert or delete a node. BSTs overcome some deficiencies of both sorted arrays and linked lists.

Recall that if we have a sorted array of elements, the "divide and conquer" Binary Search algorithm allows us to find any value in the array quickly. We take the middle element of the array, compare it with the target value, and, if they are not equal, continue searching either in the left or the right half of the array, depending on the comparison result. This process takes at most $\log_2 n$ comparisons for an array of *n* elements. However, inserting values into the array or deleting them from the array is not easy — we may need to shift large blocks of data in memory. The linked list structure, on the other hand, allows us to insert and delete nodes easily, but there is no quick search method because there is no way of getting to the middle of the list easily.

> **Binary search trees combine the benefits of sorted arrays for quick searching and the benefits of linked lists for inserting and deleting values.**

As the name implies, a binary search tree is a kind of binary tree: each node has no more than two children. Recall that the subtree that "grows" from the left child is called the *left subtree* and the subtree that "grows" from the right child is called the *right subtree*. The tree's nodes contain some data values for which a relation of order is defined; that is, for any two values we can say whether the first one is greater, equal, or smaller than the second. The values may be numbers, alphabetized strings, some database record index keys, and so on. Sometimes we informally say that one node is greater or smaller than another, actually meaning that that relationship applies to the data values they contain.

What makes this tree a <u>binary search tree</u> is the following special property: for any node, the value in the node is larger than all the values in this node's left subtree and smaller than all the values in this node's right subtree (Figure 23-8).

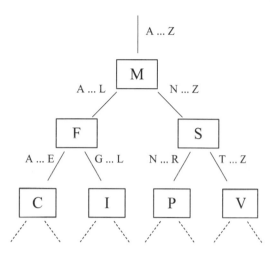

Figure 23-8. The ordering property of a binary search tree

A binary search tree is specifically designed to support a divide and conquer search algorithm. Suppose we need to find a target value. First, we compare the target to the root. If they are equal, the value is found. If the target is smaller, we continue the search in the left subtree. If larger, we search the right subtree. We will find the target value (or conclude that it is not in the tree) after a number of steps that never exceeds the number of levels in the tree. If our tree is rather "bushy," with intermediate levels filled to near capacity with nodes, the number of steps required will be close to $\log_2 n$, where n is the total number of nodes.

In a binary search tree, it is also easy to find the smallest and the largest value. Starting at the root, if we always go left for as long as possible, we come to the node containing the smallest value. Similarly, if we always keep to the right, we come to the node containing the largest value (Figure 23-9). The smallest node, by definition, cannot have a left child, and the largest node cannot have a right child.

For a BST, inorder traversal (left-root-right) visits the nodes of the tree in ascending order of values.

(The proof of this fact is left as one of the exercises at the end of this chapter.)

Traversing a BST in decreasing order of values is also easy (see Question 21 in the exercises for this chapter.)

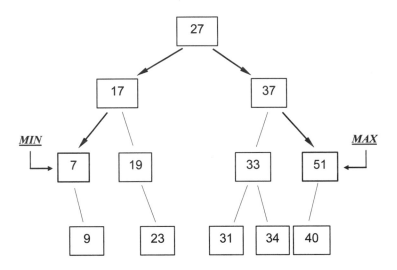

Figure 23-9. Locations of the smallest and largest values in a BST

23.5 A Do-It-Yourself BST

Figure 23-10 shows a fragment from a simple class that implements a BST. The field `root` refers to the root of the tree. The no-args constructor creates an empty tree by setting `root` to `null`. We have provided four public methods: `contains`, `add`, `remove`, and `toString`. This implementation assumes that the nodes of the tree hold `Comparable` objects, but it would be easy to provide another constructor that takes a comparator as a parameter.

Each of our four methods (`contains`, `add`, `remove`, and `toString`) uses a respective private recursive helper method, which takes an additional parameter: the root node of a subtree for which the method is called (Figure 23-11).

```java
// Implements a BST with TreeNode nodes.
public class MyTreeSet
{
  private TreeNode root;   // holds the root of this BST

  // Constructor: creates an empty BST.
  public MyTreeSet()
  {
    root = null;
  }

  // Returns true if this BST contains value; otherwise returns false.
  public boolean contains(Object value)
  {
    return contains(root, value);
  }

  // Adds value to this BST, unless this tree already holds value.
  // Returns true if value has been added; otherwise returns false.
  public boolean add(Object value)
  {
    if (contains(value))
      return false;
    root = add(root, value);
    return true;
  }

  // Removes value from this BST.  Returns true if value has been
  // found and removed; otherwise returns false.
  public boolean remove(Object value)
  {
    if (!contains(value))
      return false;
    root = remove(root, value);
    return true;
  }

  // Returns a string representation of this BST.
  public String toString()
  {
    String str = toString(root);
    if (str.endsWith(", "))
      str = str.substring(0, str.length() - 2);
    return "[" + str + "]";
  }
  ...   // other methods
}
```

Figure 23-10. Public methods from MyTreeSet
(J_M\Ch23\BST\MyTreeSet.java)

```java
// Returns true if the BST rooted at node contains value;
// otherwise returns false (recursive version).
private boolean contains(TreeNode node, Object value)
{
  if (node == null)
    return false;
  else
  {
    int  diff = ((Comparable<Object>)value).compareTo(node.getValue());
    if (diff == 0)
      return true;
    else if (diff < 0)
      return contains(node.getLeft(), value);
    else // if (diff > 0)
      return contains(node.getRight(), value);
  }
}


// Adds value to the BST rooted at node. Returns the
// root of the new tree.
// Precondition: the tree rooted at node does not contain value.
private TreeNode add(TreeNode node, Object value)
{
  if (node == null)
    node = new TreeNode(value);
  else
  {
    int  diff = ((Comparable<Object>)value).compareTo(node.getValue());
    if (diff < 0)
      node.setLeft(add(node.getLeft(), value));
    else // if (diff > 0)
      node.setRight(add(node.getRight(), value));
  }
  return node;
}


// Removes value from the BST rooted at node.
// Returns the root of the new tree.
// Precondition: the tree rooted at node contains value.
private TreeNode remove(TreeNode node, Object value)
{
  int  diff = ((Comparable<Object>)value).compareTo(node.getValue());
  if (diff == 0)  // base case
    node = removeRoot(node);
  else if (diff < 0)
    node.setLeft(remove(node.getLeft(), value));
  else // if (diff > 0)
    node.setRight(remove(node.getRight(), value));
  return node;
}
```

Figure 23-11 `MyTreeSet.java` *Continued* ☞

```
// Returns a string representation of the tree rooted at node.
private String toString(TreeNode node)
{
  if (node == null)
    return "";
  else
    return toString(node.getLeft()) + node.getValue() + ", " +
                        toString(node.getRight());
}
```

Figure 23-11. Recursive helper methods in ᴶM\Ch23\BST\MyTreeSet.java

Actually, the contains, add, and remove methods have simple iterative versions as well, because in these methods at each step we either explore the left subtree or the right subtree, but not both. For example:

```
// Iterative version:
private boolean contains(TreeNode node, Object value)
{
  while (node != null)
  {
    int  diff = ((Comparable<Object>)value).compareTo(node.getValue());
    if (diff == 0)
      return true;
    else if (diff < 0)
      node = node.getLeft();
    else // if (diff > 0)
      node = node.getRight();
  }
  return false;
}
```

The add helper method adds a new node as a leaf, appending it either as the root (if the tree was empty) or to the left or to the right subtree, depending on the value.

The remove helper method is a little more involved. The complicated part is the base case, when the target value to be removed is found at the root (of some subtree). We have isolated this case into a separate method, removeRoot. It removes the root node, repairs the tree, and returns a reference to the root of the new tree. The idea of the algorithm is to replace the root with the smallest node in the right subtree. Such a node can have only one child (right), so it is easy to unlink that node from the tree by promoting its right child into its place. Figure 23-12 illustrates this algorithm. (In a slightly different version, we would replace the root with the <u>largest</u> node in the <u>left</u> subtree.)

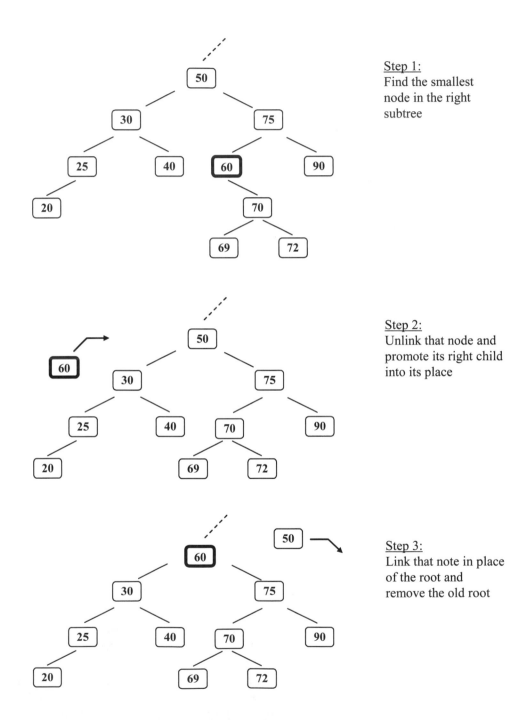

Step 1:
Find the smallest
node in the right
subtree

Step 2:
Unlink that node and
promote its right child
into its place

Step 3:
Link that note in place
of the root and
remove the old root

Figure 23-12.   Removing the root node from a subtree in a BST

The `contains`, `add`, and `remove` methods take, in the worst case, an amount of time proportional to the number of levels in the tree. When the tree is reasonably "bushy," this is $O(\log n)$, where n is the number of nodes in the tree.

> **In our simplified implementation, if the values to be added to the BST arrive not in random order but close to ascending or descending order, the tree may lose its shape and deteriorate into an almost linear structure.**

A more sophisticated implementation would use algorithms that keep the tree "balanced" (but such algorithms are outside the scope of this book).

As a lab exercise, fill in the blanks in the `removeRoot` method in `JM\Ch23\BST\MyTreeSet.java`. For "extra credit," make `MyTreeSet` `Iterable` by implementing an `iterator` method and a `MyTreeSetIterator` class. See Section 20.3 for an example. Your iterator should perform inorder traversal of the tree: left subtree, root, right subtree. Use a `Stack<TreeNode>` in your `MyTreeSetIterator` class. Do not implement the `remove` method for your iterator.

23.6 *Lab:* Morse Code

Morse Hall, the Mathematics Department building at Phillips Academy in Andover, Massachusetts, is named after Samuel F. B. Morse, who graduated from the academy in 1805. (According to the Encyclopedia Britannica, "he had been an unsteady and eccentric student.")

In 1838, Samuel Morse devised a signaling code for use with his electromagnetic telegraph. The code used two basic signaling elements: the "dot," a short-duration electric current, and the "dash," a longer-duration signal. The signals lowered an ink pen mounted on a special arm, which left dots and dashes on the strip of paper moving beneath. Morse's code gained wide acceptance and, in its international form, might be still in use. (Samuel Morse also achieved distinction as an artist, particularly as a painter of miniatures, and between 1826 and 1845 served as the first president of the National Academy of Design.)

In 1858 Queen Victoria sent the first transatlantic telegram of ninety-eight words to congratulate President James Buchanan of the United States. The telegram started a new era of "instant" messaging — it took only sixteen and a half hours to transmit via the brand new transatlantic telegraph cable.

In this project, we will simulate a telegraph station that encodes messages from text to Morse code and decodes Morse code back to plain text. The encoding is accomplished simply by looking up a symbol in a `TreeMap<Character, String>` that associates each symbol with its Morse code string. The decoding is implemented with the help of a binary "decoding" tree of our own design (it is <u>not</u> a BST). The Morse code for each letter represents a path from the root of the tree to some node: a "dot" means go left, and a "dash" means go right. The node at the end of the path contains the symbol corresponding to the code.

The *Telegraph* program is implemented in two classes: `Telegraph` and `MorseCode`. In addition, `MorseCode` uses the `TreeNode` class described in Section 23.2. The `Telegraph` class opens two windows on the screen, "London" and "New York," and handles the text entry fields and GUI events in them. We have written this class for you. The `MorseCode` class implements encoding and decoding of text. <u>All the methods in this class are static</u>. The `start` method initializes the encoding map and the decoding tree; the private method `treeInsert` inserts a given symbol into the decoding tree, according to its Morse code string; the public `encode` and `decode` methods convert plain text into Morse code and back, respectively. Your task is to supply all the missing code in the `MorseCode` class.

The `Telegraph` class and the unfinished `MorseCode` class are in `JM\Ch23\MorseCode`. `TreeNode.java` is provided in `JM\Ch23`. Put together a project with `Telegraph`, `MorseCode`, and `TreeNode`, finish `MorseCode`, and test your program.

23.7 *Case Study and Lab:* Java Messenger

In 1996, America Online introduced its subscribers to the "Buddy List," which allowed AOL members to see when their friends were online. A year later, AOL introduced the *AOL Instant Messenger* (*AIM*). In this case study we implement our own instant "messaging" application, *Java Messenger*. In our application, the same user logs in several times under different screen names, and messages are sent from one window to another on the same screen. Also, in this toy version, all other logged-in users are considered "buddies" of a given user.

Our program allows you to send messages to yourself under different aliases. This can compensate for your friends' absence when your Internet connection is down. It also has the advantage of always connecting you to a person just as smart and thoughtful as you are! (Another advantage of our program is that it illustrates the use of `java.util`'s `TreeSet` and `TreeMap` classes.)

Our *Java Messenger* application consists of five classes and the `Login` interface. (Figure 23-13). As usual, we split the work evenly: we supply the `Messenger`, `LoginWindow`, and `MsgWindow` classes, which deal with GUI, and the `Login` interface; you'll write the `Server` and `MsgUser` classes.

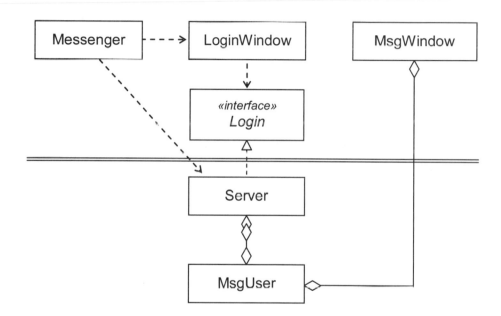

Figure 23-13. *Java Messenger* classes

The `Messenger` class's `main` method creates the server and logs in a few users:

```
Server server = new Server();
server.addUser("vindog1981", "no");
server.addUser("apscholar5", "no");
server.addUser("python2008", "no");
server.addUser("lucytexan", "no");
```

After that it opens a login window on the screen.

Your `Server` class should implement the `Login` interface. It must use a `TreeMap<String, MsgUser>` to associate screen names with users and a `TreeSet<MsgUser>` to hold `MsgUser` objects for all currently logged-in users.

A user is represented by an object of the `MsgUser` class. `MsgUser` implements `Comparable<MsgUser>`: its `compareTo` method compares a user to another user by comparing their screen names, case blind. When a new user logs in, the server calls its `openDialog` method, which creates a new `MsgWindow` and attaches it to that user.

A `MsgWindow` handles GUI for the user: a text area for typing in messages and displaying received messages and a "buddy list" for all logged-in "buddies."

The detailed specs for the *Java Messenger* classes have been generated from the Javadoc comments in the source files and are provided in the `MessengerDocs.zip` file in `JM\Ch23\Messenger`. Open `index.html` to see the documentation.

You might notice that the *Java Messenger* setup looks familiar: it looks like a part of the class diagram for the *SafeTrade* project in Chapter 19. This is not a coincidence: we want to reuse as much of the *SafeTrade* code here as possible. In particular, we can reuse the `LoginWindow` class and the `Login` interface without any changes. Recall that the purpose of the `Login` interface was precisely to make `LoginWindow` reusable. The `Messenger` class is similar to the `SafeTrade` class; the `Server` class can be adapted from `Brokerage`; the `MsgUser` class plays the same role in this project as `Trader` in *SafeTrade*.

23.8 Summary

A *tree* is a structure of connected *nodes* where each node, except one special *root node*, is connected to one parent node and may have one or more child nodes. Each node has a unique path ascending to the root. A tree is an inherently recursive structure because each node in a tree can be considered the root of its own tree, called a *subtree*. A *binary tree* is a tree where each node has no more than two children. These are referred to as the *left child* and *right child*. In the linked representation, each node of a tree contains references to its child nodes. Each node of a tree holds a data value.

The nodes of a tree are arranged in layers: all nodes at the same level are connected to the root by a path of the same length. One important property of trees is that they can hold a large number of values in a relatively shallow structure. A binary tree with h levels, with all levels filled with nodes, contains 2^h-1 nodes.

A *binary search tree* (*BST*) is a binary tree whose data elements have some relation of order defined for them and are organized so that the data value in each node is larger than all the values in the node's left subtree and smaller than all the values in its right subtree. The binary search tree combines the benefits of a sorted array for quick binary search with the advantages of a linked list for easy insertion and deletion of nodes.

Due to the recursive structure of trees, it is convenient to use recursive methods when working with them. The base case in such methods is when the tree is empty and, sometimes, when the tree consists only of the root. The method is usually applied recursively to the root's left and/or right subtrees.

Tree *traversals* can be easily implemented with recursion. *Preorder* traversal first visits the root of the tree, then processes its left and right subtrees; *postorder* traversal first processes the left and right subtrees, then visits the root; *inorder* traversal first processes the left subtree, then visits the root, then processes the right subtree. Inorder traversal of a BST processes its nodes in ascending order.

Exercises

Sections 23.1-23.3

1.   Define the following tree-related terms:

root	*parent*
child	*ancestor*
leaf	*subtree*

2.   What is the smallest number of levels required to store 100,000 nodes in a binary tree? ✓

3.   What are the smallest and the largest possible number of leaves
        (a)   in a binary tree with 15 nodes?
        (b)   in a binary tree containing exactly six non-leaf nodes?

4.■   Prove using mathematical induction that a binary tree with h levels cannot have more than 2^h-1 nodes. ✓

5. ▪ Prove using mathematical induction that in a binary tree with n nodes

$$L \le \frac{n+1}{2}$$

where L is the number of leaves.

6. Write a method

```
public boolean isLeaf(TreeNode node)
```

that returns `true` if `node` is a leaf and `false` otherwise. ✓

7. Write a method

```
public int sumTree(TreeNode root)
```

that returns the sum of the values stored in the tree defined by `root`, assuming that the nodes hold `Integer` objects.

8. What does the following method count? ✓

```
public int countSomething(TreeNode root)
{
  if (root == null)
    return 0;
  if (root.getLeft() == null && root.getRight() == null)
    return 1;
  else
    return countSomething(root.getLeft()) +
               countSomething(root.getRight());
}
```

9. Write a method

```
public int countPaths(TreeNode root)
```

that returns the total number of paths that lead from the root to any other node of a binary tree.

10. ▪ Write a method

```
public int depth(TreeNode root)
```

that returns the length of the longest path in a binary tree. ✓

11.■ Let us call the "bush ratio" the ratio of the number of nodes in a binary tree to the maximum possible number of nodes in a binary tree with the same number of levels. Using the `countNodes` method that returns the number of nodes in a tree and the `depth` method from the previous question, write a method

```
public double bushRatio(TreeNode root)
```

that calculates and returns the "bush ratio" for a given binary tree. The method should return 0 if the tree is empty.

12. (a) Write a method

```
public TreeNode copy(TreeNode root)
```

that creates a copy of a given binary tree and returns a reference to its root. (Assume that the nodes hold immutable objects, so there is no need to copy them.) ✓

(b) Write a method

```
public TreeNode mirrorImage(TreeNode root)
```

that creates a mirror image of a given binary tree and returns a reference to its root.

13.■ (a) Write a method

```
public boolean sameShape(TreeNode root1, TreeNode root2)
```

The method should return `true` if binary trees with the roots `root1` and `root2` have exactly the same shape and `false` otherwise.

(b) Using `sameShape` from Part (a), write a method

```
public boolean hasSameSubtree
        (TreeNode root1, TreeNode root2)
```

`root1` and `root2` refer to the roots of two binary trees. The method should return `true` if the second tree (rooted in `root2`) is empty or has the same shape as the subtree of some node in the first tree; `false` otherwise.

14.⬥ (a)   Write a method

```
public TreeNode buildFull(int h)
```

that builds a binary tree with *h* levels and all levels completely filled with nodes. The method should set the values in all the nodes to `null` and return a reference to the root of the new tree.

(b)   Write and test a method

```
public void fillTree(TreeNode root)
```

that appends new nodes (with `null` values) to the tree until all existing levels in the tree are completely filled.

15.   An algebraic expression with parentheses and defined precedence of operators can be represented by a binary tree, called an *expression tree*. For example:

Expression	Tree
| $a + b$ | ```
  +
 / \
a   b
``` |
| $(a + 1)(a - 1)$ | ```
     *
    / \
   +   -
  /\   /\
 a  1 a  1
``` |

In an expression tree, leaves represent operands and other nodes represent operators.

(a)   Draw an expression tree for

$$\frac{2}{\dfrac{1}{x} + \dfrac{1}{y}} \quad \checkmark$$

Continued ⇨

(b)   Draw an expression tree for

```
yr % 4 == 0 && (yr % 100 != 0 || yr % 400 == 0)
```

(c)   Write a class `ExpressionTree` extending `TreeNode`. Assume that the nodes contain `Strings`: operands are strings that represent integers and operators are `"+"` or `"*"`. Add a method that determines whether a node contains an operand or an operator and another method that extracts an integer value from the operand string.

(d)■   Write a recursive method

```
public static int eval(ExpressionTree root)
```

that evaluates the expression represented by this tree.

(e)■   Conventional algebraic notation is called *infix* notation. In infix notation, the operator is placed between the operands:

```
Infix:       x + y
```

Write a method

```
public static String toInfixNotation(ExpressionTree root)
```

that generates a fully parenthesized infix expression from a given expression tree. For example:

Continued ➱

(f)   There are two other ways to represent expressions which are useful in computer applications. They are called *prefix* and *postfix* notations. In prefix notation we place the operator before the operands; in postfix notation we place the operator after the operands:

```
Prefix:      + x y
Postfix:     x y +
```

As you can guess, prefix and postfix notations can be generated by traversing an expression tree in preorder and postorder, respectively. The prefix and postfix notations are convenient because they do not use parentheses and do not need to take into account the precedence of the operators. The order of operations can be uniquely reconstructed from the expression itself. Prefix notation is also called *Polish* notation after the Polish mathematician Łukasiewicz, who invented it, and postfix notation is sometimes called *Reverse Polish Notation* (*RPN*). RPN is used in some calculators and compilers.

Rewrite in postfix notation:

```
(x - 3) / (x*y - 2*x + 3*y)
```

(g)   Prove that the operands appear in the same order in the infix, postfix, and prefix notations — only the position of the operators is different. (This is a good test when you have to convert one notation into another manually.) ✓

(h)▪   Write and test a method

```
public static int eval(String[] tokens)
```

that evaluates a postfix expression. The `tokens` array contains operands — string representation of integers — and operators (such as `"+"` or `"*"`). ⸨ Hint: go from left to right, save "unused" operands on a stack. ⸩

(i)◆   Write a method

```
public static
        ExpressionTree toExpressionTree(String[] tokens)
```

that converts a postfix expression represented by the array `tokens` into an expression tree and returns the root of that tree.

Sections 23.4-23.8

16.   Mark true or false and explain:

(a)   The smallest node in a binary search tree is always a leaf. _____

(b)   If a binary search tree holds integers (with the usual order of comparison) and the root holds 0, then all the nodes of the left subtree hold negative numbers. _____ ✓

(c)   The number of comparisons necessary to find a target node in a binary search tree never exceeds $\log_2 n + 1$, where n is the number of nodes. _____ ✓

17.   (a)   Swap two nodes in the following binary tree to obtain a binary search tree.

```
        H
       / \
      C   R
     /   / \
    A   E   S
```

(b)   What will be the sequence of nodes when the resulting binary search tree is traversed inorder? Preorder?

18.   Suppose we start with an empty binary search tree and add nodes with values

```
475, 474, 749, 623, 292, 557, 681
```

(in that order). Draw the resulting tree. How can we arrange the same numbers in a balanced binary search tree (with three levels)? ✓

19.   Draw the binary search tree created by inserting the letters

```
L O G A R I T H M
```

(in that order) into an empty tree. List the nodes of this tree when it is traversed inorder, preorder, and postorder. ✓

20.■   Using mathematical induction, prove that inorder traversal of a BST visits the nodes in ascending order.

21.   Write a method that traverses a BST in the decreasing order of values.

22. ■   Write a non-recursive method

```
public TreeNode maxNode(TreeNode root)
```

that finds and returns the largest node in a BST. ✓

23. ◆   (a)   Write a method

```
public TreeNode buildNCT(TreeNode root)
```

that takes a binary tree and builds a new tree. The shape of the new tree is exactly the same as the shape of the original tree, but the values in its nodes are different: in the new tree the value in each node is an `Integer` object that represents the total number of nodes in the subtree rooted at that node. (For example, the value at the root is equal to the total number of nodes in the tree.) The method returns the root of the new tree.

(b)   Suppose you have a BST and a companion "node count" tree (NCT) as described in Part (a). Write an efficient method

```
public Object median(TreeNode bstRoot, TreeNode nctRoot)
```

that finds the median of the values stored in the BST. The median here is the $((n + 1) / 2)$-th node in the tree, in ascending order, where n is the total number of nodes, and the nodes are counted starting from 1. ⸮ Hints: write a more general helper function that finds the k-th node in the tree for any given k. Use recursion or iterations to build parallel paths in the BST and the NCT from the root to the node you are looking for. ⸮

Chapter →  → **24**

Lookup Tables and Hashing

24.1 Prologue

In this chapter we continue our discussion of different ways to store and retrieve data in programs. But first let us briefly review what we already know about data structures.

In a list, data elements are arranged in a sequence; each element has an index assigned to it, its position in the sequence. If we want to find a given value in a list, we can do a sequential search, traversing a list from the beginning until we find the value. If we represent a list as an array, it is easy to get access to an element with a given index, but inserting and removing values at the beginning or in the middle of the list takes some time. In a linked list we have to follow the links to get access to an element with a given index, but it is easy to insert and remove elements.

Stacks and queues are used for temporary storage. In these structures, access to values is defined by the order in which they were stored. A stack provides immediate access to the value stored last, whereas in a queue values are retrieved in the order of their arrival.

BSTs (Binary Search Trees) support quick searching, similar to Binary Search in a sorted array, and relatively easy insertion and removal of values, as in a linked list.

Is there a way to store and retrieve data even faster than in a BST? The answer is yes, if we can set up a *lookup table* or a *hash table*. In the remainder of this chapter we will discuss lookup tables and hashing and get more practice with `java.util`'s `HashSet` and `HashMap` classes, which use hashing.

24.2 Lookup Tables

A lookup table implements a map. The idea is to avoid searching altogether: each key in a map tells us right away where we can find the value associated with it. A lookup table is simply an array that holds the values. The key is converted either directly or through some simple formula into an integer, which is used as an index into the lookup table array, and the associated value is stored in the element of the array with that index. One special reserved value (for example, `null`) may be used to indicate that a particular slot in the table is empty — the key is not used. The indices computed for two different keys must be different, so that we can go directly to the corresponding lookup table entry and store or fetch the data.

Suppose, for example, that an application such as entering shipping orders requires a database of U.S. zip codes that would quickly find the town or locality with a given code. Suppose we are dealing with 5-digit zip codes, so there are no more than 100,000 possible values, from 00000 to 99999. Actually, only a fraction of the 5-digit numbers represent real zip codes used by the U.S. Postal Service. But in this application it may be important to make the zip code lookup as quick as possible. This can be accomplished using a table with 100,000 entries. The 5 digit zip will be used directly as an index into the table. Those entries in the table that correspond to a valid zip code will point to the corresponding record containing the locality name; all the other entries will remain unused (Figure 24-1).

Figure 24-1. A lookup table for zip codes in the United States

This type of data access takes $O(1)$ time, but some space may be wasted if many lookup table entries are empty.

Lookup tables are useful for many other tasks, such as data compression or translating one symbolic notation into another. In graphics applications and in hardware, for example, a "logical" color code (usually some number, say, from 0 to 255) can be converted into an actual screen color by fetching its red, green, and blue components from three lookup tables.

Another common use of lookup tables is for tabulating functions when we need to speed up time-critical computations. The function argument is translated into an integer index that is used to fetch the function value from its lookup table. In some cases, when the function argument may have only a small number of integer values, the lookup table may actually take less space than the code that would be needed to implement the function! If, for example, we need to compute 3^n repeatedly for $n = 0,...,9$, the most efficient way, in terms of both time and space, is to use a lookup table of 10 values:

```
private static int[] n_thPowerOf3 =
    {1, 3, 9, 27, 81, 243, 729, 2187, 6561, 19683};
...

// Precondition: 0 <= n < 10
public int powOf3(int n)
{
    return n_thPowerOf3[n];
}
```

In another example, an imaging application may need to count quickly the number of "black" pixels (picture elements) in a scan line (for instance, in order to locate lines of text). In a large black and white image, pixels may be packed eight per byte to save space. The task then needs a method that finds the number of bits in a byte that are set to 1. This method can easily do the job by testing individual bits (using the bit-wise "and" operator and hex constants 0x01, 0x02, 0x04, etc. for integers that have a single bit set — see Chapter 17):

```
// Count the number of bits in byte b that are set to 1:
int count = 0;
if ((b & 0x01) != 0) count++;  // bit 0
if ((b & 0x02) != 0) count++;  // bit 1
if ((b & 0x04) != 0) count++;  // bit 2
...
if ((b & 0x80) != 0) count++;  // bit 7
```

But, if performance is important, a lookup table with 256 elements that holds the bit counts for all possible values of a byte (0–255) may be a more efficient solution:

```
private static int[] bitCounts =
{
    0,1,1,2,1,2,2,3,1,2,2,3,2,3,3,4,    // 00000000 - 00001111
    1,2,2,3,2,3,3,4,2,3,3,4,3,4,4,5,    // 00010000 - 00011111
    ...                                 ...
    4,5,5,6,5,6,6,7,5,6,6,7,6,7,7,8     // 11110000 - 11111111
};

...
int i = (int)b;
if (i < 0)          // In Java, byte-type values are signed:
    i += 128;       //    -128 <= b <= 127; we need 0 <= i <= 255
int count = bitCounts[i];
```

24.3 *Lab:* Cryptogram Solver

Almost everyone is sooner or later tempted to either send a message in code or to decode an encrypted message. In a simple cryptogram puzzle, a small fragment of text is encrypted with a substitution cipher in which each letter is substituted with another letter. Something like: "Puffm, Cmafx!" To solve a cryptogram we usually look for familiar patterns of letters, especially in short words. We also evaluate frequencies of letters, guessing that in English the most frequent letters stand for 'e' or 't', while the least frequent letters stand for 'j' or 'q'. The purpose of this lab is to solve a cryptogram and to master the use of lookup tables in the process.

Our *Cryptogram Solver* program is interactive. After opening an encrypted text file, the user sees the encrypted text on the left side of the screen and the decoded text on the right. Initially, nothing is decoded — the decoded text has only dashes for all the letters. The user then enters substitutions for one or several letters, clicks the "Refresh" button, and immediately sees an updated version of the decoded text. In addition, the program can offer decoding hints based on the frequencies of letters in the encrypted text.

Cryptogram Solver can also create cryptograms. If you enter random substitutions for all letters (or click the "Encode" menu item) and then enter your text fragment on the left side (by typing it in, loading it from a text file, or cutting and pasting it from another program), then the text shown on the right side will be an encrypted version of your text.

Your task is to write a class `Enigma`, named after the famous German encryption machine.※enigma Enigma was invented in 1918 and was first used in the banking business, but it very quickly found its way into the military. Enigma's codes were considered "unbreakable," but they were eventually broken, first by Polish codebreakers in 1932 and later, during WWII, by the codebreakers of the Bletchley Park project in Great Britain, led by Alan Turing,※turing one of the founders of modern computer science. The battle between Enigma codemakers and codebreakers lasted through WWII, and the dramatic successes of Allied cryptanalysts provided invaluable intelligence information.

Your `Enigma` class should maintain a lookup table for substitutions for the letters 'A' through 'Z'. For example:

```
    private char[] lookupTable;
```

Initially the lookup table contains only dashes. As decryption proceeds, the table is updated and gradually filled. You can change your guess for a letter as often as you want.

The `getNumericValue(char ch)` static method of the `Character` class returns consecutive integers for letters 'A' through 'Z' (10 for 'A', 11 for 'B', etc., 35 for 'Z'; 0 though 9 are returned for characters '0' through '9'). Therefore, if `ch` is an upper case letter, then

```
    int i = Character.getNumericValue(ch) -
                             Character.getNumericValue('A');
```

sets `i` to an integer in the range from 0 to 25, which can be used as an index into our lookup table.

Your `Enigma` class should define a constructor with one `int` parameter — the number of letters in the alphabet — and three public methods:

```
    void setSubstitution(int i, char ch);
    String decode(String text);
    String getHints(String text, String lettersByFrequency);
```

The first two methods support decoding (or encoding) of text; the last one supports computer-generated hints based on letter counts.

The `setSubstitution(int i, char ch)` method should set the *i*-th element of the lookup table to `ch`.

The `decode(String text)` method decodes all the letters in `text` according to the current lookup table. `decode` should leave all characters that are not letters unchanged and preserve the upper or lower case of letters. It should return the decoded string, which has the same length as `text`.

The `getHints(String text, String lettersByFrequency)` method returns computer-generated hints for each letter in the encrypted text. It works as follows. First it counts the number of occurrences for each of the letters 'a' through 'z' in `text` (case blind) and saves these 26 counts in an array. Write a separate private method for that:

```
    private int[] countLetters(String text)
```

You should count all letters in one sweep over `text`. Start with zeroes in all counts, then increment the appropriate count for each letter.

After getting the counts for all letters, `getHints` creates and returns a `String` of "hints." The returned string `hints` should hold a permutation of letters 'A' through 'Z'; `hint.charAt(k)` will be displayed as a computer-generated hint for decoding the *k*-th letter of the alphabet. The hints should be based on comparing the order of letters by frequency in letter counts in encrypted text with the order of letters by frequency in plain (unencrypted) text. The `lettersByFrequency` parameter contains the letters 'A' through 'Z' arranged in increasing order of their frequencies in a sample text file. Suppose `lettersByFrequency`, passed to `getHints` is `"JQXZKBVWFUYMPGCLSDHROANITE"`. Then 'J' should be the hint for the least frequent letter in `text`, 'Q' for the second least frequent letter, and so on. The method's code is quite short once you figure out the algorithm. Try to figure it out yourself or read the (encrypted) hint below.

Kwy ep efhjdxqct wxtxfed qj "wjdqxph iv ajkpqxph," sywadxiys xp Aceuqyd 18. Ojd yeac yfytypq `ajkpqw[x]` xp qcy fyqqyd ajkpqw eddev oxps qcy pktiyd jo yfytypqw `ajkpqw[r]` wkac qceq `ajkpqw[r]` < `ajkpqw[x]` jd `ajkpqw[r]` == `ajkpqw[x]` eps r < x. Qcxw pktiyd (aeff xq depz) xw qcy depz jo qcy *x*-qc fyqqyd jo qcy efuceiyq xp qydtw jo xqw odynkypav xp qcy ypadvuqys qygq. Wj `cxpqw[x]` wcjkfs iy wyq qj `fyqqydwIvOdynkypav.acedEq(depz)`.

(The above paragraph is also available in `JM\Ch24\Cryptogram\hint.txt` file. You can use *Cryptogram Solver* on it even before you get the hints part working correctly. Just use a "stub" method for `getHints` that returns an arbitrary string of 26 characters.)

We generated our `lettersByFrequency` string by counting occurrences for the 26 letters in the file `sample.txt`. Therefore, if you load `sample.txt` (a plain text file) into the program, the hint displayed for each letter should be that same letter. This is an easy way to test your `countLetters` and `getHints` methods.

Combine your `Enigma` class with the `Cryptogram` and `CryptogramMenu` classes located in `JM\Ch24\Cryptogram`. Test your program with `sample.txt`, then try to decode `secret.txt`. Both these files are in `JM\Ch24\Cryptogram`, too.

Unfortunately, as you can see, our computer-generated hints turn out to be entirely unhelpful, except for the most frequent letter 'e'. Apparently we need a more sophisticated tool for solving cryptograms automatically — perhaps counting 2-D distributions for all pairs of adjacent letters, or even 3-D distributions for all triplets of letters, or a way to look for other patterns in the text.

24.4 Hash Tables

The technique of *hashing* builds on the lookup table concept. In a lookup table, a key is either used directly or converted through a very simple formula into an integer index. Different keys translate into different indices in the lookup table. This method is not practical, however, when the range of possible key values is large. It is also wasteful when the mapping from keys to integer indices is very sparse — many lookup table entries remain unused.

We can avoid these problems by using a tighter system of mapping from keys to integer indices in the table. We can try to map all possible key values into a narrower range of indices and to cover that range more uniformly. Such a transformation is called a *hash function*; a table used with it is a *hash table*.

The price of hashing is that we lose the one-to-one correspondence between keys and table entries: two different keys may be mapped into the same location in the hash table. Thus when we try inserting a new value into the table, its slot may already be occupied. These situations are called *collisions*. We have to devise some method of dealing with them. When we retrieve a value, we have to verify that its key indeed matches the target; therefore, the key must be explicitly stored in the table with the rest of the record.

The design of a hash table thus hinges upon successful handling of two problems: how to choose a good hash function and how to handle collisions. There is room for ingenious solutions for both.

A good hash function must have the following properties:

1. It must be easy to calculate.

2. It must map all possible values of keys onto a range that is not too large.

3. It must cover that range uniformly and minimize collisions.

To devise such a function, we can try some "random" things akin to the transformations used for generating random numbers in a specified range. If the key is a string of characters, we can use some numeric codes (for instance, Unicode) for them. We can then chop the key into pieces and combine these together using bit-wise or arithmetic operations — hence the term "hashing." The result must be an integer in the range from 0 to `tableSize-1`.

Overly simplistic hash functions that simply truncate the key or take it modulo the table size —

```
public int hashCode(long key) { return (int)(key % tableSize); }
```

— may create unexpected clusters of collisions resulting from some peculiar clustering in the data. Fortunately, we can evaluate our hash function on some simulated and real data before using it in an application.

There are two principal approaches to resolving collisions. In the first approach, each entry in the hash table is itself implemented as a structure that can hold more than one value. This approach is called *chaining* and the table entry is referred to as a *bucket*. A bucket may be implemented as a linked list, a sorted array, or even a binary search tree (Figure 24-2). This approach works well for densely populated hash tables.

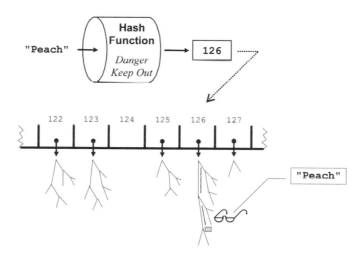

Figure 24-2. Resolving collisions in a hash table by chaining

The second approach to resolving collisions is by storing the colliding value in a different slot of the same hash table. This approach is known as *probing*. We calculate the index into the table using the hash function as usual. If the slot is already occupied, we use some *probing function* to convert that index into a new index; we repeat this step until we find a vacant slot:

```
    . . .
    int index = hashCode(target.getKey());
    while (hashTable[index] != null)
      index = probe(index);
    hashTable[index] = target;
    . . .
```

The same probing function, of course, must be used for retrieving a value:

```
    . . .
    int index = hashCode(key);
    while (hashTable[index] != null &&
           !key.equals(hashTable[index].getKey())
      index = probe(index);
    target = hashTable[index];
    . . .
```

The simplest form of the probing function is to increment the index by one or by some fixed number:

```
    int probe(index) { return (index + INCR) % tableSize; }
```

This is called *linear probing* (Figure 24-3). After the table has been in use for a while, linear probing may degrade the uniform distribution of the hash table population — a condition called *clustering*. In so-called *quadratic probing*, the sequence of examined slots is

```
    index, index+1, index+4, index+9, ...
```

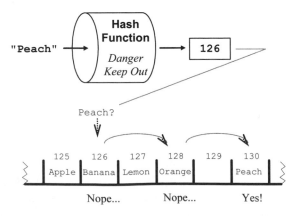

Figure 24-3. Resolving collisions in a hash table by linear probing

In more elaborate probing schemes, the next location may depend not only on the consecutive number of the attempt, but also on the value of the key. In addition, some rehash function may be used instead of `% tableSize`:

```
...
int index = hashCode(target.getKey());
int attempt = 1;
while (hashTable[index] != null)
  index = rehash(index, hashTable[index].getKey(), attempt++);
...
```

Probing should be used only with relatively sparsely populated hash tables so that probing sequences are kept short. The sequence of probing attempts required to insert a value is repeated each time we search for that value.

As we can see, the performance of a search in a hash table varies greatly with the details of implementation. Usually data access is $O(1)$. But with many collisions, the performance may deteriorate. The ratio of the number of items stored in a hash table to the number of buckets is called the hash table's *load factor*. If a load factor is too small, a lot of space is wasted. When the load factor becomes very high, all the advantages of hashing are lost. Then it may be time to rehash all the items into a new table with a larger number of buckets. A reasonable load factor may range from 0.5 to 2.0.

> **One disadvantage of a hash table as compared to a binary search tree or a sorted list is the difficulty of quickly traversing the table in ascending order of keys. This may be a serious consideration in some applications.**

24.5 java.util's HashSet and HashMap

> **java.util's HashSet and HashMap classes resolve collisions through chaining.**

`HashSet`'s no-args constructor creates an empty hash table with a default initial capacity (the number of buckets) of 16 and a load factor limit of 0.75. If you know in advance the maximum number of entries to be stored in the table, it is better to use another constructor, `HashSet(int initialCapacity)`. Otherwise, when the table becomes too crowded, the `HashSet`'s `add` method has to allocate a larger array and "rehash" all the elements into it. `initialCapacity` is the number of buckets to be used in the table; it should be roughly twice the number of entries expected to be stored. The third constructor takes two arguments, the initial capacity and the load factor limit.

The HashMap class provides similar constructors.

The main difference between Java's BST classes and hash table classes is that objects stored in a HashSet and keys mapped in a HashMap do not have to be Comparable and do not use comparators. An iterator for a hash set traverses the set's values in no particular order. Instead of the ordering among the set elements, you have to pay attention to providing a reasonable hash function for them.

When an object is added to a HashSet or serves as a key in a HashMap, that object's hashCode method is called. hashCode is a method of the Object class, so every object has it. Unfortunately, this method is hardly usable because it is based on the object's current address in memory and does not reflect the object's properties. Programmers usually override Object's hashCode in their classes.

> **It is important to override Object's hashCode method with a hashCode method appropriate for your class if you plan to store the objects of your class in a HashSet or use them as keys in a HashMap.**

Java library classes such as String, Double, and Integer have suitable hashCode methods defined for their objects. For example, String's hashCode method computes the hash code as

$$s_0 \cdot 31^{n-1} + s_1 \cdot 31^{n-2} + \ldots + s_{n-1}$$

where s_i is Unicode for the *i*-th character in the string. (This computation is performed using integer arithmetic, ignoring overflows; hashCode returns 0 for an empty string).

> **Normally, you do not have to invent your own hash code formula for your class from scratch but can rely on the library hashCode methods available for one or several fields of your class.**

For example:

```
public class MsgUser
{
  ...
  private String screenName;
  ...
  public int hashCode()
  {
    return screenName.hashCode();
  }
}
```

But, no matter how simple it is, it is important not to forget to supply a `hashCode` if you plan to use your objects in a `HashSet` or a `HashMap`.

`HashSet` and `HashMap` also use the `equals` method when they look for a target within a bucket.

> **To successfully store and retrieve objects from a `HashSet`, or to use them as keys in a `HashMap`, the objects must have the `hashCode` method and the `equals` method. `hashCode` method must agree with `equals`: if `x.equals(y)` is true, `x.hashCode()` == `y.hashCode()` must also be true.**

You don't have to worry about the range of values returned by a `hashCode` method.

> **The `hashCode` method returns an integer from the whole integer range. `HashSet` and `HashMap` methods further map the hash code onto the range of valid table indices for a particular table (by taking it modulo table size).**

24.6 *Lab:* Search Engine

We have already built a couple of games, a browser, and a messaging program, but one can hardly imagine life without a search engine. In this lab we'll design and program our own miniature search engine, which we'll call "Giggle." Rather than searching the Internet for keywords or phrases, *Giggle* searches a single file for all lines of text that contain a given word. *Giggle*'s code uses lists, BSTs, and hash tables. More precisely, it takes advantage of `java.util`'s `List`, `Set`, and `Map` interfaces and `LinkedList`, `TreeSet`, and `HashMap` classes.

Before you start searching, you need to create an index of all the words in the file you are going to search. This is analogous to the indexing process in which real search engines constantly update their indices and "crawl" the web looking for new web pages. In *Giggle*, the index is a map that associates each word in a text file with a list of all lines in the file that contain that word. With a little more work, we can upgrade *Giggle* to build an index for multiple files.

As usual, we will supply a GUI class, `Giggle`, that loads files, accepts user input, and displays the search results. You'll write the `SearchEngine` class that builds the index for a file and generates the search results. Your class <u>must</u> use a `HashMap` to hold the word index. In this map, a key is a word (in lowercase letters) and the associated value is a `List<String>`. The list holds all the lines in the file that contain the corresponding keyword.

Here are the specs for your class:

<u>Fields:</u>

```
private String myURL;
  // holds the name for the "url" (file name)

private Map<String, List<String>> myIndex;
  // holds the word index
```

<u>Constructor:</u>

```
public SearchEngine(String url)
```

> Saves `url` in `myUrl`; initializes `myIndex` to an empty <u>HashMap</u> with an initial capacity of 20,000. Note: this constructor does not load the file; the `Giggle` class reads the file and passes one line at a time to `SearchEngine`.

<u>Public methods:</u>

```
public String getURL()
```

> Returns `myUrl`. I call this method from `Giggle` to display the name of the file in which hits were found. In the present version I already know the file name, but eventually an expanded version of `Giggle` may need to index several files.

```
public void add(String line)
```

> Extracts all words from `line`, and, for each word, adds `line` to its list of lines in `myIndex`. This method obtains a set of all words in `line` by calling a private method `parseWords(line)` described below. Use a `LinkedList<String>` object to represent a list of lines associated with a word.

```
public List<String> getHits(String word)
```

> Returns the list of lines associated with `word` in `myIndex`.

Private method:

```
private Set<String> parseWords(String line)
```

> Returns a set of all words in `line`. Use the same technique for extracting all the words from `line` as you did in the *Index Maker* lab in Section 12.9: call `line.split("\\W+")`. Add all the elements from the resulting array to a `TreeSet`. Skip empty words and convert each word to lower case before adding it to the set. `parseWords` uses a set, as opposed to a list, because we don't want to index the same line multiple times when the same word occurs several times in it. When we add words to the set, duplicates are automatically eliminated.

Combine your class with the `Giggle` class, located in JM\Ch24\Giggle. Test `Giggle` thoroughly on a small text file. Be sure to try searching for words that are not in the file as well as those that appear in several lines and multiple times in the same line.

24.7 Summary

In a *lookup table*, each key is converted through some simple formula into a non-negative integer, which is used as an index into the lookup table array. The associated value is stored in the element of the array with that index. Lookup tables can be used when the keys can be easily mapped onto integers in a relatively narrow range. All allowed keys correspond to valid indices in the table, and different keys correspond to different indices. Lookup tables provide access to data in $O(1)$ time, but a sparsely populated lookup table may waste a lot of space.

In the *hashing* approach, a hash function converts the key into an integer that is used as an index into a hash table. Different keys may be hashed into the same index, causing *collisions*. The *chaining* technique resolves collisions by turning each slot in the hash table into a "bucket" that can hold several values. The *probing* technique stores the colliding objects in alternative slots chosen according to a predefined probing function. The performance and space requirements for hash tables may vary widely depending on the implementation. Data access time in a hash table is usually $O(1)$, but the performance may deteriorate with a lot of collisions. One disadvantage of a hash table as compared to a binary search tree or a sorted list is the difficulty of quickly traversing the table in ascending order of keys.

java.util's HashSet and HashMap classes implement the Set and Map interfaces, respectively, using hash tables. The objects kept in a HashSet and the keys in a HashMap do not have to be Comparable and do not use comparators. Instead, you have to make sure that these objects have a reasonable hashCode method defined for them, which agrees with the equals method. Java library classes, such as String, Double, and Integer, have suitable hashCode methods defined. You can often write a reasonable hashCode method for your own class by calling library hashCode methods for one or several fields of your class.

A hashCode method may return an integer from the whole integer range. HashSet and HashMap methods further map the hash code onto the range of valid table indices for a particular table.

Exercises

Sections 24.1-24.3

1. A class LookupState implements a lookup table that helps to find full names of states from their two-letter postal abbreviations (in which both letters are uppercase). The lookup table is implemented as an array of 676 entries (676 is 26 times 26), of which only 50 are used.

    ```
    public class LookupState
    {
      private static String[] stateNames = new String[676];

      public static void add(String abbr, String name)
      { ... }

      public static String find(String abbr)
      { ... }

      private static int lookupIndex(String abbr)
      { ... }
    }
    ```

    Devise a method for mapping a two-letter state abbreviation into an integer index from 0 to 675 returned by the lookupIndex method, write the add and find methods, and test your class. ⸌ Hint: Recall from the Cryptogram lab in Section 24.3 that Character.getNumericValue(ch) returns consecutive integers for letters 'A' - 'Z'. ⸍

2.   Write a method

```
public List<String> sortByFirstLetter(List<String> words)
```

that takes a list of words, all of which start with capital letters, and returns a
new list (a `LinkedList`) in which all the words that start with an "A" are
followed by all the words that start with a "B," and so on. All the words that
start with a particular letter must be in the same order as in the original list.
Use the following algorithm:

1. Create an `ArrayList` of 26 queues.

2. Scan `words` once from the beginning and put each word into the
   appropriate queue based on its first letter.

3. Collect all the words from the queues into a new `LinkedList`.

3.   The class `PhoneCall` represents a record of a telephone call:

```
public class PhoneCall
{
  . . .
  public int getStartHour() { ... }   // European time: 0 -- 23
  public int getStartMin() { ... }
  public int getDuration() { ... }    // in seconds
  . . .
}
```

Write a method

```
public int busiestHour(List<PhoneCall> dayCalls)
```

that returns the hour (a value from 0 to 23) in which the largest number of
calls originated. Count only those calls that lasted at least 30 seconds. Your
method must scan the list only once, using a "for each" loop or an iterator. ✓

4.◆   Implement *Radix Sort* for a list of words.

Radix Sort is a sorting method that is not based on comparing keys but rather
on applying the lookup or hashing idea to them. Suppose we have a large list
of integers with values from 0 to 9. We can create 10 buckets, corresponding
to the 10 possible values. In one pass through the list we add each value to
the appropriate bucket. Then we scan through the ten buckets in ascending
order and collect all the values together. The result will be the list sorted in
ascending order.

Continued

Now suppose we have some data records with keys that are integers in the range from 0 to 99999. Suppose memory limitations do not allow us to use 100000 buckets. The Radix Sort technique lets us sort the keys one digit at a time: we can complete the task with only 10 buckets, but we will need five passes through the list. We have to make sure that the buckets preserve the order of inserted values; for instance, each bucket can be a list with the values inserted at the end (or a queue). We start with the least significant digit in the key (the units digit) and distribute the data values into buckets based on that digit. When we are done, we scan all the buckets in ascending order and collect the data back into one list. We then take the second digit (the tens digit) and repeat the process. We have to make as many passes through the data as there are digits in the longest key. After the last pass, the list is sorted.

The Radix Sort method works for data with any keys that permit positional representation. For integers, using hexadecimal digits or whole bytes is actually more appropriate than decimal digits. To sort words in lexicographic order we can use radix sort with a bucket for each letter or symbol. We have to pad (logically) all the words with "spaces" to the maximum length and start sorting from the rightmost character position.

Write the method

```
public LinkedList<String> sort(LinkedList<String> words)
```

The method should take a list of words and return a linked list of these words sorted alphabetically in ascending order, using Radix Sort. Assume that all the words are made up of uppercase letters 'A' through 'Z'. Recall that `Character.getNumericValue(ch)` returns consecutive integers for letters 'A' through 'Z'. Use an `ArrayList` of `List<String>` to hold the temporary buckets (each bucket is a `LinkedList` of words). Don't forget to "pad" (logically) shorter words with spaces: the first bucket should be reserved for words that are shorter than the letter position at the current pass, so you'll need to use 27 buckets. Use a "for each" loop for each bucket to append the words from that bucket to the new list (or use `LinkedList`'s `addAll` method).

Sections 23.4-23.7

5.   Define:

hashing	*chaining*
hash function	*bucket*
collisions	*probing*

6.   Mark true or false and explain:

(a)   Access time in a lookup table of size *n* is $O(n)$ _____ ✓

(b)   Probing is feasible only when the population of a hash table is relatively sparse. _____

(c)   It is easy to traverse a hash table in ascending order of keys. _____

(d)   One of the advantages of hash tables over binary search trees is the faster access time when adding and removing data values. _____ ✓

7.   A class `RecordsHashTable` implements a set of `Record` objects as a hash table —

```
private ListNode[] buckets = new ListNode[1000];
```

It resolves collisions by chaining, with buckets implemented as linked lists (references to `ListNode`).

(a)   Assuming that a class `Record` has a method `hashCode` that returns an integer from 0 to 999 and a method `equals(Object other)`, write a `RecordsHashTable`'s method

```
public boolean contains(Record record)
```

that returns `true` if `record` is found in the set; `false` otherwise.

(b)■   Suppose a reference takes 4 bytes and `Record` information takes 20 bytes. The average number of collisions is 5. Suppose we can convert our hash table into a lookup table by using 12 times more slots and a different `hashCode` method. Will we use more or less space? By approximately what percentage? How many times faster, on average, will the retrieval operation run, assuming that computing the old and the new `hashCode` method and comparing two records takes the same time? ✓

8.■   A hash table has sixty entries. Devise and test a hash function for English words such that all the different words from this paragraph are hashed into the table with no more than four collisions. Do not call any `hashCode` methods.

Compare the performance of your method with the more standard `Math.abs(word.hashCode()) % 60`.

9.■   Write a `hashCode` method for the `TicTacToeBoard` class. An object of this class represents a tic-tac-toe position. It has a method

```
public char charAt(int row, int col)
```

that returns the character at the (`row`, `col`) position ($0 \leq$ `row` < 3; $0 \leq$ `col` < 3): space, `'o'`, or `'x'`. There are 3^9 possible configurations on a 3 by 3 board (although only a fraction of them can occur in a real tic-tac-toe game). Define your `hashCode` method in such a way that it returns different values for all 3^9 board configurations.

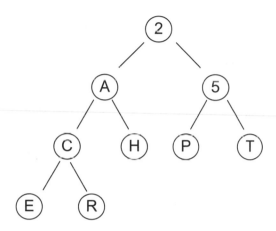

Heaps and Priority Queues

25.1 Prologue

When you are swamped with requests and can't keep up with them, perhaps you need to respond to the most pressing ones first. Some computer applications, too, need to maintain a list of items ranked in order of priority so that they can access the top-priority item quickly. A structure that supports this functionality is called a *priority queue*.

In everyday life we talk about "top priority" or "high priority," but in computer science by convention the <u>smallest</u> value has the highest priority. This is not very important, of course — what is smaller and what is bigger depends on how you rank or compare items. A priority queue is allowed to hold equal values.

> **We will follow the same convention: the <u>smallest</u> value has the highest priority.**

In the following sections we will discuss different implementations of priority queues, learn about heaps, and implement our own efficient priority queue class based on a heap. The `java.util.PriorityQueue` class in the Java collections framework is based on a heap, too.

25.2 Implementations of Priority Queues

One obvious way of implementing a priority queue is to keep all the items in an ordered list. In an array list we would put the smallest item last; in a linked list, first. This would make it very easy to access and remove the highest priority item, but to insert a new item in order, we would need to scan through the list until we found the spot corresponding to its rank, then insert the item at that location. If the list were long, this could take considerable time. In an application where values are frequently inserted and removed, the insert operation would create a bottleneck that would offset the advantage of instantaneous removal.

If the priorities of objects stored in a queue take only a small number of discrete values, then a priority queue can be implemented as an array or list of regular queues. Suppose, for example, an object `Message` has an `int` method `getPriority`, which returns a value from 0 (top priority) to 4 (lowest priority). Then we can use an array of five queues, one for each priority level. Question 7 in the exercises at the end of this chapter asks you to implement such a priority queue class and to state the average time big-O for `peek`, `add`, and `remove` operations.

A binary search tree can store items according to their rank, and it takes relatively little time to insert a new node and to remove the smallest node (just follow the left-child link as far as you can go — see Figure 23-9 on page 586). However, if we use a BST (modified to allow duplicate values) as a priority queue, with lots of removals and insertions of values, our BST may quickly deteriorate into a nearly linear structure. We will need to spend time re-balancing our tree back into shape.

It turns out that binary trees of another type, called *heaps*, help us implement priority queues in such a way that both insertion and removal of items is quick and the tree always stays in shape. In a heap, the smallest node is in its root, and each node holds the smallest value of the subtree rooted in it. (More precisely, this ordering property describes a *min-heap*. In a *max-heap*, the largest value is in the root.) In a heap each subtree is also a heap. Inserting or removing a value takes a number of steps that is less than or equal to the number of levels in the tree, which is only $\log_2 n$ for a tree with n nodes. For a tree with a million nodes, for example, we would have to run through at most 20 steps, as opposed to the average of half a million steps in a sequential list implementation.

The algorithm for quick insertion of nodes into a heap requires going from a node to its parent. In the linked representation of a tree, we could add to the node structure a reference to the node's parent. A more efficient way of implementing heaps, however, is based on a non-linked representation of binary trees. In this approach, all nodes are stored in an array in a certain order so that it is easy to find the children and the parent of any given node. We will talk about heaps in Section 25.4.

> The `java.util.PriorityQueue<E>` class is implemented as a
> min-heap.

Recall from Chapter 19 that `java.util.PriorityQueue<E>` implements the `java.util.Queue<E>` interface with `isEmpty`, `peek`, `add`, and `remove` methods. A `PriorityQueue` holds `Comparable` objects (or a comparator is passed to `PriorityQueue`'s constructor as a parameter).

25.3   Binary Trees: Non-Linked Representation

A binary tree is called *full* (or *perfect*) if all its levels are filled with nodes. A full tree with h levels has $2^h - 1$ nodes. Each level contains twice as many nodes as the preceding level; the number of nodes in the bottom level is 2^{h-1}.

A binary tree is called *complete* if it has no gaps on any level, except the bottom level, which may have some leaves missing on the right. Figure 25-1 shows the shapes of a full tree and a complete tree.

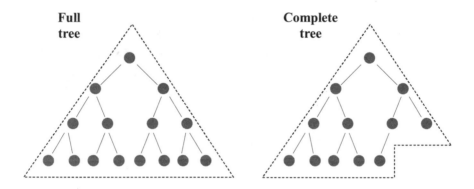

Figure 25-1.   The shapes of *full* and *complete* binary trees

If we have a complete tree, we can number all its nodes starting from 1 at the root, then proceeding from left to right at each consecutive level (Figure 25-2). Since the tree is complete, there are no gaps between its nodes, so a node's number tells us exactly where in the tree we can find it. The left and right children of the i-th node, if they are present, have the numbers $2i$ and $2i+1$, and its parent has the number $i/2$ (truncated to an integer).

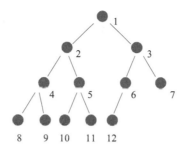

Figure 25-2. Numbering of the nodes in a complete tree

We have numbered all the nodes of a complete tree from 1 to n in such a way that knowing the number of a node lets us easily find the numbers of its left and right child and its parent. This property allows us to store a complete tree in an array where the element `items[i]` corresponds to node number i (Figure 25-3). This is one of a few cases where it is convenient to count the elements starting from 1, as opposed to the Java convention of indexing the elements of an array starting from 0. In the Java implementation, it is convenient to leave `items[0]` unused.

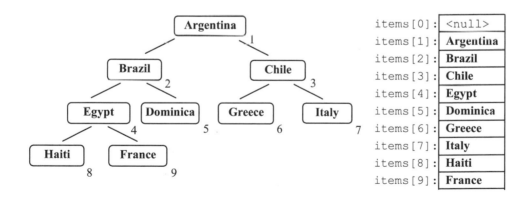

Figure 25-3. Representation of a complete binary tree in an array

In the following section, we will see how a special type of a binary tree, stored in an array, can be used for implementing a priority queue with $O(\log n)$ time for adding and removing elements.

25.4   A Do-It-Yourself Priority Queue

A *heap* is a binary tree that satisfies two conditions:

1. It is a complete tree;

2. The value in each node does not exceed any of the values in that node's subtree.

Unlike binary search trees, heaps are allowed to have more than one data item with the same value, and values in the left subtree do not have to be ranked lower than values in the right subtree.

> **The root of a heap holds its smallest value. This fact, together with efficient algorithms for adding and removing nodes, makes a heap a perfect data structure for implementing a priority queue.**

The best way to program a heap is by using the array representation of a complete binary tree, discussed in the previous section. We will use an array of `Objects` called `items` to hold the items. The element `items[1]` of the array corresponds to the root node. The element `items[0]` remains unused, as shown in Figure 25-3 above. Figure 25-4 shows a fragment from our `HeapPriorityQueue` class: its fields and the `isEmpty` and `peek` methods.

This class assumes that the array `items` holds `Comparable` objects or that a comparator is supplied for them. Two of the constructors take a comparator object as a parameter.

The `peek` method is really simple — since the smallest value in a heap is in its root, it is not too difficult to find it. The `remove` method is more involved: we need to repair the heap, restoring both its shape as a complete tree and its node ordering property. The shape is restored by cutting off the rightmost leaf at the bottom level and placing it into the root. To repair the order we apply the "reheap down" procedure, in which the value from the root moves down the heap until it falls into place. At each step down that value is swapped with its smaller child. In the actual code, the swapping is logical: the root is saved and an "empty node" moves down the tree until it falls into place, then the saved root value is stored in that node. Figure 25-5 illustrates the procedure.

The `add` method works in a similar way but in the opposite direction: first we add the new node as the rightmost leaf at the bottom level, then apply the "reheap up" procedure to restore the ordering property of the heap. "Reheap up" moves the new node up the tree, swapping places with its parent until the order is restored. Figure 25-6 shows the code for the add and remove methods.

```java
// Implements a priority queue based on a min-heap.

import java.util.*;

public class HeapPriorityQueue
{
  private static final int DFLT_CAPACITY = 101;
  private Object[] items;
  private int numItems;
  private final Comparator<Object> comparator;

  < constructors not shown >

  /**
   *   Returns true if this priority queue is empty;
   *   otherwise returns false.
   */
  public boolean isEmpty()
  {
    return numItems == 0;
  }

  /**
   *   Returns the highest priority element without removing
   *   it from this priority queue.
   */
  public Object peek()
  {
    if (numItems == 0)
    {
      throw new NoSuchElementException();
    }
    return items[1];
  }

  < other methods not shown >
}
```

**Figure 25-4. A fragment from the `HeapPriorityQueue` class
(`JM\Ch25\Heap\HeapPriorityQueue.java`)**

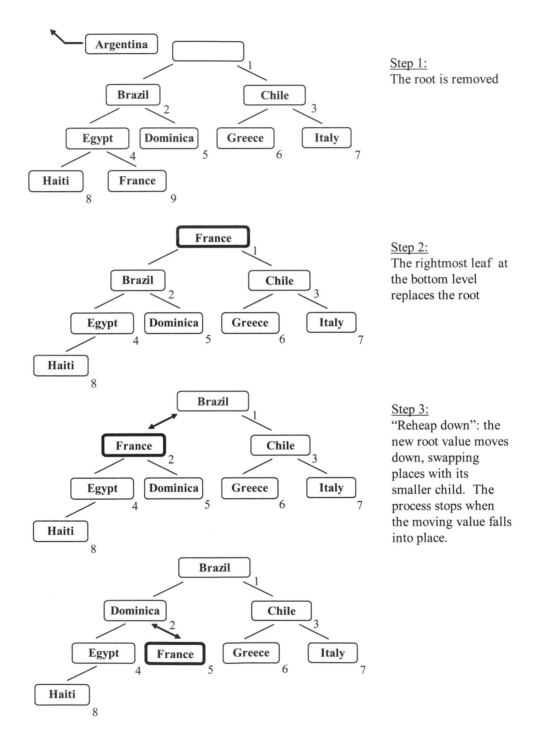

Step 1:
The root is removed

Step 2:
The rightmost leaf at the bottom level replaces the root

Step 3:
"Reheap down": the new root value moves down, swapping places with its smaller child. The process stops when the moving value falls into place.

Figure 25-5. Removing the root node from a heap

```
...

/**
 *  Adds obj to this priority queue; returns true.
 */
public boolean add(Object obj)
{
  numItems++;
  if (numItems >= items.length)  // items[0] is not used
    growCapacity();
  items[numItems] = obj;
  reheapUp();
  return true;
}

/**
 *  Removes and returns the highest priority item.
 */
public Object remove()
{
  if (numItems == 0)
  {
    throw new NoSuchElementException();
  }

  Object minObject = items[1];
  items[1] = items[numItems];
  numItems--;
  reheapDown();
  return minObject;
}

...
```

Figure 25-6. add and remove methods in HeapPriorityQueue

Note that if the items array runs out of space, we have to allocate a new, larger array and copy all the items into it. In this case we'll double the size of the array. If the approximate maximum heap size is known in advance, it is better to construct a heap of sufficient capacity at the outset, using a constructor that takes the initial capacity as a parameter.

The code for the HeapPriorityQueue class is available in JM\Ch25\Heap. As a lab exercise, supply the missing code for the reheapUp and reheapDown methods.

25.5 *Lab:* Heapsort

As we saw briefly in Chapter 19, a priority queue can be used for sorting. All you have to do is add all the items to a priority queue in any order, then remove them one by one. The items will be returned in ascending order. If the priority queue is implemented as a min-heap, this sorting algorithm will run in $O(n \log n)$ time.

It is possible to apply this algorithm to an array, without creating a separate priority queue. This efficient algorithm, proposed by J. Williams in 1964, is called *Heapsort*.

Suppose you have an array a and you need to sort its elements in ascending order. Heapsort is performed in two phases. In the first phase, the elements are rearranged to form a <u>max-heap</u> with the root (the largest element) in a[0]. This is accomplished by calling the reheapDown procedure for every node that has children, starting with the last one:

```
int n = a.length;
for (int i = n/2; i >= 1; i--)
  reheapDown(a, i, n);  // reheap down the subtree with the
                        //   root in a[i-1]
```

In the second phase, the root element is swapped with the *n*-th element of the array, the size of the heap n is decremented by one, and the heap is repaired by applying the reheapDown procedure to the root:

```
while (n > 1)
{
  // swap a[0] with a[n-1]:
  double temp = a[0], a[0] = a[n-1], a[n-1] = temp;

  n--;
  reheapDown(a, 1, n);
}
```

As a lab exercise, write a class Heapsort with a method

```
public static void sort(double[] a)
```

and a private method reheapDown. Add your Heapsort to the *Benchmarks* program from Chapter 13 to compare it with the other sorting algorithms.

25.6 Summary

A binary tree is called *complete* if all its levels are completely filled with nodes without gaps up to the bottom level, which may have nodes missing on the right. A *min-heap* is a complete binary tree that holds some ranked data items in such a way that the root holds the smallest item and each node holds an item ranked not higher than all the items in its subtree. A heap is allowed to have several items of the same rank. The heap structure is an efficient way of implementing a *priority queue* in which we can insert items in any order and remove the smallest item (the item of the highest priority). The heap allows us to insert or remove an item in $O(\log n)$ time, where n is the total number of items in the heap.

A good way of implementing a heap is through the non-linked representation of a complete binary tree. In this implementation the tree nodes are represented by the elements of an array. If `items` is the array, the root corresponds to `items[1]`; subsequent elements in the array store the nodes in each consecutive level from left to right. In a Java implementation, it is convenient to leave `items[0]` unused. With this numbering of nodes, the children of the node `items[i]` can be found in `items[2*i]` and `items[2*i+1]`, and the parent of `items[i]` is in `items[i/2]`.

In Java, the `java.util.PriorityQueue` class implements a priority queue using a min-heap. We have sketched a similar implementation in our own class `HeapPriorityQueue`. The `add` and `remove` methods rearrange a number of nodes in the heap to preserve the heap structure, keeping it a complete tree with the heap ordering property. `add` uses the "reheap up" procedure, and `remove` uses the "reheap down" procedure. These elegant algorithms involve no more than one node at each level and therefore require a number of steps no greater than the number of levels in the tree. They can be implemented in concise iterative code.

The efficient *Heapsort* algorithm sorts an array by first rearranging the array elements into a max-heap, then removing them one by one and storing them back in the array, starting at the end.

Exercises

1.   Mark true or false and explain:

    (a)   A heap is a kind of binary search tree. _____ ✓
    (b)   All nodes in a heap must contain different values. _____
    (c)   The largest value in a min-heap, if unique, is always a leaf. _____ ✓
    (d)   At most one node in a heap may have one child. _____
    (e)   If a heap has n nodes, a new node can be inserted using at most $\log_2 n + 1$ comparisons. _____ ✓
    (f)   The most economical implementation of a heap is a linked binary tree with references from each node to its parent. _____

2.   The nodes of a complete binary tree are represented by the following array (starting with the first element):

```
12 17 4 65 50 17 2 76 72 74 73 18 57
```

    (a)   Draw the tree.
    (b)   Swap the root with one of the leaves to obtain a heap.

3.   In an array representation of a complete binary tree, x[0] is unused, x[1] represents the root, and so on. The heap contains n nodes.

    (a)   Write the indices of the parent, left child, and right child of the node x[i] in terms of i. ✓
    (b)   Write a condition for i that determines whether x[i] is a leaf. ✓
    (c)▪   Write an expression for the number of levels in the tree in terms of n.

4.▪   Write and test a method

```
public void traverseInOrder(int[] x, int n)
```

that would traverse inorder a heap of integers with n nodes and with the root in x[1]. ⟨ Hint: use a recursive helper method with a third argument. ⟩

5.■   Consider a heap

```
        5
      /   \
     8      34
    / \
   21  55
```

Nodes are inserted by appending them at the bottom level and then using the "Reheap Up" procedure. Nodes are removed by removing the root, putting the rightmost leaf from the bottom level at the top, and then using the "Reheap Down" procedure.

(a)   Draw the resulting heap after inserting 13, then 3. ✓
(b)   Start with the result of (a). Now remove the smallest value three times. Draw the resulting heap.

6.■   Implement a priority queue of Integer objects as an ArrayList<Integer>, sorted in descending order. Use Binary Search to find the place where a new value is to be inserted. Is this implementation more or less efficient than a heap? Explain.

7.■   (a)   The class Message has a method int getPriority() that returns an integer from 0 to 4 (0 being the highest priority). Write and test a class MessagePriorityQueue that implements a priority queue of Message objects based on the value returned by the getPriority method. Use an array of five queues, one queue for each priority value.

(b)   How does the time efficiency of this implementation compare to a heap?

(c)◆   Using MessagePriorityQueue, write a simulation in which a Message event with a random priority from 0 to 4 occurs with a probability of 0.2 each "minute" (iteration). Pretend that processing of a message takes four "minutes." Determine the average waiting time for messages of different priorities. ⸱ Hint: add a "time of arrival" field and a getArrivalTime method to Message. ⸲

8.♦   Modify the *Giggle* program in Section 24.6 so that it displays the lines that contain a search word in descending order by the number of hits in each line. Modify the `getHits` method in the `SearchEngine` class: rather than returning a list of lines that contain a given word, make `getHits` scan the list and build and return a priority queue. Use a `java.util.PriorityQueue<String>` constructed with a comparator. Provide a comparator class that compares two strings based on how many times a search word occurs in each of them; provide a comparator's constructor that takes a search word as a parameter. The updated `Giggle` class is provided for you in J_M\Ch25\Exercises\Giggle.java.

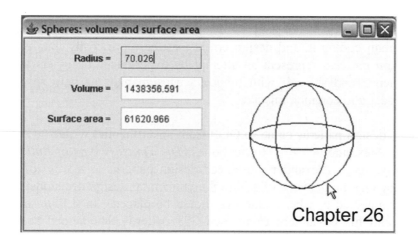

Design Patterns

26.1 Prologue

Object-oriented design is not easy — designing a software application often takes more time than coding it, and design errors may be more costly than errors in the code. *Design patterns* represent an attempt by experienced designers to formalize their experience and share it with novices. Design patterns help solve common problems and avoid common mistakes.

The idea of design patterns came to OOP from an influential writer on architecture, Christopher Alexander.☆alexander In his books, *The Timeless Way of Building*[*] and *A Pattern Language*,[**] Alexander introduced design patterns as a way to bring some order into the chaotic universe of arbitrary architectural design decisions: how rooms should be connected or where windows should be placed. In *A Pattern Language*, Alexander and his co-authors catalogued 253 patterns that helped solve specific architectural problems and offered standard ideas for better designs.

No one has a good formal definition of a "pattern" — somehow we recognize a pattern when we see one. In fact, we humans are very good at pattern recognition. We recognize a pattern as some recurring idea manifested in diverse situations. We talk about organizational patterns and patterns of behavior, grammatical patterns, musical patterns, speech patterns, and ornament patterns. Recognizing patterns helps us structure our thoughts about a situation and draw on past experiences of similar situations.

Experts, researchers, and volunteers have published some OO software design patterns in books, magazine articles, and on the Internet. The first and most famous book on the subject, *Design Patterns*, was published in 1995.[***] Since then, hundreds of patterns have been published, some rather general, others specialized for particular types of applications. Apparently many people enjoy discovering and publishing new design patterns. The great interest in design patterns is evident from the numerous conferences, workshops, discussion groups, and web sites dedicated to collecting and cataloguing patterns.☆patterns

A more or less standard format for describing patterns has emerged. A typical description includes the pattern name; a brief statement of its intent or the problem it

---

[*] C. Alexander, *The Timeless Way of Building*. Oxford University Press, 1979.

[**] C. Alexander, S. Ishikawa, and M. Silverstein, *A Pattern Language*. Oxford University Press, 1977.

[***] The famous "Gang of Four" book. *Design Patterns: Elements of Reusable Object-Oriented Software*, by Erich Gamma, Richard Helm, Ralph Johnson, and John Vlissides. Addison-Wesley, 1995.

solves; a description of the pattern and the types of classes and objects involved; perhaps a structural diagram; and an example, sometimes with sample code.

With too many patterns around, there is a danger that a novice may get lost. It is a good idea to start with only a handful of the most commonly used patterns and to understand exactly when and how they are used. Don't feel inadequate if your initial design doesn't follow an "officially" named pattern. But if the design runs into a problem, you can try to find a pattern that deals with that kind of problem, fix the design, and follow the pattern in the future. Fortunately, unlike buildings, programs are not set in concrete — it is often possible to change the design through minor restructuring of classes while keeping most of the code intact. If you find a standard pattern that fits your situation really well, it may bring you great satisfaction.

Being aware that OO design patterns exist helps you pay more attention to the design stage of your project before rushing to write code.

In the following sections we briefly review and illustrate six common design patterns: Façade, Strategy, Singleton, Decorator, Composite, and MVC (Model-View-Controller).

26.2 - 26.7

These sections are online at http://www.skylit.com/javamethods.

❖   ❖   ❖

OO design patterns and tools represent a bold attempt to turn the art of software design into something more precise, scientific, and teachable. But, behind all the technical terms and fancy diagrams, some art remains an essential ingredient. Software structures are largely hidden from the world. Still, something — not only the need to finish a project on time — compels a designer to look for what Christopher Alexander called "the quality without a name": order, balance, economy, fit to the purpose, and, in Alexander's words, "a subtle kind of freedom from inner contradictions." Let us join this search — welcome, and good luck!

Exercises

1.▪ Many people have found that the Java library classes `Calendar` and
`GregorianCalendar`, which handle date and time, are hard to use.
Sketchy documentation, a few unfortunate choices for method names, and
the fact that the months are counted starting from 0 — all add to the
confusion. The calendar classes are rather general, yet lack some useful
methods that one would expect in a date class (such as methods that tell you
the number of days between two dates and make dates `Comparable`).

To get the current month (an integer from 1 to 12) and day you need to get a
`GregorianCalendar` object first, then call its `get` method with the field ID
parameter for the field you need:

```
import java.util.Calendar;
import java.util.GregorianCalendar;
...
    Calendar calendar = new GregorianCalendar();
    int month = calendar.get(Calendar.MONTH) + 1;
    int day = calendar.get(Calendar.DATE);
    int year = calendar.get(Calendar.YEAR);
```

To find the number of days from one date to another date, you need to get a
calendar object for each date, get the time difference in milliseconds, and
convert it into the number of days. Something like this:

```
Calendar calendar1 =
    new GregorianCalendar(year1, month1 - 1, day1);
Calendar calendar2 =
    new GregorianCalendar(year2, month2 - 1, day2);
long ms = (calendar2.getTimeInMillis() -
        calendar1.getTimeInMillis());
int days = ... // convert ms to days,
            // rounding to the nearest integer
```

Continued

Write a simple Façade class `EasyDate` with fields for the month, day, and year. Make `EasyDate` objects immutable and `Comparable`. Supply a no-args constructor that creates an `EasyDate` with settings for the current date, another constructor that creates a date with a given month (1 to 12), day, and year, and a copy constructor. Provide three corresponding accessor methods, `getMonth`, `getDay`, and `getYear`. Add a `toString` method that returns a string for the date in the format `"mm/dd/yyyy"`, and a method

```
public int daysTo(EasyDate otherDate)
```

that returns the number of days from this date to `otherDate`. ✓

2.▪ The game of Goofenspiel is played by two players. Each player has the same set of cards, let's say 13 (one full suit), represented by values from 1 to 13. On each move the players simultaneously open one card. The bigger card wins and the player takes the trick (both cards). In case of a tie, neither player gets the trick and the cards are discarded. The player with most tricks wins.

In the computer version, the cards are open but the computer plays "honestly," not using the information about the opponent's current move.

Devise a couple of different strategies for the computer and implement the game in accordance with the Strategy design pattern. Make the computer switch strategies if it loses two or three games in a row.

The images of 52 playing cards are available in `JM\Ch26\Exercises\deck.zip`. Extract the images for all spades and hearts and place them into the `cards` subfolder of the folder that holds class files for the project. ✓

3. Test whether the `java.util.Calendar` class and its `getInstance` method follow the Singleton design pattern: that is, whether the same `Calendar` object is returned by all calls to the `Calendar.getInstance()` method.

4.   Write and test a Singleton class `FavoriteColor`, with methods

```
public static void set(Color c)
public static Color get()
```

The `set` method should throw an `IllegalArgumentException` if an attempt is made to reset the previously set favorite color.

5.■   Define an abstract Decorator class for `EasyDate` from Question 1. Write a Decorator class for `EasyDate` (extending the abstract decorator) that is aware of the English names for the months and whose `toString` method returns the date in the format `"<Month name> d, yyyy"` (for example, `"May 10, 2007"`). Write another decorator class with methods

```
public int getDayOfWeek()
public String getDayOfWeekName()
```

`getDayOfWeek` returns this date's day of the week (`0` for Sunday, `1` for Monday, etc.) and `getDayOfWeekName` returns the name of this date's day of the week (for example, `"Sunday"`). ⸨ Hint: January 1, 1970 was a Thursday. ⸩

Test your two Decorator classes in a small program that prints out the full dates (including month names) of Labor Day (the first Monday in September) and Thanksgiving (the fourth Thursday in November) for a given year.

6.   (a)   Let's define an "expression" as either a simple variable or the sum or product of two expressions (of any kind). Write an interface `Expression` with one `int` method, `getValue`.

       (b)   Write a class `Variable` that implements `Expression`. Provide the fields to hold the variable's name and its `int` value, appropriate constructors, and the `getValue` and `setValue` methods. Also provide a `toString` method that returns the variable's <u>name</u>.

       (c)   Write the `SumExpression` and `ProductExpression` classes that implement `Expression` in accordance with the Composite design pattern. Provide a constructor for the `SumExpression` class that makes a sum expression out of two given expressions. Do the same for the `ProductExpression` class. For each of the classes, provide a method `toString` that converts this expression into the standard infix notation, adding parentheses around sums. Consider for example, the following code:

```
Variable a = new Variable("A");
Variable b = new Variable("B");

Expression aPlusB = new SumExpression(a, b);
Expression aPlusBsquared =
              new ProductExpression(aPlusB, aPlusB);

a.setValue(2);
b.setValue(3);

System.out.println(a + " = " + a.getValue());
System.out.println(b + " = " + b.getValue());
System.out.println(aPlusBsquared + " = " +
        aPlusBsquared.getValue());
```

       Its output should be:

```
A = 2
B = 3
(A + B) * (A + B) = 25
```

7.   Make sure the program for Goofenspiel from Question 2 complies with the MVC design pattern and revise the code making use of `Observer/Observable`.

8.■   Put together `HanoiTowerPuzzle.java`, `HanoiTowerModel.java`,
      `HanoiTowerView.java`, and `HanoiTowerMove.java` from
      JM\Ch26\Exercises to make a simple GUI application that solves the
      Tower of Hanoi puzzle, described in Section 22.5. This implementation,
      however, is contrary to the MVC design pattern: the model is created and
      controlled by the view. Modify this program to make it comply with MVC,
      using `Observer` and `Observable`.

9.♦   Explain why MVC and Composite (for the model) don't go together well.
      For example, the `SumExpression` or `ProductExpression` classes from
      Question 6 may fail as a model in MVC. Can you think of a way to make it
      work? ✓

❀ Appendices ❀

The following appendices are online at

> http://www.skylit.com/javamethods

❀ Solutions to Selected Exercises ❀

Solutions to exercises marked with a ✓ are on *Student Disk* downloadable from

> http://www.skylit.com/javamethods

Download `studentdisk.zip`, extract all files and folders, then click on `JM\SolutionsToExercises\index.html`.

Index of Tables and Figures

Tables:

Figures:

Index